Hanging Together

Hanging Together

Unity and Diversity in
American Culture

JOHN HIGHAM

Edited by
Carl J. Guarneri

YALE UNIVERSITY PRESS   NEW HAVEN & LONDON

Published with assistance from the Louis
Stern Memorial Fund.

CHAPTER 5: Reprinted from John Higham,
"Integrating America: The Problem of
Assimilation in the Nineteenth Century,"
Journal of American Ethnic History 1 (Fall
1981): 7–25. © 1981 by The Immigration
History Society.
CHAPTER 8: Reprinted from John Higham,
"Coda: Three Reconstructions," in *Civil
Rights and Social Wrongs: Black-White
Relations Since World War II*, ed. John
Higham (University Park: Pennsylvania State
University Press, 1997), 179–89, 207–8.
© 1997 by The Pennsylvania State University.
Reproduced by permission of the publisher.
CHAPTER 13: Reprinted from John Higham,
"Multiculturalism and Universalism: A History
and Critique," *American Quarterly* 45 (June
1993): 195–219. © 1993 by the American
Studies Association.

Designed by James J. Johnson and set in
New Caledonia Roman types by Keystone
Typesetting, Inc., Orwigsburg, Pennsylvania.
Printed in the United States of America by
Sheridan Books, Chelsea, Michigan.

*Library of Congress Cataloging-in-Publication
Data*

Higham, John, 1920–
   Hanging together : unity and diversity in
American culture / John Higham ; edited by
Carl J. Guarneri.
   p. cm.
   Includes bibliographical references and
index.
   ISBN 0-300-08818-3 (alk. paper)

   1. Pluralism (Social sciences)—United
States. 2. Group identity—United States.
3. United States—Race relations. 4. United
States—Ethnic relations. 5. United States—
Civilization. 6. National characteristics,
American. 7. Historiography—United States.
I. Guarneri, Carl, 1950– II. Title.
E184.A1 H488 2001
305.8′00973–dc21   00-049540

A catalogue record for this book is available
from the British Library.

The paper in this book meets the guidelines
for permanence and durability of the
Committee on Production Guidelines for
Book Longevity of the Council on Library
Resources.

10 9 8 7 6 5 4 3 2 1

To the students at six American universities and
overseas who have made my life of learning
an adventurous companionship

Contents

Preface   ix
Introduction   xiii

I   *Tracing Unities*

1. Hanging Together: Divergent Unities in American History   3
2. America in Person: The Evolution of National Symbols   23
3. Rediscovering the Pragmatic American   57
4. Specialization in a Democracy   67

II   *Integrating Diversity*

5. Integrating America: The Problem of Assimilation at the Turn of
   the Century   85
6. Immigration and American Mythology   101
7. Pluralistic Integration as an American Model   111
8. Three Postwar Reconstructions   135

III   *Turning Points*

9. From Boundlessness to Consolidation: The Transformation of
   American Culture, 1848–1860   149
10. America's Utopian Prophets   167
11. The Reorientation of American Culture in the 1890s   173
12. The Long Road to the New Deal   199

IV   *Prospects*

13. Multiculturalism and Universalism: A History and Critique   221
14. The Future of American History   241

Notes   259
Index   307

Preface

Only connect! That was the whole of her sermon.

E. M. FORSTER, *Howard's End*

Watching this book take shape in the hands of a talented group of former students has made me more aware than I had earlier been of the overall shape and direction of my career as historian. Without my knowledge, Carl Guarneri and his associates had gathered together a selection of my essays that I had always regarded as belonging to two distinct realms of inquiry. One group of papers dealt with American history and culture in their largest dimensions. The other sprang from a special interest in immigration and ethnic history. Read together, however, all the essays now seemed to have a common goal or point of view.

I now perceived that both lines of inquiry, though strongly marked by the changing contexts that Guarneri's Introduction illuminates, are parts of a long-term personal project: a need to make connections. Everybody knows that American history has fallen apart. Even the *New York Times* says so ("The Humpty Dumpty of Scholarship," August 26, 2000). For years scholars avoided talking about the breakup, probably because it stemmed in large measure from attitudes that many historians maturing in the 1970s and 1980s brought by the subject of national identity. These younger scholars felt to a greater or lesser degree a general sense of the oppressiveness of nations and dominant elites. Many of them therefore devoted themselves to a laudable but overreaching celebration of minorities. As popularized, this has turned "diversity" into a vested interest and specialization into a new provincialism. I now realize that I have devoted my academic career throughout to resisting specialization and escaping provincialism. I haven't made any great breakthrough, devised any new paradigm, or discovered any fundamental resolution of conflicts between freedom and solidarity.

But I have pursued, through many shifting circumstances, a persistent goal. From the outset I have aimed at an apprehension of the wholeness of history: an apprehension attainable now and then by arranging some of history's fragments into a richer design than they used to have, one that opens outward. My work in ethnic history is therefore intended to connect the experience of ethnic groups with one another and with American institutions, whatever the nature of the connection may be.

Before any history interested me much, I felt those connections personally. At a wonderfully multiethnic New York City high school in the mid-1930s I shared in the joyous esprit and interactions of many second-generation-American classmates. All of us learned together to see beyond our respective provincialisms, and I have never forgotten that.

My other line of inquiry, into the large patterns of American history, has a more bookish origin. It goes back, oddly enough, to the European history (or Occidental Civilization, as it was called) that I studied as an undergraduate. Reading European history in college, I was enthralled by the sweep and intellectual challenge it offered, along with the literature and philosophy we studied simultaneously. Then in graduate school I plunged into American history, guided by advice about the job market but also, regrettably, by my own inaptitude for foreign languages. I found this new field to be sadly provincial, though with important exceptions. Studying political conventions or the building of railroads or the intracacies of constitutional law was not for me. I wanted to emulate the professors who had introduced me to great thinkers, religious wars, and class struggles. The best way, I concluded, was to find the powerful and encompassing themes in American history. And nationalism was surely one of them. Again, as in high school, I was looking for connections.

In the middle years of the twentieth century there was much progress in American historiography, especially in bringing history together with the social sciences and, on the other side, building cultural history as a bridge to the humanities. I was involved in all that and thrived. Then, in the late sixties, turmoil and alienation produced an array of new fields of study. But the new fields brought with them inward-looking agendas that resurrected what my generation had scorned as "filiopietism." Connection-making on any considerable scale fell off sharply.

Today we are emerging from the negativism of those oppositional years. Nations are again a commanding subject for study, calls for synthesis are being voiced, and my students have chosen an exciting moment to do me the great service of bringing my fragments together. I hope this book may provide some evidence—against the gloomy lucubrations of the *New York Times*—that a history of all Americans is not only possible but under way.

Acknowledgments

My foremost obligations are to those immediately involved in the making of this book: first to my editor, Carl Guarneri, who designed the project, supervised the headnoting, and provided absolutely dependable advice, criticism, and general availability every step of the way; then to the other former students who joined so helpfully and enthusiastically in writing headnotes; and finally to the larger company of my students to whom we could offer no editorial work but whose initiative and collaboration produced the memorable dinner party in my honor at which the seeds of the enterprise were planted. I am much indebted also to the people we worked with in the publishing process: to the instant enthusiasm of John G. Ryden; to Lara Heimert's supervision and Mary Pasti's impeccable taste and dazzling speed in copyediting; and, on the outside, to Jack G. Goellner's advice on contract negotiations.

Over the years of writing these essays my chief reliance has been on The Johns Hopkins University and the University of Michigan, together with their exceptional libraries (with a special salute to the William L. Clements Library in Ann Arbor for the research that produced Chapter 9). No less precious have been the fellowships I have received from the National Endowment for the Humanities and the Guggenheim Foundation and the wonderful residencies I have enjoyed at the Center for Advanced Study in the Behavioral Sciences, the Institute for Advanced Study, the Woodrow Wilson Center for Scholars, the National Humanities Center (as a Mellon Senior Fellow), and most recently at the Bellagio Center of the Rockefeller Foundation.

Other institutions that have given guidance as well as access to unique materials are the Prints and Photographs Division of the Library of Congress and the American Antiquarian Society, where Georgia Barnhill was my cicerone. For sponsoring enlightening international meetings and teaching engagements I thank the Nobel Foundation in Sweden, the Fulbright Commission, the Free University of Berlin, the Austrian American Studies Association, the Korean American Studies Association, the Ecole des Hautes Etudes en Sciences Sociales in Paris, the Commonwealth Fund at the University of London, the American Studies seminars at Sapporo and Kyoto, and the Bicentennial Conference at the Hebrew University of Jerusalem.

In this country I am indebted further to Cornell University for appointment as Newman Visiting Professor in American Civilization, to the University of Virginia for an invitation to give the Page Barbour Lectures, to Rutgers University for an invitation to give the Mason Welch Gross Lectures, and to the Center for the Study of Democratic Institutions for Chapter 7 in this book.

Staunch friends and doughty colleagues have been mainstays of a career that must sometimes have seemed erratic. For their friendly criticism and longtime encouragement I thank above all Stuart Bruchey, Otis Graham, Michael Kammen, Eric McKitrick, and Trygve Tholfsen. I am much indebted also to Jeffrey Brooks, Avrom Fleishman, Louis Galambos, Jack Greene, Macie Hall, Bradford Perkins, Dorothy Ross, David Spring, Stephen Tonsor, and Katherine Verdery at my own universities, to Joyce Appleby, Alan Brinkley, Reinhard Doerries, John Hope Franklin, Gary Gerstle, Philip Gleason, David Hollinger, Kenneth Kusmer, Elise Marienstras, Henry May, and Alfred Young at others, and to my dear mentor Merle Curti. Finally, my greatest indebtedness is to Eileen.

Introduction

This book of essays embodies three decades of reflection by one of America's foremost historians. After completing important works on attitudes toward immigration and on American historiography, *Strangers in the Land* (1955) and *History* (1965), John Higham added a third, equally ambitious line of inquiry to his historical explorations. Its object was to trace the changing contours of American culture as a whole. The case studies that Higham undertook are sampled in this collection. Ranging widely in their quest to encompass Americans' diversity, the essays also offer broad interpretations of the ideas and habits that have bound Americans as one people. The topics include the evolution of national symbols, the course of race relations, and the increasing bureaucratization of society. Chronologically, the essays span three centuries, moving from European images of the New World in the colonial era to the debate over multiculturalism in the 1990s. They are unified by a remarkably consistent focus on the ways a dynamic national culture has caused divergent ethnic, class, and ideological groups to "hang together" as Americans. In the face of tendencies toward a divisive pluralism, Higham insists that there is a common American culture, although it has diverse strains, is always contested, and is constantly changing.

Higham's practice of cultural history centers around several polarities that describe shifts undergone by the discipline in the second half of the twentieth century. The first—in chronology and perhaps in importance—is the struggle between consensual and conflict-oriented versions of the American past. Higham's own historiographic essays of the 1950s helped to define this generational dispute. The dual inheritance of the Progressive history of the 1930s and the post–World War II "consensus school" that repudiated it forms the background of Higham's attempt to integrate continuity and change in his essays on cultural themes. Rather than rejecting consensus concepts of an American ideology or national character, Higham's essays try to historicize them and to inject elements of complexity and conflict into their development. In Higham's work, Americans are not a "People of Plenty," as the consensus historian David Potter once wrote, but a "People of Paradox," as Michael Kammen has called them; the "American Creed" is not fixed by consensus but emerges as the outcome of struggle between competing visions. Cross-national comparisons are similarly complicated. It was consensus historians such as Louis Hartz and Daniel Boorstin who first made the proposition of American uniqueness explicit in our historiography by proclaiming the nation's course an exception to developments elsewhere. Higham's essays seek to improve upon their work by suggesting more nuanced comparisons that trace connections and parallels as well as points of American difference.

The relation between ideas and social forces is a second context for Higham's writings. During the 1960s and the early 1970s he explored cultural history as a middle ground between the history of ideas and the history of society, two approaches that were competing for dominance among historians. Higham brought special resources to this task. As a student at the Johns Hopkins and Wisconsin Universities in the 1940s, he had imbibed both the "internal" and the "external" approaches to intellectual history. The former, epitomized by Arthur O. Lovejoy's subtle discrimination between versions of "unit ideas" through history, followed the conversation among leading thinkers across the centuries. The latter, exemplified by Higham's mentor Merle Curti, was more open to popular currents of thought, and its proponents explored the social contexts and political ramifications of ideas. Higham's work in cultural history combines the careful distinctions of Lovejoy with Curti's interest in social questions. Higham seeks to enlarge both, however, by searching for collective mentalities and cultural systems. His essays from the 1960s correlate diverse phenomena with the object of defining a dominant zeitgeist. Within a few years this method was modified through the influence of social history. In essays such as "Hanging Together" (Chapter 1) and "Specialization in a Democracy" (Chapter 4), Higham extends his cultural approach to analyze how concepts and norms influenced, and were influenced by, the changing configuration of social groups.

By the mid-1970s, however, the triumph of social history called into question the key assumption that had underpinned Higham's quest for a cultural synthesis: the very existence of a unified American culture. Higham responded by examining forces of adhesion as well as fragmentation in our past. First, he turned his attention to ethnicity, one of the social historians' main exhibits in the case against a unitary culture. In his first book, *Strangers in the Land*, Higham had already surveyed his particular subject—the relations between ethnic groups and the larger American environment—across a span of forty tumultuous years. Returning to this inquiry in the mid-1970s and after, he now looked for the quiet connections that surrounded and interlaced the dramatic story of conflict that *Strangers* had told. National and ethnic history, he was now convinced, should not prioritize conflicts over connections.

In the 1970s Higham's search for a dynamic middle ground produced studies of assimilation and pluralism as changing ideals. His more recent essays incorporate data from social history. But they continue to make the case for "pluralistic integration" and an interactionist framework for discussing group identities.

In the 1990s Higham's response to social history entered a second phase. Concerned that social historians were too absorbed in local contexts and subgroup identities, Higham reasserted the importance of the nation for understanding American history. A new research project charted changing symbols of American nationhood. New narratives traced the evolving history of American "universalism," an egalitarian social ideal that gradually expanded through the impact of depression, wars, and protests. It remains, in his view, a viable basis for an inclusive national identity. To scholars of other persuasions, Higham argues that national frameworks are still indispensable in connecting "subnational particulars" with "supranational patterns."

Conflict and consensus, intellectual and social history, assimilation and pluralism, national versus subgroup history—these polarities are distinctive but they are also overlapping and analogous. They all represent ways of framing the tension between unity and diversity in American history. To trace the contours of American culture, as Higham has conceived that task, is to incorporate this tension without denying or superficially harmonizing it. There is always in some measure a choice of emphasis: injecting conflict and contradiction into an American story that has become too celebratory and monochromatic (as Higham did in the 1950s), or reasserting the case for national history when historians avoid or repudiate it (as Higham's recent essays do). Over the years, he has repeatedly tried to pull the pendulum of historians' discourse back when it has swung too far in one direction. In *Writing American History* (1970), he defended this "habit of taking positions in the center" as locating "not a mere intermediate zone but a center of gravity, where one can stand and prepare to move forward." From the middle he can take the measure of both extremes and incorporate their insights without echoing their exaggerations.

Yet Higham's approach reflects more than a judicious temperament, important as that is for writing good history. It also arises from the belief that American culture itself revolves around polarities: idealism and materialism, freedom and organization, the nation and the world—above all, the one and the many. To practice cultural history is thus to look for the shifting center between such poles, to chart the ways that unity and diversity have shared the same gravitational field in our past. The essays collected here demonstrate Higham's mastery of the skills that this kind of cultural mapping requires: sensitivity to paradox and symbiosis, the ability to connect seemingly disparate phenomena, a willingness to examine larger contexts and longer time spans, receptivity to concepts from other disciplines, interest in international comparisons, perceptive reading of visual evidence, and, not least, clear and graceful prose. The range and depth of these writings suggest why reviewers themselves have resorted to polarities to describe Higham's work, calling it both fresh and authoritative, panoramic and precise.

The chapters in this book are grouped by shared themes rather than date of origin. Part I, "Tracing Unities," opens with two sweeping essays that track the evolving and overlapping ways Americans have bonded together as a people. Beginning with a primordial sense of ties through kinship and descent, Higham argues, Americans created a nation that relied heavily on a set of principles to attract popular allegiance. By enlarging the principles and investing allied symbols (like the Statue of Liberty) with new meanings, they forged a more inclusive nationality in the early twentieth century. By then, however, the force of technological progress was channeling Americans' lives away from encompassing ideologies toward techniques of organization, efficiency, and specialization. The modern world's reliance upon what Higham calls "technical unity" challenged traditional notions that American culture was uniquely pragmatic and resolutely egalitarian. Some effects of that challenge are discussed in the second pair of essays in Part I.

Part II, "Integrating Diversity," examines a crucial nexus of American culture: the relation between ethnic and racial groups and the larger society. As in *Strangers in the Land,* Higham focuses on changing definitions of group boundaries, for both the ethnic group and the host society, and the implications of such changes for national myths and values. Acutely aware of the ongoing tension in American history between openness and exclusiveness, Higham offers "pluralistic integration" as our best tradition for binding together such a kaleidoscopic culture. The final essay of this section, "Three Postwar Reconstructions," extends a version of this ideal to the history of race relations.

The essays grouped in Part III, "Turning Points," uncover social and cultural transitions, not always apparent to observers, which underlie shifts in behavior and attitudes from one era to another. Encompassing popular and elite culture, Higham's essays on the 1850s and 1890s show how diverse cultural expressions illustrate the "spirit of an age." He attempts to avoid the static quality of most studies of national character by concentrating on transition points from one system of beliefs and values to another. In contrast to these studies of pivotal decades, the last essay of this section traces the gradual, forty-year process of ethnic mobilization that culminated by transforming the American polity during Franklin Roosevelt's New Deal.

Finally, a pair of provocative essays in Part IV, "Prospects," confront aspects of the "culture wars" still simmering at the close of the twentieth century. In the first, Higham criticizes the multiculturalist movement for hardening group identities and for lacking a coherent vision of what the nation, as a larger collective entity, should become. As an alternative, he sketches a tradition of American democratic "universalism" that flourished in the mid-twentieth century and, he argues, ought to be revitalized for the twenty-first. In the final essay, Higham promotes an agenda for historians in the coming century of global interdependence. Asserting the continued importance of nations, Higham urges scholars to revive a national framework for historical analysis, which has lapsed in recent decades as social historians have focused on local or subgroup identities, and to enhance it by analyzing international connections and comparisons.

This book presents a substantially new selection of Higham's work. His article-length contributions to American historiography were published in *Writing American History,* and his major essays on immigration and nativism were collected in *Send These to Me* (1975; rev. ed., 1984). But his essays treating more general themes in American culture, several of which are located in hard-to-find journals or anthologies, have never been gathered together to reach a wider audience.

The idea of doing so originated among Higham's former graduate students as a way to honor their mentor upon his retirement. Accordingly, each essay in this collection is introduced by one of those students, who are now historians in their own right. These headnotes contextualize the presentation that follows by indicating the genesis of its topic and approach, and they also suggest differences from, or influences upon, work by other scholars.

Initial publication dates for the essays are provided in brackets on the first page of each chapter. Chapter 2 has been enlarged and updated for this collection, but retains its original date. Chapter 7 is followed by a postscript (dated 1999) written expressly for this volume. Chapter 9 was originally published without notes; they have been added. Chapter 12 is published here for the first time. All the other essays are reprinted in their original form, except for minor corrections and editorial changes.

The following list gives the source for each chapter:

Chapter 1. "Hanging Together: Divergent Unities in American History." In *Journal of American History* 61 (June 1974): 5–28.

Chapter 2. "America in Person: The Evolution of National Symbols." An earlier version was published in *Amerikastudien* 36 (Spring 1992): 473–93. New text and illustrations have been added.

Chapter 3. "Rediscovering the Pragmatic American." In *Pragmatism as an American Way of Life* (in Korean), ed. Korean Association for American Studies (Seoul: n.p., 1986), pp. 207–220.

Chapter 4. "Specialization in a Democracy" [originally titled "The Matrix of Specialization"]. In *The Organization of Knowledge in Modern America, 1860–1920,* ed. Alexandra Oleson and John Voss (Baltimore, Md.: Johns Hopkins University Press, 1979), pp. 3–18.

Chapter 5. "Integrating America: The Problem of Assimilation at the Turn of the Century" [originally titled "Integrating America: The Problem of Assimilation in the Nineteenth Century"]. In *Journal of American Ethnic History* 1 (Fall 1981): 7–25.

Chapter 6. "Immigration and American Mythology" [originally titled "The Movement of Peoples, 1788–1989"]. In *Commonality and Difference: Australia and the United States,* ed. Glenn Withers (Sydney: Allen and Unwin, 1991), pp. 1–10, 126–128.

Chapter 7. "Pluralistic Integration as an American Model" [originally titled "Another American Dilemma"]. In John Higham, *Send These to Me: Jews and Other Immigrants in Urban America* (New York: Atheneum, 1975), pp. 231–246. The postscript is previously unpublished.

Chapter 8. "Three Postwar Reconstructions" [originally titled "Three Reconstructions"]. In *Civil Rights and Social Wrongs: Black-White Rela-*

tions Since World War II, ed. John Higham (University Park: Pennsylvania State University Press, 1997), pp. 179–189, 207–208.

Chapter 9. *From Boundlessness to Consolidation: The Transformation of American Culture, 1848–1860* (Ann Arbor, Mich.: William Clements Library, 1969).

Chapter 10. "America's Utopian Prophets." In *Virginia Quarterly Review* 60 (Summer 1984): 507–513.

Chapter 11. "The Reorientation of American Culture in the 1890s." First published in *The Origins of Modern Consciousness,* ed. John Weiss (Detroit: Wayne State University Press, 1965), pp. 25–48, this essay was expanded in John Higham, *Writing American History: Essays on Modern Scholarship* (Bloomington: Indiana University Press, 1970), pp. 73–102, 187–192. The latter version is used here.

Chapter 12. "The Long Road to the New Deal." This heretofore unpublished essay draws upon material and insights from two articles: "The Mobilization of Immigrants in Urban America," *Norwegian-American Studies* 31 (1986): 3–33; and "From Process to Structure: Formulations of American Immigration History," in *American Immigrants and Their Generations: Studies and Commentaries on the Hansen Thesis After Fifty Years,* ed. Peter Kivisto and Dag Blanck (Urbana: University of Illinois Press, 1990), pp. 11–41.

Chapter 13. "Multiculturalism and Universalism: A History and Critique." In *American Quarterly* 45 (June 1993): 195–219.

Chapter 14. "The Future of American History." In *Journal of American History* 80 (March 1994): 1289–1307.

Carl J. Guarneri

PART I

Tracing Unities

For the 1974 presidential address before the Organization of American Historians, Higham chose a large and deliberately contrarian theme: "Adhesive Forces in American Culture." By the mid-1970s the shock waves of a decade of protest had shaken the academy, and historians were beginning to challenge consensual theories of American culture. With energy and sometimes anger, young scholars stirred the melting pot, bringing to the surface issues of race, class, locale, ethnicity, and gender that eventually called all general frameworks for understanding American history into question. Without directly critiquing this trend, Higham set out to revive historians' sense of the commonalities that had held together an amorphous national culture despite myriad forces of fragmentation.

Disillusioned scholars of the 1960s and 1970s had chronicled the "eclipse of community" in studies of colonial settlements and nineteenth-century cities. Higham argued that their jeremiads missed the point: the key to capturing enduring unities in American culture was not to fix upon one version of community—this inevitably led to a narrative of decline—but to explore changing forms of cultural integration. Combining typologies from the American anthropologist Clifford Geertz and the French sociologist Jacques Ellul, Higham divided American cultural history into three overlapping phases: primordial, ideological, and technical. His schema neatly accommodated important events and established interpretations. It accounted for America's first and second "foundings": the peopling of the colonies in clusters of primordial folk, then their linkage under common religious and political beliefs. It described the marriage of Protestant and national ideologies in the early republic, thereby synchronizing religious and republican interpretations of the American experience. And it traced the roots of our modern technical mentality to the mid-nineteenth century, to soil that the historians Alfred Chandler and Daniel Boorstin were sifting and that Higham himself had excavated in his essay "From Boundlessness to Consolidation" (reprinted here as Chapter 9). Among the present essay's freshest interpretations was its reading of Progressivism as an ideological revival in the midst of modernization, a view that corrected Robert Wiebe's widely influential portrayal in *The Search for Order* (1967).

Retitled "Hanging Together" when published, Higham's sketch of the nation's cultural center was largely ignored by cutting-edge historians of the 1970s and 1980s, who were intent upon giving voice to long-neglected groups outside the mainstream and who viewed with skepticism any pronouncements about American culture as a whole. In recent years, however, the synthesis that Higham proposed has regained its relevance as influential scholars like Robert Wuthnow and Daniel Rodgers return to the task of describing and affirming the "loose connections" and "contested truths" that tie Americans together.

Carl J. Guarneri
Saint Mary's College of California

1

Hanging Together
Divergent Unities in American History
[1974]

For about a decade American historical writing has been characterized by a repudiation of consensus and an invocation of community.
Present-day historians seem substantially agreed that many of their
predecessors overemphasized unities in American history and society. Yet
perhaps never before have so much interest and effort gone into a search
for those times and places in which a high degree of solidarity obtained. On
first notice, we have here a curious contradiction. The repudiation of consensus was supposed to permit a rediscovery of profound conflicts in our
past. It has done so only to a very limited degree. The exciting advances in
contemporary scholarship have more to do with understanding cohesive
structures: the New England town, the family, the ethnic subculture, the
professional and trade associations, the political machines.

A moment's reflection dispels the paradox. Historians who are interested in the issues of consensus and community are actually trying to
distinguish between true and false communities, between the social arrangements that sustain participants and those that coerce or scatter them.
The term "consensus" is commonly applied to a factitious conformity, arising from manipulation and acquiescence. When we speak of "community"
we refer to a more authentic, more truly shared bond. To look at American
historiography in this light suggests that for some time historians of quite
different persuasions have been asking the same questions, though giving
different answers. The so-called consensus historians who came to the fore
in the 1950s—Richard Hofstadter, David Potter, Louis Hartz, and Daniel
Boorstin—created the conceptual universe their present-day critics and

successors inhabit. Both groups have been studying the possibilities and the limits of social solidarity in our peculiarly amorphous country.

A striking feature of this grand enterprise is the high proportion of negative conclusions it has so far produced. At first many historians described an all-embracing community, shaped by a common national character.[1] Before long this kind of community began to seem too thin, even illusory, to have much significance. Interest in national character has survived only to the extent that it can be treated—as Michael Kammen does—as a bundle of contradictions.[2] The locus of community has shifted to smaller, presumably more homogeneous entities. The more closely these are examined, however, the more they reveal their own fissures and stultifications. A remarkable number of recent studies focus on the points at which or the ways in which American communities have failed. A small army of historians has been trying to determine how and when the early New England towns came apart. Some say it was during the era of the Great Awakening; but Michael H. Frisch argues that Springfield, Massachusetts, kept its organic wholeness until the middle of the nineteenth century. Michael Zuckerman, on the other hand, insists that the cohesiveness of the New England towns was always contrived, that it rested on an intolerance of differences, and that it has never broken down but rather has spread throughout American group life. Survival of "the massive coercion of the monolithic community," Zuckerman sternly remarks, "belies the belief that we are a liberal society." Taking a different tack but reaching an equally gloomy verdict, Sam Bass Warner, Jr., portrays the entire span of American urban history as a story of "endless failures . . . to build and maintain humane cities."[3] With some important exceptions[4] the search for community has led American historians either to a rediscovery of consensus or to a scene of alienation and disorder.

Bemused with so much failure, a reader must wonder what kind of social integration, what experience of unity, might qualify as successful. By what criteria do our historians distribute praise and blame among different kinds of communities? May we call one parochial because it is small and self-sustaining and another weak because it is large and nonexclusive? Under what conditions should we expect a unifying force to bind people more closely together, or to respect their partial autonomy, or release them completely? I ask these questions to suggest that the quality and nature of social cohesion pose fundamental dilemmas for Americans. Historians cannot resolve the dilemmas, but they can ask the past to clarify their shape and duration.

America has exhibited not only an enormous variety of communities but also some underlying differences in the forms of unity our peoples have sought. Much of the confusion in current scholarship seems to arise from a propensity to judge one pattern of social integration by criteria derived from another, and thus to demean the first at the expense of the second. American history has been in considerable measure a struggle between rival ways of getting together. In actual experience the alternatives have overlapped very greatly. Instead of facing a clear choice between commensurate loyalties, Americans have commonly been enmeshed in divergent systems of integration. That is not a condition peculiar to America. It is intrinsic to modern life. This essay sketches in barest outline three adhesive forces that have pulled people in different directions wherever the process of modernization has occurred. I intend to point up, not the uniqueness of American experience, but rather the special salience here of disparities every modernizing society seems to confront. I shall concentrate on the sequential unfolding of three forms of unity, which American historians have studied only in fragmentary ways. Obviously I shall not take account of all cohesive structures. In particular I leave aside the working of sheer political or economic domination, in order to concentrate on types of integration that function through consent, whether tacit or explicit.

At the most elementary level, the peoples of America have participated in what Clifford Geertz has called "primordial" unity: a corporate feeling of oneness that infuses a particular, concrete, unquestioned set of inherited relationships. The primordial tie is so much taken for granted that it may be nameless. It binds one to kin, to neighbors, to memories of a distinct place, and to the symbols and rites and customs associated with that heritage. It is therefore localized, specific, yet undefinable. Primordial consciousness differs in its intimacy and unbounded concreteness from what we ordinarily describe as ethnic feeling. The modern ethnic group is a federation of primordial collectivities. It depends on a conceptual simplification and extension of primordial sentiments. It comes about through encounters with outsiders and reflects in part their perceptions.[5]

Primordial ties vary enormously, in character and strength, between groups and over time. In American history the primordial bond has probably been most intense and pervasive within the separate Indian tribes and kin groups. Among Indians primordial unity permeated every dimension of life. As a result, the development of a wider ethnic consciousness—a pan-Indian identity—came very slowly;[6] and when primordial solidarity has

given way under pressure from the dominant white society, the psychological consequences have often been unbearably painful and demoralizing.

Primordial attachments flourished also among those immigrants who
arrived in America with little, if any, sense of nationality, who knew themselves as the people of a particular Norwegian valley, the sons of a certain
Calabrian village, the members of an eastern European shtetl, the country
folk of one small district on the Chinese coast. So far as their circumstances
permitted, immigrants re-created those local solidarities in the New World.
Chinese clustered under the shelter of their warring district companies.
Eastern European Jews ordinarily limited their synagogues, their mutual
aid societies, and often their workshops to "landmen," so that the whole
round of daily life could occur within a circle of fellow townspeople. Italian
peasants grouped themselves by village or province on the streets of New
York. Often the people from a particular locality would maintain a conspicu-
ous conformity in dress and avoid competing with one another in business.[7]

It would be a mistake to suppose that primordial identities have originated only outside native white American society and have lingered only on
its fringes. Solidarities of this kind emerge wherever people live together
long enough to enclose their daily experience in a skein of common memories. Perhaps the most tenacious primordial attachments among American
whites developed in the eastern counties of the South in the late seventeenth and eighteenth centuries and spread into the lower Mississippi
Valley in the nineteenth century. There alone the archaic Elizabethan term
"kinsfolk" survived, slightly Americanized into "kinfolks."[8] It was a constant
reminder that complex networks of personal relationships extend far beyond the household. No sharp line separates antecedents from neighbors,
kin from community. In the world of kinfolks, vestiges of a folk society and
a folk memory endured. Here is the root of that concrete sense of place and
belonging which Thornton Wilder and C. Vann Woodward have described
as one of the hallmarks of a southerner. Whereas most Americans sought
their identity in abstractions, southerners resisted the abstract in clinging
to "the blessing of being located—contained."[9]

Other Americans, abstract and dislocated, have sometimes greatly envied that attachment to past and to place and have contributed enthusiastically to the celebration of it. American yearnings for a lost primordial
world shaped the northern image of the South in the nineteenth century
and invested it with immense nostalgia. It was an Ohio-born minstrel who
composed what became the war song of the Confederacy and a polyglot
New York audience that first popularized it:

I wish I was in de land ob cotton,
Old times dar am not forgotten;
Look away, look away . . .[10]

In adverting to southerners and to the land of cotton, we are indeed looking away. We are looking away from New York; but we are also looking beyond the primordial matrix. We have entered a larger universe, where primordial experience is transmuted into a collective image that can focus the allegiance of people with roughly similar linguistic and geographical origins. The creation of group identities grounded in primordial life has continued to be a significant industry in American popular culture: it has given us the Down-Easter, the Hoosier, and the cowboy, to name but a few; and our own time has brought forth new species, such as the hippie, which have not yet acquired a stable geographic base. But the multiplication of ethnic and regional groups cannot disguise a long-term tendency for primordial ties to come apart. The peopling of America required at the very outset a profound rupture in primordial solidarity, and the enormous mobility that has churned American society ever since has given special importance to other integrative mechanisms. The most powerful of these in the eighteenth and nineteenth centuries was ideological.

Since I propose to talk at some length about the importance of ideology in American history, I must say at the outset how I am using that elusive term. I do not, like many of the critics of ideology, restrict it to rigid, totalistic outlooks; nor do I limit it to secular political creeds. On the other hand, I wish to avoid also the looser usage that describes any rationale for a social loyalty as an ideology. A culture or a group may or may not have an ideology, depending on the degree to which its goals are explicitly formulated and also endowed with transcendent significance. Ideology is therefore a variable in history; perhaps it may even give us a measure of the importance of ideas in motivating and directing a society. American historians, defending their particular bailiwicks and points of view, have characteristically argued over the causal force of ideas in history without sufficiently appreciating that ideas may be enormously more significant in one era or society than in another. We have therefore overlooked one of the great systemic changes in American history.

To come more directly to the matter of definition, I wish to designate as ideologies those explicit systems of general beliefs that give large bodies of people a common identity and purpose, a common program of action, and a standard for self-criticism. Being relatively formalized and explicit, ideology contrasts with a wider, older, more ambiguous fund of myth and tradition. It includes doctrines or theories on the one hand and policies or prescriptions on the other. Accordingly, it links social action with fundamental beliefs, collective identity with the course of history. This combination of generality with directional thrust has enabled ideology to function as an important unifying force. Arising in the course of modernization when an unreflective culture fractures, ideology provides a new basis for solidarity.[11]

Ideological unity assumed its special importance in America at the outset. One large part of early American society was founded upon an ideology. Elsewhere ideologies arose out of dissatisfaction with the existing social order. In the Old World this was the case with Puritanism. It constituted the first great ideological movement in English history. As a revolutionary force, it cut through established institutions and relations like a laser beam.[12] Yet Puritanism ultimately failed in England, and after its shattering defeat in 1660 ideology never again provided the primary basis for social integration. America, on the other hand, had no preexisting structure for Puritans to overthrow. Here ideology arrived not as a subversive or divisive force but as a bedrock of order, purpose, and cohesion.

If ideological unity was from the outset fundamental in New England, primordial unity was correspondingly weak. The researches of Sumner Chilton Powell suggest that the early settlers of New England towns could not rely very much on the local familiarities and affinities of primordial experience. The first settlers of Sudbury came from widely scattered parts of England; they melded together a surprising variety of customs and practices.[13] In addition to a common English culture, however, they possessed an ideology that put a heavy stress on mutuality and discipline. It bound them with written covenants, taught them formal creeds, and commanded them to subordinate all private concerns to one collective end. Since the New England colonies adopted a loose, decentralized government in both church and state, they entrusted to ideology much of the regulative function that elsewhere belonged in the hands of constituted rulers. In place of hierarchical authority, the Puritans substituted a voluntary mobilization of belief. In doing so, they originated an especially American combination: institutional decentralization and ideological uniformity.

Although Puritanism was never overthrown, its pristine vitality ebbed toward the end of the seventeenth century. The remarkable social cohesion of the preceding decades in New England diminished.[14] During the next half-century a rising consciousness of the common English heritage uniting all parts of the British Empire helped to stabilize colonial life.[15] But the programmatic fervor of ideology subsided. About this first decline of ideology in American history we know very little, except that it proved short-lived. American Christianity recovered in the eighteenth century an ideological thrust that sustained it into the early twentieth. With the dispersion of population from the clustered settlements of the seventeenth century, the original Puritan reliance on ideological mobilization revived and intensified.

The Puritans had needed the discipline of ideology to hold their ranks, to stave off fragmentation. Their descendants had to cope with a society already fragmented. To encompass a people rushing away from one another—a people straining the last ligaments of a common life in their pursuit of land and freedom—Americans put their ideological inheritance to expanded uses. What had been a discipline became also an incitement. Exploding churches turned the full power of the Word outward to reach the unconverted and to penetrate a culture no single group could dominate. This produced, of course, enormous conflicts. It split congregations and multiplied competing sects. Like any other integrative mechanism, ideology divides as well as unites. Nevertheless, the point remains: the Great Awakening marks the moment in American history when ideology undertook the task of forging a new solidarity among individuals who had lost through migration and competition any corporate identity.[16]

The new solidarity was very difficult to achieve and not fully worked out until the Second Great Awakening in the early nineteenth century. Gradually, however, the impulse toward union broke through the theological and ecclesiastical fences that had separated Protestant bodies in the past. Whereas the Puritans had generally insisted that a single comprehensive faith should enclose a tightly knit society, eighteenth-century Christians developed an intellectual framework that accommodated unprecedented diversities. What I shall call the Protestant ideology had as its working principle a distinction between two levels of belief. Specific creeds and confessions adorned the more formal, visible level. They served as identifying marks for particular segments of the population and as concrete symbols of a pervasive freedom of choice. At a deeper level, unaffected by the clash of creeds, dwelled the inclusive truths, which required neither debate nor strict definition. Thus the Protestant ideology accepted conflict between "denominations" as permanent, legitimate, and inspiriting, for the conflict could be seen to rest on and to demonstrate the worth of certain unifying ideals.[17] As time passed, theological doctrines acquired a largely honorific, ceremonial status in America's pantheon of religions. The basic ideology stood guard, and one could question its tenets only at the risk of heresy.

This dynamic relation between ideals shared by the great majority of people and distinct creeds that attracted only limited followings helps to explain an anomaly puzzling to European observers of nineteenth-century America. How could intense religious activity proceed unobstructed in a setting that seemed largely secular? In actuality secular life was suffused with a pan-Protestant ideology that claimed to be civic and universal. Pledged to leave private beliefs undisturbed, it was vague enough that increasing numbers of Jews and Catholics could embrace it. But it infused a generalized piety in school textbooks and civic oratory.[18] At the same time the Protestant ideology gave a special focus and initiative to the Protestant churches. It offered them a unifying purpose. It encouraged their members to feel a praetorian responsibility for the whole society.[19]

Necessarily, the tenets of the Protestant ideology were few and simple. First among them was the conviction that no compulsion should rule the choice of faith. Genuine religious commitment is a private and voluntary act. While it remains so, a pure religion and a sturdy morality will undergird American institutions. The great diversity of churches guarantees that no one of them can corrupt this truth or reduce an energetic people to apathy.

Second, the Protestant ideology offered Americans a collective task and a sustaining hope. Aiming at nothing less than the redemption of humankind, it held that God had assigned to America the leading role in the enterprise. America's history and destiny assumed a sacred character, which the great historian George Bancroft captured in making providential guidance the grand theme of his ten-volume epic.[20] In origin, this sense of divine mission flowed straight from the millennialism of seventeenth-century Puritans; nothing more clearly revealed the continuity of the Protestant ideology with the Puritanism from which it sprang. All Calvinists looked forward to the coming of a new order. Those who emigrated to New England identified themselves as a people especially chosen to advance it. The Scriptures promised an ultimate reign of holiness, peace, and happiness, and the New England Puritans knew they were summoned to do some special work toward the end—perhaps to build, in Edward Johnson's ringing words, "a new Heaven, and a new Earth, in new Churches, and a new Commonwealth together."[21] In the seventeenth century, however, the millennial promise held as much terror as hope. An oppressive sense of the insufficiency of their own efforts made the Puritans particularly sensitive to signs of failure and to prophecies of premillennial doom. Beginning with the Great Awakening, Alan Heimert tells us, the millennial idea lost for many people its cataclysmic implications. The awakening that was already under way was securely building Christ's Kingdom on earth. America began to be seen as the spiritual center of Christendom.[22] Thus the Protestant ideology, instead of enshrining a single creed, exalted a sacred place.

We ordinarily think of ideologies as jealous masters, contending with one another for exclusive possession of a society. Yet American history offers a striking exception. The two ideologies that exercised the widest influence eventually overlapped and reinforced one another to the point almost of complete convergence. By giving the millennium a temporal and secular character, the Protestant clergy identified the Kingdom of God with the American republic; and the Protestant ideology thereupon attached itself to American nationalism. In principle and in origin the two were different. The national ideology was primarily political and secondarily social. It was born in the struggle for, and dedicated to the defense of, an independent republic. It drew heavily on non-Christian sources, notably the Enlightenment and the tradition of classical humanism.[23] The Protestant ideology, for all of its entanglement with American culture, was supranational. It subordinated all political structures and all territorial communities to the will of God. Still, each came to supplement the other. Together, they forged the strongest bonds that united the American people during the nineteenth century.

Collaboration pivoted on a mutual commitment to an American destiny. Both systems of belief posited a national mission to realize the hopes of humankind. Like the patriotic clergy of the Revolutionary era, secular leaders construed America's character and promise in universalistic terms. On a secular plane, the Founding Fathers grounded their independence in the laws of nature. They ransacked historical experience in framing institutions suitable to the universal tendencies of human nature; and they conceived of their enterprise as a new beginning for humankind. Quoting Virgil, the Continental Congress in 1782 designed the Great Seal of the Republic, which proclaimed "Novus Ordo Seclorum"—A New Order for the Ages.[24] From both points of view—Protestant and classical-republican—Americans defined themselves as a people who had broken out of a traditional mold in order to fulfill certain general truths. The significance of the American people, therefore, belonged more to the future than to the past. Their very identity inhered in their abstractions.

The interlacing of American nationalism and American Protestantism extended far beyond their common invocation of an ideological mission. It may be observed also in the symmetry of other major tenets. Where Protestantism endorsed a diversity of denominations and confessions, the national ideology asserted the importance of a multiplicity of political bodies and social interests. Profoundly distrustful of centralized authority, Americans relied on a separation and division of powers in the political sphere, just as they relied on a wide distribution of ecclesiastical power in the religious sphere. "The security for civil rights," James Madison wrote in the *Federalist*, "must be the same as that for religious rights. It consists in the one case in the multiplicity of interests, and in the other in the multiplicity of sects. The degree of security in both cases will depend on the number of interests and sects."[25] Variety became fundamental to the dominant American ideal of unity: E Pluribus Unum.

No less fundamental was a shared passion for individual liberty. If the theoretical goal of American ideology was to exemplify and disseminate universal truths, and if the chief structural principle was a dispersion of power, surely the animating idea was a belief in the equal rights of individuals in the interest of maximum personal autonomy. The Protestant stress on unfettered personal choice as the key to true religion had its corollary in the American stress on the free individual as the source of energy and the seat of value in the good society.[26] The adherents of the American ideology could thus feel united by their common possession of equal rights and their common opposition to artificial inequalities.

The three beliefs I have touched on—a collective mission, a dispersal of power, an individual locus of opportunity—made for a large, loose faith. It could not easily become an orthodoxy. It explicitly denied a unified past; it had no single, authoritative text; its own premises prevented any single agency or group from establishing an official formulation. Its early history was tempestuous. From the struggle over the Constitution to the Civil War and beyond, American political history was in considerable degree a conflict between rival versions of the American ideology.

In rejecting the Beardian thesis that American history turns on a continuous, essentially unchanging division between two antithetical ideologies, historians for many years closed their eyes to all ideological conflicts. We are only now discovering how seriously Americans took the differences of principle that arose within the framework of a common ideology as they strained to enact its cloudy imperatives. To understand the passion and ferocity of early American politics is to see how desperately convinced Americans were that the very survival of the Union depended on the triumph of the true version of its basic ideals. Torn loose from primordial unity and committed to finding a new solidarity in a set of beliefs they knew they had as yet only begun to realize, the Americans revealed their enormous dependence on ideology by quarreling chiefly over its implications and mandates.[27] In sum, the terrible fears and anxieties that embittered political life in the Jeffersonian period reflected not only the frailty and the ambiguities of the national ideology but also the psychological vulnerability of a people who had little else to hold them together.

Though fluctuating from year to year, the tensions within the American and Protestant ideologies persisted; they were intrinsic. The stress on a common purpose clashed in both cases with an unrelenting opposition to consolidated power. In the American ideology the differentiating thrust of individualism pulled against the leveling belief in equality. Above all, the American ideology was beset with contradiction because its basic task of building solidarity was not compatible with the competitive, acquisitive values the ideology also legitimized. In spite of these enduring strains, however, the main trend in the pursuit of an American identity from the time of Thomas Jefferson to the time of Abraham Lincoln was a strengthening of its power and a deepening of its emotional resonance.

Still thin and uncertain in the 1790s, ideological unity may have reached its fullest development around the middle of the nineteenth century, about one hundred years after its rebirth in the Great Awakening. It was the erosion of traditional loyalties by mobility and acquisitiveness that left Americans dependent on ideology for their sense of identity, and by the mid-nineteenth century the dispersion of population had attained awesome proportions. Travelers noticed that a truculent, gasconading patriotism was especially characteristic of newly settled parts of the country, but everywhere ideological commitment compensated to some extent for the weakness of local ties. The American, observed Alexander Mackay in 1849, "exhibits little or none of the local attachments which distinguish the European. His feelings are more centered upon his institutions than his mere country. He looks upon himself more in the light of a republican than in that of a native of a particular territory. . . . Every American is thus, in his own estimation, the apostle of a particular political creed, in the final triumph and extension of which he finds both himself and his country deeply involved."[28]

The strengthening of ideological bonds in the first half of the nineteenth century came about partly through the development of rituals and symbols. Beginning with relatively unadorned, disembodied ideologies, Americans developed two crucial sets of rituals: on one side, the camp meeting and associated devices for mass conversions; on the other side, the

annual electioneering carnival of conventions and torchlight parades. Ideological mobilization was further assisted by the elaboration of symbols,
such as the portrait of George Washington, the eagle, and the flag. By the
1860s flagpoles in American towns were said to be almost as common as the
chimneys on houses.[29] The unifying abstractions acquired by these means a
compelling concreteness.

Meanwhile the dominant ideologies also advanced by raising their goals.
On many fronts aspirations soared in the nineteenth century. Instead of
viewing the American polity as an uncertain experiment, patriotic spokesmen elevated it to an ultimate, indissoluble necessity.[30] Instead of seeing
only a new beginning for humankind, many now thought they as individuals
could attain a state of total righteousness. Instead of anticipating a gradual
betterment of society, reformers now insisted on immediate liberation.[31]
Instead of waiting for the American example to be imitated, more and more
citizens clamored for direct action to hasten the triumph of freedom and
Christianity in benighted parts of the country and beyond its expanding
frontiers. Ironically, this escalation of ideological demands was largely responsible for bringing the greatest schism in American life to a violent
climax. As the desire for ideological unity increased, slavery—a flat denial of
the American ideology—became less and less tolerable. In that broad sense
the Civil War, like the expansionism that preceded it, was the result of a
general intensification of ideological forces in nineteenth-century America.

Even before the Civil War demonstrated that ideology could not by
itself permanently hold the country together, another system of integration
was emerging. The new pattern was one of technical unity. By that I mean a
reordering of human relations by rational procedures designed to maxi-
mize efficiency. Technical unity connects people by occupational function
rather than ideological faith. It rests on specialized knowledge rather than
general beliefs. It has had transforming effects in virtually every sphere of
life. As a method of production, technical integration materialized early in
the factory system. As a structure of authority, it has taken the form of
bureaucracy. As a system of values, it endorses a certain kind of interdependence, embodied in the image of the machine. Technical relations are
machinelike in being impersonal, utilitarian, and functionally interlocking.[32] Since the Civil War the growth of technical unity has been the most
important single tendency in American social history; and its end is not yet
in sight.

Before the twentieth century few articulate Americans recognized a
serious incompatibility between their ideological principles and their eager
elaboration of technical networks. As early as the 1790s, according to Alex-

ander Hamilton, it was often remarked that the genius of the American people included "a peculiar aptitude for mechanic improvements."[33] There was also a peculiar enthusiasm for such improvements. The industrialization of New England and the middle Atlantic states went forward unopposed by the machine wrecking of Luddites or the moral indignation of Tories. Even the troubled response to technology of an occasional Nathaniel Hawthorne or Herman Melville pales in comparison with the outrage of a Thomas Carlyle or a John Ruskin. America's affection for the machine, accompanied as it was by a cheerful submission to industrial discipline, cannot be explained simply by economic incentives or by the prevalence of materialistic attitudes in American society. In nineteenth-century America even the critics of materialism—the intellectuals who, generation after generation, assailed luxury and acquisitiveness as the deadliest national evils—rarely implicated technology in their indictment.[34]

One cause, generally overlooked, for the responsiveness of Americans to technical values was their ideological cast of mind. As ideologists, Americans from the outset were attuned to universal principles and to their implementation in programs of action. Ideology had largely emancipated Americans from the matrix of primordial life. It had dissolved the entanglements of tradition—the local particularistic identities—which elsewhere have constituted the principal obstacle to industrialization and modernization. Moreover, an ideological orientation taught Americans to internalize their norms in the form of conscience and thus freed them to a great extent from dependence on other persons or external institutions.[35] Their ends already infixed in their hearts, Americans adopted technical means without fear of personal loss. Thus technical integration spread under the shelter of the American ideology; and the resulting innovations were embraced as ever more powerful instruments for attaining familiar goals. Throughout the nineteenth century what Leo Marx has called the technological sublime reverberated in American rhetoric. Acclaiming the arrival of the "Mechanical Epoch," American spokesmen invested it with millennial promise. Technological progress quickens the mind, uplifts the masses, and demonstrates the superiority of republican government. In subjugating matter through the aid of mechanism, human beings come more and more to resemble God.[36]

The origins of the technical order run back to the thirteenth century and before. But not until the middle of the nineteenth century do we find the various strands (rationality, specialization, etc.) coming together in a social pattern that extended beyond the factories. In the 1850s, amidst a surge of urbanization and industrialization, technical integration became a significant force in American life. The railroads, the first big corporations, developed the elaborate administrative arrangements necessary to coordinate the flow of traffic and to supervise their personnel. In the public sphere a similar organization of large bodies of people within a strictly graded hierarchy of ability and authority was beginning in the urban public school systems and in urban police forces. An exemplar of technical prowess was the civil engineer, who designed and managed complex projects for cities and private corporations alike. Trained in the new polytechnic institutes and scientific schools and imbued with a professional spirit, engineers rose to the status of planners and administrators.[37] Another key figure was the inventor. During the decade before the Civil War the rate of innovation—as measured by the number of inventions patented annually—made its first great leap, proportionately the largest in the nineteenth or twentieth centuries (see table 1).[38]

This, of course, was only a beginning. A gradual but relentless diffusion of technical values went forward throughout the succeeding decades. The two most influential social philosophers of the post–Civil War era, Herbert Spencer and Henry C. Carey, were both prophets of a technical culture. For all of their differences on economic policy, Spencer and Carey shared a common commitment to a rational social order of interlinking specialists. Both argued that humanity progresses through the growth of occupational differentiation and the correlative forms of association that result. The evolutionary process develops specialization on one hand and interdependence on the other.[39] Nature is an evolving bureaucracy.

Accordingly, Spencer argued, successful adaptation requires habits of mind that are orderly and systematic, yet also innovative. Those were precisely the intellectual habits the new educational institutions of postwar America inculcated. At the lower level, urban public school systems taught regularity, punctuality, and above all acceptance of a rigid grading of students by ability and age. Simultaneously, the value of innovation was instilled at a higher level: the secularized universities enshrined an ideal of critical thinking in place of the older dependence on eternal verities.[40] At all levels of urban culture, Americans were learning to think more matter-of-factly about cause and effect. There is no clearer index of the spread of technical values than the increasing use of statistics as a basis for analysis and decision making.[41] To give but one example, the U.S. census of 1850, sometimes called the first modern census, was contained within one volume; the census of 1900 filled ten.

In that matter-of-fact age of technical knowledge, it was not long before

INVENTIONS IN PROPORTION TO POPULATION, 1800–1960

Years	Total number of patents issued for inventions	Number of patents per 10,000 population	Percentage increase or decrease
1800–1809	911	1.7	
1810–1819	1,998	2.8	64
1820–1829	2,697	2.8	0
1830–1839	5,605	4.4	57
1840–1849	5,508	3.2	− 27
1850–1859	19,591	8.4	163
1860–1869	71,679	22.1	163
1870–1879	124,672	31	40
1880–1889	195,104	39	26
1890–1899	221,277	35	− 10
1900–1909	304,696	40	14
1910–1919	381,198	41	3
1920–1929	414,923	39	− 5
1930–1939	442,856	36	− 8
1940–1949	307,634	23	− 36
1950–1959	425,990	28	22

SOURCE: United States Bureau of the Census, *Historical Statistics of the United States: Colonial Times to 1970* (Washington, D.C., 1976), 8–9, 958–59.

a subtle but unmistakable deflation of ideological thinking became evident. The dominant ideologies depended on an idealistic worldview; they assumed that ideas shape events. In a technical world, however, a preoccupation with means has tended to take the place of the ends those means were originally designed to serve. One notices a despiritualization of life, visible already in the 1850s but more marked after the Civil War. Both painting and literature revealed a loss of heroic affirmation, together with a refinement of technique.[42] The clinical point of view that shaped the superbly articulated novels of Henry James and the objective canvasses of Thomas Eakins stemmed from technical values quite as much as did the philosophy of Spencer. Likewise in popular literature the sphere of the ideal contracted. Triumphing over one's own moral shortcomings dwindled as a primary theme in best-selling novels; the challenge of external barriers came to the fore. Similarly the emphasis on moral teaching in children's textbooks declined drastically between 1840 and 1880.[43] In the handbooks on success a comparable shift occurred a little later. By the end of the nineteenth century getting ahead seemed to require a panoply of techniques more than a set of principles.[44] The whole ideological framework receded, and utilitarian rules took over part of the function that ethical absolutes had performed.

The American ideology also suffered a special disadvantage. It asserted that America is uniquely entrusted with humanity's ideals and hopes. In a technical age, however, American intellectuals became more humble about the limitations of their own spare culture and more aware of common problems emerging in all industrial societies. For solving those problems the insufficiency of the old republican faith became painfully apparent.[45] By the 1890s society seemed to be tearing apart, and the American ideology was in need of reconstruction.

It is a commonplace of current historiography that the first two decades of the twentieth century brought a dramatic advance of complex organizations depending on specialized knowledge. Consequently, a "bureaucratic orientation" triumphed in American politics. The hallmarks of the period were the entry of the scientific expert into the governmental process at all levels and the diffusion of "scientific management" in industry. "Efficiency" promised a remedy for personal inadequacies as well as social injustices. So salient has this perspective become that many historians no longer take very seriously the Progressive era's rampant evangelism, its romantic celebration of freedom, equality, and heroism.[46] For too long, it is true, the old-fashioned rhetoric of progressives obscured the calculus of their social engineering. Nevertheless, in a long-term perspective the distinctive feature of the period from 1898 to 1918 is not the preeminence of democratic ideals or of bureaucratic techniques but rather a fertile amalgamation of the two. An extraordinary quickening of ideology occurred in the very midst of a dazzling elaboration of technical systems. Instead of continuing to retreat as technical relations expanded, the old ideological framework was temporarily revitalized. For a time it seemed that a modernized Americanism and a social gospel could be the moving spirit of a technical society.[47] After World War I that hope waned; and we have yet to deal adequately with its failure.

The revival of ideology at the turn of the century released more than one kind of political energy. Progressivism, in the conventional sense of middle-class reform, contained only part of that energy. Some of it took the form of imperialism; some of it was expressed in an ideological kind of racism; some of it went into the remarkable upsurge of an American socialism. This last is a particularly revealing sign of the ideological passion of the Progressive era, for Marxist ideologies had until then failed to penetrate beyond small immigrant groups. The socialism of Eugene Debs, effervescent rather than doctrinaire, seems to have gained a mass following because it was a vehicle of the ideological revival. The American ideology was undergoing a reconstruction that enabled socialism to offer itself as a new version of a familiar faith, a new means of realizing the old dream of a promised land.[48]

Two alterations were basic to the renewal of the American ideology in the Progressive era. The first was a revised definition of freedom. Like socialists, the leading progressive intellectuals interpreted individual rights as a function of participation rather than autonomy. Not the absence of legal restraint but the capacity to share as widely as possible in the common good of the whole society makes us free and equal. Secondly, progressive intellectuals thought, scientific techniques can take the place of universal a priori principles. To identify the common good, we may rely on scientific inquiry. Since it is both flexible and objective, science can build a self-correcting mechanism into the American ideology. Moreover, science implements the concept of freedom through participation. Collaborative by their very nature, science and technology are extending the communications network, which in turn is widening a common life.[49] From the point of view of many progressives and most socialists, democracy and technical rationality were interdependent.

It was an exciting vision, and the disillusions that engulfed the ideological renaissance after 1918 did not destroy it completely. Most thoughtful Americans still believe in harnessing scientific-technical methods to democratic ideals. What we have lost is any belief in an inner affinity between the two, such that together they can unite a divided society. What the progressives hailed as complementary we must wrestle with as contradictions; for technical integration has tended in the long run to replace ideological unity instead of reinforcing it.

I have already mentioned in a cursory way one reason why that is so. The utilitarian effectiveness of technical relationships made an overarching faith seem less important. This is not just a problem of means and ends. Moral commands yielded to functional requirements not only because of the demonstrable effectiveness of the latter for immediate purposes but also because specialization has separated one part of the culture from another in a new way. In the twentieth century every activity has developed, more and more, its own conceptual basis. Thus an increasing segmentation of society weakens the hold of those universal beliefs that are the linchpins of ideological unity.

A second reason for the incompatibility of the two types of unity has to do with the particular values affirmed by the American ideology. Contrary to what the progressives supposed, technical organization is essentially undemocratic. Not equal rights but the hierarchical articulation of differentiated functions is its working principle. The more complex the knowledge required for maintaining a system, the further the professional expert is detached from the common life and the more the centers of power are hidden from public view.[50] It is not surprising that the technological utopians, from Saint-Simon to B. F. Skinner, have abolished conflict and choice by subordinating everyone else to a technical elite.

A widespread, overt consciousness of the opposition between ideals and techniques emerged in the United States in the 1920s. Henry Adams's *Education* sounded the keynote: we have passed from unity to multiplicity, from the Virgin to the Dynamo, from an age of faith to an age of uncontrollable technological power.[51] Folk heroes like Henry Ford and Herbert Hoover might insist that the partnership of machines with American ideals was stronger than ever, but the passion of their advocacy betrayed a spreading doubt. In different ways various groups repudiated the progressive synthesis. Disillusioned writers described a mechanized, routinized society that turned humane values and national ideals into bitter travesties. For John Dos Passos, Elmer Rice, and Aldous Huxley technocracy crushed ideology or perverted it.[52] In contrast to these wounded idealists, many academic intellectuals kept an enthusiastic allegiance to the technical order, but in doing so they, too, sacrificed any long-range social goals. By insisting that science is strictly a method, the rapidly expanding social sciences tended to relieve themselves of concern with values, political programs, and ideologies.[53] A similar disjunction between ideals and techniques appeared in the popular culture of the time. Between 1905–1909 and 1925–1928 the proportion of articles published in general American magazines on topics relating to applied science increased more than sevenfold. The proportion of articles dealing with religion, philosophy, and pure science markedly declined. So we observe a common trend after World War I in American literature, in the social sciences, and in public opinion. The ideological bonds that had united Americans in the nineteenth century slackened, while technical integration accelerated. "The machine process," a young academic administrator glibly declared in 1924, "has captured practically every field of men's behavior."[54]

Since the 1920s the United States has moved farther in the same direction, but not steadily or irreversibly. A second ideological revival welled up in the mid-1930s. It lasted, like the first, for about twenty years, and during that time it mitigated the compulsions of technical authority. Again, as in the Progressive era, the revival produced a reassertion of democratic ideals, an upsurge of nationalism, and a return to religion. Among its exemplars were Lewis Mumford, Reinhold Niebuhr, and Ralph Ellison. The revival infused into history and the social sciences a renewed belief in the primary importance of ideas, norms, and values. But the content of this second revival—the principles and programs it espoused—was never as sharply defined as the substance of the progressive revival had been. From the outset this latter-day idealism had to serve the defensive purposes of global warfare. Plunging from one crisis to another, its advocates could not fix on a clear set of goals.[55] Shriveled remnants of the American ideology fell increasingly into the hands of demagogues and cold warriors. Eventually, battered intellectuals were glad to announce the end of ideology.[56] As ideological passions cooled, however, the emptiness and desolation of a technocratic world were felt more crushingly than ever before.

The experience of the sixties and since has not demonstrated that ideology is once more efficacious, only that it is still in demand. Looking back, it is possible to conclude that the age of ideology has indeed passed. Perhaps, in the long perspective of world history, the ideological age will prove to be only an intermediate stage between the primordial community and a thoroughly technical society. An alternative conclusion, however, seems to me equally possible and more attractive.

Conceivably, a deeper examination of historical experience than I have here attempted may reveal a continuing struggle to bring the primordial, the ideological, and the technical dimensions of culture into some kind of workable counterpoise with one another. American history suggests that none of these linkages can stand alone and that an alliance between any two of them will also fail. The efforts of racists and ethnic nationalists to save primordial solidarity by imposing an overlay of ideological unity have never been wholly successful. The efforts of progressives to save ideological unity by undergirding it with technical structures have also broken down. But each of these adhesive forces—the primordial, the ideological, and the technical—has something to contribute to our complex society; and each of them survives within it. If we can discover how to align the technical with the primordial so that each offsets the other, and give to ideology the task of challenging both, we may raise to a new level one of the great and enduring principles of our ideological heritage: the importance of diversity, the value of countervailing power.

Higham's intellectual pursuit of what has held Americans together took an iconographic turn in the 1980s. Invited by the University of Virginia to deliver the Page-Barbour Lectures for 1989, Higham examined various personifications of America, including an Indian Princess, Columbia, Uncle Sam, and the Statue of Liberty. Revised into a single illustrated narrative spanning the length of American history, his vignettes grew into the essay reprinted here.

Higham's synthesis made its debut across the Atlantic, in Germany. Higham has lectured widely in Europe, South America, and Asia, and many of his essays were first published overseas. His travels have reflected and also stimulated his long-standing interest in comparative approaches to the study of the American past. It is not surprising, then, that this essay begins with the German-American historian Hans Kohn's characterization of the differences in nationalism between western and central Europe. Higham then introduces a schema of his own, distinguishing among symbols that represent the nation as a place, a set of principles, a polity, and a people. He proceeds to explore the particulars of how each of the various symbols for America was created, institutionalized, disseminated, and changed over time.

Whereas "Hanging Together" (Chapter 1) appeared just as American historians were turning away from questions of national identity, "America in Person" emerged amid a wave of new scholarship on the topic. By the time the essay was published, Benedict Anderson's *Imagined Communities: Reflections on the Origins and Spread of Nationalism* (1983) had found its way onto American historians' reading lists; the *Journal of American History* and *Representations* had published special issues on memory that addressed questions of national consciousness (1989); Michael Kammen had completed *Mystic Chords of Memory: The Transformation of Tradition in American Culture* (1991); and John Bodnar's *Remaking America: Public Memory, Commemoration, and Patriotism in the Twentieth Century* had just appeared. Several of these authors questioned the treatment of national symbols as collective representations by focusing on the creation and manipulation of public memory or by dissecting the problematic relation between symbol and audience. Higham, extending an older American Studies tradition of myth-and-symbol analysis, bypasses these methodological concerns in a quest for cultural connections and generalizations.

Readers encountering this essay for the first time will be intrigued by the illustrations. Higham's eye for the telling image is also evident in the political cartoons accompanying *Strangers in the Land* (1955) and his essay on the transformation of the Statue of Liberty in *Send These to Me* (1975).

David Glassberg
University of Massachusetts, Amherst

2

America in Person
The Evolution of National Symbols
[1992]

For about twenty years, from the late 1960s to the late 1980s, there was relatively little scholarly study of American *national* consciousness and *national* identity. Intellectual and cultural historians turned so sharply away from the problem of nationalism that it remained on the agenda of research only in the form of a delusion that still needed debunking. For example, the only recent, full-length historical study of early American nationalism treats it as "the most repressive of all abstractions," and Laurence Veysey noted with satisfaction in 1979 that social historians were now focusing almost entirely on subnational groups "because the parts are seen as the realities, the whole as an artificial construction sustained by politicians and financiers."[1]

The notion that the only real communities are smaller than a nation, and closer to the self, has never had so strong a grip on European historians or on historians of the Third World. There the "national question" has been inescapable. In American history those who seek to reopen the national question have much to gain from a comparative perspective drawing on the history of Germany, of eastern Europe, and of the Third World.

A good starting point for comparison is the contrast that Hans Kohn proposed forty-five years ago between nationalism in western Europe on the one hand and in central and eastern Europe on the other. In Britain and France nationalism infused an already existing state and became a means of democratizing it. In central and eastern Europe, national movements were blocked by older empires that legitimized local rulers. Eastern European nationalists were compelled, therefore, to build their claims and hopes on a supposedly unique ethnic culture rather than on a malleable state adaptable to rational principles.[2]

American nationalism was an outgrowth of the western European pattern. In little more than a decade (1775–1789) the movement for independence created a state that theoretically belonged to everyone because it rested on universal principles. Yet cultural nationalism, in the sense of a deep popular consciousness of being a single people, hardly existed. In the United States, therefore, we observe at the beginning of the nineteenth century a weak but popular national state loosely connecting a fragmented, ethnically heterogeneous society.[3] In Germany we see the opposite: a strong ethnic tradition frustrated by political fragmentation. The resulting contrast between the ideological identity of the Americans and the ethnic identity of the Germans is summed up in the language of the people. The United States was not, and was never called, a fatherland. Until sometime in the mid-nineteenth century, there was even considerable reluctance to label it a nation, although George Washington and others occasionally did so. In popular parlance it was "the Union." And the Union was above all a republic: a state in which (as Roger Sherman said at the time) power depends "on the *public* or *people at large*, without any hereditary powers."[4]

On both sides of Kohn's east-west line his distinction between the liberal nationalisms of the West and the intensely ethnic nationalisms of the East was surely drawn too sharply. Every national movement has both a political orientation and *some* ethnic basis, real or supposed. Yet the centrality of a political creed, rather than a people, in the structure of American nationalism has been truly remarkable, and so has the extent to which that creed has counterbalanced ever-present longings for a higher, more comfortable level of ethnic solidarity. We can see these ongoing tensions dramatically played out in the visual symbols Americans have employed to personify their country.

Over the course of American history, image makers have crafted a small number of real or imaginary human beings to symbolize the nation and so to shape its meaning and character. I shall take up the meanings so portrayed roughly in the chronological order in which they came into prominence. At the outset America was simply a *place*, a new world. In the eighteenth century it came to represent a body of *principles,* and soon thereafter a distinctive *polity*—that is, the system through which the principles operate. Finally, nationality seemed to require a *people.* Those are my four categories: place, principles, polity, and people.

For the reasons sketched above, representing a people—in effect, defining a national type—turned out to be the most difficult task for my gallery of symbolic Americans. In a population as heterogeneous as that of the United States, what image could embody the social solidarity that nationalists wanted? Who could personify a single people? Of all of the patterns emergent in national consciousness that one proved the slowest to crystallize.

Let us begin when America was only a place, a vague, little-known place existing on the margins of the European mind.[5] It was perceived then as one of four great land masses, and it was seen as more backward than the other three—Europe, Africa, and Asia. A domain of barbaric cannibals, America alone was personified as a savage. It was necessarily female because all of the principal parts of the world were so defined in the classical tradition and languages that European humanists employed. Gender, however, was less essential to her persona than were the attributes of savagery: partial or complete nudity, bow and arrows, and the close presence of some exotic, wild animal.

An early predilection for exhibiting this primitive America as a naked cannibal gave way in the seventeenth century to less threatening but still muscular images. She might appear, for example, as a barbaric queen, borne aloft in a giant conch shell, scattering largess from her cornucopia to the European adventurers crowding below (Fig. 1).[6] Then, in the eighteenth century, as the New World became less threatening to Europeans, its personification grew softer, more decorative, more Arcadian. Amazons gave way to graceful innocence. In the standard handbook on iconography, however, the contrast between a Europe loaded with symbols of culture and power and an America endowed with nothing but her bow and arrows and the gifts of nature endured (Fig. 2).

This is the form in which British mapmakers appropriated the Indian Princess—the noble savage par excellence—as the key symbol of their American colonies. American colonials became familiar with her as a ubiquitous, allegorical presence in the fanciful cartouches displayed on the maps of their own provinces (Fig. 3).[7]

When conflict erupted in the 1760s between the British government and the American colonists, English caricaturists were just then finding an avid market for satirical prints on contemporary life and politics, which were sold through stationery shops in London and elsewhere.[8] Since the caricaturists were incorrigibly critical of the blunders of their own government, they naturally seized on the innocent Indian princess as their standard personification of the restive British colonies in North America. A simplified version of the idealized Indian that Europeans had invented

Fig. 1. America imagined as a land of untold riches, where Europeans may join in the scramble for favors but have the grim power of a fortress close at hand. Frontispiece by Jacob van Meur for Arnoldus Montanus, *Die Unbekante Neue Welt oder Beschreibung des Welt-teils Amerika und des Sud-Landes* (Amsterdam, 1673). Special Collections, Milton S. Eisenhower Library, The Johns Hopkins University.

Fig. 2. Medieval geographers had divided the world they knew into three parts, centering on Jerusalem. The discovery of the Americas added a fourth. In traditional European iconology the continents ranked from European civilization (*upper left*) to American savagery (*lower right*), with Asia and Africa occupying intermediate positions. Africa sits in front of a pyramid and a camel. Yet a common humanity bathes these symbols of cultural difference. George Richardson, *Iconology,* 2 vols. (London, 1779), vol. 1, plate 16. Library of Congress.

Fig. 3. Cartouche of John Mitchell's map of 1755. Created by a Virginia-born physician and naturalist who emigrated to England in 1746, the famous Mitchell map was commissioned by the Board of Trade to define English territorial rights in North America. It is generally regarded as the most important single map in the history of American cartography. An elaborate cartouche culminates in cherubs displaying British and French emblems overhead, while the Indian Princess and her consort (?) gaze upward, presumably in supplication or gratitude. Their headdress of vertical feathers (which European artists had persistently copied from early woodcuts of the Tupinamba Indians of Brazil) remains to this day, in altered form, a key emblem of the idealized Native American. *A Map of the British and French Dominions in North America with the Roads, Distances, Limits, and Extent of the Settlements* (London, 1755). Library of Congress, Geography and Map Division [G3300 1755 .M5].

proved an effective device for depicting the American colonists as victims of evil British policies.

Accordingly, the Indian Princess was a much abused maiden when London printmakers denounced coercive measures by their own government. Playing on the mother-daughter theme, English artists might present Britannia as an enraged lady of fashion clawing at her half-naked Indian daughter. More commonly, both of them were harrassed by wicked politicians. In an especially powerful criticism of British enforcement of the new tax imposed on tea in 1774, Britannia weeps in helpless shame as

Nº X   Engraved for Royal American Magazine.   Vol. I.

The able Doctor or America Swallowing the Bitter Draught.

Fig. 4. The Able Doctor, or America Swallowing the Bitter Draught, 1774. In December 1773 rebellious American colonists, disguised as Indians, dumped a shipment of British tea into the waters of Boston Harbor, thereby defying a tax that Parliament had levied on the tea. Outraged, the British government closed the port of Boston and imposed a kind of martial law. The American Revolution was under way. Engraving by Paul Revere for *Royal American Magazine,* 1, no. 10 (1774). Library of Congress, Prints and Photographs Division [LC-USZ62-39592].

the Prime Minister forces hot tea down America's throat, she spews it back, and the Lord of the Admiralty peers lecherously up her skirt. On the sidelines, France and Spain consider what advantage they may gain (Fig. 4).[9]

The colonies lacked good cartoonists of their own, so American engravers like Paul Revere occasionally copied for local distribution these English prints featuring the tribulations of the Indian Princess. But the rebellious colonists never felt comfortable about a symbol that linked them with uncivilized natives whose land they were seizing. To Anglo-Americans the Indian signified only a place, and a contested place at that. As soon as American colonials declared independence, they required a symbolic affirmation of their *own* cause and of their parity with Europe, not a reminder of their former dependence and continuing backwardness. As a new nation, America had to be more than a place. It had to embody a principle.

Fig. 5. Pocahontas averts the fatal blow. Depicted here as white in contrast to her dusky, bloodthirsty father, Pocahontas further assured her place in American history by converting to Christianity and in 1614 marrying a prominent Jamestown colonist. It was the first interracial marriage in Anglo-America. Anonymous print (n.d.), Warshaw Collection, National Museum of American History.

In the mid-nineteenth century, after Indian resistance to the expansion of white settlement was largely overcome, white Americans once more looked back with a certain nostalgic fondness to those Indians whose gifts they had taken. Some space was thereupon created in American iconography for Indian peacemakers, such as Pocahontas, depicted often in romantic, nineteenth-century prints as saving the life of Captain John Smith just when her father was about to beat out his brains (Fig. 5).[10] In this resonant legend of the first permanent English settlement on the American mainland, Pocahontas could be understood as the primal American woman—the native princess who, by rescuing the leader of the settlement and later marrying another English colonist, united the land and its conquerors through the mediation of her body and spirit.

Nevertheless, the Indian could never play more than a minor role in personifying the American republic. Too much enmity, suffering, and inequality divided the two races to allow the Indian more than a compensatory presence among the symbols of an independent nation that was proud of its

European origins. After 1776 another woman came to the fore. Reaching back into the iconographic heritage of classical republicanism, Americans embraced a Roman goddess who epitomized both their separation from Britain and their common inheritance. The goddess of liberty, with whom Marius and other leaders of the Roman republic had prominently identified themselves, had reappeared in eighteenth-century England. She emerged in the 1730s, in the midst of a political rhetoric that dwelled on the glories of English liberty and the dangers threatening it. Liberty had become, the English widely agreed, the distinctive genius of British institutions and the birthright of the English people. In truth, liberty and nationality were forming a fateful partnership, which spread from England to America and eventually around the world.

The crucial attribute of the goddess, as preserved on Roman coins and medals, was a close-fitting cone-shaped cap, a *pileus,* carried on a staff as Roman priests had done to bestow on slaves at the ceremony of their emancipation. Otherwise, Liberty presented a severely simple image. In marked contrast to the exotic or luxurious objects that accompanied personifications of the four continents, Liberty wore a plain, white classical gown. She was the visualization of a disembodied principle.

In seizing on Liberty as their national goddess, the Americans appropriated a familiar English symbol. The English goddess, Britannia, who was also a Roman invention, began in the mid-eighteenth century to display a liberty cap, usually held aloft on a staff to signify her solicitude for the rights of all the English.[11] After 1776 the Americans obviously had no use for Britannia. But instead of appointing a new national deity to be (like Britannia) the guardian of liberty, Americans chose Liberty herself as the female personification of the nation. On the first map that published the official boundary of the United States as established in 1783, the cartouche displayed an attractive young goddess holding proudly aloft her cap-topped staff while waving farewell to a blindfolded and weeping Britannia (Fig. 6). At the beginning of the peace negotiations the year before, the American commissioners had used a prerevolutionary map which had retained the Indian Princess.[12] The shift from one symbolic system to another could not have been more dramatically declared. America had become a principle as well as a place.

In creating a U.S. mint in 1792, Congress formalized the choice of Liberty as the embodiment of national consciousness. At first the Senate intended, in conformity with European dynastic precedents, that all coins should bear the image of the current president and identify his

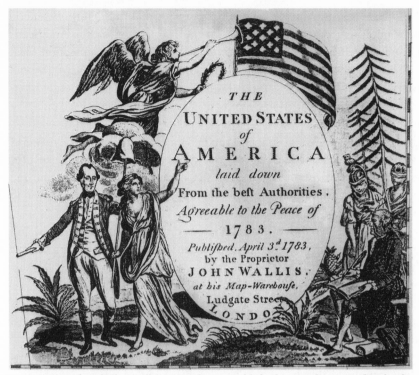

Fig. 6. Cartouche of John Wallis's map of 1783. Published in London immediately after the Peace of Paris was signed, this map lacks entirely the imperial grandeur that pervaded its great predecessor (see Fig. 3). Instead we find George Washington in military dress leading Liberty off to the west, as Benjamin Franklin—the most notable of the American plenipotentiaries—signs a glorious peace. *The United States of America Laid Down from the Best Authorities Agreeable to the Peace of 1783* (London, 1783). RG 76 [Records Relating to International Boundaries, Series 8, No. 21], National Archives, Washington D.C.

administration in a numerical sequence of presidencies. But fears of an imperial presidency persuaded Congress to require coins to be stamped, not with the visage of the president, but with "an impression emblematic of liberty [and] with an inscription of the word Liberty."[13] That is why almost all of the coins of the United States throughout the nineteenth century featured a neoclassical female profile labeled "Liberty."

As a symbol of principle that was serving also as an emblem of place, Liberty was entangled in contradictions. She represented what America was, but also spoke for what Americans thought their country could be. In this wider persona Liberty signified and promoted a national commitment to human rights.

Fig. 7. Samuel Jennings, *Liberty Displaying the Arts and Sciences*, 1792. The painting still hangs in the general reading room of the Library Company of Philadelphia. Library Company of Philadelphia.

The interplay of nationalism and universalism suffuses Samuel Jennings's painting of 1792, *Liberty Displaying the Arts and Sciences.* Surrounded by symbols of the arts, a matronly Liberty in contemporary dress is showing a pile of books to several newly freed slaves (Fig. 7). Although the whole painting is obviously an allegory of hopes for the new nation, it nowhere identifies the central figure as uniquely American. She can be viewed as either national or universal, or both.[14] The picture documents the rise of an antislavery movement and proudly identifies it with the American republic.

While Liberty remained a vital symbol, its capacity to blur distinctions between nation and humanity was one of its special strengths. Yet the supranational persona of Liberty was also a handicap. By herself, without concrete associations such as those that Jennings supplied, she presented a bland, generalized image that was ill suited to rouse and unite a particular people. In much early American symbolism the goddess of liberty does not seem to belong to any specific setting.

Throughout the nineteenth century Americans strove to attach their goddess to the reality of a place and the identity of a people. One gambit

Fig. 8. Edward Savage, *Liberty in the Form of the Goddess of Youth Feeding the American Eagle,* 1796. This stipple engraving was based on Greek mythology as interpreted in 1790 by the Italian academic painter Gaspare Landi. Hebe, goddess of youth and spring and the cup bearer of Olympus, offers her cup to the eagle, a bird sacred to Zeus. Savage energized and nationalized the scene by putting the eagle in flight—descending upon the uplifted cup—and by adding a liberty pole and a church steeple attracting lightning. No other contemporary work succeeded in humanizing Liberty so well. She was a real woman in contemporary dress and imbued with humanly engaging emotions. Yet her ideal significance as embodiment of a principle was assured by her location in semisacred space, midway between earth and heaven. Worcester Art Museum, Worcester, Mass.

was to rename Liberty "Columbia" and to apply the same high-sounding name to everything from colleges to state capitols and patriotic songs. Another way of giving Liberty a national habitat was to require her to carry an American flag or lean on a shield emblazoned with stars and stripes or, best of all, to be the mistress of the American bald eagle, which Congress designated in 1782 as the official emblem of the United States. Since the eagle was always assumed to be male, his close association with Liberty could suggest a sexual as well as a national bond, as in Edward Savage's famous engraving of 1796, in which the hovering eagle is about to plunge his aggressive beak into Liberty's uplifted cup, as lightning plays on a church steeple below (Fig. 8).[15]

Liberty touched the high point of her career as a personification of national principles in the era of the Civil War, when an epochal struggle for national unity became a struggle to make liberty truly national. Both the idealism and the human expressiveness that America's goddess occasionally reached in this period were displayed most powerfully in the drawings of Thomas Nast. Nast's fame as a cartoonist was originally built on his depiction of Columbia during the war and during the period of radical reform immediately following. Perhaps his most influential cartoon was published in 1871 at the height of his furious campaign against the political bosses of New York City (Fig. 9). Here Columbia lies prostrate in a Roman arena under the violating paws of the Tammany Tiger, Nast's symbol for the ruling machine. Columbia's diadem is broken. Blood trickles from her head. From seats of honor in the stands, imperial political bosses look down smugly on the spectacle. The *New York Times* called the cartoon "the most impressive political picture ever produced in this country."[16]

Ultimately, however, the representation of national principles was not enough to satisfy the growing nationalism of the nineteenth century. Americans also wanted ways of personifying the polity—that is, the state they had created—and, finally, some way of representing an American people. For both of these symbolic tasks, male figures came to the fore in the nineteenth century. By personifying universal, unchanging principles and the enduring bonds of humanity, female symbols made Americans aware of connections between the nation-state and all of humanity, or between the nation and God or the nation and the family.[17] Males, on the other hand, characteristically symbolized great deeds, achievements, initiatives. They dramatized action and change rather than universal principles. They embodied the power of government and the active propensities of the people.

George Washington was the first male figure who personified the

Fig. 9. Thomas Nast, *The Tammany Tiger Loose*, in *Harper's Weekly*, November 11, 1871. Many cartoons of the Civil War era presented Columbia (Liberty by another name) in militant postures, brandishing a sword, for instance, while riding her eagle. Nast allowed her righteous anger, but he specialized in grief. His first great success as a cartoonist, when the Democratic National Convention in 1864 proclaimed the Civil War a failure, was a scene, *Dedicated to the Chicago Convention,* in which Columbia is crumpled at the grave of Union heroes while a smug Confederate officer plants his foot on the mound. Endlessly reprinted, the drawing helped Lincoln's reelection.

United States. No other would ever do so to the same degree. None of the later heroes who became national idols, from Andrew Jackson to Charles A. Lindbergh, need detain us. But Washington, at the very beginning of his career on a nationwide stage, turned into a living allegory of the new American republic. Why that happened helps to explain the slow maturation of Uncle Sam, who remained an uncertain figure of small consequence so long as Washington, together with our goddess Liberty, satisfied the symbolic requirements of American nationalism.

Washington's appointment in 1775 as commander in chief of military operations for the Continental Congress dramatically transformed a Virginia colonel into a singular and complete incarnation of the patriot cause. This was partly because his instinctive dignity and self-possession suited the part. But more important, Americans needed a commanding male to succeed the king as the symbolic center of their political firmament.

Prior to the rise of modern nationalism, loyalty to a state functioned through an ingrained attachment to a monarch, to the royal house and family, and in the case of colonies to the royal governors. Everything in this traditional order was done in the king's name. When their colonial rebellion turned reluctantly against the king, Anglo-Americans hungered for an equivalent personification of loyalty and legitimacy—a leader who might give an uncertain experiment a touch of the divinity that still hedged a king. Washington, while carefully repudiating the powers and pretensions of monarchy, provided a psychic substitute in republican dress.

At the outbreak of the Revolution no real person other than George III was shown on the coins and currency that Americans used. The paper money issued by the Continental Congress in 1776 depicted a chain of states. During the 1780s, however, Washington's visage replaced that of George III on coins and tavern signs. An elaborate allegory in the *Boston Magazine* showed Liberty proudly displaying a medallion of Washington in much the same way that Britannia exhibited a medallion of the king in similar British compositions.[18] It is little wonder that as early as 1778, Washington, like the king before him, began to be styled the Father of His Country.[19]

The ceremonial veneration long accorded to kings and princes also collected around Washington. Fervent public celebrations of his birthday spread spontaneously from the army to major towns everywhere. His travels through the states became royal progresses, replete with triumphal arches for him to pass under. "Through all the land," a French correspondent marveled, "he appears like a benevolent god."[20]

Fame came to him partly because he received it so well. Washington knew that he must demonstrate repeatedly an extreme reluctance to hold office, a scrupulous respect for limitations on executive power, and an abhorrence of personal aggrandizement. Though regal in style, in substance he must be a plain republican (Fig. 10). The artists of the time gladly depicted him driving Liberty's coach and receiving her honors and gratitude; but he never sat at her side, as George III sometimes did in English caricatures, and certainly never ranked above her.[21]

Character, rather than accomplishments, was always at the heart of Washington's reputation, and as his influence widened, the uses that were made of his celebrated virtues multiplied. From the outset he personified the fragile American republic, to which he lent a prospect for stability. He was unwavering, persevering, unshakably rooted. The most famous of the nineteenth-century representations of Washington, Emanuel Leutze's *Washington Crossing the Delaware* (1851), gained its dramatic power by

APOTHEOSIS of WASHINGTON

Fig. 10. David Edwin, *Apotheosis of Washington*, 1800. In death (1799) as in life, George Washington was a nation-making force. For several weeks large mourning ceremonies in every American city called forth a national feeling that could mitigate the partisan wrangling of those early years. In response to the sorrow and celebration of the occasion, a number of American artists turned to a European convention in history painting: the apotheosis of great poets and heroes to heaven. Edwin gave Washington a setting of republican simplicity. Clad in the plainest of robes, he rises from his country home to rejoin two young military comrades killed in the first year of the Revolution. National Portrait Gallery, Smithsonian Institution.

presenting the general with his fist clenched, improbably erect in a small boat, in the midst of struggling oarsmen, all buffeted by wind and threatened by ice floes. A contemporary art critic acclaimed the work for giving Washington a distinctive American look, expressed through "a peculiar contraction of the brow and . . . a mouth which denoted indomitable perseverance."[22]

By building his career on an austere ethic of disinterested public service, Washington gained early and cultivated relentlessly a reputation for independence from rival factions and clashing interests. By the time of his death many Americans looked on Washington not only as the oracle of common interests but as the mainstay of a common culture. "When Washington lived," lamented the *Pennsylvania Gazette* after he died, "we had one common mind—one common head—we were united—we were safe."[23]

In the early nineteenth century the yearning for that imagined solidarity seemed to increase. At the same time old fears of the overweening power latent in Washington's fame could be forgotten. As the Washington panegyric poured forth from schoolbooks, orations, and histories, the exaltation of his character as a pattern for Americans passed all bounds.[24]

This posthumous adulation may have served the country well by strengthening the presidential office. As Washington's successors followed one another, each in turn became the chief guardian of the republic. This inheritance of charisma is writ large in the many nineteenth-century prints that linked the presidents to one another in patriotic tableaux. Beginning with Washington's inauguration in 1789, American printmakers developed a market for large patriotic pictures offering a "Display of the United States of America," to borrow the title of the first of them. Sold as "domestic embellishments," the engravings centered on a bust of Washington, surrounded initially by an interlocking chain of states, then later by a circle of all the presidents who followed him.[25] Typically, the design incorporated additional national symbols and carried a title such as *National Galaxy, Our Presidential Portrait Gallery,* or *A Family Picture for the Million* (Fig. 11).

All in all, Washington's lasting achievement was the building of a national state. For the project of molding a national character his image was far less efficacious. As a model *for* Americans, Washington reigned supreme throughout the nineteenth century, but as an embodiment *of* America, he lost credibility in the democratic era signaled by the election of Andrew Jackson.[26] By then something like a national character *was* emerging, and it bore no close resemblance to Washington's. Where he appeared selfless and abnegating, Americans in the large were acquisitive and aggressive.

Fig. 11. The American Union, 1861. The most beautiful and haunting of the "Displays" is an anonymous lithograph published in Cincinnati in 1861, appealing for peace and union but overtaken by war. Blessed by angels above, flanked by woodland scenes of the Indian and the advancing pioneer, and located in a national landscape of prosperity and order, Columbia displays the chain of presidents and the encircling shields of the states. Her own shield bears this inscription:

> A union of hearts, a union of hands,
> A union which none may sever,
> A union of lakes, a union of lands,
> The American Union forever.

Library of Congress, Prints and Photographs Division [15756-USZ62].

Where he stood for harmony and mediation, theirs was a culture of enterprise and contention. Where he was rooted, they were mobile. Washington
had personified the male side of America magnificently in a patrician age,
when an elite culture still functioned as a powerfully integrative force in
society and supplied the lifeblood of an emerging nationalism. By Jacksonian times, however, Americans wanted not just an exemplary hero tower-
ing above them but an incarnation of the people, flaunting their rough
edges and rejoicing in their gritty vitality.

Uncle Sam was invented during the War of 1812. That is a well-known
historical fact.[27] What has not been understood so well is that more than
fifty years were required to transform him from a mere name for the
federal government into a recognizable personification of the nation. As a
mere name, Uncle Sam had no graspable identity. Cartoonists who tried to
visualize Sam in the early nineteenth century achieved only a blank, fea-
tureless male in contemporary dress with no specific attributes other than a
bodily shape contrasting with John Bull's.[28] Sam had to be tall and thin
because John was short and fat. And Sam, in addition to his original and
continuing personification of the U.S. government, had to become a folk
symbol—a man of the people—as John Bull was at the time.

The difficulty was that Americans, unlike the English, had no collective
image of themselves as a people. England's John Bull could be seen at the
end of the eighteenth century as a stolid, long-suffering taxpayer who
phlegmatically supports a crushing military and political establishment, or
as a loyal Englishman who resolutely refuses French demands for surrender.[29] In the nineteenth century John Bull evolved into a general symbol
of the government as well as the people, but he was always basically an
image of the English people.

American publicists in the early nineteenth century knew that there
was as yet no national type; they frequently bemoaned its absence. America
is too young a country, they said, to have yet developed a national character.[30] We may add that it was not only young but also highly decentralized
and spread thinly over a vast space. What stood out in American consciousness was the variety of regional types. Through comic almanacs, theatrical
farces, and the ethnic jokes that circulated in the oral culture, Americans
everywhere absorbed regional stereotypes. They could recognize the New
England Yankee, the southerner, the frontiersman, and the eastern factory worker or urban roughneck. The blandness of Uncle Sam images
in the 1830s and 1840s contrasts strikingly with the concrete vitality of

Fig. 12. E. W. Clay, *The Downfall of Mother Bank,* 1833. Jack Downing, seen here as President Andrew Jackson's boon companion, is applauding the old general's order to remove federal funds from the Second Bank of the United States and thereby ruin it. This was a dramatic moment in the Jacksonian attack on privileged monopolies, and a raw country lad like Jack could be expected to savor it. In 1830, to amuse local readers, an editor in Maine had invented Jack as a fictitious contributor who blunders into the seats of power and reports weekly on the strange doings there. Reprinted everywhere, his letters inspired countless imitators and provided Yankee impersonators with a fresh character to portray on stage. Within a decade the country tired of Jack, but the striped trousers and beaver hat that his impersonators wore passed on to Brother Jonathan and thence to Uncle Sam. Courtesy American Antiquarian Society.

James Akin's New England fisherman, replete with the long nose and nasal speech of the regional Yankee, who sasses the imperious Duke of Wellington during the dispute between Britain and the United States over the boundary of Maine.[31]

As the most prominent and nationalistic of the regional stereotypes, the New England Yankee slowly expanded into Uncle Sam. At the beginning of that process a newspaper editor in Maine invented a hugely popular folk character named Major Jack Downing. The rustic Downing supposedly took his Yankee wit and shrewdness to Washington, D.C., where he became an adviser to President Andrew Jackson. Downing bears on my theme because countless theatrical productions in the 1830s featured him in the clothes that later became the trademark of Uncle Sam: striped pants and a tall, fuzzy beaver hat (Fig. 12).[32]

Another personification of rural New England was Brother Jonathan, a cocky stage character who emerged directly from America's rivalry and connection with Britain. At Bunker Hill in 1776 British troops mocked the country bumpkins they confronted there as "Brother Jonathan," presumably meaning a younger relative of John Bull. Picking up the phrase, American playwrights delivered their riposte in a vein of theatrical braggadocio that contrasted the artificiality of British society with the untutored integrity of America. For a generation Jonathans delighted American audiences. They capered and brayed in the supposed accents of a backcountry trader, but were also aggressively American.[33]

During the 1850s, in humor magazines and theatrical skits, the stereotypical Yankee lost his specifically New England dialect and rustic manners. He became more broadly identifiable as a native-born inhabitant of the northern states.[34] Downing was forgotten while Uncle Sam gradually absorbed and replaced Brother Jonathan. Distinctions between northerner and southerner persisted in Civil War cartoons, of course, though rarely with the insight that Frank Bellew showed in his depiction of a dandified, youthful Brother Jonathan mocking a tattered, embittered southern rebel (Fig. 13). But shortly after the war, Uncle Sam settled into the national mold by which we know him today.

In Thomas Nast's drawings we do not find Uncle Sam fully realized until 1872, when he acquired the white chin whiskers and the maturity that completed his identity. Uncle Sam, like the nation, was no longer young. Beginning in 1872, Nast brought Sam together with his beloved Columbia, making them joint defenders of the American home and family against the supposed menace of Irish Catholicism (Fig. 14).

This slow, halting evolution of a slang term for the federal government into a national type reflects, I believe, an actual social process that gradually subordinated regional and local identities to the consciousness of an American family. When the image of Sam and his family appeared in advertisements, we know that the process was well advanced. A poster advertising kitchen stoves in 1876 showed Sam and Columbia, together with their children—North, South, and West—and their black servant boy, gathered around their kitchen table on the new American holiday of Thanksgiving. Their guest, the World, with a happy smile on his great global head, is eating his way through a long menu of American foods.[35]

The lessening of sectional asperities in the post–Civil War decades ran

Fig. 13. Frank H. T. Bellew, *That's So!* ca. 1864. Against a background of rich farmland, a dapper Brother Jonathan sneers at a ragged, starving Confederate ("Old Secesh") with nothing but a ruined countryside behind him. "You're only walking about to save your funeral expenses!" Courtesy American Antiquarian Society.

parallel to a similar decline in social distance between the older immigrant groups and the white Protestant majority. A backlash against large-scale immigration did start in the 1880s; but the civic recognition that many German and Irish Americans were winning from the Civil War onward prompted a cheerful mingling of ethnic and national symbols in immigrant neighborhoods and newspapers (Fig. 15). The rabid anti-Irish feeling that Nast had fostered in the 1870s faded away.

   In the late nineteenth century new tensions developed in the American

ROMISH INGRATITUDE.—[Drawn by Thomas Nast.]

Fig. 14. Thomas Nast, *Romish Ingratitude,* in *Harper's Weekly,* July 13, 1872. Having cast Uncle Sam and Columbia as joint and equal defenders of the American home and the public school, the most powerful cartoonist of the day shocks our contemporary sensibilities by designating Irish Catholics as the deadly enemy. This is not racism as we know it today. Sam and Columbia, under their household motto "Equal Rights to All," are defending children of all colors against a different kind of intruder. One way of reading this picture is to see it as an example of the rapidity with which burning antagonisms can fade if circumstances change. The George Peabody Library of The Johns Hopkins University.

family. Sam swelled into an aggressive figure, kicking troublesome ethnic children out of his bed, challenging Britain's domination of international trade, and strutting past his envious European rivals with an exotic
Miss Hawaii hanging on his arm. In the tropical islands where he now
strolled, Sam's costume grew ostentatious. His once simple Jacksonian
dress sprouted frills. A boutonniere decked his flaring lapels. His plain

Fig. 15. Cudahy Bros. Packers, ca. 1880s. In densely German Milwaukee, the patrons of meat markets were presumably pleased to learn from this poster-sized advertisement that Uncle Sam had discovered another playmate in Miss Germania, their recently invented national spirit. For us today the poster is striking evidence of rapidly advancing Americanization. Warshaw Collection of Business Americana, Video Disk #44284, NMAH Archives Center, Smithsonian Institution.

old riding boots turned into dancing slippers, and his outsize watch fobs sparkled (Fig. 16). Anti-imperialists depicted Sam as gorged with conquests, but a perhaps more deeply felt response was a kind of piety toward this godlike figure, dispensing justice by fiat (Fig. 17). The era of imperialism and expanding national power was indeed Uncle Sam's apogee.[36]

As for Columbia or Liberty, she remained in the 1890s the same nurturant spirit she had been in the 1790s, although now her humane sympa-

Fig. 16. Bernhard Gillam, *The Champion Masher of the Universe,* in *Judge,* February 25, 1893. An American-supported scheme to overthrow the Hawaiian monarchy failed when the newly elected U.S. president, Grover Cleveland, disavowed it a few days after this cartoon was published in *Judge,* a reliably Republican organ. The expected enhancement of America's international status was delayed for five years. The "masher" (in the slang of the period, an ardent pursuer of attractive women) is visibly envied by John Bull, Emperor William of Germany, King Humbert of Italy, and President Carnot of France.

thies masked an American pursuit of power (Fig. 18). In the early twentieth century she would share the fate of all of the classical goddesses of the nineteenth century. Like Germania, Britannia, and the interchangeable goddesses of civilization, justice, and peace, she was too vaporous, too idealized, to survive in an age of realism and materialism. As late as 1916, Charles Dana Gibson's cartoons were still relying on Columbia as the good, steadying influence on Uncle Sam. Criticizing Wilson's policy of neutrality as German-inspired, Gibson showed a beefy, helmeted Germania distracting a blinded Uncle Sam from the attentions he should be paying to his true love, the willowy Columbia (Fig. 19). But that may have been one of the last occasions on which the American couple appeared together in complementary and interdependent roles.[37]

From World War I onward, a great new personification of liberty more than counterbalanced the passing of Columbia. At first the Statue of Liberty, a

Fig. 17. William Allen Rogers, *An Example to All Nations,* in his *Hits at Politics: A Series of Cartoons* (New York, 1899). A truly worshipful drawing presents Uncle Sam clad in a judicial robe and weighing the alternatives of peace or war against Spain as the USS *Maine* goes down in the background. Print Collection, Miriam and Ira D. Wallach Division of Art, Prints and Photographs, New York Public Library, Astor, Lenox and Tilden Foundations.

gift from France erected in New York Harbor in 1886, seemed little more than a stupendous enlargement of the traditional personification of liberty. In origin, of course, Frédéric Auguste Bartoldi's Statue was the same classical goddess that Americans had earlier conjured in words and pictures. Yet the form and location of the Statue, and the associations that accumulated around it, created a separate, tangibly American identity; and that enabled it to survive the general recession of nineteenth-century idealism. For one

Fig. 18. Grant Hamilton, *Miss Columbia's School,* in *Judge,* February 18, 1893. In another drawing anticipating the annexation of Hawaii, the island kingdom is a repentant child asking for admission to Miss Columbia's School while Canada stands in line to be next. During this distraction, however, the students whom Miss Columbia has already admitted revert to stereotypical misbehavior: a gleeful Russian(?) is pushing an Indian from his swing; a southern ruffian terrorizes a black child with a bayonet; an Irish man punches a Chinese, who drops his opium pipe; goose-stepping Germans carry a socialist flag and a bomb; an Italian organ-grinder is apparently ducking out; and a Mexican in the corner is gambling.

thing, the Statue was a material reality. It was therefore vulnerable: the symbol of a freedom no longer assumed to be immortal or divinely guaranteed. Joseph Pennell's apocalyptic World War I poster, imagining the destruction of the Statue and of the city behind it by enemy bombers, dramatized the danger to liberty in an age of global conflict.[38] Nineteenth-century Americans had felt little need to monumentalize a liberty that seemed secure in their hearts. For twentieth-century Americans liberty was powerfully represented as a strong but destructible work of human hands.[39]

In rescuing Liberty from ungrounded ideality, the Statue at last gave this personification of principle a truly American identity. Standing at the eastern gateway to this country and facing outward to the commerce of the world with the skyline of the nation's greatest city rising behind her, the Statue became in the early twentieth century an essential local landmark. Recognizable everywhere through postcards, magazine covers,

Fig. 19. Charles Dana Gibson, *The Charmer,* in *Life,* June 22, 1916. By this time the famous "Gibson Girl" has lost the youthful vitality and independence she projected in the 1890s, but her anxious concern for Uncle Sam's fidelity and rectitude remains appealing. On the cover of *Life* in 1920 Gibson resurrected Columbia for at least one more time. There, in celebrating the final enactment of nationwide women's suffrage, she offers an affectionate, matronly handshake to a young suffragist. Mostly, however, the scattered survivals of Columbia in the 1920s tend to be demeaning, as in Rollin Kirby's sketch of her as a stenographer taking a letter from Uncle Sam.

travel writings, and New York State license plates, it was not an ancient goddess but rather the centerpiece of a fabled American place. It became our contemporary equivalent of the Indian Princess, announcing the presence of a "continent . . . commensurate to [man's] capacity for wonder."[40]

To complete its Americanization, the Statue of Liberty absorbed still another layer of meaning. For the millions of eager immigrants who passed

Fig. 20. Welcome to the Land of the Free, in *Frank Leslie's Illustrated Newspaper,* July 2, 1887. American history textbooks have made this early scene of immigrants' first view of the Statue of Liberty a familiar and affectionate sight. Apparently, however, there is no other picture like it in late nineteenth-century American mainstream publications. The statue was originally viewed by Americans (and its French sponsors) as radiating freedom outward to the world. Not until American public schools in the early twentieth century began cultivating (and reenacting in pageants) the immigrants' own view of a glorious welcome did the Statue of Liberty fully absorb this major extension of its significance as a great American icon.

beneath the uplifted torch, interpreting its message as a welcome to themselves, the Statue symbolized a uniquely inclusive nation in which newcomers of many different origins could be at home. For the first two decades after its erection this immigrant perception of the Statue as symbol of an inclusive America made little or no impression on native American opinion (Fig. 20). During the First World War and the Americanization campaign that followed it, however, government propaganda celebrating the loyalty of new citizens gave public legitimacy to their personal response (Fig. 21).[41] As a result, the Statue of Liberty came to personify a multiethnic people more convincingly than any of its predecessors. Today it speaks for all the meanings of America: for place, principles, people, and— imprinted as it is on every check issued by the U.S. Treasury—for the polity as well (Fig. 22).

From the story I have told much too briefly, two conclusions may be

IL CIBO VINCERÀ LA GUERRA!
Venite qui a cercare la libertà
Dovete ora aiutare a conservarla
Il PANE è necessario agli alleati
NON SPRECATE NULLA

Fig. 21. C. E. Chambers, *Il Cibo Vincerà la Guerra!* ca. 1917. During World War I the U.S. government drew heavily on the immigrants' sense of connection with the Statue of Liberty by distributing posters in numerous languages urging support of "liberty" bonds and other wartime needs. Here the U.S. Food Administration appeals for conservation of food. "Don't waste anything." United States Food Administration.

drawn, the first based chiefly on Uncle Sam. Unlike the Indian Princess and the goddess of liberty, Uncle Sam endures into our own time. His presence and role have greatly shrunk, however. As early as the 1930s some cartoonists were calling for a less stern and deaconish character who might look and act more like "the real American" of the twentieth century. There was no agreement, and among American political cartoonists Uncle Sam remained a heavily worked device. Nevertheless, the genuine affection that Americans had felt before World War I for that craggy Yankee figure was slipping away.[42] The Vietnam War hastened Uncle Sam's decline (Figs. 23–24). Since then he has rarely represented national strength and has become more often a target of criticism. By the 1990s the frequency of his appearance has diminished, too.[43]

Fig. 22. U.S. stamps, 1922, 1954. The Statue of Liberty, in its first appearance on a U.S. postage stamp in 1922, was just one among many American places that series of stamps depicted. It received no special emphasis. By 1954, when the statue adorned the basic stamp for ordinary letters, it had become a radiant embodiment of the nation's faith.

He remains nonetheless a reliable vehicle for either applauding or criticizing the American people and their government. Depending on the context, Uncle Sam may stand for both or for either (Fig. 25). American cartoonists never firmly established a separate male personification of the people, comparable to Germany's der Deutsche Michael or Portugal's Zé Povinho. Even today, when the state is increasingly distrusted, Americans do not seem to want to differentiate clearly between state and people. On a cover of the *New Yorker,* Uncle Sam wears an apron emblazoned with historic mottoes of public endeavor while devoting himself contentedly to the private pleasures of a holiday picnic.[44] The picture seems to say that Americans have no trouble mixing and matching professions of patriotism with personal indulgences.

Thus, in the structure of American nationalism, Uncle Sam reveals a persistent though declining identification of the people with the state.

Figs. 23 and 24. James Montgomery Flagg, *I Want You,* 1917, and Committee to Help Unsell the War, *I Want Out,* ca. 1971. As the full burden of the Vietnam War came home to Americans in the late 1960s, and college students were evading conscription in droves, James Montgomery Flagg's famous World War I recruiting poster fell subject to widespread mockery. Among the scores of images ridiculing and demonizing the U.S. government, however, a few such as *I Want Out* made serious appeals to end the war. The pathos of this anonymous product of advertising professionals provides a measure of the decline of patriotism and the weakening of the Uncle Sam image in this period. Yanker Poster Collection, Prints and Photographs Division, Library of Congress [LC-USZ C4-3860].

When people and state diverge, or when a failure seems too pervasive to blame on particular politicians or interest groups, Uncle Sam in our political cartoons exhibits the sickness or stupidity of both the state and the people.[45] So closely intertwined are the two meanings of the symbol that American political cartoonists are largely debarred from representing Uncle Sam as the oppressor of his own people. In other parts of the world cartoonists can more readily depict a malevolent Uncle Sam without intending to implicate the American people.

A second conclusion is actually a question that hovers over the female figures of liberty and concerns their persistent display of a universalizing dimension in the symbolic order of a particular people. I have already touched on the positive aspect of this dimension; it has given American

Fig. 25. Steve Sack, *Untitled*, 1983. Uncle Sam never fully recovered from the Vietnam War. Here we find him as Jonah in the whale's belly, awash in the federal deficit of the 1980s and unable to think of a way out. He is now short and pudgy and doesn't look very bright. Reprinted with permission of the *Minneapolis Star Tribune*.

nationalism an unusual responsiveness to transnational ideals of freedom and to multiethnic definitions of American society. Since World War I the statue's uplifted torch and flaring crown have repeatedly vivified struggles for civil liberties at home while promoting the extension of American influence abroad. The same multivalent symbol that can simply represent the United States has inspired the feminist movement in this country; and it electrified people everywhere when reborn in 1989 as the "Goddess of Democracy" in Beijing's Tiananmen Square.

But there is also a negative side to the conflation of American nationalism with human freedom. It tempts Americans to confuse the welfare of humankind with their own national interests and so to assume the universal acceptability of American leadership and goals. Is this confusion worse than a hard-boiled differentiation between national interest and human need? Does the ethnocentric universalism that runs through American history still offer a significant counterpoise to national egoism? These are pregnant questions for the history of nationalism.

When Higham was invited to a meeting of the Korean Association for American Studies in 1984, he was asked to address the theme of pragmatism as an American way of life. By this time, several historians were writing important books on the philosophical pragmatism of John Dewey, William James, and Charles Peirce; and contemporary intellectuals such as Stanley Fish, Hilary Putnam, and Richard Rorty were reviving pragmatism as a vital element in the debate over postmodern philosophy. Korean scholars, however, were working in an older tradition in which philosophers were seen as American prophets, and pragmatism was viewed as a cultural pattern rather than a formal system of thought.

Returning to this earlier view, Higham recalled his graduate student days at the University of Wisconsin in the late 1940s, when the philosophy professor Max Otto declared that the grand epistemological ideas had come from Europe but that American philosophy had turned them into guidelines for ethical living. Higham's essay parses this looser construction of pragmatism as a practical approach to life. Analyzing the ways that commentators have used "pragmatism" to praise or to blame Americans, Higham suggests that the concept has served as a site for rehearsing the conflict between materialism and idealism, two symbiotically related impulses in the American character.

This is, in fact, the only essay in this volume that addresses squarely the theme of American national character, a popular subject in the 1950s and early 1960s, when consensus was the watchword. In the next two decades, the concept of national character was discarded by historians, who were preoccupied with Americans' internal differences and suspicious of the ties between exceptionalist theories and American imperialism. Higham himself had warned as early as 1959 that consensus history went too far in dismissing American conflicts and diversities. But he also believed that national character remained an undeniable cultural reality with genuine explanatory power. If national character was construed in terms of the conflicts it contained and the changes it resisted, it could help to make sense of Americans' divisions as well as their common culture. This essay was meant to demonstrate such a middle path between the consensus history of the 1950s and the conflict-driven history of subsequent decades.

Whether Higham has explained the paradox of being American or simply restated it more elegantly is up to the reader to decide. He does, however, suggest a provocative answer to the question of why pragmatism no longer stirs intense debate in America: it is built into the bureaucratic structures that have increasingly replaced ideology as the cement of our modern society. What Higham calls technical unity in Chapter 1 of this book has rendered less visible and less controversial the moral dilemmas associated with pragmatic idealism. Beginning the essay by asking why American scholars have forgotten the pragmatic American, Higham ends by noting that practicality may be losing its distinctively American identity as it accompanies modernization and specialization around the world.

William L. Joyce
Pennsylvania State University

3

Rediscovering the Pragmatic American
[1986]

S ome years ago, when the Korean Association for American Studies convened a meeting in Seoul, its sponsors asked me to address the theme of their conference. The topic, "Pragmatism as an American Way of Life," was both familiar and strange. It brought suddenly back to mind debates of yesteryear that no longer engaged my colleagues at home. Why had I and other Americans almost forgotten what my Korean hosts wanted to understand? Their theme seemed to me both appealing and freshly provocative.

I found it appealing because it would focus attention on an aspect of American life and thought that foreign observers had often contrasted, for better or worse, with the more traditional ways of their own societies. The contrast was important, I believed, and admirably suited to an international colloquy. At the same time the subject was disconcerting. Why had I and nearly all of my fellow Americanists in the United States lost interest completely in a feature of our national culture that had so strongly impressed generations of foreign and domestic observers alike? How could we, over the past three decades, have abandoned the pragmatic American whom we had once celebrated and reviled? The disappearance of the pragmatic American from American Studies was an intriguing puzzle.

When I began teaching American intellectual history in 1948, the allegedly practical temper of American civilization was one of the basic themes on which I relied. The great intellectual initiatives had arisen in Europe, I suggested, but Americans had made them effective and useful. In taking this line I was simply following my teachers and a long succession of critics and commentators stretching back to Alexis de Tocqueville and before. "A

thousand special causes," Tocqueville had written, "have singularly con-
curred to fix the mind of the American upon purely practical objects. His
passions, his wants, his education, and everything about him seem to unite
in drawing the native of the United States earthward; his religion alone bids
him turn, from time to time, a transient and distracted glance to heaven."[1]

The only question I remember explicitly posing about this alleged
predilection had to do not with its truth (which I took for granted) but with
its consequences. Had America's pragmatic cast of mind served the country
well or ill? The same question reverberated in the famous teaching aids
that were produced in the early 1950s by the Department of American
Studies at Amherst College, *Pragmatism and American Culture* and *Benjamin Franklin and the American Character.*[2] With these booklets we invited our students to consider whether pragmatic ways of thinking had led
Americans into a crass expediency or had guided them in solving problems.

Yet few historians, it now seems to me as I look back, were genuinely
curious about America's pragmatic heritage. It did not engage us as a
problem. We knew American history also encompassed contrary tendencies that clashed with the image of the flexible, calculating Yankee, and
those were the impulses that young historians wanted to study. One knew
that Tocqueville was badly mistaken in lightly dismissing the intense re-
ligiosity of Americans as a transient and distracted glance to heaven. One
knew that practicality had nothing to do with the fanatical defense of slavery in the Old South, with the founding of scores of utopias in the nineteenth century, with Woodrow Wilson's crusade to make the world safe for
democracy, or with the discontents of modern American writers and intellectuals. Some of the contrary tendencies were wildly visionary, some
cruelly repressive, some laden with destruction and despair. Whatever
value judgment one reached on American practicality, the contrary tendencies—which Henry May in 1959 called the Other Tradition—seemed to
most historians in the 1950s and 1960s far more interesting and exciting.[3]
Consequently it was the Other Tradition in its many guises that historians
concentrated upon, from the 1950s onward, in exploring the variousness
and the possibilities of their national heritage. It is true that Daniel J.
Boorstin celebrated a native pragmatism in the first two volumes of his
monumental three-volume work, *The Americans* (1958–1973). But Boorstin's was an exceptional voice; and even he quietly abandoned the pragmatic theme in the late 1960s and 1970s, when the success of American
institutions could no longer be regarded as self-evident.[4]

Thus the tumult of the 1960s seems to have accelerated a shift of
attention that was already under way, and somehow the subject of pragma-

tism as a way of life disappeared from the agenda of American scholarship. What was once taken for granted as a social or cultural reality—and disputed as a value—is now remembered, if at all, as an unmanageably diffuse notion belonging to an outmoded debate about national character. In 1980, David Hollinger's excellent article "The Problem of Pragmatism in American History" made clear at the outset that the significant historical problem for him was to explain the origin and popularity of philosophical pragmatism in a particular era. An understanding of the philosophy associated with William James and John Dewey, Hollinger declared, could "scarcely be expected to come about so long as pragmatism is . . . stretched to cover all of America."[5]

I regretted this narrowing of the scope of inquiry, and I saluted my Korean colleagues for placing the question of pragmatism in its broadest sense once more before us. The importance of precision and specificity is often cited as a good reason for avoiding the misty generalities of national character. But that does not seem to me sufficient justification for abandoning altogether the inquiry of Tocqueville, Bryce, and our greatest historians into the characteristics of the American people. To reject out of hand (as most historians and social scientists now do) any reference to an American character is to imply that nationality does not shape individual identities or major historical tendencies in any profound way and that national feeling is some kind of colossal popular mistake. Most Americans still believe they are a people, and register that belief in action in countless ways. During much of our history since 1776, Americans have affirmed their peoplehood with fervency. Since those who feel themselves joined in a common destiny are highly susceptible to the formation of a common culture, a history that looks only at divisions and diversities may not succeed in making much sense of them.

Returning to a topic that has been brushed aside for more than a quarter of a century necessarily presents that topic in a fresh light. As I look back at the strange disappearance of an American pragmatic temper from the discourse of American scholars, two questions suggest themselves as starting points for analysis. One question has to do with the persistent doubleness of American culture, the other with the changes this divided culture may have undergone in recent years. The first question is simply: How can we explain the apparent fissure in American culture that Henry May observed over three decades ago? How are we to account for the prominent coexistence in the United States of cool practicality and its antitheses? Can America somehow be a nation of pragmatic Lockeans who are also tormented saints?[6] The critics and historians who have written about this contradiction have been content with stating a paradox. It is time to ask for historical explanation.

The second question that needs to be addressed if pragmatism as a way of life is to be restored to the agenda of American scholarship is this: Why did it drop off that agenda? Does the disinterest of late twentieth-century scholars in the subject of American pragmatism help to explain its salience in an earlier era? Is pragmatism, like other aspects of a nation's character, a fixed trait, or is it a changeable disposition? To deal with either of these problems—the continuing schism and the recent changes—we will have to be as precise as possible in defining the pragmatism we are talking about.

To that end let us look at some of the more notable descriptions that American intellectuals have written of their nation's pragmatic mentality. The commentaries seem to fall into two overlapping but somewhat distinct categories. Each category rests on a basic antithesis. For one group of commentators practicality contrasts with idealism. The subject of lament among this group is the prevalence in America of pragmatic materialism. For a second group of commentators practicality contrasts with fixed or constraining beliefs. These writers associate pragmatism with experimentalism.

Let us begin with materialism. According to the critics of American materialism, all the circumstances that have made Americans autonomous have exposed them to the debasing influence of immediate, crass self-interest: the absence, from the earliest days, of any strong constraints on capitalism; the accessibility of abundant natural resources; and the migratory habits of a people with only shallow roots in any fixed community. I suspect that throughout the whole span of American history no rhetorical theme has resounded more continually than the warning that a grasping practicality betrays the underlying ideals that Americans have cherished.

An influential modern example is Van Wyck Brooks's argument that American culture suffers from a stultifying separation between disembodied ideals and a "current of catchpenny opportunism, originating in the practical shifts of Puritan life, becoming a philosophy in Franklin, passing through the American humorists, and resulting in the atmosphere of contemporary business life."[7] Lewis Mumford wrote in the same vein when he excoriated the self-interest and expediency that had brought American intellectuals to a "Pragmatic Acquiescence" in an ugly social order. Richard Hofstadter gave us a far more sophisticated account of how the anti-intellectualism of business leaders fostered an excessively practical bias, which in turn (Hofstadter thought) has permeated every area of American life.[8]

It is unfortunate that Hofstadter and other modern critics have attributed a crass, short-sighted practicality so largely to the influence of business leaders. Many nineteenth-century Americans thought politicians at least equally responsible. A deeply ingrained distrust of government contributed to the sinister connotations that the word "politician" acquired in the United States. To "play politics" is, in American usage, to betray principle for the sake of personal or group advantage. "Politics is, as it were, the gizzard of society, full of grit and gravel," Henry David Thoreau wrote. And H. L. Mencken, quoting an anonymous source, added that a politician is "an animal who can sit on a fence and yet keep both ears to the ground."[9]

Thus when pragmatism has implied a sacrifice of idealism in business, politics, or any other sphere, it has been taken to signify a glaring and fundamental contradiction in American culture. Even in our own time, in spite of certain changes I will discuss shortly, this opposition between pragmatism and idealism continues to prick American consciences. Some years ago an article in the *New York Times* argued that higher education in America has long oscillated between two poles, the ideal and the pragmatic. In lean times students become pragmatic, flocking to courses in business administration; and the universities themselves increasingly resemble businesses. In more prosperous times the students express more idealism by moving into philosophy, political science, and literature; and universities project a more lofty image.[10]

The other general context in which America's pragmatic bent is discussed usually puts that inclination in a much more positive light, at least among American commentators. When pragmatism signifies an experimental attitude, practicality contrasts with fixed, a priori principles. In this context a practical outlook partakes not of a slavish, mean-spirited materialism but rather of a self-reliant, clear-eyed empiricism. Here practicality connotes freedom from hidebound rules, whether those rules take the form of traditional shibboleths or abstract doctrines remote from everyday experience. "Abstract reasonings they dislike," declared James Bryce, "subtle reasonings they suspect; they accept nothing as practical which is not plain, downright, apprehensible to an ordinary understanding."[11] Robin Williams characterized the pragmatic orientation as a "short-range adjustment to immediate situations," and Boorstin has lyrically described the innovations it inspired in creating resources, organizing production, and reshaping the law.[12] Pragmatism in this sense is associated with the attainment of industrial efficiency on one hand and the flexible negotiation of political compromises on the other.

The distinction I have sketched between two types of pragmatism may help to clarify positions that American intellectuals have taken. But the two versions have blurred together in popular consciousness, especially in the ethos of American business. The business culture has celebrated both material reward and empirical flexibility, each buttressing the other. Consider, for example, how William Allen White, a rising small-town editor in Kansas at the turn of the twentieth century, presented to a railroad promoter his own qualifications for handling the printing jobs the railroad would require in that part of the state. White's letter broached the subject as "a practical business scheme that will make you some money and me some money." The editor continued: "I am a practical printer and have made the newspaper business a financial success and I know how to run a printing office. I want to form a stock company with you to do all the printing for the Orient Railroad in Emporia."[13] Here White equates practicality with both material gain and operational skill. He has the know-how to run a printing office. Though a newspaper editor, he is no dreamy idealist. Millions of Americans must have defined themselves in just that way.

Coming back to the experimental dimension of American practicality, let us not suppose that American intellectuals have always thought well of it. A pragmatic fixation on immediate operational choices can seem as stultifying as a pragmatic fixation on material self-interest. For about a century a myth prevailed that utilitarian priorities were diverting Americans from doing basic, theoretical work in science. Nathan Reingold has shown that American scientists were themselves among the leading propagators of the myth.[14]

Pragmatism in the sense of a worship of technique has also been held responsible for major failures in American foreign policy. In terms reminiscent of Van Wyck Brooks and Randolph Bourne, Stanley Hoffmann, for example, has argued that a fatal disjunction separates the narrow pragmatism of policy makers from the simple, inflexible principles that Americans honor. The "American Style" in foreign policy, Hoffmann tells us in *Gulliver's Troubles*, has treated ends as fixed and sacrosanct while allowing means to be chosen by purely technical criteria. "The pragmatic approach," Hoffmann says, "means, all too often, priority to what is urgent over what is important. Events, not policy makers, appear to order the issues." In wartime, for example, the urgency of winning displaces the importance of shaping the postwar world.[15]

In spite of these criticisms of a "short-range adjustment to immediate situations," I have the impression that pragmatic experimentalism was never as loaded an issue as pragmatic materialism. It never engaged American consciences as deeply. If my impression is correct, many Americans in the nineteenth and first half of the twentieth century gladly acknowledged a pragmatic bent when it contrasted with prescription or theory, but found it troubling and problematic when it cast doubt on their idealism. Perhaps what was truly distinctive about pragmatic Americans was not their concentration on either facts or tangible rewards, since both forms of calculation may be a consequence of capitalism in all countries. The distinctive feature of Americans' pragmatism may have inhered rather in their intense need to embrace both practicality and idealism: for each to be at once a pragmatic Lockean and a tormented saint.

If there is in American history an intimate, mutually sustaining connection between materialistic practicality and unworldly ideals, the American intellectuals who have noticed only the threat of the former to the latter have taken too simple a view of their culture. To be sure, practicality and idealism have been arrayed against each other in many specific contexts, as in the Jeffersonian Embargo, the antislavery movement, and the campaign to drive Richard Nixon from the presidency. On a wide and deeper level, however, practicality and idealism have been symbiotic in America; each has nourished the other. That is what George Santayana meant in describing the American as "an idealist working on matter." Henry Adams struck the same note in his famous description of the United States in 1800: "the hard, practical, money-getting American democrat, who had neither generosity nor honor nor imagination, and who inhabited cold shades where fancy sickened and where genius died, was in truth living in a world of dream, and acting a drama more instinct with poetry than all the avatars of the East, walking in gardens of emerald and rubies, in ambition already ruling the world and guiding Nature with a kinder and wiser hand than had ever yet been felt in human history. . . . Even on his practical and sordid side, the American might easily have been represented as a victim to illusion."[16]

What Adams and Santayana described so vividly let us now venture to explain. The American people developed in the nineteenth century a lively consciousness of themselves as a highly mobile population of heterogeneous origins. This migratory people lived in a loose-knit, scattered society with weak central institutions. They lacked the dense fabric of tradition and the overbearing structures of power that held other countries together. Their one great bond of unity was a set of national ideals that endowed them with the transcendent purpose of realizing the hopes of humankind. This intensely ideological orientation, this need to conceive of themselves as holders of a sacred trust, made Americans sensitive to criticism of their narrow self-interest and often acutely guilty about it. Idealism flourished in nineteenth-century America at least partly to deny and overcome the menace it confronted in the American pragmatic temper.

Yet idealism also had the paradoxical effect of encouraging the practicality it tried to restrain. In most of the modernizing world a short-range adjustment to immediate situations has been impeded by entanglements of local customs, ceremonies, superstitions, taboos, and the like. Americans, however, being ideologists from the outset, were attuned to universal principles. Rational calculation, as a means of translating objectives into programs, came easily to them. Thus an ideological orientation emancipated individuals from the matrix of tradition. Norms were internalized in the form of conscience. This in turn freed Americans to calculate practical strategies, and to adopt new devices, without fearing the atrophy of old customs. If an ideological bent gave Americans a bad conscience about some of their hungry appetites, it also cleared their way toward a worship of technique.[17]

My interpretation of how and why traditional American culture was at war with itself is phrased in the past tense because I want to take up in conclusion the second question posed early in this essay. Why has discussion of American practicality faded away? I suspect that loss of interest in the question of pragmatism in recent decades lends some inferential support to my belief in the deeply felt importance of idealism in an earlier era. In the twentieth century the United States underwent an organizational revolution. This revolution has created vast bureaucracies. It has centralized power, tying together regions, classes, and groups as never before. America now has the interlocking structures of authority so notably absent from the decentralized republic of a century ago. Reliance on national ideology—indeed, on any scheme of ideals—to hold the country together and animate the energies of its people has correspondingly diminished. Pragmatism is now built into the organizational complex. It has become more an attribute of the system than a trait of the people. One might even go so far as to say that the organizational revolution is changing a nation of saints and pragmatists into a nation of specialists, ruled over by a pragmatic elite.

Consider, for instance, how unlikely it would be today for a newspaper editor to assert his practical business sense the way William Allen White did nearly a century ago. No honest editor today would be proposing money-making schemes to a railroad president. Today's editors are professional or quasi-professional experts who market their special skill and leave to the publisher the selling of services and the building of profitable relationships with other community leaders. The publisher in turn hands over most of these chores to advertising agencies, public relations counselors, trade associations, and investment bankers. Nobody with any authority has to convince anyone else that he or she is a hardheaded pragmatist rather than an ineffectual idealist. Even the editors, now shorn of the multiple roles they once had, are unlikely to feel the continual strain that White experienced in being an idealist working on matter.

Of course the moral dilemmas that were phrased in the nineteenth century in the language of national character have not gone away. But those dilemmas now present themselves more urgently as institutional problems. Pragmatic calculation (however defined) is very likely as widespread as ever in the United States. But it is less discussed, and therefore less visible, because the idealism that spurred its development no longer confronts it with so stark and absolute a challenge.[18]

If the Americans are less inclined than they once were to think of themselves as a preeminently practical race, it would seem plausible that the rest of the world, too, might modify that image. The evidence I have gathered on this point is scanty but suggestive. In a public opinion poll in 1952 people in six western European countries were asked to pick from a long list the five traits that best describe the Americans. Practicality and receptiveness to progress headed the list. Both traits turned up in all but one of the six national surveys.[19] Twenty years later, in a poll of British opinion, the Americans got high marks for efficiency and friendliness; but practicality was no longer explicitly inquired about. In the interim a British poll of 1967 solicited opinions about several nations by presenting a list of twenty-four qualities, including practicality. Receptiveness to progress still headed the list of American traits in British eyes; but practicality ranked only sixth among the twenty-four choices. In this poll both the Germans and the Russians received higher scores for practicality than did Americans. More recently, an international poll conducted for the American magazine *Newsweek* to determine how others see the United States failed to include either practicality or efficiency in its list of fourteen American characteristics.[20] Apparently the United States is losing its reputation as the world headquarters of pragmatism.

We all know how misleading national stereotypes can be. Yet they are important aspects of a nation's culture, as well as lenses through which the nation is perceived. When stereotypes change, historians would do well to take seriously what the shift may be signaling. In the case before us a pragmatic culture may be losing its distinctively American configuration as it spreads through the modernizing world.

Intellectual history held a preeminent place among historians after World War II by virtue of its claim to identify the unifying framework of ideas and values that had ostensibly created a distinctive and triumphant American people. When the concept of national character came under attack in the 1960s and 1970s, historians of ideas were compelled to defend their approach in the face of a new social history employing rigorous social science methods and emphasizing the experience of previously marginalized groups. In this setting, Higham helped bring focus to a major reformulation of intellectual history when he and Paul K. Conkin organized a conference and coedited the ensuing book of essays, *New Directions in American Intellectual History* (1979). This symposium demonstrated that many historians of ideas were responding to recent criticisms by abandoning the search for broad generalizations and defining their subject as the work of carefully delimited intellectual communities.

The possibilities of this approach had already been suggested by a long-term study of the institutional structures of American science and scholarship sponsored by the American Academy of Arts and Sciences. First presented in a symposium in 1975, the case studies appeared in *The Organization of Knowledge in Modern America, 1860–1920* (1979). Higham, who had served on the advisory committee for the project, was asked to provide an introductory overview. A seemingly simple commission, it was complicated by the strong sentiment of the moment against generalization. Drawing on his own study of the historical profession, Higham produced a synthesis that was both anchored in an understanding of institutional structures and informed by a wide-ranging interest in cultural patterns in America.

Identifying the "rampant growth of specialization" in the period 1860–1920 as a pervasive theme in the history of knowledge, he noted that this pattern involved an "extraordinary reversal" in American attitudes toward specialization. This accommodation to "technical unity" was possible, he argued, because expertise in America was democratized through broad decentralization, which allowed everyone within a profession to carve out an autonomous domain. The contrast between European and American academic departments and learned societies illustrated this Tocquevillian insight. Higham pointed out that a peculiarly horizontal structure in America accommodated both a proliferation of specialties and a dislike of centralizing authorities. These tendencies were counterbalanced in the twentieth century by the appearance of large private foundations and mediated by a wide range of new reference tools.

Higham referred to his essay as a kind of prospectus for "a still unwritten general history of specialization," but subsequent historians of the professions have followed other paths. An exception is Thomas Bender, whose works exploring the relationship between intellectuals and public life share Higham's interest in combining close study of particular communities with broader social questions. Yet the cogency of Higham's analysis is attested by the continuing proliferation of academic fields in the face of persistent complaints of overspecialization, and the vehement charges of elitism that greet any observation about the need for synthesis in American history.

Sally F. Griffith
Franklin and Marshall College

4

Specialization in a Democracy
[1979]

B etween 1860 and 1920 the modern organization of knowledge came into being. It is true that some foundations for wide collaboration in sustained, self-correcting research were laid before the Civil War—the Smithsonian Institution, for example, under Joseph Henry's inspired direction, and the American Association for the Advancement of Science, which provided after 1848 a general clearinghouse for scientific reports. Also, in the first half of the nineteenth century a few professors had won the right to be judged primarily on their original investigations.[1] Yet these were mere beginnings. In 1860 there was no American university fully worthy of the name. The United States had no libraries of national or international renown, no industrial laboratories or great private foundations, no widely based learned societies devoted exclusively to the advancement of knowledge within a single limited field. In the late nineteenth and early twentieth centuries all these agencies took shape. Interlocking with one another, they constituted a matrix for research that has survived to this day.

Efforts to account for this enormous and complex reordering of intellectual life have characteristically viewed it from outside, as a change in conditions of employment. Amateur scholars and gentlemen-scientists gave way to professionals. A "professional outlook" thereupon reshaped the production and conservation of knowledge.[2] Accordingly we now have a growing literature, with its own internal controversies, on the history and sociology of the academic and scholarly professions. Historians, while differing in their definitions of "professionalization," have largely agreed in assigning it preeminent importance.

Undeniably central though it is, the theme of professionalization does not go to the heart of this great transition. As Laurence Veysey reminds us, the professions already composed an influential sector of American society before scholarly disciplines became professionalized. The reorganization of the professions in such a way as to vest new authority in emerging academic groups must have been an effect of antecedent changes as well as a cause. It is necessary therefore to ask: What distinctive characteristic of nineteenth-century knowledge impelled its creators and custodians to turn their particular competences into professions? The obvious answer is specialization. The multiplication and differentiation of bodies of esoteric knowledge made the new professions possible. Indeed, the rampant growth of specialization pervades, as no other theme does, the history of knowledge in the period under examination. It is so ubiquitous that historians have taken it for granted, as if it were one of the constants of nature, like the speed of light, rather than one of the riddles of history.

The essays in *The Organization of Knowledge in Modern America, 1860–1920* (1979), edited by Alexandra Oleson and John Voss, may be read, therefore, not only as separate chapters in the variegated history of science and scholarship but also as contributions to a still unwritten general history of specialization. What such a history might embrace—what illumination it might give to the most fundamental problems of modern society—we can only begin to guess. But the materials before us do yield some clues to one aspect of the topic—they tell us something about the shape that intellectual specialization has assumed in the United States. Most particularly, they compel attention to an extraordinary reversal in American attitudes toward specialization.

Before looking at attitudes and institutions, something should be said about specialization as a process that would bring about a greater division of intellectual labor, a process that went on continuously throughout the nineteenth century. Before the Civil War, a professor of natural philosophy in the smaller colleges might have taught all the sciences, but in the larger ones the responsibility was more and more divided. Thus Yale created a professorship of mathematics in 1836, separated chemistry from natural history in 1853, and eleven years later divided natural history between a professor of botany and a professor of geology. Some "men of science" hailed the trend. Others regretted it.[3] Until after mid-century, however, these reactions seem to have done little to shape or direct the process. In the second half of the century specialization acquired a programmatic thrust. The institutional matrix, which had earlier accommodated increasing specialization, was now transformed by it. This happened as effective resistance to specialization markedly declined.

In the early nineteenth century, specialization went against the grain of American culture. To parcel out segments of work or knowledge, so that the responsibility of each person contracts while dependence on others increases, violated the American ideal of the untrammeled individual and its corollary, the jack-of-all-trades. Moreover, the intellectual specialist affronted egalitarian values by dealing in secrets only a few could share. In Jacksonian America, disdain for esoteric knowledge and hostility toward any narrow delimitation of competence flourished. Both the learned professions and the colleges were distrusted as bastions of privilege. Under the pressure of populistic criticism both lowered their standards. Commencement speakers assured their audiences, as Gulian C. Verplanck did at Union College in 1836, that science was no longer "a thing mysterious and solitary . . . but . . . familiar and popular to a degree which the recluse scholar of former days could never imagine."[4] The true American scholar, as described by Ralph Waldo Emerson a year later, was not the learned specialist cut off from life but the active, unbounded individual.[5] These sentiments struck contemporary European observers forcefully because they were so very American. More than one foreign traveler marveled that "every man you meet [in America] thinks himself capable of giving an opinion upon questions of the most difficult kind."[6]

Yet the last third of the nineteenth century saw the virtual overthrow of effective resistance to specialization. The year 1869 may serve as a turning point. Harvard inaugurated an elective system. Simultaneously the American Medical Association officially resolved "that this Association recognizes specialties as proper and legitimate fields of practice."[7] The elective system, by shattering the classical curriculum, opened every aspect of higher education to the incursion of specialists. Within the medical profession the official recognition of specialized practices soon led to the subordination of the general practitioner in income and prestige, as many of them had feared. Rural spokesmen in backward areas of the country continued to complain about the high costs of specialized services and the self-importance of those who provided them. But libraries swelled to bursting, the Ph.D. Octopus (as William James called it) reached out to every reputable college, and the number of occupations listed in the U.S. census multiplied time and time again. "In all of our large cities and densely populated districts," a writer marveled in 1880, "specialism revels in tropical luxuriance."[8]

A large part of this transformation was unavoidable. It flowed in good measure from modernizing tendencies that penetrated all advanced societies. Yet the American case was exceptional in the extent to which established norms were seemingly reversed. Of the leading countries in the Western world, the United States in 1830 was perhaps the least specialized and surely the most committed to the omnicompetence of the ordinary citizen. By 1920, however, America had embraced the specialist and sanctified the expert with an enthusiasm unmatched elsewhere. For European critics and imitators alike, the American assembly line with its minute subdivision of labor and the American university with its cafeteria style of education were becoming emblems of the future. Literature reinforced the lessons of experience when Sinclair Lewis produced in Martin Arrowsmith the most compelling literary hero of the 1920s: a scientist whose narrow, ruthlessly focused intelligence was as distinctively American as Emerson's Scholar had once seemed.[9]

Whereas American opinion shifted from one extreme to another—often repudiating specialization in the early nineteenth century and embracing it uncritically in the late nineteenth century—European intellectuals displayed a persistent ambivalence. The Scottish philosophers of the eighteenth century grasped the contradiction that specialization posed. They acclaimed it as the prime cause of the rise of civilization, while, at the same time, they feared it as a profound threat to civic virtue and social solidarity.[10] Without using the term "specialization," Adam Ferguson was perhaps the first to comment on its incursion into intellectual life. In his *Essay on the History of Civil Society* (1767) he observed that "a continued subdivision," already so productive in the mechanical arts, could extend to every art and profession, "and thinking itself in this age of separations may become a peculiar craft."[11]

Adam Smith a few years later welcomed "this subdivision of employment in philosophy." As in every other business, Smith said, each individual "becomes more expert in his own peculiar branch, more work is done upon the whole, and the quantity of science is considerably increased by it." But no one has written a more searing commentary than Smith's on the brutalizing effects that industrial specialization was having on the masses. Though stimulating the minds of the few to an extraordinary degree, specialization, according to *The Wealth of Nations*, was reducing the great body of the people to mental torpor and moral flaccidity.[12]

The warnings of the Scottish philosophers swelled into a more immediate and pervasive concern in the "synthetic philosophy" of Auguste Comte. It was he who apparently minted the word "*spécialisation*"; from him it passed into English. Comte accepted a division of labor among scholars and scientists as essential to intellectual progress. For him the crux of the problem was not (as for Smith) increasing inequality but rather the "dispersive" tendency of empirical research and the consequent fracturing of intellectual authority.[13] Comte's entire system may be understood as a strategy for harnessing the energies of specialization while overcoming its disintegrative effects.

In England, Comte's line of thought was taken up by John Stuart Mill and Thomas Huxley—champions of science who were nevertheless distressed over the narrowness of mind that seemed likely to result from the runaway growth of research.[14] In the United States, however, the criticism of specialization during the late nineteenth and early twentieth centuries came from other quarters. It came from outside the scientific culture. Among American intellectuals it was a lament, a protest, and a rearguard action, usually associated with the Genteel Tradition and mounted by those who sought to preserve as the central purpose of higher education the making of gentlemen. These proponents of "liberal education" complained unceasingly of a "dissevering of sympathy and dehumanizing of scholarship, the lowering of tone which comes from losing one's view of knowledge in its unified grandeur."[15]

In shaping American colleges the power of the gentlemanly ideal was substantial and lasting, but it worked largely to protect a certain jurisdiction. Instead of bringing a larger dimension into specialized thought, the champions of liberal education for the most part concentrated on holding their own within the setting in which they felt at home: the undergraduate college. In doing so, they conceded to specialists the control of graduate and professional studies. Although we customarily regard American universities of the late nineteenth century as forums of conflict between opposing educational ideals, it may be more accurate to observe how a doctrine of two spheres inhibited an effective challenge of one to the other. In 1898, William T. Harris, a leading theoretician of "liberal education," placed his blessing on this historic compromise: "Higher education seeks as its first goal the unity of human learning. Then in its second stage it specializes. . . . The first part of higher education, that for the B.A. degree . . . shows how all branches form a connected whole and what each contributes to the explanation of the others. . . . After . . . comes the selection of a specialty. . . . We accordingly rejoice in the fact of the increasing popularity of the university in both of its functions—that of culture and that of specialization."[16]

If the beleaguered defenders of gentility were somewhat compro-
mised, outside their ranks the trend toward intellectual specialization in the
late nineteenth and early twentieth centuries provoked little serious discussion of any kind. No American who identified with the scientific culture
seems to have published a book on the subject. The few authors of the
articles I have discovered were content with declaring that specialization is
an inviolable law of nature, or at least an inescapable condition of modern
life, and people should take full advantage of it. In 1882 a young graduate
student at Johns Hopkins, in a letter to a friend, caught the euphoric note of
the time: "vive la specialization! Go to, let us centrifugate."[17]

For many Americans Herbert Spencer provided all the explanation
that was desired. Among the nineteenth-century system builders, Spencer
stands out for his comforting faith in specialization as the universal law of
progress. All structures, according to Spencer, are organic. All organisms
evolve by a more and more complex differentiation of their parts. Specialization, therefore, is a beneficent necessity making for ever greater articulation and interdependence.[18] There is nothing to worry about. The unique
enthusiasm for Spencer's philosophy in late nineteenth-century America
fits neatly with the American proclivity for specialization.

When the spell of Spencerian determinism was broken at the end of
the nineteenth century, one might have thought that a significant reappraisal of specialization would arise. No one was better prepared for the
task than John Dewey. His whole cast of mind worked against the separation of one realm of experience from another, against the compartmentalization and fragmentation of culture. Throughout a long life, Dewey circled
warily around the question of specialization; yet he touched it only in
glancing ways. Intellectual specialization, he believed, could and should be
compatible with breadth. "Overspecialization," on the other hand, is "unnatural." Dewey never made the difference between the two altogether
clear. But he always associated overspecialization with institutional barriers
that separate thought from practical activity.[19] Faced with the problem of
intellectual differentiation, Dewey spoke of social divisions. He relied so
heavily on scientific inquiry as the means of integrating experience that
when it failed, the blame had to lie somewhere outside the scientific enterprise—among those who resist inquiry rather than those who practice it.

Spencer and Dewey—one of them at the beginning and the other at the
end of the era we are examining—illustrate the intellectual strategies that
shielded America's proliferating specialists from probing self-appraisal and
criticism. Both of these leaders of opinion offered assurance that scientific

inquiry, in demonstrating the interrelatedness of all things, was rendering obsolete the profound theoretical questions that had engaged men in the past. Otherwise very different from each other, Spencer and Dewey alike encouraged a cheerful outreach of research in every direction, with a minimum of theoretical guidance.

The degree to which that actually happened is hard to judge. For many decades foreign critics contended that American scholars and scientists were bypassing broad conceptual issues and plunging instead into concrete applications or trivial particulars. In one version of the indictment, a version that Americans often echoed, they charged that pure science was neglected in this country because of an excessive concentration on practical applications.[20] In another version they alleged that American scholars sacrificed theoretical breadth and coherence because of their addiction to a narrow factuality. In a lecture delivered in 1929, the outstanding Anglo-American sociologist Robert MacIver described the antitheoretical bent of his American colleagues with detachment and elegance:

> It might be maintained that one thing which American and German sociologists have in common is a preoccupation with method. But method means an entirely different thing to American and to German investigators. To the American, method means preeminently research technique, a device for collecting, recording, sorting, classifying, tabulating or counting facts. To the German, method is a principle in terms of which he arranges facts in categories, determines the relation of the categories to one another, analyses a social situation or a large-scale social movement into its essential factors, and offers a synthetic interpretation to the world. In a word, the American is eager for new facts and new verifications, whereas the German seeks new formulations and new thought-constructions. It is not that the German is careless of facts; it is certainly not that he is less thorough. It is that his main objective is different. His voyage of exploration seeks the far horizon of new principles whereas the American does coasting voyages from facts to facts. Consequently, the German is often more preoccupied with the interpretation of old facts than with the discovery of new ones, while the American is often so keen for new facts that he is apt to neglect the established ones.[21]

There seems little doubt that MacIver's characterization applied in a rough way to some fields, notably history, political science, and sociology. Where it did apply, the conclusion might plausibly follow that coasting voyages scattered the explorers and therefore promoted specialization. Yet caution must be exercised in attributing a high degree of specialization in the late nineteenth century to habits of mind (such as an antitheoretical bias) that have persisted in one form or another throughout American history.

An indifference or hostility to the role of theory and hypothesis in the formulation of knowledge was actually most blatant and presumptuous during the early nineteenth century. Far from encouraging specialized inquiry, this naive empiricism validated egalitarian resistance to specialists. In Jacksonian America reliable knowledge was widely believed to be immediately available through the direct observation of surface appearances. This was the meaning of the "Baconian method" celebrated in the magazines of the period; it was the upshot of the commonsense philosophy propagated in all the colleges. Both taught that science is nothing more than a classification of the evidence of the senses. Anyone, therefore, could participate in the scientific enterprise.[22] Science, as Verplanck said, had become "familiar and popular."

The leading American scientists were never altogether comfortable with the belief that Everyman can trust his senses, that science is everybody's business. Looking enviously to Europe, scientific leaders complained more and more loudly, as the century progressed, of the mediocrity of American science and the dispersion of scientific resources. The rapid advance of specialization never figured in their complaints; that was not part of the problem, it was part of the solution.[23]

The matrix of specialization was built by people who were deeply dissatisfied with the status of science and scholarship in America and who set out deliberately to remodel their own situation along European lines. Their object was partly to elevate men of science and men of letters to the dignity of a European elite. At the same time they sought to purify science and scholarship (as well as art and literature) by making those enterprises more rigorous and sophisticated and thus removing them from common understanding and participation. Intellectual specialization inevitably challenged egalitarian values by conferring new authority on technical elites. Accordingly it assisted the strong post–Civil War reaction among the cultivated classes against the alleged excesses of the democratic revolution. Outraged by the corruption and materialism that democracy had spawned, and rallying around the watchwords "civilization" and "culture," the "better sort" of Americans—upholders of education and respectability—mounted a counteroffensive in the late nineteenth century to recoup some of the authority they had lost in preceding decades. Over and over again, one finds a common idealistic and elitist motive among the leading scholars and scientists of the late nineteenth century: a zeal to make "a higher order of things" prevail over "the base votáries of Mammon," a determination (as another young aspirant said) to tread "the path of science, though alone and exposed to the sneers of the vulgar and ignorant."[24] Men and women of this persuasion were implicitly redefining science. Explicitly they were detaching themselves from the loosely structured, nontheoretical, community-based culture of Jacksonian America. Specialization, entrenched in newly created professional guilds, provided a means to those ends.

Yet the outcome was not European. It was different in ways that have become intelligible only in retrospect. However much American scholars and scientists aspired to transplant the structure of authority they observed abroad, egalitarian traditions could not be swept aside. Nor could the empirical and pragmatic temper that infused those traditions be altogether reversed. A new set of relations between intellectual elites and the social order would have to be worked out.

A crucial incompatibility between the European pattern and the American milieu is revealed in the ill-starred attempts of American intellectuals to group themselves into national academies like the Royal Society of London or the French Academy of Sciences. These were quasi-official bodies, their membership sharply limited to a fixed number of supreme experts drawn from various fields of learning and supposedly capable of setting standards for all the lesser authorities. Thus the national academy in European countries constituted a pinnacle of eminence, through which intellectual leadership was recognized, reinforced, and consolidated. By contrast, A. Hunter Dupree reviews the ineffectual career of the first American venture along these lines, the National Academy of Sciences.[25] Laurence Veysey sketches other efforts to create centralized academies in the humanities in the 1880s and 1890s. Margaret Rossiter shows how the Society for the Promotion of Agricultural Science functioned as an academy during the same period. In medicine, the Congress of Physicians and Surgeons, founded in 1888, tried to play a similar role.[26] Without exception, these enterprises failed to flourish, if they survived at all.

When Lord Bryce, who was then the British ambassador to the United States, suggested in 1907 a new attempt to set up an honorific body that would preside over the destinies of the humanities, J. Franklin Jameson wisely discouraged him. "I told him," Jameson later recalled, "that I did not believe such a plan was consistent with American ways, and that what such an Academy might accomplish was being achieved well enough by our various humanistic societies, with their broad membership, and the representative and elect quality of their guiding officers."[27]

Broad membership . . . representative and elect! Jameson saw that organized specialization in the United States needed to conform to the national style. The European centralist approach disqualified itself by emphasizing the vertical dimension of specialization. It made the hierarchical structure of intellectual authority overt by setting an apex on the pyramid. As the experience of the late nineteenth century demonstrated, the best strategy for American specialists was to play down vertical relationships, expand horizontally, and thereby erect a great decentralized democracy of specialists. The conflict between a Jacksonian distrust of privileged elites and the advance of specialization was resolved by widening immensely the opportunity to specialize and restricting the opportunity to dominate. The way to overcome resistance to specialization, Americans discovered, was to create a superabundance of it. That may explain why, in the second half of the century, a sharp reversal of attitudes occurred.

To resolve the apparent contradiction of a democracy of specialists called for major innovations. Learned societies with broad membership and representative officers were necessary but not sufficient. The institutional matrix would have to be flexible and polycentric, yet capable somehow of coordinating an infinite variety of research activities. The pattern that developed between 1870 and 1910, in an apparently ad hoc way, was one of the remarkable achievements of American civilization. It had these features:

1. *A standard entrance requirement.* In transplanting the German Ph.D. to the United States, Americans altered it to suit their own needs. The doctor's degree in Germany meant two things: that a student had received a broad education and imbibed a love of pure "science" and that he had at some point probed the frontiers of knowledge—an attainment characteristically (but not quite universally) demonstrated in the form of a dissertation. Americans downplayed the first aspect of the Ph.D. and accentuated the second. The Ph.D. became in effect a certification that the candidate was an academic specialist, and thereby sanctified specialization as the supreme object of American higher education.

American educational historians have never quite realized that the Ph.D. in a German university was not the highest on an ascending scale of academic degrees, as it proudly became in America. It was the basic and almost the only degree the philosophical faculty (i.e., arts and sciences) awarded. There was no B.A., no graduate school, and no clear differentiation between the few students who hoped for a career in science or scholarship and the many students who were simply preparing themselves for secondary school teaching or for some other profession. The German Ph.D., although it was the first requisite for appointment to a professorship, was really designed to serve this much wider constituency: most students who took the degree were destined to be *Gymnasium* teachers. In addition to writing a brief dissertation, candidates underwent examination in three broad subjects, such as history, geography, and mathematics. Neither the dissertation nor the examinations were very concentrated or demanding.[28] Rather, they partook of the encompassing spirit of *Wissenschaft*.[29]

The Americans converted the Ph.D. into an advanced degree for students already committed to a career of research in a single field. Consequently, when Johns Hopkins formalized requirements in 1877–1878, it stipulated two years of study beyond the baccalaureate in "one main subject" and "one subsidiary subject." Moreover, the Hopkins authorities demanded "an elaborate thesis" requiring "labor for the greater part of an academic year" and showing "powers of independent thought as well as of careful research.[30] Subsequently, standards were further raised, so that the doctorate became a three-year rather than a two-year degree prior to World War I.[31] William James could see no serious purpose in all of this—he called it "a sham, a bauble, a dodge whereby to decorate the catalog of schools and colleges."[32] Actually it was a conscientious rational means of ensuring that a decentralized system would produce fully qualified specialists in every field of knowledge.

As a regulative mechanism in America, the academic degree had a very serious limitation, however. In the absence of governmental supervision, degrees could be altered, multiplied, and debased by any institution to serve any purpose. As the importance of degrees increased in the second half of the nineteenth century, their number and variety passed all bounds. The commissioner of education counted fourteen different degrees in use in 1872. Fifteen years later the first American handbook on degrees complained of more than sixty. To attach a uniform meaning to the Ph.D. and to fight off alternative degrees required a sustained struggle. In the 1890s graduate students at the leading universities organized clubs that affiliated as the Federation of Graduate Clubs and pressed for the adoption of uniform requirements. In 1900 the Association of American Universities was founded "to protect the dignity" and secure "greater uniformity" in the American doctorate. Gradually the awarding of honorary Ph.D.'s was stamped out. The rival degree, doctor of science (D.Sc.), which Harvard introduced in 1872, was converted into an honorary degree.[33] The doctorate of philosophy prevailed in this welter of multiple possibilities because it signified the ability to do original work of a scientific order in any field.[34]

2. *The university department as a society of equals.* Once certified, the Ph.D.'s needed an institutional setting in which each could pursue a specialty with a maximum degree of independence. Americans assumed that every academic person should not only have a distinct specialty but be able to aspire to a sphere of influence. Every Ph.D. who chose to teach should be able some day to become a professor. That was not the case in European universities. In Europe, one professor represented a whole field. Professors were few, and each was likely to have his own research institute staffed by apprentices and assistants. To become a professor, therefore, was not a normal career expectation but a sacred calling reserved for a very few exceptional individuals. So jealously were professorial prerogatives guarded that provision for new fields of study usually came slowly and reluctantly. Specialization was confined within strict limits.

The formation of departments in American universities permitted an entirely different set of relationships.[35] In a department, several relatively autonomous teachers shared responsibility for a field of knowledge. Every one of them could have unchallenged control of a little subdivision of the field. By the 1890s departments were developing a busy, independent life which they conducted for the most part on a collegial basis. The department could easily expand to accommodate new specialties, it facilitated the coexistence of a considerable number of full professors, and its self-governing procedures acknowledged the juridical equality of all specialists. As the departments rose in importance after 1900, they acquired power that had earlier belonged to the university presidents. The age of strong presidents passed, and that too promoted specialization.[36]

3. *Multipurpose agencies to sponsor research.* Another way to promote specialization without concentrating authority was to give the sponsoring institutions a mixture of purposes and a multiplicity of constituencies. Here again the universities were a model. They loudly proclaimed an allegiance to ideals of public service and cultural conservation as well as research. They catered to gentlemen, aspiring accountants, civil reformers, and young women escaping from the farm while nourishing every species of scientist and scholar. Astounded by this variety, French observers thought it wasteful and chaotic.[37] Yet it made possible a profusion of specialists inconceivable elsewhere. And by intertwining their work with other objectives, the American "multiversity" neutralized opposition.

Similarly, the libraries on which scholars depended made themselves accessible to everyone while amassing the resources that specialists required. John Cole describes how American libraries turned from the mere acquisition and preservation of books to a new policy of actively stimulating and facilitating their use.[38] This popular outreach did not for a moment divert the libraries from accumulating materials that specialists wanted. On the contrary, the widening utility of American libraries to the whole community justified the ever-increasing appropriations that book-loving librarians lavished on their research collections. Even the rare-book libraries, which guarded their holdings from indiscriminate use, did not restrict themselves entirely to a scholarly clientele—they functioned also as museums, appealing to a larger public by displaying their treasures under glass.

The great private foundations that appeared in the early twentieth century at first seemed to resist the heterogeneous intermixture of purposes that transfigured universities and libraries. Customarily, charitable trusts were set up for a narrowly defined object, as in the case of the Rockefeller Institute for Medical Research (1901) and the Carnegie Foundation for the Advancement of Teaching (1905). Nathan Reingold points out that the Carnegie Institution of Washington (1902), though breaking new ground in its commitment to fundamental research in a wide variety of fields, followed European precedent in becoming strictly a research center without any practical or pedagogical objective. It was not until John D. Rockefeller in 1909 earmarked fifty million dollars to promote "any and all of the elements of human progress" that the distinctive flexibility and many-sidedness of the modern American foundation began to emerge. From this grant developed the Rockefeller Foundation (1913), which gradually learned to avoid fixed and limited goals by making outside agencies responsible for executing the projects it funded.[39] The very word "foundation" came to signify a new kind of institution with exceptional latitude in disbursing its funds.[40]

4. *Rule by reference works.* The problem of specialization is inevitably one of communication among fields. In America this difficulty was aggravated by the diffusion of authority throughout a horizontal system. Since all of the above arrangements tended to obscure the visibility of leaders, only an experienced insider could say with reasonable accuracy where the influential ideas and investigators within a discipline were to be found. The crucial challenge to the American system, therefore, was to coordinate specialized knowledge and to give outstanding scholars and ideas a wider hearing. The challenge was met with a new panoply of reference tools.

Instead of vesting leadership in an academy, Americans called on the neutral services of bibliographers and librarians.

Certain types of reference works were done better in Europe than in the United States. The great nineteenth-century encyclopedias were European. Americans also lagged far behind the French and Germans in the production of comprehensive guides to a single specialized field, like the *Quellenkunde der deutschen Geschichte*, which was first published in 1830 and enlarged and improved under a succession of editors. Works of this kind, surveying a large subject and evaluating the leading materials for it, expressed the stability and concentration of intellectual authority that existed in a European research institute. By contrast, Americans excelled in producing open-ended reference works designed to acquaint a miscellaneous variety of users with what was current outside their own specialties. The notable American achievements in the organization of knowledge were indexes, catalogs, and directories.

The model of American reference tools was the public card catalog. Today we take it so much for granted that we have forgotten how revolutionary a dictionary catalog of loose cards was when introduced at the Harvard Library in 1861. Infinitely flexible, it could accommodate any degree of specialization. In the next half-century improvements in the organization and cataloging of printed matter came with increasing rapidity, the most notable being the Dewey decimal system of classifying books (1876) and the sale of printed cards by the Library of Congress (1901).[41] Card catalogs have facilitated the distribution of specialized knowledge by permitting anyone, starting either with the name of an author or with a topic, to become acquainted with the current authorities on any subject a library encompasses. At the same time, card catalogs have added to the prestige of specialized knowledge by guiding readers to the most up-to-date and specific works. Because the card catalog is so obviously designed for quick inclusion of new publications, it confirms the premium on contemporaneity that is inherent in the specializing process.

While Melvil Dewey and Charles A. Cutter worked out the modern principles of book classification in the 1870s, other Americans developed similar controls over the vast literature of medicine and law. Publications in both law and medicine were proliferating in so many directions that they posed, in an acute form, the problem of communication between specialties. In the field of law, perhaps the outstanding achievement was the modern digest, essentially an elaborate subject index to law reports. The *American Digest: Century Edition* (fifty volumes, published between 1897 and 1904) established a uniform classification of the law which became the recognized standard for all subsequent indexes and digests. For its contribution to indexing techniques and for its sheer magnitude—a half million cases assimilated to one topical arrangement—the *Century Digest* was hailed as "the magnum opus of American law."[42]

Meanwhile, John Shaw Billings, librarian of the Surgeon General's Library in Washington, was building the largest collection of medical literature in the world and devising an index to all of the books, pamphlets, theses, and journal articles the library held and was receiving. The result was the monumental *Index-Catalogue of the Surgeon General's Library* (1880–1955), for which Billings and his successor, Dr. Robert Fletcher, are said to have indexed, by subject, 168,000 books and more than one-half million articles before Fletcher's death in 1912.[43] This they supplemented with a monthly bulletin, the *Index-Medicus* (1879–1926).

What Billings and Fletcher accomplished for medical literature, a former farm boy and bookseller did for other current publications. Following in the footsteps of several less successful predecessors, Halsey William Wilson launched in 1900 the *United States Catalog*, a trade list of books in print. The following year he inaugurated the famous *Readers' Guide to Periodical Literature*. By 1900 American libraries were so numerous and avid for reference services that current, ongoing bibliographies could be produced for a profit. Wilson proved himself a master in articulating detailed subject entries. One project reinforced another and his efforts expanded rapidly. Incorporating as the H. W. Wilson Company in 1902, his office absorbed rivals, created such new serials as the *Book Review Digest* (1906) and the *International Index to Periodicals* (1907), and built a staff that filled a five-story plant in New York City. By the 1930s the Wilson publications indexed, reviewed, and catalogued more than 1,200 periodicals and all books printed in the English language in all countries of the world.[44] Nothing approaching this bibliographical empire existed anywhere else.

What remained teasingly unanswered, after the indexes and catalogs were on hand, was the elusive issue of individual merit and importance. Who matters? What counts? These were questions no reference work could objectively arbitrate, but it is suggestive that one of the foremost American scholars of the early twentieth century tried to produce just such an instrument. James McKeen Cattell was a psychologist with a special interest in measuring individual mental differences and a passion for organizing and promoting science. In 1906 he combined both objects by creating *American Men of Science: A Biographical Directory*. "There is here given for the first time," Cattell announced, "a fairly complete survey of the scientific activity of a country at a given period." Cattell hoped that the directory's main service would be to make scientists better acquainted with one another.[45] To that end he starred the names of the most notable figures in twelve principal sciences, as determined by an elaborate analysis of the rank orderings that leaders in each field supplied. Cattell's directory began publication in the same year that Wilson launched the *Book Review Digest,* and the stars in the former correspond functionally to the plusses and minuses in the latter.

A new edition of *American Men of Science* appeared every few years. Its total number of biographies grew from 4,000 in 1906 to 34,000 in 1943. To be starred in its pages gave a scientist dramatic visibility and benefited his career and his university alike. According to some admirers, Cattell's directory not only opened a window into the compartmentalized life of specialists but also provided a major incentive to the advance of American science.[46] The grandiose nature of the idea takes us beyond the obvious hunger for recognition felt by thousands of obscure specialists. The belief that a handbook of classified information could exercise a significant influence in organizing and inspiring the march of science bespeaks a trust that bordered on piety. It suggests that reference works were the icons of a redemptive empiricism.

In reviewing the peculiarly American institutions called forth by specialization, I have not tried to be exhaustive. Further analysis should uncover others.[47] The four I have touched upon present a most miscellaneous appearance: a strengthened Ph.D. degree, the departmentalization of universities, the funding of research by agencies with nonresearch purposes, and the development of reference tools designed to open the latest specialties to outsiders. What could these oddly assorted devices have in common? What linked the American doctorate, the American academic department, the American foundation, and the American card catalog? On close inspection the answer seems clear. Each provided a means of reconciling the elitist tendencies of intellectual specialization with the egalitarian requirements of American society. Together they demonstrate that Americans, while failing to *discuss* the deeper problems of specialization in the late nineteenth century, nonetheless *reacted* with vigor and inventiveness. Not in ideas but in institutions did the onrush of specialization produce a creative response.

PART II

Integrating Diversity

Higham's *Strangers in the Land* (1955) has become a historical classic, but Higham has reassessed its analysis of changing American attitudes toward immigration on several occasions: in an afterword to a new edition (1988), for example, and in three essays on anti-Semitism included in *Send These to Me* (1975). The following essay, published as the first article in the inaugural issue of the *Journal of American Ethnic History*, continues his reworking of the history of nativism. It offers a new interpretation of a crucial moment in the story that *Strangers* tells.

Higham had never felt fully satisfied with the multicausal explanation he had given for the dramatic escalation of antiforeign feeling from 1905 to 1915. Somehow race was at the heart of the nativist revival. But what started this wave of bigotry that swelled to a crest in the early 1920s? The conventional explanation—a new scientific racism among academic elites—could hardly account for the crude, popular race-feelings that were awakening in the country at large. Why, at a time when the economy was growing vigorously and Progressivism in its various forms was winning over the American middle class, did segregation, race riots, immigration restriction, and aggressive nationalism coalesce? Higham looked for a common factor and decided that a large part of it would have to be found in the character of Progressivism itself.

Higham introduced his argument obliquely by fixing on the problem of assimilation as a new feature of the Progressive years. Before then, ethnic minorities had largely been left to remain unassimilated or to assimilate themselves. In the early twentieth century, however, Progressive policies and concerns promoted institutional consolidation and national pride. This in turn brought to light an underlying crazy quilt of local cultures and ethnic minorities. The heterogeneity that had earlier been accepted or ignored now lay exposed to a widely popular animus in Progressive reform: a Puritan zeal to cleanse and purify, whether in blood or in disease, whether in corrupt institutions or in face-to-face encounters. A generalized racism gave the problem of assimilation a very scary look.

Exclusionist and universalist versions of America polarized, one may now add, and they grew in definition and intensity. Was the critical question how to restore the lost "purity" of American culture, or was it how to cultivate an inclusive Americanism? In the first two decades of the twentieth century the attack on impurity and diversity predominated, and nativism triumphed.

In this essay Higham views ethnic relations from a national cultural context that most ethnic historians put aside in the 1970s and 1980s. Except for Robert Crunden's *Ministers of Reform* (1982), the role of religious ideas in Progressive politics has also received little attention. Yet younger historians are turning back to the problem of race and Progressivism, most strikingly in Gail Bederman's *Manliness and Civilization* (1995). And studies of the 1920s, such as Ann Douglas's *Terrible Honesty* (1995), are documenting a later stage in the ongoing revolt against the equivocations and hypocrisies of the Victorian Age.

Josef Barton
Northwestern University

5

Integrating America

The Problem of Assimilation at the Turn of the Century

[1981]

To speak of assimilation as a problem in nineteenth-century America is, in an important sense, to indulge in anachronism. That is because nineteenth-century Americans seemed for the most part curiously undaunted by, and generally insensitive to, the numerous and sometimes tragic divisions in their society along racial and ethnic lines. Leaving aside some significant exceptions, the boundaries between groups with different origins and distinct cultures caused little concern. Assimilation was either taken for granted or viewed as inconceivable. For European peoples it was thought to be the natural, almost inevitable outcome of life in America. For other races assimilation was believed to be largely unattainable and therefore not a source of concern. Only at the end of the century did ethnic mixing arouse a sustained and urgent sense of danger. Only then did large numbers of white Americans come to fear that assimilation was *not* occurring among major European groups and that it was going too far among other minorities, notably blacks, Orientals, and Jews.

This acute consciousness of assimilation as a problem marked a great crisis in ethnic relations. Extending from the 1890s to the 1920s, the crisis persisted until a new ethnic pattern came into being. The objects of this essay are, first, to describe the ethnocultural system of the nineteenth century in a way that may help us to understand more fully the ensuing crisis and, second, to glimpse within that crisis the origins of a new system of ethnic relations that has unfolded in subsequent decades.

Before considering assimilation as a newly perceived problem at the end of the nineteenth century, it will be necessary to give some account of assimilation as a process in earlier decades. Here we may note in passing that the blending, merging, and incorporation of peoples has occurred on many levels in the United States, not just on the level of nation-building that historians and politicians ordinarily have in mind when they speak of assimilation. Surely the most impressive instances of assimilation in American history are to be found in the formation of racial or national minorities from more particularistic antecedents. The African slaves imported into the English colonies in the late seventeenth and eighteenth centuries were a medley of peoples, differing widely in appearance, traditions, and language. In their own minds they belonged to distinct tribes, not to a race. Their English masters threw them together quite indiscriminately, however, and gave them a single, inclusive name: Negroes. Accordingly, the plantations of the colonial South functioned as a remarkable melting pot, in which distinctions between Mandigoes, Ibos, Angolans, and other African peoples were largely obliterated.[1] Partly because the English ascribed a common identity to them, and partly because certain common themes in West African cultures facilitated their amalgamation in spite of disparate languages and customs, the Afro-Americans gradually became a single people in spite of enormous differences in their circumstances and their exposure to Anglo-American influences.[2]

Although the slaves present the most striking example, a similar process of assimilation entered into the making of major European ethnic groups as well. Most of the peasants and villagers who came to the United States in the nineteenth century brought with them very little sense of having belonged to a nation. At first they thought of themselves as the people of a particular local area—a village or at most a province. They were not Germans but Württembergers, Saxons, and Westphalians; not Italians but Neapolitans, Sicilians, Calabrians, and Genoese; not Chinese, but members of particular districts and clans.[3] Speedily in most cases, slowly in a few, these localized attachments were submerged within the wider identities we know today: identities that demonstrate both the special bond a common language provides and the special respect Americans have accorded to the principle of nationality as a basis of social identification.

When we turn from this very successful, intermediate level of assimilation, which Victor Greene has called ethnicization,[4] and consider the higher level on which an overarching American consciousness has formed, we find a more confusing and complicated situation. An enormous amount of interethnic assimilation did in fact occur in the experience of individuals. Even while the emerging ethnic groups of nineteenth-century America were crystallizing, each of them was losing highly mobile families who cast off the old ways and the old identity, became in speech and manners indistinguishable from the native white population, and gradually faded into it. In the South, for example, many German Jews in the nineteenth century were so fully accepted into the white society that their descendants ceased to be Jewish. Meanwhile, in the North, miscegenation and mobility made possible a continual, silent passing of light-skinned African Americans across the color line. According to a black physician in 1844, at least six of his former classmates at the New York African Free School were then living as whites.[5]

Even more important, entire ethnic groups lost much of their distinctiveness in the course of time. In upper New York State the asperities between the old Dutch settlers and incoming Yankees from New England gradually softened. By the 1802s the descendants of the French Huguenots in New Rochelle and elsewhere retained little more than their names to mark their origin.[6] By the end of the nineteenth century the Irish Catholics, though still keenly distrusted in New England, were elsewhere sufficiently accepted and well established that comic magazines no longer felt free to portray them as drunken louts with the faces of gorillas.[7] In the twentieth century the crumbling of the great German-American community is the most familiar and spectacular case of collective assimilation. In some degree a multiethnic melting pot indubitably *has* worked—but so imperfectly, so inconsistently, so incompletely! It worked, but it did not prevail. Whereas virtually all of the local or tribal identities that the people of this country brought with them from other lands have been obliterated, every one of the racial and national groupings that was created in America has stubbornly persisted. It is not an outright failure of assimilation that needs to be understood in comprehending nineteenth-century America, but rather the peculiar contradictions the process of assimilation displayed.

The most obvious of these contradictions was between theory and reality. The theory of assimilation, as formulated by J. Hector St. Jean de Crèvecoeur in the Revolutionary era, seemed to allow for no exceptions. "Here individuals of all nations are melted into a new race of men," this wandering Frenchman declared.[8] The Revolutionary belief that America offered a new start for humanity acquired, from Christian and classical sources, rich millennial overtones. Listen, for example, to Herman Melville's musings as he watched German emigrants boarding ships for America: "We are not a nation, so much as a world. . . . Our ancestry is lost in the Universal paternity; and Caesar and Alfred, St. Paul and Luther, and Homer and Shakespeare are as much ours as Washington, who is as much the world's as our own. We are the heirs of all time, and with all nations we divide our inheritance. On this Western Hemisphere all tribes and peoples are forming into one federated whole; and there is a future which shall see the estranged children of Adam restored as to the old hearthstone in Eden."[9] More prosaically, Oliver Wendell Holmes described his compatriots as "the Romans of the modern world—the great assimilating people." This was not enough for George Bancroft, the first great historian of the United States, who declared: "Our country stands . . . as the realisation of the unity of the [human] race."[10]

In actuality, of course, white Americans had no intention of translating a national myth into a literal command. Even the most radical abolitionists shrank from the accusation that they were promoting an amalgamation of races.[11] Yet some kinds of assimilation did bridge the chasm between blacks and whites; and the relations of both blacks and whites with other minorities varied enormously. What needs to be explained is not a simple opposition between theory and practice but rather a baffling mix of inconsistencies.

Consider, for instance, how white Americans behaved and felt a century ago toward the Indian tribes. U.S. Indian policies, as one commissioner of Indian affairs confessed, were "hopelessly illogical." In some situations expediency dictated a resort to warfare; in others it produced a mixture of subsidies and neglect. In still other situations the federal government pursued a conscientious (though often misguided) program of assimilation.[12] Private attitudes ranged from a special respect for Indians to outright contempt. Throughout the nineteenth century the Currier and Ives prints, which often treated blacks condescendingly, never demeaned or ridiculed Indians. They appeared always as dignified human beings with a legitimate life of their own. Similarly it was not uncommon in the southern states for upper-class whites of both sexes proudly to claim descent from Indian ancestors.[13] Yet middle-class tourists at the same time were sneering at the Indians they saw at transcontinental railroad stops; and a leading historian in the 1870s urged his readers to appreciate the fascination their forebears had had with Indians, although "To us, of course, the American Indian is no longer a mysterious or even an interesting personage —he is simply a fierce dull biped standing in our way."[14]

Education is another sphere in which paradox and contradiction abounded. Americans characteristically viewed the common school as the one instrumentality essential for molding a common citizenry, education of the young being the only organized effort the nation needed to make to promote assimilation. Yet many public schools also served contrary objectives that had more to do with maintaining segregation or preserving minority cultures. In some parts of the country control of the local schools gave ethnic minorities substantial protection from the dominant culture. In rural areas of the Middle West where Germans predominated heavily, some public schools were taught mainly or even entirely in the German language—a practice that aroused little notice or objection before the 1890s.[15]

In other parts of the country assimilation through education was vigorously supported as a national goal but severely qualified in local practice. Nowhere was public education stronger, or zeal for social integration greater, than in New England. During the post–Civil War decades New England educators and reformers threw themselves into campaigns to inculcate the ex-slaves of the South, the Indians of the Great Plains, and the Chinese of California with the knowledge and the values they would need to become effective participants in a free society.[16] At the same time, however, these New Englanders showed scant interest in assimilating the French Canadians—contemptuously described as "the Chinese of the Eastern States"—who were pouring into their own towns and cities. Like the Chinese, the French resisted the culture and society they encountered in the United States and did not send their children to public schools. The Yankees, no doubt glad to have the schools to themselves, allowed their own school-attendance laws to go unenforced.[17]

The examples I have chosen have in common a feature that is central to the contradictions in nineteenth-century America. In responding to Indians and in formulating educational strategies, white Americans showed particularly receptive attitudes toward people who were distant in time or in space from themselves: people whose disembodied remoteness made them suitably abstract objects of an abstract faith in assimilation. Toward outsiders who crowded into one's immediate environment—like the French Canadians in New England and the Indians who asked for handouts at railway stations—a greater distrust or resistance was manifested. Some of this difference between sympathy at a distance and repulsion on closer contact may be inescapably and perennially human, but the glaring contrasts we find in nineteenth-century America owe their salience to a distinctive combination in American culture of jealous localism and universalistic beliefs.

By localism I mean both a condition and an attitude. I mean a condition of decentralization, enabling towns and other local districts to be largely autonomous communities. I mean also a reinforcing attitude that such autonomy is the key to liberty. The settlements from which the United States emerged shared nothing more than an animus against remote, consolidated power. Scattered along 1,300 miles of the Atlantic coast, the English colonies in the eighteenth century were separated from one another to a degree hard to imagine today. Few people traveled from one province to another. Little news passed between them. Most colonists also felt remote from their own provincial capitals. While colonial assemblies continually chipped away at the power of royal governors and London officials, within each colony districts that were relatively distant from centers of trade felt a similar distrust of the more cosmopolitan towns. In every colony the revolutionary impulse sprang from a profound suspicion of consolidated power.[18] No wonder it took well over a decade before the patriots of 1776 could bring themselves to create a national government, and then only with great difficulty and reluctance.

Once established, the new government merely stabilized and perpetuated the traditional dispersal of power. As late as 1831, to serve a population of thirteen million people who were spreading rapidly over a territory of 1,750,000 square miles, the U.S. government employed just 11,491 civilians. Only 666 of them resided in the raw little capital on the banks of the Potomac.[19] The rest were scattered across the country and beyond—a few staffing customs houses and embassies while nearly all the others operated the tiny post offices of which contemporary genre painters have given us many charming glimpses. It would not be unfair to say that the U.S. government in the nineteenth century consisted during peacetime mostly of post offices, and to conclude with Robert Wiebe that America was "a society without a core."[20]

The point was made more colorfully by Henry James: "No State, in the European sense of the word, and indeed barely a specific national name. No sovereign, no court, no personal loyalty, no aristocracy, no church, no clergy, no army, no diplomatic service, no country gentlemen, no palaces, no castles, nor manors, nor old country houses, nor parsonages, nor thatched cottages, nor ivied ruins; no cathedrals, nor abbeys, nor little Norman churches; no great universities nor public schools—no Oxford, nor Eton, nor Harrow; no literature, no novels, no museums, no pictures, no political society . . ."[21]

By putting first among America's shortcomings the absence of a state in the European sense of the word, James's litany suggests that this was the most embracing of the symbols of legitimacy, the most fundamental of the structures of authority, that he missed. A society lacking that kind of state might have to do without all of the rest.[22] Such was the situation of the American republic. Very scantily endowed with the outward trappings of power and social connection, it had almost no visible means of instilling allegiance. There was a flag and a Capitol, but no capital city in a European sense. Even the Capitol building was, at the time of the Civil War, still undergoing major alterations. The flag was not yet fully defined.[23] The only really imposing memorial in the country, the Washington Monument, was not completed until 1885.

Nevertheless, this almost disembodied state lived as an idea—resonant, compelling, and universally espoused. The Americans depended on an ideology—a set of abstract principles—to hold their country together. Although nationalism everywhere in the nineteenth century acquired an ideological thrust, it seems unlikely that any other country defined itself so preeminently as a community of belief, a nation gathered around a creed.[24] Americans who lived or traveled in Europe sometimes regretted the relative abstractness of American patriotism. To Nathaniel Hawthorne it seemed "as cold and hard . . . as the steel spring that puts in motion a powerful machinery," and he contrasted it with the human warmth and rich concreteness of an Englishman's sense of nationality.[25] Yet the non-specific and therefore universal aspect of American nationalism served a loose-knit, heterogeneous society well. A national ideology enabled Americans to do without—and even told them why they did not need—the unitary state, the imposing monuments, and the dense social fabric that James observed in Europe.

We are now in a position to understand how the localization of power in nineteenth-century America allowed innumerable separations to flourish within a matrix of national unity. First, decentralization encouraged ethnic groups to act differently in different contexts. As a result, none of them— neither the powerful nor the weak—could present a united front against the rest of society. The dominant segment of the population was of course severely handicapped, in defining an exclusive identity or maintaining an exclusive preeminence, by the absence of a centralized state and its accoutrements. Who were these Anglo-Americans, to call them by a name that always sounded slightly foreign or presumptuous? There was little to mark them as anything but a miscellany of regional and local types— southerners and northerners, easterners and westerners, rural and urban folk—all intensely conscious of their differences from one another. Similarly, ethnic minorities in the United States could not close ranks in stubborn resistance to assimilation because they did not, as in Europe, confront a centralized state controlled by others. At most, ethnic groups might hope to gain preponderance in particular localities; when that happened, decentralized power came easily into their hands.[26] The system worked for them, and elicited their allegiance.

Secondly, decentralization fostered a scattering of population. This enabled local ethnic clusters to keep a certain distance from one another, particularly where economic competition could be acute. For a homogeneous people to have sprung from America's diversities, extensive interaction would have been required *between* the subordinate groups in addition to the contacts each might have with the dominant majority. It is true that minorities could not escape some involvement with one another, but the attention that historians have given to spectacular incidents of conflict, like the New York Draft Riots of 1863, has made us overlook the great extent to which ethnic groups in the nineteenth century kept out of one another's way. Moving west, European immigrants avoided areas where blacks were concentrated. At the same time, the presence of huge immigrant populations in northern cities discouraged the northward migration of blacks.[27] The principle of mutual avoidance also influenced the distribution of German and Irish immigrants, the former settling in the Middle West and the latter in the Northeast. Where large concentrations of both groups materialized, as in Detroit and Milwaukee, they clustered in widely separated divisions of the city.[28] Thus, in a decentralized society mutual avoidance checked *both* conflict *and* assimilation.

The conditions that limited conflict between ethnic groups while promoting differences within each group were admirably suited to an ideological definition of America as a whole. A single canopy of beliefs made an otherwise loose-knit society of dissociated towns and neighborhoods comprehensible. Violations of the ideological norms could usually be understood as pragmatic adjustments to local realities rather than fundamental contradictions. Public schools could segregate minorities or preserve their cultures, depending on the particular ethnic accommodation in each locality, while all of them taught the same promises of the American ideology.

In addition to these disparities between a national ideology and localized institutions, there was also a deep fracture in the substance of the ideology itself. Any fully developed ideology provides its believers with a collective image of themselves, and in this respect the American ideology was profoundly split. On the one hand, nineteenth-century Americans conceived of themselves—in the images I have already quoted from Melville and Bancroft—as a cosmopolitan and unbounded people. On the other hand, the overwhelming majority were white Protestants, whose culture and religion permeated American institutions. On this second and more parochial level of consciousness white Protestants regarded the United States as a white and Protestant country, and so had no special name for themselves because they *were* the Americans and all others were outsiders, although the same people on another level of consciousness took pride in the United States as an open and free society resting on universal, self-evident principles rather than any exclusive origins, a society dedicated to the separation of church and state and the elimination of all barriers to mobility and opportunity, a society of individuals rather than groups.

A capacity to entertain both of these sets of beliefs, applying them selectively to different situations and avoiding any ultimate reckoning by all manner of equivocation, evasion, and compromise—that capacity to minimize, ignore, and defuse the contradictions—was essential to the stability of American society in the nineteenth century. The one serious attempt to resolve an elemental contradiction tore the nation apart in 1861.

I may run a risk here of overstating the contradictions in nineteenth-century American culture. In principle at least, the exclusionary image of a white Protestant nation could be reconciled with the eclectic image of a universal homeland by identifying the former with the past and the latter with the future and then projecting as the nation's destiny a gradual enlargement of one into the other. Idealists did just that. They depicted a "United States of the United Races," an unfinished nation that was creating a composite people on a sturdy Anglo-Saxon base.[29] Over the very long run, this synthesizing vision has expressed a basic truth. It is a truth of historical continuity: a reminder that the American identity has proved capable of enormous extension partly because it never required a drastic transformation. From its narrowest Anglo-Protestant beginnings, the new society carried an evangelical and messianic outreach, which made possible its eventual conversion into a heterogeneous and cosmopolitan republic.

In spite of this undeniable continuity between the relatively restrictive national consciousness that goes back to our Puritan origins and the more embracing national consciousness that we usually attribute to the Enlightenment, the tensions between the two in daily life and in the ways people thought about themselves were profound. A host of ambiguities and divisions in nineteenth-century culture arranged themselves around these opposing visions of a national community. There was endless uncertainty over the attributes an American should have as a legal category, a social type, and a moral ideal.

The difficult legal questions were about citizenship. Who was eligible? In keeping with the cosmopolitan idea of nationality, Americans rejected the English presumption that people belong immutably and naturally to a political community, as they do to a family. One became an American by subscribing to the principles of republican government. Thus membership in the new nation derived from individual choice; and the newcomer, casting off the encumbrances of a personal past, served as the model of American citizenship. Since the logic of these assumptions worked against discriminations in terms of origin or previous condition, free blacks claimed the full rights of citizenship. Some states grudgingly recognized the claim. Others from the outset restricted citizenship to whites, and so did the federal government. After the Civil War compelled the extension of citizenship to people of African descent, confusion continued over the status of other nonwhites and over the privileges and immunities that citizenship should guarantee. The United States never had in the nineteenth century a single standard of membership in a national community.[30]

Nor had it a literature that was concrete and unambiguous in interpreting national character. In contrast to their generalized rhetoric about national purposes and institutions, American writers rarely attempted specific descriptions of an American people or a national type. When Henry James dared in 1877 to define the American type, he produced an extraordinary mélange of contrarieties. The American, as he appeared in the opening pages of the novel by that name, had straight brown hair, brown complexion, aquiline nose, cold grey eyes, flat jaw, and above all a "typical vagueness" of expression, a "blankness which is not simplicity, that look of being committed to nothing in particular . . . so characteristic of many American faces."[31] Notice that James's American combines the gray eyes that used to suggest a man of destiny with other features that are typically Indian; yet his vague expression is not what we expect either of an Indian or of a man of destiny. What an eclectic image!

Significantly, Christopher Newman's character was a compound of opposites. He was, according to James, both frigid and friendly, both frank and cautious, both shrewd and credulous, both positive and skeptical, both confident and shy. His eye "was full of contradictory suggestions. . . . You could find in it almost anything you looked for." Such was the ambiguous figure who, James assures us, "filled out the national mould [with] almost ideal completeness."

At the same time, a reader can hardly miss in Christopher Newman the qualities associated with a white Protestant and specifically English heritage: above all, a simple consciousness of preeminence and rightful possession.

Of all the complexities that Christopher Newman projected, none are more intriguing than those imbedded in his moral values. Like Huckleberry Finn, Newman was tolerant, open-minded, easygoing, and shrewd. A maker of washtubs, he belonged to an eminently practical world. On the other hand, Newman also revealed an unconditioned goodness that James

called innocence and others described as purity. Here again Newman resembled Huck Finn and Deerslayer as well. Each of these mythic figures in
American literature harmoniously united purity with practicality. But was
that not because an opposition between purity and practicality was so
fundamental to the contradictions in American life?

A practical turn of mind—fertile in expedients, adaptive to circumstance, skilled in collaboration and compromise—was long regarded as
characteristically American. According to Frederick Jackson Turner, it
arose on the frontier. Others have traced it to the ethos of unimpeded
capitalism. Still others attribute the American pragmatic temper to the
interactions among a heterogeneous population under conditions of mobility and freedom. Whatever its social roots, this open and flexible mentality
infused the ideas and institutions of America's "moderate" Enlightenment.
Through Franklin and Jefferson a system of thought designed to allay
religious strife became the means of tolerating and eventually legitimizing
conflict and variety of every sort.[32] Enshrined in the lives and words of the
Founding Fathers, pragmatic values have provided a common standard for
a polyglot society.

The tolerant, practical attitudes that relaxed and enlarged the boundaries of an extended national identity clashed with another moral tradition
that sometimes stiffened an exclusive American identity. A yearning for
purity has always been a central feature of the Puritan mentality. A burning
zeal to purify the church, the community, and the self inspired the earliest
New England settlements. A religion based on a sharp separation between
the elect and the damned, Puritanism induced a horror of contamination;
and it assigned major importance to expunging "all manner of *Unclean-
ness.*"[33] For Puritans and their spiritual descendants, purity meant both a
deliverance from evil and the attainment of unity. It meant keeping distinct
the categories of creation while maintaining absolute conformity to a single
moral standard.

These impulses survived the breakup of a more complex Puritan culture and were carried down into the nineteenth century by evangelical
Protestantism. The quest for purity was not always defensive in the nineteenth century, but it did sustain among white Protestant Americans the
old Puritan vision of an elect nation: God's chosen people, summoned like
their biblical ancestors to struggle against enemies without and corruption within.[34] In this struggle they would need to close ranks against an
evil world.

How nineteenth-century Americans dealt with opposing injunctions to
be practical and to be pure is too large and unexplored a subject to take up

here in a serious way; but it may be suggested that this basic contradiction touched not only the problem of national identity but also other vital social relationships. One major strategy for coping with the contradiction, especially in the late nineteenth century, was to narrow the idea of purity, focusing it chiefly on the private world of home and family. In that context purity meant freedom from irregular sexual indulgence; it implied a sanctification of womanhood.[35] The identification of purity with private life and with women seems to have permitted an almost free reign of practicality in the public world of work, politics, and men.[36] This segregation of the two moralities was heavily underlined in popular fiction and the theatre. On the stage and in the sentimental novel practical choices were never allowed to compromise a sacred sphere in which spotless virtue always triumphed over unmitigated evil.[37]

By assigning to purity a separate and private sphere of influence, nineteenth-century Americans may have checked the impulse to purify the entire national community, but the separation of spheres was always imperfect. Throughout the nineteenth century a hunger for purity more or less constantly threatened the worldly compromises and the double standards that structured Victorian society. Americans still wanted to think of themselves as innocent and to perceive their history as a redemptive quest. Only by elaborate compartmentalization, much compromise, and a certain measure of hypocrisy could they value purity while practicing it only in limited and special ways.

Let us return now to our main concern with assimilation. I have suggested that nineteenth-century Americans developed no consistent theory of how they should behave. The decentralization of society and the disjunction of values and traditions made every alternative feasible and no one policy authoritative. Issues could not crystallize; discontents could not converge. The ethnic crises of the 1850s present a major exception, but still a partial one. In all essential respects the antebellum pattern survived until the 1890s. Then a general and prolonged upheaval in ethnic relations, lasting from the nineties into the 1920s, marked the breakdown of that pattern and the beginning of a new social order.

The clearest indication of a fundamental change at the end of the nineteenth century was the interlinking of racial and religious tensions that had formerly been discrete. During the 1850s, for example, the Know-Nothing movement had been unable to formulate a national program. In the North, Know-Nothings focused almost exclusively on foreign Catholics as the subversive element in American society. Southerners, living in dread of slave conspiracies and of abolitionists, were completely unresponsive to the Catholic issue. Californians, preoccupied with the problem of the Chinese, cared nothing about the phobias of the South or the fears of the Northeast; and the indifference was reciprocated. In contrast, the ethnic hostilities that developed around the beginning of the twentieth century acquired a more generalized character. One fed into another. Southern whites became aroused for the first time about Catholics, Jews, and immigrants. Midwesterners and Far Westerners started to think of themselves as defenders of an America beleaguered on all sides. A sweeping rejection of all outsiders—of everyone who deviated from a conservative, Protestant, northern European pattern—gave a new, comprehensively ethnocentric meaning to the term "prejudice."[38]

What was happening? In brief, the conditions that had sustained the intricate segmentation of the nineteenth century no longer prevailed. The local community lost much of its cherished autonomy, leaving Americans feeling increasingly vulnerable to the intrusion of outsiders. At the same time that the separateness of groups and localities diminished, the wall of separation between opposing values in American minds gave way as well.

The first of these two changes, the shift away from localism, is the more obvious and familiar. Recent interpretations of the political, economic, and cultural turmoil of the 1890s have highlighted, as the critical change in American life at that time, a new awareness of interdependence.[39] Under the inroads of industrialism, bureaucracy, and specialized knowledge, the self-sufficiency of the "island communities" was irretrievably passing. As national organizations crisscrossed an increasingly crowded terrain, more and more of the American people became integrated into economic networks and status hierarchies that drastically reduced the significance of the local arena. On the international level also, the world contracted alarmingly, and the entanglements of interdependence multiplied. Wherever one looked, the state was becoming a palpable reality. All this could be enormously stimulating to Americans who were ready and eager to move outward into a larger, less provincial milieu. It could also be very threatening. Either way, a consciousness of racial, national, and ethnic differences dramatically intensified.

The tightening mesh of interdependence goes far to explain why the internal disjunctions within nineteenth-century culture also broke down. The willingness of Americans to live with a divided heritage and an ambiguous national identity declined. A demand for consistency and sincerity—for an end to lies, deception and hypocrisy—swept through the tangled underbrush of American opinion in the first two decades of the twentieth century. Baffled by the obscure, complex forces that filled the modern world, millions of Americans cried out for light in dark places, for simplicity and wholeness, and finally for purification of the entire society.[40] This was one of the meanings of Progressivism.

It was a sure instinct for cultural definition that inspired Lewis Mumford to call the 1870s and 1880s the Brown Decades.[41] The period that ended with the Chicago World's Fair of 1893 seemed, from a point of view located in the early twentieth century, as dingy in physical appearance as in moral hue. The dazzling luminescence of the White City—as the Chicago Exposition was popularly known—heralded an era of light. American cities glowed at night as never before. White, symbolizing purity and unity, became the essential color of the exterior of government buildings and the interior of hospitals. Windows were enlarged and domestic interiors swept clean of clutter.[42] Campaigns against disease, dirt, darkness, ignorance, "tainted" money, and moral pollution formed a continuous sequence of public endeavor. The zeal of progressives for "clean-ups," which were understood to be simultaneously physical, moral, and social, suggests how a passionate desire to re-create a homogeneous society could evolve into the exclusionary spirit of the Ku Klux Klan. The old American passion for purity burst the compromises and constraints of the Victorian Age.

Historians have conventionally interpreted the repressive waves of nativism and racism from 1890 to 1924 in more concrete terms. They have emphasized class antagonisms, economic dislocations, and Darwinian ideas.[43] All of these were present. Yet the phenomena to be explained transcend these categories. We have to ask why the period from the nineties through the First World War witnessed both a systematic campaign to humiliate and ostracize blacks and a sweeping drive for immigration restriction. These campaigns did not correlate with any sustained economic crisis. Rather, they went along with the triumph of prohibition, the criminalization of prostitution, an intense concern about personal hygiene, pure foods and drugs, public sanitation, and infectious diseases, and a national effort to wipe out corruption of every sort.

The great evil that native white Americans associated with blacks in this era was essentially identical to what they discerned in immigrants. The evil in both cases was pollution: politically, through the sale of votes; socially, through the spread of crime, disease, and immorality; racially, through contamination of the very body of the nation.[44] In the racism of the early twentieth century the critical factor was surely not its scientific rationale, to which most people paid little attention, but rather a new feeling of defilement through contact with what was dark and unclean. The ultimate defilement was that of rape, since it directly violated "purity of blood," and the southern white woman's quite unprecedented fear of rape in the early twentieth century had a more generalized parallel in the growing belief that alien peoples were polluting the bloodstream of the nation. Both of these anxieties interlinked with the prohibition movement, which came alive in the South only when whites became convinced that cheap whiskey was responsible for turning blacks into ravenous beasts.[45] The polluters had been themselves polluted.

Thus a broad movement for purification offered a way of overcoming the contradictions in American life and making the hegemony of the white Protestant culture impregnable. But this was not the only path toward a more consistent society, and ultimately it was not the path Americans chose. Progressivism also had a humanistic side, rooted in the ideology of equal rights and congenial to the cosmopolitan idea of nationality. This side of Progressivism showed itself in the cooperative ethic of the settlement houses and the civil rights initiatives of the newly formed National Association for the Advancement of Colored People. The purity crusades of the early twentieth century therefore widened the old rift in the American ideology instead of closing it. The compartmentalization of differences gave way to bitter ideological conflict. In politics the conflict led to a mobilization of minorities on an unprecedented scale. In thought and culture the boldest advocates of an inclusive Americanism were driven to new positions that would be labeled pluralism and modernism.

What I have in mind especially is the emergence in the early twentieth century of a number of young cultural rebels, like Randolph Bourne and Hutchins Hapgood, for whom any ethnic identity—any distinct group allegiance—had become an encumbrance. Provincialism of all kinds was the enemy.[46] The point to be emphasized is that both sides, both cosmopolitans and puritans, had rejected the Victorian compromise. Both were in revolt against equivocation and complexity. Critical thought, from the Muckrakers onward, concentrated fiercely on exposing sham and pretence. The characteristic hypocrisies, dualisms and double standards of the nineteenth century became intolerable both to those who would revitalize and those who would radicalize the traditional culture. A passion for exposés, for unmasking underlying realities—the very assumption that reality is always hidden—this became the leitmotif of intellectual life in the twentieth century.[47]

In sum the Progressive era brought finally into the open the challenge that a divided heritage and an ambiguous, dualistic national identity posed to the American people. The problem of assimilation could no longer be evaded.

An invitation to the Fulbright Fortieth Anniversary Conference planned for 1989 in Canberra, Australia, offered Higham an opportunity to consider the role of immigration in American history broadly and in comparative perspective. He restated ideas he had elaborated elsewhere, but there were new insights, too. They sprang from juxtaposing the two societies formed on the frontier of Europe's expansion in the modern era.

Although the United States and Australia can both be considered immigrant societies, Higham contends, only in the former did immigration become a powerful symbol that dominated national identity. There were, in fact, rival myths of American origins, each corresponding to a different "founding." The colonial myth of Anglophile identity and the Revolutionary myth of melting-pot Americanism coexisted uneasily after the 1780s and created continual tension between "ethnic" and "civic" versions of American nationalism. Higham showed in *Strangers in the Land* (1955) that the first tends to resurface during periods of national crisis, whereas the second is allowed freer play when economic opportunity appears unlimited. Here Higham adds the point that the melting-pot idea gained popularity by merging with another potent American legend, the myth of the frontier. In the United States, but not in Australia, the frontier and immigration coalesced into a single national story of westward migration and gradual assimilation. So successful was this merger that it became commonplace to claim, as Oscar Handlin does, that the saga of the immigrants *is* the story of American history, not a particular aspect of it.

This master-myth of a "nation of immigrants" Higham debunks succinctly in the second part of his essay, which is distilled from a chapter he contributed to C. Vann Woodward's pioneering anthology, *The Comparative Approach to American History* (1968). By defining immigrants as voluntary entrants into a preexisting polity, Higham clears the way for an inquiry into the specific impact of immigration on American society. What made the United States different from other immigrant receivers, according to Higham, was the extraordinary variety of its incoming population. Together with geographic mobility and other pressures toward assimilation, this diversity muted the impact of foreigners on American life. Higham ends with the paradox that massive immigration had surprisingly limited effects on American society, contrary to the claims of many ethnic historians, although it may have mitigated divisions of race and class.

Higham does not undertake a sustained comparison between the United States and Australia. Nor does he deal with the huge shift—taking place as he wrote—in the sources of immigration to the two countries. Still, his conclusions about the earlier migrations have been confirmed by Walter Nugent's *Crossings* (1992), which finds that the ethnic variety and absorptive capacity of the United States were unique among immigrant destinations. Recently, scholars have interpreted ethnicity itself as a cultural construction that is continually reinvented to define individual and group identities. Further work may reveal how the process of "inventing ethnicity" that has been outlined by Kathleen Conzen and others may impinge on Higham's chronology of changing national myths. Meanwhile, his emphasis on the "fluid diversities" and "weak boundaries" of American ethnic groups may help to promote a new candidate for national mythology: the vision of a cosmopolitan "postethnic America" that David Hollinger introduced in 1995.

Robert Lewis
University of Birmingham (U.K.)

6

Immigration and American Mythology
[1991]

Migration is one of the great forces in history. People have always been on the move. In the history of nations, migration can play various roles. It sometimes constructs, sometimes sustains, sometimes disrupts or alters, sometimes destroys. My chief interest is in the first and second of these, specifically in the construction of two nations, rather than the discrete experiences of particular peoples in those settings. For the sake of clarity I shall focus on one kind of migration—namely, immigration. And there I can make only tentative allusions to the Australian side. Comparison, nevertheless, frames my subject. Australia and the United States are new nations, formed by men and women who emigrated from Europe, evicted the native population, and relied on a continuing inflow from overseas—both voluntary and coerced—for the help they needed in tapping the wealth of a continent. Yet a major contrast has long differentiated the way Americans and Australians think about this common experience.

Whatever their attitudes toward the latest arrivals from Latin America and Asia, Americans recognize that immigration has been a major force in shaping the kind of society and consciousness their country has developed. Today the proposition that every American has two homelands can be offered as a self-evident truth; and not so long ago the foremost historian of American immigration aroused no visible dissent when he declared grandly "that the immigrants *were* American history," not a special aspect of it.[1] These views bespeak a powerful national myth. I shall explain shortly why the myth exaggerates and simplifies the reality it also celebrates and shapes. For now, however, it is sufficient to note that Australia has no comparable myth of immigration as a great nation-making experience and profound human adventure. There is no Australian national icon similar to America's Statue of Liberty, facing out to the world as a symbol of promise and hope to people in other lands.

National myths are not, of course, singular, monolithic, or uncontested. Typically, a national myth glorifies a certain group of founders or a transcendent hero. To later generations either becomes a basic referent of collective identity. But rival myths may construe the founding experience quite differently. One American myth has had to do with exclusive possession rather than the openness and fluidity of migration. Before Americans learned to think of themselves or even of others as immigrants—before the very word existed—an incipient national consciousness celebrated the early English settlers who had staked out for themselves and their descendants a domain where their own particular way of life could be defended and perpetuated. We find the myth of exclusive possession in the Hebraic side of Puritanism, conveying the early New Englanders' strong sense of being a chosen people. We meet it again on the eve of the American Revolution among the colonial elites who were proudly defending what they viewed as an ancient English heritage lately endangered by the perfidy of a corrupt regime. "The Americans," John Randolph declared in 1774, "are descended from the Loins of *Britons,* and therefore may, with Propriety, be called the Children, and *England* the Mother of them." At the very beginning of the quarrel with the home government, James Otis had pointed out that Americans were not "a compound mongrel mixture of *English, Indian,* and *Negro,* but . . . freeborn *British white* subjects."[2]

The contradictions between this restrictive, Anglophile identity on one hand and a cosmopolitan Americanism on the other are familiar but still not sufficiently understood. The American Revolution is often said to have created a new people who made an abstract philosophy of universal rights the definition of their kinship and purpose. Arthur Mann, for example, declared that "American nationality has nothing to do with an earlier folk identity. It is purely ideological."[3] Unfortunately, history is not that simple. Although the delegates who gathered in Philadelphia in 1776 and 1787 designed a national state on the basis of universal principles, the colonial societies they linked together remembered an earlier founding. That first founding of the Anglo-American world had occurred piecemeal throughout the seventeenth century. It was in each case accomplished by people committed to enhancing their own well-being at any cost, including expulsion of the native inhabitants and a massive importation of African slaves. The second founding, in contrast, sanctioned a myth of national inclusiveness, according to which the American is, in Crèvecoeur's words, a "new man . . . who, leaving behind him all his ancient prejudices and manners . . . becomes an American by being received in the broad lap of our great *Alma Mater*. Here individuals of all nations are melted into a new race."[4] Yet the second founding, and the evolving, open-ended identity it projected, did not expunge the memory of the first. One was superimposed on the other, and the two have been entangled ever since.

To suggest how vividly the older myth of exclusive possession infused the patriot cause during the American Revolution I need only quote a few lines of doggerel from an anonymous broadside published in Danvers, Massachusetts:

> Now unto who belongs this Land?
> It was gain'd by our Fathers Hands:
> This Land they did their Children give,
> That they a free born Race might live.
> This Land they won themselves alone,
> The Blood shed for it was their own;
> They thank none that dwelleth around,
> For Help from them they never found.
> Now let us keep it as our own,
> For it belongs to us alone:
> And let us stand firm like a Tree,
> That never can removed be.[5]

Whenever Americans feel that some powerful outsider may take away something they deeply cherish, we can expect the myth of exclusive possession to revive. Through most of the past two hundred years, however, it has been at a disadvantage. The first founding of America in the seventeenth century had involved so many disparate groups, separated from one another by religion, country of origin, local institutions, and geographical distance, that no coherent, overall image of those original founders could crystallize. Every attempt in the nineteenth century to define an old American type, an autochthonous, pre-Revolutionary American, splintered on the rock of irreducible particularism.

The lack of a suitable name is perhaps the best evidence of the amorphousness of an indigenous core population. Unlike colonial Latin America and the Caribbean islands, North American society never developed a basic distinction between "creoles," that is, old settlers in a colonial society who, with their progeny, feel superior to, and more rooted than, newcomers from the homeland.[6] In contrast also to Australia, the United States never produced an American Natives' Association. To us "natives" are Indians. The nearest thing in the nineteenth century to an organized defense of the native-born against the foreign-born was the mid-century nativist movement, but this anti-Catholic crusade carefully avoided identifying "true" Americanism with any place of birth or ethnic origin. It could appeal to Protestant and Jewish immigrants because the prejudices of the Know-Nothings were packaged in a universalistic, libertarian ideology. Their hero was George Washington.

On the early American stage the character who came closest to projecting a national identity—a homespun American image—was the Yankee, a rural New Englander whom some actors tried to inflate to national proportions by adding a western inflection. Outside the United States, "Yankee" caught on as a national name; in domestic discourse it did not. Among Americans the specifically regional meaning of the word was too emphatic for it to signify a national identity. At most the Yankee became the northener, who was known south of the Mason and Dixon Line by the obligatory epithet "damn Yankee."[7]

Meanwhile a rival myth, emerging during the Revolution, acknowledged the multiple origins of the American people. At first the new myth was largely ideological. It attributed the common posture of American patriots to a set of political ideas, that is, to the republican principles their otherwise diverse ancestors had passionately espoused.[8] Yet ideology, no matter how inspiriting, seemed a frail basis for national unity in the loose-knit society of the early republic. Nationalistic rhetoric was shrill in those antebellum decades because national institutions were weak and a national culture thin and undeveloped. Talking obsessively about the need for a distinctive American literature, cultural elites worried about the incompleteness of a national character.[9] From the 1820s onward, however, an answer to the problem of an American focus was found increasingly in the epic of migration westward.

It is well known that both the United States and Australia have drawn copiously on the image of the frontiersman as the national type par excellence. In legend and to some extent in reality, the bush workers of Australia and the pioneers of the American West formed a model of national traits. The great distinction between them, in Russel Ward's classic interpretation, is that democracy carried different meanings in the two contexts. For the bush rangers, in a land of vast ranches and restrictive land policies, it meant strong class solidarity and hostility to any control or patronage from above. For Americans on a frontier that encouraged competition and small holdings through most of the nineteenth century, democracy meant self-reliance; and self-reliance entailed an insouciant disregard for the bonds and constraints of class.[10]

In addition to a contrast between the collectivism of one folk image and the individualism of the other, there was a second difference between the two frontier types—a difference less noticed by historians but more rele-

vant to our subject. Australia's frontiersmen, according to the legend, belonged exclusively to the interior. They scorned the effete coastal cities and
the English newcomers who inhabited them. Thus Australian national consciousness, in resisting the strong pull of the British connection, posited a
wholly endogenous type: a "nomad tribe," in Anthony Trollope's telling
phrase. The American frontiersman—though also shaped by the land—
came from somewhere else. He was, for example, the Virginian in the most
famous of American cowboy novels.[11] Characteristically, the American pioneer was seen not as a nomad but as the spearhead of a continuous migratory process: a westward march of the people in all of their multitudes,
which had settled the older parts of the country as well. Instead of repress-
ing the memory of earlier migrations, the American pioneer extended and
fulfilled them.[12] The legend of the pioneer easily blended with the legend
of the American as immigrant.

Walt Whitman's universalizing of the westward movement in the poem
"Pioneers! O Pioneers!" reflects this well:

> All the pulses of the world,
> Falling in they beat for us, with the Western movement beat,
> Holding single or together, steady moving to the front, all for us,
> Pioneers! O pioneers!
>
> Life's involv'd and varied pageants,
> All the forms and shows, all the workmen at their work,
> All the seamen and the landsmen, all the masters with their slaves,
> Pioneers! O pioneers![13]

The synergy between the two themes—the pioneer and the immigrant—
arose from their common promise of rebirth and renewal. By moving
farther west, Americans repeatedly reenacted a ritual of deliverance, which
for some had begun in the original departure from the Old World. However
much their migrations were impelled by desperately worsening conditions
in familiar habitats, the magic of hope buoyed their movement onward.
American national self-consciousness, Paul Nagel has remarked, "has been
mostly a spirit of anticipation."[14] Although this hope for a better life and an
improved society was certainly grounded in the political and religious ideas
of the Revolutionary era, it acquired an everyday reality and a deeply
personal significance from the energies of geographical and social mobility.
As images of pioneers, immigrants, and other supposedly self-made men
fleshed out the new liberal ideology that Americans proclaimed in 1776, it
flowered into a myth of an unbounded society. America is the place where
anything is possible, where no one is irrevocably fenced in.[15]

The special contribution that immigration made to this dominant national myth was the vision of the nation as a great melting pot. Of all those who were caught up in the migratory process, immigrants underwent the most visible alteration. Few foreign observers failed to note, and many immigrants proudly proclaimed, the changes in dress, demeanor, and status the newcomers displayed after a few years in America, particularly in the West. Immigration dramatized the rebirth and self-transformation that the myth of boundlessness celebrated.[16]

It is little wonder, then, that the frontier and the melting pot came to the fore in historical writing concurrently and under similar auspices. Although pioneers and immigrants had lived, as stereotypical figures, in the popular imagination for decades, the most reputable scholars largely ignored both types until 1893, when Frederick Jackson Turner brought them together. His famous paper "The Significance of the Frontier in American History" spelled out the myth of American boundlessness with a new analytical clarity. Here and in the work of Turner's colleagues at the University of Wisconsin the immigrant was placed squarely on the agenda of professional scholarship. "In the crucible of the frontier," Turner declared, "the immigrants were Americanized, liberated and fused into a mixed race, English in neither nationality nor characteristics."[17] A similar fusion actually occurred in the Australian bush; but neither scholars nor mythmakers (if they can be separated) seemed to think it was very important.

Turner's association of the immigrant with the frontier and with a redemptive process of becoming American defined an era in the scholarly study of immigration in American history. The first major academic studies were published between the two world wars by midwesterners, two of them Turner's own students, while Turner's successor at Harvard, also a midwesterner, sketched the common framework within which their work was cast. The two grand themes of American history, Arthur M. Schlesinger wrote in his very influential *New Viewpoints in American History,* are the influence of immigration on American life and institutions and the influence of the American environment on the ever-changing composite population.[18] From there it was an easy but also a significant step to Oscar Handlin's conflation of the immigrant *with* American history. In the immigrant's painful liberation from the traditional securities of the Old World, Handlin argued, we find the key experience of all Americans. From Turner to Handlin, the myth of an unbounded society permeated American approaches to the study of immigration.

In the 1960s the myths that had long shaped the ways Americans thought about themselves were badly shaken. Both the myth of exclusive possession and the myth of an unbounded society had begun to lose intellectual credibility as early as the 1930s: exclusive possession challenged by an increasingly egalitarian acceptance of ethnic and racial diversity; boundlessness mocked by recognition of the finitude of nature's bounty and the recalcitrance of institutions.[19] What the 1960s added was an *anti*-American myth, that is, a belief that all affirmative myths about America are entrapments. Identities should therefore be grounded in more tangible allegiances that are closer to the self. The immigrant as a prototypical individual dissolved. The melting pot shivered into a thousand pieces. But the study of ethnic groups and their subdivisions flourished as never before. There is an instructive irony about the dramatic proliferation of ethnic studies once the myth that had sponsored them lost general credence.

Between myth and anti-myth, is it now possible to see that there are limits to the role of immigration in American history and that the scope of that role is best understood in terms of its limits? Believing that a comparative perspective can help us to *delimit* the influence of immigration, I want now to suggest how certain distinctive features of the immigrant stream as we have known it to date have cushioned its impact on the larger American society.

Even to begin to make comparative judgments requires an understanding of ethnic groups that escapes from the mythic clutch of the cliché that all Americans are immigrants. If they are, we have no specific component of the U.S. population to compare with similar segments of other societies. I propose therefore that the immigrant sector be defined as people whose status and behavior reflect a consciousness that they or their antecedents joined a preexisting society by a voluntary act of migration. This usage distinguishes immigrants from ethnic groups of an involuntary or native origin; and it is congruent with sociological distinctions between first-generation, second-generation, and third-generation immigrants.

The ethnic communities that immigrants form to keep their traditions alive undergo erosion through assimilation. At times the erosion is reversible, and in some groups it is slow. But the proportion of the American people who feel significantly conscious of foreign origins has always been limited. Census statistics show that the foreign born have never quite reached 15 percent of the U.S. population. The total body of immigrants and their offspring (first and second generations) has fluctuated between a high of almost 36 percent of the American people in 1930 and a low of 16.5 percent in 1970. These figures, compared to those from some other immigrant-receiving countries, do not appear exceptionally large. In the years just before World War I the foreign-born alone made up 22 percent of Canada's population and almost one-third of the people of Argentina.[20]

For most of the white population of the United States the significance of a particular foreign origin diminishes greatly after the second or third generation. How many, through intermarriage or in other ways, have relinquished the Old World identities of their ancestors in favor of affinities formed from native materials cannot be calculated. But it is significant that the efforts of survey and census takers in recent years to induce people to report some non-American birthplace for their ancestors have shown that about 10 percent of all whites either don't know or won't admit to any origins outside the United States.[21] Since a mere knowledge of where one's ancestors came from is ordinarily a very slight indicator of ethnicity, the actual number of unhyphenated Americans must be far larger than these figures show.

While assimilation has confined the influence of immigration in one direction, a related feature of American society—mobility—has offset that influence in another direction. Since immigrants by definition come from somewhere else, they are an unsettling force wherever they appear. But in America their arrival has often been less stressful than it would be in other countries because here most of the older, supposedly more settled population have themselves been engaged in an endless round of relocations. From east to west, from town to city, from city to suburb, and from one neighborhood to the next, Americans have always been an extraordinarily migratory people. International migration has invigorated this larger process *but has also been absorbed in it.* Internal mobility has accustomed Americans to living among strangers; it has lessened the social distance between one kind of newcomer and another. Although the amazing levels that internal mobility reached in the nineteenth century have declined in recent decades, Americans are still a people perpetually on the move.[22]

Some observers, in fact, tell us that historical statistics cannot capture the increasing stressfulness of mobility. A global economy compels firms to become flexible and modular. Fewer jobs last; couples accept commuter marriages. Amid fast-moving and constantly changing markets, we live with an ever-increasing premium on speed.[23] All of this makes what remains of dissolving communities all the more precious.

Together with mobility and assimilation, there is a third great factor that characterizes but also limits the influence of immigrants in America. This is simply the exceptional diversity of their origins. America's immigrants have differed from those drawn to other new countries most strikingly in the variety of peoples who have come, not in the sheer size of the influx. Until after World War II, certain favored nationalities dominated the immigrant stream that flowed to Argentina, Brazil, Canada, Australia, and smaller countries like Fiji and Malaya. Where the way of life of the predominant immigrant group contrasted markedly with that of the older inhabitants, a deep, enduring schism could split the receiving society. The United States has largely escaped such cleavages not only because internal mobility encouraged assimilation but also because our many ethnic minorities have differed too much from one another to form a compact body.

In the nineteenth century the biggest single immigrant stream was German; but only for two decades—the 1850s and 1860s—did the Germans amount to as much as a third of the total number of arriving immigrants.[24] The huge German-speaking quarters in some American cities worried older Americans less than the aggressiveness of Irish politicians in other cities; but more important than either circumstance was the fact that the Germans and the Irish could rarely see eye to eye. In quarreling with one another, immigrant groups have time and again sought allies among the older native population, and in doing so have speeded their own Americanization.

Observing this process in the politics of his city, a Chicago newspaper editor marveled in 1874 that a natural law—a "law of compensation"—made the German and Irish immigrants who were pouring into the Windy City "so thoroughly opposed to each other" that they "act as counterpoises." Warming to his subject, the editor continued: "That these opposites come in quantities that so balance each other, enables the native population—and by native we mean all those born in, and identified with, the country whether of foreign or native parentage—to hold the balance of power and to prevent affairs from gravitating either in the direction of the one or the other. This of course applies only to the first or second generations of the emigrants for the reason that the grandchildren, and often the children of both, are anxious for nothing so much as to drop their ancestral line, and to regard themselves wholly as Americans."[25]

Paradoxically, then, the diversity that immigration has so greatly nourished in America has been self-limiting. The ethnic groups that immigration has spawned have been fluid rather than static, dispersive rather than rooted, overlapping and interpenetrating instead of congealing in ancient territories. At the same time, these fluid diversities stemming from immigration have cross-cut other divisions in American society and blurred them as well. Without immigration, racial and class differences would surely have been sharper than they are. Although the myth of an unbounded society has lost much of its viability, there is an enduring truth in the association of immigration, as experienced historically in the United States, with weak rather than strong social boundaries.

In this essay, first presented at a small conference at the Center for the Study of Democratic Institutions in Santa Barabara, California, in 1974, Higham addresses head-on the problem of assimilation that "Integrating America" (Chapter 5) leaves the reader with. Here he proposes the concept of "pluralistic integration" to encompass the dynamic relation between shared and distinct cultures in American society.

Higham chose initially to call his essay "Another American Dilemma" because he sought to restore a missing element in Gunnar Myrdal's construction. The "American Dilemma," as Myrdal had explained in the 1940s, is the distance separating Americans' democratic creed from their undemocratic conduct. Higham examines this formulation and in effect asks, Can we spell "creed" in the singular? The contest between assimilationist and pluralist perspectives suggests that there may be no unitary national credo, or at least that it embodies opposing social ideals.

At the California conference, Myrdal, upholding his assimilationist version of the "American Creed," launched an impassioned attack on the "romantic ethnicity" of the 1970s. Rudolph Vecoli, a leading immigration historian, countered by pressing the case for preserving ethnic subcultures. By proposing "pluralistic integration," Higham emerged as a radical of the center. He restored diversity without declaring war on unity, and pointed to the multiple trajectories and shifting identities that the tension between integration and pluralism could create. There is no compromise here, but a shrewd and perceptive insight into the dynamics of American society.

The timing of the gathering made Higham's resolve to pursue usable concepts all the more urgent. The Center for the Study of Democratic Institutions, founded by former University of Chicago President Robert Hutchins, was headed by the journalist and civil rights activist Harry Ashmore, who had done much to fight segregation in the South. But hopes for a peaceful resolution of racial issues had faded quickly. By the end of the 1960s the civil rights coalition had splintered, and young black leaders were preaching separatism and violence. Large parts of Detroit had gone up in flames in 1967, only thirty miles from the University of Michigan, where Higham was teaching. As he prepared his paper, Higham felt a renewed sense of urgency about understanding American diversity. New concepts would help clarify the debate about social justice.

For this volume, Higham has written a postscript to his original essay that reflects his engagement over the past quarter of a century with a broad and diversified social history as well as his continuing search for synthetic concepts. Surveying recent developments in immigration, public policy, and private life, he points to the continuing significance of pluralistic integration.

Olivier Zunz
University of Virginia

7

Pluralistic Integration as an American Model
[1975]

A season of struggle and hope, of turmoil and guilt, in American racial and ethnic relations has passed. In its place has come a time of apathy, cynicism, exhaustion, and near despair. The civil rights movement has collapsed, a victim at least in part of its successes. The demands for ethnic power and recognition, which exploded in the wake of the civil rights movement, have used up the hectic energies of posture and intimidation. This is a moment, then, for reflection and reconsideration. It is most especially a moment to reckon with an impasse in our thinking about ethnicity. Until the clash between two ways of looking at ethnic problems is resolved, it is hard to see how further advances can take place. The conflict between those contending points of view is paralyzing because it divides the creative minority of Americans who actively seek a more just social order.

The clash is old and familiar, although (as I shall argue later) most American writing on ethnic relations seeks to suppress or avoid it. One form of the basic dilemma occupied the New England Puritans. For them the problem of the one and the many centered on the difficulty of maintaining a unified society while guarding the purity of independent congregations. On another level the issue crystallized in the structure of the American Constitution. The Founding Fathers not only left us the problem of reconciling national supremacy with state and local rights but provided a matrix for dealing with it. The importance of reconciling ethnic diversity with national unity, though no less crucial, is much less attempted. The Constitution laid down no explicit guidelines for adjudicating issues of social integration—we have no court of ethnic rights—and an appreciation of the complexities in this troubled area is rarely met. Here the dilemma is both sociological and moral. It has to do with what we are and what we wish to be, with the possibilities of our social heritage and circumstances and with the kind of identity we would like to have.

I propose, first, to state the crux of the dilemma as we confront it today; second, to review two characteristic strategies that American intellectuals have used to escape from the dilemma; and finally, to suggest a third strategy that may not suffer from the shortcomings of the other two. Doubtless there are other fruitful approaches to the perplexities of a multiethnic society. I intend not to be exhaustive but to concentrate on the leading tendencies in American liberal thought in the twentieth century. In proposing a third formulation I do not suppose I am settling anything. Fundamentally the issues of ethnic life are never settled. But a clear grasp of unacceptable alternatives and some sense of direction can help us to move beyond the constraints of received opinion.

The essential dilemma, of course, is the opposition between a strategy of integration and one of pluralism. Although the contrast has many dimensions, it can be summed up as a question of boundaries. The integrationist looks toward the elimination of ethnic boundaries. The pluralist believes in maintaining them. Their primary difference, therefore, concerns the scale and character of the community each takes as a model. Integration is pledged to the great community yet to be realized: the community of humankind. Pluralism holds fast to the little community: the concrete sodality rooted in the past. Integration in its modern form expresses the universalism of the Enlightenment. Pluralism rests on the diversitarian premises of romantic thought.[1]

From this fundamental distinction others flow. In the United States both integrationists and pluralists claim to be the true champions of democracy; but democracy means different things to them. Consistent with its universal criteria, integration lends itself to a majoritarian emphasis. The integrationist expects a simple majority to approximate the general will. Pluralism, on the other hand, is always a philosophy of minority rights. It represents an effort to generalize the particular claim of a small part of society. It resists the conformity that majorities encourage; it is likely to dispute the legitimacy of any simple majority. Pluralism conceives of democratic politics as a process of building coalitions between minorities.

The democracy of integration is an equality of individuals; pluralist democracy, an equality of groups. For the assimilationist the primary social unit and the locus of value is the individual. What counts is the individual's right to self-definition. Individuals must therefore be free to secede from their ancestors. This is exactly what happens in the process of assimilation: individuals or families detach themselves one by one from their traditional communities. For pluralists, however, the persistence and vitality of the group comes first. Individuals can realize themselves, and become whole, only through the group that nourishes their being.[2]

The priority that one side assigns to the individual and the other to the group affects their respective views of what binds a people together. For integrationists the linchpin of a rightly ordered society is a set of ideals, a body of principles—in our own case, what Gunnar Myrdal called an "American Creed." A people who aspire to universality and consist largely of detached and mobile individuals will rely heavily on the beliefs they hold in common. Indeed, they may share little else, for all who subscribe to the official creed should be received into membership. Pluralists care much less what people believe; they want to know who they are. The most important social bond is inherited, not adopted, the work of ancestors, not of abstractions. In a multiethnic society, therefore, assimilationists stress a unifying ideology, whereas pluralists guard a distinctive memory.

When the two positions are stated so baldly, the undesirability of either—at least without heavy qualification—becomes manifest. For one thing, both positions are unrealistic. Assimilationism falsely assumes that ethnic ties dissolve fairly easily in an open society. On this score the melting-pot idea—the standard metaphor of assimilation—presents the same weakness that vitiated Frederick Jackson Turner's frontier thesis. Just as Turner underestimated the toughness of the entire social heritage that pioneers carried westward, so the melting-pot theory fails to appreciate the durability of their ethnic allegiances. Even Mary Antin, the most ecstatic of assimilationists, who claimed to "have been made over," to be "absolutely other than the person whose story I have to tell," could not exorcise the past. "The Wandering Jew in me seeks forgetfulness," she confesses in her autobiography. "I am not afraid to live on and on, if only I do not have to remember too much."[3] Other immigrants never wished to forget. Many groups resist for generations the assault of technology and modern education on their sense of ethnic selfhood. No ethnic group, once established in the United States, has ever entirely disappeared; none seems about to do so. People are not as pliant as assimilationists have supposed.

Pluralism makes the opposite mistake. It assumes a rigidity of ethnic boundaries and a fixity of group commitment that American life does not permit. Although immigrants like Mary Antin could not forget the past, some of their children and more of their grandchildren could detach themselves from the old ethnic base. All American ethnic groups perpetuate themselves, but none survives intact. Their boundaries are more or less porous and elastic. All of them lose people who marry out and whose offspring cease to identify with the rejected strain. This is so patently true that loud assertions of pluralism almost invariably betray fears of assimilation.

Pluralism encourages the further illusion that ethnic groups typically have a high degree of internal solidarity. Actually, many of them are unstable federations of local or tribal collectivities, which attain only a temporary and precarious unity in the face of a common enemy. On top of sharp localistic differences, an ethnic group is likely to be split along religious, class, and political lines. For example, the American Dutch, a relatively small immigrant group, belonged in the nineteenth century to three rival churches (Reformed, Christian Reformed, and Roman Catholic), many distinct speech communities (Zeelanders, Groningers, Friesians, Gelderlanders, Limburgers, Noord-Brabanters, East Friesians, Flemings, Utrechters, people of Graefschap, and those who spoke the Drenthe and Overijsel dialects), and totally dissimilar generations (colonial descendants versus nineteenth-century immigrants). No American ethnic group, Arthur Mann has pointed out, has created an organized community capable of speaking for all its members.[4]

In addition to being unrealistic, both integration and pluralism are morally objectionable. From the point of view of the individual, integration is an ethic of self-transformation—an Emersonian summons to "shun father and mother and wife and brother when my genius calls me." It teaches a rejection of one's origins and a contempt for those parts of the self that resist transformation. It sacrifices love and loyalty to autonomy and mastery, only to find those elusive goals dissolving in a pervasive conformity. In sum, for individuals outside the mainstream the process of assimilation is identical with the pursuit of individual success. It gives an edge to private ambition and a spur to personal aggrandizement. In actuality only a thin line separates Mary Antin's idealistic renunciation of the past from the queasy evasions of the traveling salesman in William Faulkner's *The Sound and the Fury*:

> "I'm not talking about men of the jewish religion," I says, "I've known some jews that were fine citizens. You might be one yourself," I says.

"No," he says, "I'm an American."

"No offense," I says. "I give every man his due, regardless of religion or anything else. I have nothing against jews as an individual," I says. "It's just the race. You'll admit that they produce nothing. They follow the pioneers into a new country and sell them clothes."

"You're thinking of Armenians," he says "aren't you. A pioneer wouldn't have any use for new clothes."

"No offense," I says, "I don't hold a man's religion against him."

"Sure," he says, "I'm an American. My folks have some French blood, why I have a nose like this. I'm an American, all right."

"So am I," I says. "Not many of us left."[5]

Assimilation makes success a species of disloyalty.

Moreover, assimilation may lay a stigma of failure on those who remain loyal to ancestral ways. The integrationist's assurance that individuals need only an opportunity to prove their worth has led innumerable underachieving ethnics into a blind alley. They may conclude either that they are indeed unworthy or that the proffered opportunity was fraudulent. The result is either self-hatred or alienation from society. It can frequently be both.

The liabilities of a pluralist ethic are equally severe. Whereas assimilation penalizes the less ambitious and successful groups and individuals, pluralism limits the more autonomous and adventurous. To young people fired by curiosity and equipped with a cosmopolitan education, the ethnic community can be intensely stultifying. It is likely to be suspicious, narrow-minded, riddled with prejudices. Pluralism adjures the young to realize themselves through the group to which they belong; but many have little sense of ethnic identity and in any case will not forgo individual opportunity in the interest of ethnic separateness and cohesion. While assimilation sacrifices the group for the sake of the individual, pluralism would put the individual at the mercy of the group.

The dangers of the latter course became manifest in the light of proposals from some pluralists for giving legal protection to ethnic differences. Harold Cruse would amend the Constitution to secure the rights of racial and ethnic groups. The Indian activist Vine Deloria has offered somewhat more concrete proposals for "tribalizing" American society by giving corporate bodies full control over local communities.[6] The threat that such arrangements would pose to the equal rights of individuals is only part of their difficulty. Raising the walls around unequal ethnic groups must surely sharpen conflicts between them while vitiating the common principles on which all rely to regulate their intercourse. A multiethnic society can avoid tyranny only through a shared culture and a set of universal rules that all of its groups accept. If integration is unacceptable because it does not allow for differences, pluralism fails to answer our need for universals.

The record of American intellectuals in clarifying the issues of race and ethnicity is less than notable. Polemics we have in abundance, but on this subject no contributions to democratic theory compare in depth or complexity with the writings of Hamilton, Madison, Dewey, and Niebuhr. Faced with the antinomies I have outlined, all but a very few theorists have simply elaborated one side of the argument. The other side is either repressed or relegated to some inactive region of consciousness.

Even before pluralism emerged as a distinct alternative to earlier conceptions of the American ethnic pattern, Americans adopted simplistic positions on the subject. In the nineteenth century the question of ethnic boundaries was argued in terms of the advantages of purity or of intermixture. Controversy centered on the merits of a unitary culture deriving from one dominant source, as opposed to a syncretistic fusion of diverse cultures. Today we honor especially the few idealists like Wendell Phillips who were genuinely all-embracing in their commitment to the mingling of races and peoples in the United States.[7] What troubles the modern reader is the assurance of such writers that every ethnic group will contribute something valuable to the amalgam without neutralizing any of the other ingredients. In this tradition there is no admission of sacrifice, strain, or loss.

Only among a few novelists and dramatists in the early twentieth century do we begin to glimpse the poignant complexities that underlay the cheerful enunciation of unambiguous ideals. Fiction has projected inner conflicts that discursive argument continues to hide. Of all modern statements of the assimilationist position, the most influential was Israel Zangwill's play *The Melting Pot*. It gave general currency to the image that has since dominated assimilationist thinking. On close inspection, however, the play reveals a riptide of conflicting values and emotions.

Before Zangwill's play opened on Broadway in 1908, the analogy between the United States and a melting pot was rarely if ever drawn.[8] Earlier tributes to America's power of assimilation had implied that the process occurred effortlessly and spontaneously. There was no point in conceiving of America as a melting pot if one supposed that the country was as yet unformed and that every current of immigration could alter it in some notable way. The traditional view of assimilation did not require a crucible—a rigid, preexisting institutional matrix—for if America was the pot, what contribution could newcomers make to it? A melting pot also implied a tender; it suggested that assimilation needs control and supervision. It was an industrial image, fraught with the menacing heat and the flaming intensity of a steel mill. In the climactic speech of the play the hero shouts, "These are the fires of God you've come to . . . into the Crucible with you all! God is making the American . . . he will be the fusion of all races, the coming superman."[9] The message was rapturous, but it came in an ambiance of fiery apocalypse. Both the symbol of the melting pot and the rhetoric surrounding it betrayed the mounting tensions Zangwill wanted to allay.

The story, too, was full of ambiguity. It told of a young Jewish violinist, David Quixano, whose parents had died in a Russian pogrom. Having emigrated to New York, he is writing a great symphony that will celebrate the American spirit. At a settlement house he falls in love with Vera, the daughter of a Russian army officer who had herself become a revolutionary before escaping to America. Their determination to renounce the "blood hatreds" of Europe nearly founders when David discovers that Vera's father was the fiendish slayer of his parents. In the end David's American ideal triumphs. The symphony, now completed and wildly acclaimed by its first audience, revives his faith in the melting pot. But others pay a price for that epiphany. "Those who love us *must* suffer," David sternly declares. "It is live things, not dead metals, that are being melted in the Crucible." Vera recognizes that even she must take second place in David's life, that his music and his "prophetic visions" come first.[10]

Thus ideals conquer memories; the abstract community of the future prevails over the tangible communities of the past. Zangwill took care, however, to blunt the painfulness of the choice. Fundamentally, what made David's willful and visionary behavior tolerable was the uniqueness of his artistic genius. It is your destiny, Vera told him, to stand "above the world, alone and self-sufficient." David's beloved uncle reinforces the point. Acquiescing reluctantly in David's flouting of ethnic loyalties, Uncle Mendel concedes that geniuses are exceptions. Through the romantic cult of the genius—"a law unto himself"—Zangwill enabled his audience to accept integration as a lovely, inspiring theory without having to face squarely the dilemmas it posed for them.

While imaginative writing began to reveal the complexity of ethnic experience, polemicists continued to simplify it. Consider, for example, John Collier's passionate plea for the group rights of the first Americans, *Indians of the Americas* (1947). As U.S. commissioner of Indian affairs in the 1930s, Collier was largely responsible for the enactment and execution of a pluralist program to revitalize tribal power and identity. Collier's program did strengthen the corporate life of the tribes; but it also had some contrary effects, which his book completely bypassed. The "New Deal for the Indians" made available to them modern techniques of administration and land utilization. In that sense it was assimilative. Collier saw that his efforts entailed assimilation as well as preservation of native culture. "I was often gripped in anxiety," he confessed late in life, "that this spiritual center of Indian life might be lost if we carried the Indians too far along with us."[11] Yet the problem is never mentioned in *Indians of the Americas,* his major book. Rather, the book was a sustained hymn to the deathless continuity of Indian culture.

The tendency of writers to seize exclusively on one side of the American ethnic dilemma was especially striking in discussions of Black Power. The classic text by Stokely Carmichael and Charles V. Hamilton rejected integrationist goals because they sap the black community's leadership while benefiting only the few who are lured away. *"Before a group can enter the open society, it must first close ranks,"* Carmichael and Hamilton declared. "By this we mean that group solidarity is necessary before a group can operate effectively from a bargaining position of strength in a pluralistic society."[12] The reader is led to suppose that ethnic groups have advanced in America only through a collective struggle against other groups, even though some of the most disunited and individualistic elements in our society—native white Protestants and Jews—have been the most successful. Moreover, when native white Protestants have mobilized self-consciously against others, as in the Know-Nothing movement and the southern Confederacy, they have usually been thrown for a loss. Pluralism works for some of the people some of the time, but not for all of the people all of the time.

In view of the obvious shortcomings of both the assimilationist and the pluralist models, a few students of ethnic problems have tried to combine the two. Let us call such intermediate schemes "pluralistic integration." Until some entirely new model turns up, pluralistic integration seems to offer the most promising approach, so we should observe carefully how it has been attempted. What nexus can be forged between individual rights and group solidarity, between universalistic principles and particularistic needs?

Robert E. Park, the first outstanding modern student of race relations, offers a clue. Comparing immigrants, blacks, and European peasants, Park proposed in the 1920s an evolutionary cycle that tends to recur (he thought) wherever different peoples meet. An initial phase of competition arouses nationalistic and racial sentiments, through which an emergent group acquires the self-consciousness to challenge the existing distribution of status and power. This brings a new accommodation between the contending groups. Once the accommodation is reached, a slow process of mutual assimilation can go forward. Thus ethnic mobilization and assimilation are alternating phases in the long history of widening human contacts. Group solidarity becomes a temporary but essential stage in the progress of assimilation.[13]

Another, not altogether dissimilar vision possessed Robert MacIver, the principal proponent of ethnic democracy in the 1940s. Writing in an era dominated by the challenge to totalitarianism, MacIver was especially concerned to reconcile unity with diversity, liberty with order. He described an "inherent tendency" in social evolution toward more and more differences, loyalties, and associations. Democracy, by affirming the common welfare with a minimum of coercion, gives maximum scope to the spontaneity of culture. A democratic ethos keeps institutions flexible and citizens responsive; it prevents difference from turning into separation. While Park construed integration and differentiation as successive stages of a dialectical process, MacIver described a way of life in which they could grow together.[14]

Fundamentally, both men relied on a common theory of history. Their writings gained persuasive force from a belief in progress. Park's benign determinism and MacIver's idealistic voluntarism offered the same assurance that a more and more humane adjustment can develop over the long run between particular communities and the great community. The problem of the one and the many, insoluble in theory, will be solved in history. Unfortunately for these optimistic assessments, the progressive interpretation of history on which they depended lost credibility in the 1950s. Evolutionism was in general rejected in history and the social sciences.

MacIver's faith in the harmonious unfolding of cultural diversity looked particularly naive as the challenge of totalitarianism was succeeded by the challenge of technological uniformity. Instead of advancing confidently against the totalitarian enemies of diversity, American intellectuals found themselves enmeshed in the more subtle but more pervasive totalitarianism of modern civilization itself. Internationally, the era was dominated by the slogans of modernization. Everywhere the plastic sterility of the International Style replaced local idioms. Rootless urban slums appeared where tribal villages had stood. In the United States television, bureaucracy, and suburbia seemed even more destructive of ethnic differences; and the first significant advances toward racial integration in American history apparently confirmed the belief that assimilation pure and simple would be our destiny. Many American intellectuals still preferred some form of pluralistic integration, but their sense of history—to say nothing of their own feelings of deracination—deprived the wish of all conviction.

In the past decade we have encountered diversity with a vengeance. It is too soon to say whether the return to ethnicity is a temporary reaction, a mere interlude in the onrush of modernization. Still, it presents an opportunity to reassess the course of history. If the sharpened ethnic assertiveness that erupted in the late 1960s is more than a passing phenomenon, it may indicate that modern history supports the theory of pluralistic integration after all, though not in quite the form either Park or MacIver suggested.

Even to consider this possibility will require a conception, clearer than we have yet formulated, of what a system of pluralistic integration might be. In contrast to the integrationist model, it will not eliminate ethnic boundaries. But neither will it maintain them intact. It will uphold the validity of a common culture, to which all individuals have access, while sustaining the efforts of minorities to preserve and enhance their own integrity. In principle this dual commitment can be met by distinguishing between boundaries and nucleus. No ethnic group under these terms may have the support of the general community in strengthening its boundaries. All boundaries are understood to be permeable. Ethnic nuclei, on the other hand, are respected as enduring centers of social action. If self-preservation requires it, they may claim exemption from certain universal rules, as the Amish now do from the school laws in some states. Both integration and ethnic cohesion are recognized as worthy goals, which different individuals will accept in different degrees. Ethnicity varies enormously in intensity from one person to another. It will have some meaning for the great majority of Americans, but intense meaning for relatively few. Only minorities of minorities, so to speak, will find in ethnic identity an exclusive loyalty.

Obviously pluralistic integration depends on a lack of precision in social categories and on a general acceptance of complexity and ambiguity. Does history give us any reason to suppose that so messy a pattern can develop enduring vitality in a world pervaded by technological rationality? I think it does. Already in some degree our situation approximates the model of pluralistic integration. Indeed, the diversity of the origins of American society provides a substantial historical base for such a pattern, although the early development of an absolute distinction between races presents an enormous obstacle. In order to take seriously the possibility that group consciousness may become more universal and less absolute, it is not necessary to suppose that a complete restructuring of American society must occur. A more modest hypothesis may be sufficient: namely, that *the trend toward a rigid, absolutistic definition of roles and identities, which arose in the eighteenth century, is now being reversed.*

This is too large a topic to do more than touch upon here. I can only suggest that modern racism, which is the principal hindrance to pluralistic integration, was itself an expression and a result of the rigidification of social boundaries during a particular era of European and American history. Prior to modern times the peoples of the West—guided by a richly elaborated world picture—seem to have lived in a hierarchy of multiple, overlapping, indistinct categories. The boundaries of the nation, the family, the age group, and the individual were vague. Even the concept of humankind was imprecise when monsters, angels, and legendary creatures also occupied the imagination. Beginning in the seventeenth and eighteenth centuries, all of these categories became much more separated from one another. "The new society," writes Philippe Ariès, "provided each way of life with a confined space in which it was understood that the dominant features should be respected, and that each person had to resemble a conventional model, an ideal type, and never depart from it under pain of excommunication."[15]

No simple explanation will account for modern racism. It arose during the great age of discovery, amid dazzling advances in science, knowledge, and freedom. Why, at such a time, did European civilization increasingly associate the physical characteristics of peoples with ineradicable inequalities of culture, morality, and status? Part of the answer must be sought in the ancient institution of slavery, now revitalized by new economic forces and warped into a strictly racial form of exploitation by overseas expansion. Racism also owed much to religious, social, and sexual predispositions in northern Europe. A complex of attitudes, emerging especially in Protestant countries, promoted greater freedom and equality among individuals and thereby made inequalities between nations and races immeasurably more difficult to deal with.

Still, in its most essential aspect, as a rigidly categorizing habit of mind, racism may require further probing. Neither slavery nor Protestant culture helps us greatly in understanding Voltaire's insistence that Indians and Negroes are unrelated to whites and incapable of civilization. Nor do the usual interpretations of modern racism explain the obsession with purity of blood (*limpieza de sangre*) in Spanish Catholicism during the sixteenth and seventeenth centuries, when religious and lay communities sought to root out anyone with a trace of Jewish ancestry.[16] It may be that the emerging classification of people by race was part of "a general tendency toward distinguishing and separating" that has characterized both modern philosophy and modern life.[17]

In the United States the absolutization of social identities may have reached an apogee in the late nineteenth and early twentieth centuries. Differentiation between the sexes was carried to an extreme. The privatized family offered itself as a refuge from and antithesis to the world outside its limits. An intense demand for purity arose in the nineteenth century. A "wall of separation" grew between church and state, between Protestant and Catholic, between sinner and saint, between black and white. In the latter decades of the century, as the interdependence of an urban industrial society was increasingly evident, the purity ethic became more and more defensive. A fear of infection, sharpened by the germ theory of disease, replaced a hope of purifying the world. It was in this context that national and racial identities acquired an absolute character. After the First World War a policy of isolationism in foreign affairs was a culmination of a two-hundred-year trend toward cultural and social apartheid.

Since that time we have witnessed what may be only the beginning of a profound shift of direction. Robert Jay Lifton has described the emergence in the 1960s of a new personality type, which he calls Protean Man and associates with a capacity to change roles and to relate flexibly to changing experience.[18] What he describes may be not a generational trait but rather part of a wider cross-cutting and interpenetration of group identities. The appeal of pluralistic and relativistic perspectives among American intellectuals in recent decades provides one indication of an increasing ability to tolerate ambiguity. Another is Robert Venturi's bold repudiation of purity and consistency in architecture. "I like elements which are hybrid rather than 'pure,' compromising rather than 'clean,' . . . inconsistent and equivocal rather than direct and clear. . . . I prefer 'both-and' to 'either-or,' black and white, and sometimes gray, to black or white. A valid architecture . . . must embody the difficult unity of inclusion rather than the easy unity of exclusion."[19] These words might equally be applied to some contemporary sensibilities in the areas of sex, race, religion, and ethnicity. In the 1973–

1974 television season the hero of ABC's most popular serial, *Kung Fu,* was neither black nor white, but a half-Chinese secularized monk.

In a cultural setting that seems so uncongenial to simple stereotypes and fixed allegiances, what can we make of the vaunted return to ethnicity? Does not the strenuous reassertion of ethnic pride at the present time partake of the very rigidities our culture is supposedly overcoming? Must not Protean Man elude the claims of ancestors as well as the coercions that would demean or obliterate them? Again, answers lie in the future. But it can be suggested that the lasting significance of the ethnic revival of the late 1960s may have to do with the strengthening of nuclei rather than the guarding of boundaries. Certainly a very large part of the ferment in contemporary ethnic life is intended to revitalize the nuclei of ethnic groups that have needed new symbols and new leadership. That is what Black Power and Black Studies are largely about; what explains the Chicano movement and accounts for the Second Battle of Wounded Knee; what inspires the appropriation of federal funds for "ethnic heritage" programs; what lies behind the annual festivals, reunions and parades of many otherwise indistinguishable Americans. In a society as fluid as ours—a society moreover in which so much that is crucial transcends ethnic categories—the quality of ethnic life depends to a very large extent on the quality of the nuclei. Pluralistic integration implies that invigoration of the nuclei can relieve the defense of ethnic boundaries.

In the 1950s, when assimilation was advancing so rapidly, there was much concern over the oppressive featurelessness of a standardized mass culture. Today the weakening of social boundaries does not suggest a further descent into uniformity, but rather a multiplication of small audiences, specialized media, local attachments, and partial identities, which play into one another in ways we cannot understand.[20] Many who are concerned about ethnic justice feel pessimistic about the ability of our society to develop the necessary appreciation of diversity. But it is possible, in view of the trend I have sketched, that our greater problem in moving toward pluralistic integration may come in rediscovering what values can bind together a more and more kaleidoscopic culture.

Postscript: 1999

The preceding pages were written twenty-five years ago, when the cultural upheaval of the late sixties was subsiding as a force but also creating a new moral landscape that I was only beginning to understand. Nevertheless, those pages still define the middle ground I occupy in the ongoing debate over unity and diversity in American history and culture. The debate is one of the truly constant features of American life. It bubbles up spontaneously in every American institution because it springs from core values that do not easily cohere: liberty and union. Some Americans commonly, even instinctively, read unity as coercion. They want to be free and unencumbered. Others regard diversity as little more than a disguise for fragmentation and disorder. They want to stand together. The American republic is an uncongealed amalgam of the two.

My special theme, the interplay between unity and diversity in American ethnic relations, is therefore—as this essay has suggested—part of a larger dialectic within the national culture. In creating the U.S. Constitution the Founding Fathers wrestled famously with the tension between liberty and union while avoiding almost completely its application to the problem of race. That the Constitution has never been fundamentally altered except to correct that one deliberate oversight is in itself a striking demonstration of the liberty-union dialectic. In early decades it divided and energized the American Protestant churches during their most expansive phase. It plunged North and South into a frightful civil war and gave us our greatest president. It shapes a perennial contrast between our two major political parties: between Republicans, who present themselves as guardians of national unity, and Democrats, who are often more ready to defend the rights of minorities.[21] Most Americans have frequently found themselves on both sides of this defining yet elusive issue. For more than a century, for example, an urge to be separate while enjoying an illusion of inclusiveness has driven the middle class outward from the dense heterogeneity of urban neighborhoods to the greater security and uniformity of suburbs.

Dealing as we are with an ongoing dilemma that Americans can never fully solve, it is not surprising that some of the seismic changes in ethnic and race relations that occurred from the 1940s through the 1970s have subsided in more recent years. Those changes went about as far as most Americans, for the time being, were willing to tolerate. The decades from World War II to the 1980s brought a profound enlargement of the principle of diversity in American culture. The terms of the social compact were renegotiated. Not only in academic theories but also in government and public opinion, racial and ethnic minorities received widening acceptance.[22]

That era of ascendant pluralism may be ending, however. If that is so, the pendulum of American culture is falling away from the protection and promotion of diversity and swinging toward a revival of commonality.

But is the shift rather a pause, hesitant and contested, within a movement toward ethnic separateness? Or, more unsettling, is the clock running down? Several indicators suggest that the clock still works, though less predictably than I once thought.

1. *Enforcement of civil rights.* From the mid-1960s to the early 1980s an elaborate structure of laws, court decisions, and administrative rules developed to enforce the equal rights of groups that had suffered discrimination. From these rules, group entitlements and racially preferential policies evolved. Inevitably, innocent individuals outside the designated categories were discriminated against. Sometimes intended beneficiaries were damaged as well.[23] As disappointments and resistance built up, the scope of enforcement activity has gradually contracted. In some situations court decisions delimited what governments could do. In others, unfortunately, a mutual resegregation of neighborhoods has left nothing to enforce. Yet the goal of rectifying historic injustices remains a spur to continuing improvement. Polls show that Americans, by a wide margin, favor "affirmative action," provided it does not go "too far."[24] Nowadays many employers do not wait to be prodded by a government agency. They are eagerly paying for training programs to encourage harmonious relations throughout a diversified work force.[25]

In various ways, therefore, governments are receding from a further institutionalization of group rights. This became crystal clear in 1993 when President Clinton dropped his own nominee for director of civil rights at the Department of Justice, Lani Guinier. In the face of widespread criticism of his choice, Clinton announced that he could not defend Guinier's scholarly writings, which proposed new constitutional devices for enhancing the power of racial voting blocs. On the other hand, standards of fairness in the distribution of offices, the behavior of police, and the administration of justice have steadily risen.

2. *Immigration controls.* An era of liberalizing reform in immigration policy, as in civil rights, followed World War II. Then, in the 1980s, while governmental empowerment of internal minorities lessened, sentiment favoring stronger protection of the country as a whole revived. The continuing openness of American borders to illegal immigration, and with it to illicit drugs and political terrorists, prompted calls for stricter controls. The

generous reception of political refugees, which had prevailed during the Cold War, lost some of its appeal with the collapse of the Berlin Wall and the ensuing eruption of ethnic wars. As in civil rights, however, the legislative status quo persists.

What is new in the present situation is a near indifference of public opinion (outside California) toward an immense influx of unskilled immigrants permitted under the Immigration Reform Law of 1965, further liberalized in 1986, 1990, and 1996. In some areas, especially those close to the Mexican border, a single immigrant group now predominates so heavily that neither pluralism nor integration can function very well. Yet Congress makes no serious effort to stanch the flow. While shrinking perhaps from the ugly ethnic antagonisms that restriction campaigns used to produce, legislators are responding more actively to Washington's present enthusiasm for laissez-faire policies and to a closely related shift of mainstream values. In recent decades attachment to the nation has greatly waned; attachment to the self has correspondingly expanded.

Still, the sharp decline of nation-building sentiments in the older native-born population and among many ethnic leaders is offset for now by the yearning of immigrants and their children to become American. One cannot witness a naturalization ceremony without feeling in the air a tingling sense of arrival and hope. In great numbers the immigrants are Americanizing themselves.

What of the future? When the clamorous prosperity of the nineties slackens, stronger controls on immigration and a richer celebration of citizenship may be expected. Today's restrictionists carefully avoid the blatant antiforeign and racist rhetoric of years gone by,[26] but there is a new concern about the long-term effects of the emerging global economy. As globalization closes American factories and reduces clerical work, it is narrowing vital intermediate levels on the social ladder between debilitating stagnation and affluence. Where in this "hour-glass economy" can the children of immigrants, brought to America from desperate conditions in less industrialized societies, find prospects for advancement?[27] And where can underprivileged, poorly educated American children, unable to cope with small farms or break out of inner-city slums, find modest urban niches like those that immigrants now occupy and even control?

There is an answer to this second question, but it is not entirely reassuring. In contrast to the wider dispersion of most migratory streams in the past, today's immigrants congregate heavily in a few very large metropolitan areas or along the southern border of the United States. At the same time, native-born youth with limited skills and education are escaping from immigrant competition by relocating in smaller cities in parts of the country that immigrants shun. If this growing separation between immigrant and native regions persists, it can sharpen a hardening division in the American electorate.[28]

3. *Social recognition and assimilation.* Ethnic groups have always sought the validation of civic honor, and the willing conferral of such recognition has contributed greatly to their identification with America. Some groups have advanced principally through political leadership and influence, others through economic and cultural attainments. The process continues unabated. The social and economic ascent of the newer European ethnic groups became dramatically visible in the 1960s as southern and eastern European names like Iacocca, Merzei, Hubschman, and Tavoulareas appeared in the boardrooms of big corporations and the dining rooms of exclusive clubs. Behind this cautious opening was an earlier history of surprisingly prompt admission of sons of northern European immigrants to the highest levels of large corporations. An intensive statistical study in 1952 showed that relative to population, the sons of foreign-born fathers were at least as likely to join the business elite as were the sons of older Americans. Its author, W. Lloyd Warner, concluded that the sons of immigrants—defying prejudice and schooled in mobility—had an advantage in moving up compared with sons who inherited an elite status. By the 1970s there was also a dawning recognition at the best business schools that a hereditary social elite can make a company stodgy and unadventurous. Now, more than thirty years later, African Americans, other nonwhites, and women are almost conventional presences on the boards of large corporations; and the nation's business elite seems to have avoided the decay that afflicts more protected upper classes in other countries.[29]

For racially designated minorities especially, recognition offers assurance of the group's capabilities vis-à-vis the older population. Colin Powell did that in commanding all of the armed forces of the United States in the Gulf War. But recognition may accrue still more from activities that contribute something new to the existing society or culture. As was true earlier for African Americans, Latinos in the 1990s have established a vivid presence in American popular music. They have invented an exciting mixture of styles derived partly from the indigenous traditions of different Latin countries and partly from rhythm-and-blues and soul-tinged ballads, all melded to make new sounds. "I don't see boundaries," one of the new Latina stars, Jennifer Lopez, told an interviewer.[30]

The crossing of boundaries is turning American popular culture, with its energy and worldwide appeal, into an irresistible medium of cultural assimilation. Social assimilation comes less easily. But it, too, after three or more decades of derision, is regaining visibility and even a modicum of approval. The one-sided celebration of diversity, which flourished from the sixties to the eighties, has steadfastly ignored three persistent and distinctive indices of assimilation.

a. *Inter-group amity.* From earliest times Americans of all antecedents, in spite of a preference for mutual avoidance, have been drawn into bloody quarrels. Competition for jobs or space could lead to riots, especially if religious or racial prejudice supervened, as in the Irish persecution of Chinese in the American West in the late nineteenth century. Such incidents, pitting one immigrant minority against another, diminished markedly in the early twentieth century. Since World War II they have faded from sight. Refugees of recent years are mostly leaving their enmities in the old country. Croats and Serbs, for example, have long lived in mixed neighborhoods around the now rusting steel mills of the Midwest. After World War II they found new ties as passionate anti-Communist Republicans. In the early 1990s ethnic cleansing in Yugoslavia drove them apart. But bloodshed was averted. At the same time a horrifying series of Hindu-Muslim riots in India produced on the streets of Chicago nothing more than a joint march of kinfolk, pledging friendship and solidarity and condemning the outbreaks in their homeland.[31] Without going that far, Jewish and Muslim leaders maintain a decent respect for each other's civil rights.

b. *Language.* Since 1968, when Congress passed the first Bilingual Education Act with the object of bringing down the school dropout rate of Mexican American children, many school districts have received special federal funds to teach English to newcomer children. Most of these funds, however, are earmarked for bilingual instruction, in which the family's traditional language becomes the principal medium of instruction. The original goal of making an early connection with the English-speaking world tends to be secondary. In the 1980s the insistence of Hispanic legislators that public education should actively maintain minority languages provoked a backlash. An English-Only movement demanded a constitutional amendment making English the official American language. To date English-Only backers have secured from twenty-two states largely symbolic resolutions declaring English to be the state's official language.[32]

Actually, neither side has altered the traditional balance between unity and diversity in American speech. English retains its unofficial preeminence as the key to social mobility and the linchpin of American culture. The involvement of state and federal governments in some degree of language maintenance has proved more controversial than effective. In 1998, California repealed a requirement that children with poor English skills be taught in their native language. Before long, statewide test scores showed significant improvement in school performance.

What remains unchanged, apparently, is a gradual but never complete erosion of immigrant languages over a span of three generations. Typically, in the first generation only professionals and entrepreneurs use English extensively and comfortably. The second generation prefers the English it has acquired in public schools and sooner or later finds its familiarity with the mother tongue deteriorating. What the third generation, grandchildren of the great migration of the 1960s and 1970s, will do is not yet clear. In the past, unfortunately, the third generation has lost the mother tongue altogether, except in certain privileged or isolated enclaves. This may change somewhat now that well-educated immigrants are stressing to their children the advantages of bilingualism. Meanwhile, the incorporative process has immeasurably enriched American English through the infusion of phrases, motifs, stories, slang, and gestures that spring in such abundance from our many cultures.[33]

c. *Intermarriage.* The ultimate step in voluntary social assimilation is the legal union of man and woman across traditional group boundaries. Such unions, building as they do on tolerance or indifference, a basic sense of human equality, and experience in social mixing, have slowly multiplied over the course of American history through gradually widening circles of relationship. Beginning in 1614 with the Anglican marriage of a powerful Algonquin chief's daughter, Pocahontas, to a prominent English colonist at Jamestown, intermarriage flickered through the dealings of fur traders with native peoples. Meanwhile, fugitive African slaves who sought refuge among American Indians produced children of mixed blood. One of these, Crispus Attucks, was the first American casualty in the Revolution. Against a ruling ideology of racial purity, the mingling of three races spread silently through the nineteenth century and beyond.[34]

A more socially accepted linkage of religious and secular identities began in colonial towns. By the eighteenth century a shortage of available marital partners within small ethnoreligious groups encouraged outmarriage. According to one study, the rate of intermarriage of Jews with non-

Jews between 1776 and 1840 was 29 percent.[35] Larger minorities living in separate neighborhoods, such as Germans and Irish in post–Civil War Detroit, rarely married one another.[36] If members did go outside their own community, they usually chose mainstream whites, whose identity—if generally Protestant—was becoming more diffuse with every migrant group encountered or migration undertaken. Since World War I a modernized mass culture has also done much to override the separateness of different ethnic and religious norms.

By the 1960s intermarriage was sweeping across religious and ethnic divisions and nearly obliterating some of them. Even before World War II young American Indians were leaving reservations in droves, and most of them married non-Indians.[37] Among American Jews intermarriage increased so dramatically after 1965 that some leaders feared (wrongly) that it was threatening the very survival of their people.[38] Data gathered in the 1970s and 1980s showed that a growing part of the entire white population no longer knew or cared what country their ancestors came from.[39]

In important ways the newer, non-European migrations to America have followed the assimilationist path laid out by their predecessors. Beginning with the second generation (native-born offspring of immigrant parents), the children of non-European parents have married whites in impressive numbers. In 1990 more than half of the American-born Asians between twenty-five and thirty-four years of age had chosen non-Asian spouses. An astonishing 35 percent of the comparable Latino population were living with non-Hispanic spouses. And in 1999 an Urban Institute demographer calculated that up to 57 percent of third-generation Hispanics were marrying outsiders.[40] One must bear in mind, however, that out-marriage often maintains the ethnic connections by bringing the outside partner in. Ethnic identities wax and wane, but memory is precious.

One strong taboo endures. The widening inclusion of European, Asian, Native American, and now Hispanic citizens in a loosely interwoven federation of peoples leaves a disturbing racial divide between African Americans and all the rest. It should be noted that black-white residential segregation did decline in the 1980s and that intermarriage increased. But both changes were small; and neither tendency toward intermixture received much encouragement from either side of the racial divide. Both sides have tired of strife, but neither feels that the gulf can be decisively narrowed. The separation is reinforced, moreover, by an unintended collaboration between the often unthinking race-prejudice that lives on among a substantial number of whites and the constant emphasis that minority politicians and ideologues put on racial oppression.

Except within a lunatic fringe, white racism is no longer easily distinguishable from economic individualism and cultural conservatism. All three contribute to a massive acceptance of the status quo, a weariness of race issues among many, and a resentment of black hostility among quite a few whites.[41] For most blacks integration remains a principle to defend but no longer a goal to pursue. As a practical objective it costs too much, and has given way to a backward-looking yearning for black solidarity. For African Americans the tensions between pluralism and integration are experienced as stark and painful.

Among activists and intellectuals a partial solution is sought through an ongoing struggle to rebuild public support for welfare programs, education, and urban renewal, all of which are thought to depend on a broad progressive coalition of minorities.[42] Unfortunately, the hope of constructing a common front of racial "victims" reflects a serious lack of realism.

The politics of protest—so exhilarating and effective when blacks stood shoulder to shoulder with white allies in the civil rights movement—founder today partly from blacks' unwillingness to appeal to whites and, still more, from enormous differences in the status and prospects of the various so-called peoples of color. In spite of the eagerness of Mexican American leaders to promote a nonwhite identity, for example, half of the Mexican Americans who were counted in the 1990 census identified themselves as white. In general, Hispanic Americans—the second largest of the officially designated minorities in America—are intricately divided over ethnic, racial, national, and class loyalties and quite susceptible to a conservative style of politics.[43]

This is still more true of the Asian nationalities, who now compose about a quarter of the foreign-born population. Many of them, especially from India, Taiwan, Iran, Korea, and Japan, have reached a remarkably high level of employment as managers, small business owners, technical specialists, and professionals.[44] These immigrants report only occasional discrimination by native-born whites, and their children flock to the leading universities. Those children are very cautious, however, about associating with black students on the balkanized campuses of today.

There are various ways to explain this failure of pluralistic integration. I prefer to focus on a failure of leadership—specifically, on a betrayal of the integrationist side of the equation. This began about 1965 with the rise of the Black Power movement. In the next few years the romance of an "oppositional" culture spread everywhere through the ghettoes of the North and the schools of the nation. It precipitated a generational rebellion against authority. In the euphoria of "liberation," integration became synonymous with repression.[45]

As the rebellion of the late sixties gradually subsided in the following decade, it left a loosened social fabric and a continuing preference for a multiplication of autonomous identities at the expense of integration. For the first time, as Philip Gleason has remarked, ethnic identities were more desirable than a national identity.[46] It is little wonder that black leaders and many specialists in ethnic studies fixated on a divisive inflation of race.

When writing the first part of the present essay, I was naively unaware that the new race-thinking was acquiring its own unyielding shape. Accordingly, I closed with a thoroughly mistaken suggestion. Ethnic leaders, I maintained, could invigorate their respective groups without resisting the surrounding culture because group life depends as much on centers as on boundaries. The boundaries can relax when the nuclei are strong.[47] This was wishful thinking. When boundaries are tightening, leaders can keep them open only if pressure to close comes chiefly from outside the ethnic group. The most visible leaders of the 1970s were imposing closure on their followers, not resisting it.

The picture of ethnic and race relations today can look different, however, if we turn it upside down. By looking at how ordinary people have behaved in the past few years instead of focusing exclusively on what elites are thinking, we may catch sight of a wider common life than one might imagine. We have already observed rank-and-file ethnics gladly crossing boundaries of language and marriage that leaders strive to protect. A remarkable book now shows us how ordinary people can also learn to cooperate with one another where space confines them all.

Roger Sanjek's fifteen-year immersion in the life of Elmhurst-Corona has yielded a richly detailed portrait of a New York City neighborhood that is undergoing racial and ethnic transition. Populated in 1960 by Germans, Irish, Italians, and older white Americans, it now has a majority of Latinos and Asians, together with some blacks (10 percent) and whites (18 percent). It may be the most ethnically mixed community in the world. Yet it has achieved an approximation of a common life. Through quality-of-life rituals that celebrate new parks and clean streets, through joint struggles against the city government, through block associations and the informal interactions of women, an ethic of civic participation has gradually developed. "Race divides," Sanjek concludes, "but people can change."[48]

In Elmhurst-Corona, and doubtless many other American communities, pluralistic integration is alive and pretty well. There are encouraging lessons in this confident study, so grandly entitled *The Future of Us All*. A historian must demur, however, from any suggestion that a single locality, caught at one moment in time, can point our way. Pluralistic integration can never be an equilibrium. It must remain, at best, a work in progress.

The final essay in Part II emerged from a symposium on black-white relations that Higham organized for the Balch Institute to commemorate the thirtieth anniversary of the Civil Rights Act of 1964. The aims of the symposium—to air disparate views on affirmative action and multiculturalism and to find common ground from which both blacks and whites could map racial progress—matched Higham's long-standing desire to find a balanced yet inspiriting middle ground between group cohesion and assimilation. In this sense, "Three Postwar Reconstructions" can be read as the extension of Higham's theme of pluralistic integration in Chapter 7. At the same time, the essay advances the rehabilitation of America's "universalist" tradition of social ideals that Higham had proposed in his critique of multiculturalism the year before (see Chapter 13).

Charting the broad course of race relations during and after the American Revolution, the Civil War, and World War II, Higham argues that real progress resulted from the upsurge in national idealism that accompanied each of these major wars. The American Revolution inspired natural rights thinking that led to the first significant legal limits on slavery. The Civil War and its aftermath abolished slavery and established political and civil rights for former slaves, however temporarily those rights were honored and enforced. And whereas World War I unleashed an anomalous outbreak of racism, the idealism of World War II culminated in the civil rights movement of the 1960s, America's "Third Reconstruction," which put the full weight of the federal government behind antidiscrimination laws and voting rights. Higham himself marched with an interracial contingent of American historians on the road from Selma to Montgomery in 1965.

While sensitive to differences among the three Reconstructions and well aware of their shortcomings, Higham stresses moments of genuine idealism and progress. In his view, the American Revolution, which established a faith in natural rights, the common good, and progress as especially American concerns, provided a viable basis for national identity and an indispensable legacy of universalist ideals for Americans to improve upon.

Higham's essay served as a coda to the collected papers of the Balch symposium, which he edited under the title *Civil Rights and Social Wrongs: Black-White Relations Since World War II* (1997). Virtually all of the contributors began with the assumptions that American public opinion is painfully divided over such issues as affirmative action and multiculturalism and that the civil rights movement ended in stalemate. But Higham concluded the volume on a cautiously optimistic note by suggesting possible preconditions for a new stage of progress. A Fourth Reconstruction, he contends, is most likely to come when whites and blacks take pains to share an overlapping agenda and a common national identity. Historians have a role to play in that process by writing a more balanced history of race relations that, without denying past injustices, helps to move Americans of all races forward by drawing upon their common inheritance.

Ted Ownby
University of Mississippi

8

Three Postwar Reconstructions
[1997]

The story of civil rights in the twentieth century has the shape of a great wave climbing a beach. A low swell, moving slowly, gains momentum. At a certain point it surges to a mighty crest that crashes with a roar. A wash of water flows onward, but the force is gone. The wave is receding. This is the pattern of modern racial reform: quiet, gradual improvement in the 1920s and 1930s; accelerating power after World War II; a dangerous, breathtaking climax in the 1960s; an aftermath of persistence and retreat.

At the crest of the wave in 1965, C. Vann Woodward called attention to similarities between what was happening at that moment and the dazzling enactment of racial reforms and civil rights exactly one hundred years earlier during the reconstruction of the defeated southern states. Woodward called the events occurring around him a "Second Reconstruction." He feared it might collapse as the first one had. But he hoped that this time the far greater power of African Americans would save the cause of racial justice from compromise, appeasement, and failure.[1]

Now, more than three decades later, Woodward's Second Reconstruction has completed the full cycle of the First. We have a longer time span before us, so we can extend Woodward's comparative perspective both forward and backward. From the vantage point of today, the accomplishments of the Reconstruction that followed the Civil War seem more than merely "rhetorical." Our present knowledge of what African Americans learned and did during the so-called Tragic Era redeems it from the dismissive judgment that historians used to pronounce.[2]

Similarly, a great advance in historical knowledge of the era of the

American Revolution has shown that the "first" reconstruction of American race relations took place then, not in the 1860s, if we define "reconstruction" as a broad postwar program for reforming the social order. Moreover, this early cycle of racial reform anticipated the pattern its successors have followed: slowly rising discontent; liberation and euphoria; breakdown and retreat. Might an examination of these resemblances yield some clue to possibilities for a fourth reconstruction? I believe they do.

Each of the three cycles that punctuate the history of black-white relations in America received a powerful impetus from a major, victorious war. In each case, war expanded the choices that black people could make. Responding to offers of liberation and protection, slaves escaped to British armies during the Revolution. During the Civil War, they found an undeclared freedom behind Union lines in such numbers that people called them contrabands—that is, confiscated rebel property. During World War II the descendants of the slaves escaped northward from the rural South in a huge migration that opened new opportunities in factories, labor unions, and politics. At the same time a million black men and women entered the armed forces. The immediate gains that accrued within a national struggle against an external enemy were, however, less significant than the great upsurge of national idealism and racial hope that each war released.

By crystallizing a distinctive national ideology, the American Revolution established the enduring dynamics of racial reform. Whether an American ideology was more a cause or a result of the Revolution, the conflict welded together an extraordinarily durable set of ideas that came to define a national purpose. One founding principle declared that the United States exists to secure the equal, unalienable rights that individuals receive from nature. Another enshrined a broadly Christian ethic of dedication to the common good. A third offered an embracing faith in human progress, with America in the lead.[3] In the absence of a homogeneous ethnic identity, this compound of secular and religious ideas—in this amalgam of liberty, nationality, and faith—was the strongest bond of unity in the new nation.

Although flatly incompatible in all respects with slavery, what Gunnar Myrdal has called the American Creed was often construed as a future promise rather than an immediate requirement. For most Americans it was more largely a conception of capacities than a claim of achievements. But advances could not be altogether postponed. The revolutionary impulse, with its appeal to human rights as well as American rights, inspired an antislavery movement abroad and at home. Never before had so many pulpits rung with condemnations of slaveholding. Nowhere earlier had blacks petitioned for their freedom on grounds of natural rights.[4]

Why did the Civil War and World War II tap and reinforce the same strain of nationalist idealism? Surely because both conflicts lent themselves to definition in the same terms. The Civil War was understood as a struggle to preserve a union based on freedom; World War II engaged Americans in resisting a new form of slavery. In all three wars did special interests manipulate patriotism for their own ends? Of course. Did intolerance of minorities produce racial barbarities and hysterical witch-hunts? Unquestionably. But that does not negate the altruistic inducement each major war held out to Americans to locate themselves within and carry forward the Spirit of '76.

In no case did war originate the impulse it popularized. Each postwar reconstruction was continuous with a gradual prewar buildup of moral disquiet over the state of race relations. Decades might pass before the fervent nationalism of a great war energized a long-standing moral concern, which had deeply troubled only a small minority of whites. In wartime the people as a whole were called to uphold the principles that had given the nation its identity. Only then, through an outpouring of national idealism, could a moral issue receive political expression.

For half a century before the American Revolution, individual Christians who were sensitive to the humanitarian tendencies of the eighteenth century had disavowed the buying and selling of human beings. Not until 1758, however, did the Philadelphia Yearly Meeting denounce Quakers who bought or sold Negroes. Then another seventeen years passed before Philadelphians, on the eve of the American Revolution, formed the first antislavery society in the Western world.[5]

Similarly, in the nineteenth century a fragmented movement for abolishing or narrowly circumscribing slavery made headway slowly, against fierce resistance, throughout the 1830s and 1840s. Not until 1848, with the formation of the Free Soil Party, did an antislavery coalition capture 10 percent of the popular vote. In the 1850s, however, an impending breakup of the Union connected the cause of liberty with the more immediately compelling issue of national survival.

The civil rights movement of the 1950s and 1960s was no less indebted to prewar antecedents. The power and confidence it radiated after World War II would not have existed without a slow accumulation of guilt and protest from the late 1920s through the 1930s, followed by an all-out global war that idealized American democracy. From a revulsion against southern lynchings in the late 1920s through the diffuse egalitarianism of the New Deal years, public opinion prepared the way for a communalizing experience of national dedication and sacrifice. If religion played a smaller role than in the earlier wars, a transfigured liberalism, celebrating the adhesiveness of a multiethnic people, amply took its place.[6]

Before examining these three encounters more closely, we cannot overlook a fourth great war, which fails completely to fit the general pattern. World War I—the Great Crusade, as ironic historians used to call it—made race relations worse rather than better. In this case, however, the exception helps to clarify the pattern of racial progress. American participation in World War I was relatively brief, just nineteen months in all, with only five months of intensive combat. Far more significant than the lighter burden that World War I imposed, however, was the absence of a significant prewar growth of racial reform.

Instead of the troubled national conscience that Gunnar Myrdal observed in 1944, nearly all white Americans from the 1890s to the 1920s displayed a colossal insensitivity to the hostility and abuse that rained down on racial or pseudo-racial minorities in the most advanced and highly industrialized nations of the world. Fears of impurity, pollution, corruption, and depravity coalesced. In this extravagantly racist milieu, Americans could try to address economic injustice (not altogether successfully as it turned out) but they were largely blind to racial oppression. When World War I ended, an explosion of racial and ethnic strife ensued. There was much talk of "reconstruction," but only among black people did it mean a reform of race relations. Among whites, "reconstruction" suggested problems of "economic serfdom," "discipline and orderly living," and "spiritual regeneration."[7]

By crushing the hopes it raised for a new dawn of peace and freedom, World War I has diverted historians from a longer linkage in American history between major wars and advances in democracy. A dichotomy between war and racial progress has seemed additionally plausible because the nation's smaller wars, such as those in Mexico and Vietnam, were indeed regressive in reasserting white supremacy. Moreover, little progress in race relations took place *during* the big wars. Each cycle of racial reform began in a long preparatory phase before the war started and climaxed in a mighty surge after it ended.

In each of the three cases reviewed here, war's immediate exigencies obscured progress in race relations. The months and years of combat allowed little latitude for altering social or political life. While raising aspirations and giving demands for change a national hearing, the wars deferred the tasks of racial reform to the postwar years. That is when the big break-throughs in race relations have occurred.

The liberating aftermath of the American Revolution was relatively modest. It simply put limits on the spread of slavery, but the limits were not inconsequential. The federal government checked the advance of slavery into the West; the states rolled it back in the Northeast. The Northwest Ordinance of 1787, which developed from an earlier proposal by Thomas Jefferson, laid down conditions for forming states north of the Ohio River. A proviso prohibiting slavery throughout the entire territory was the first national legislation that set bounds on the expansion of slavery. Meanwhile, beginning with Pennsylvania in 1780, every northern state by 1804 had adopted plans for gradual emancipation of its slaves. Two years later, federal legislation completed a similar process that banned the African slave trade from all American ports.

During the same years, antislavery sentiment persuaded state legislatures in the South to loosen existing restrictions on manumission. Especially in the Upper South, numerous slave owners freed their slaves voluntarily. In doing so they quickened a yearning for freedom among those who were left behind. Accordingly, manumission inspired a larger flight from the slave states. Nationally, the free black population rose from a mere handful—probably less than 5,000 in 1780—to 186,000 in 1810, most of whom gathered in the larger towns and cities of the mid-Atlantic region. Their communities produced such institutions as fraternities, churches, and mutual aid societies, through which freed people could manage their own affairs. The creation of autonomous black congregations from the 1780s onward, sometimes within existing denominations and sometimes entirely independently, was an important step in the building of self-sustaining African American communities.[8]

This early freedom movement was cautious and circumspect. It merely nibbled at the edges of slavery. Its Civil War counterpart was dramatic, impetuous, and visionary. Even more than during the Revolution, the main body of northern Protestants was convinced that their cause was holy. In "the glory of the coming of the Lord," Julia Ward Howe wrote that she could see him "trampling out the vintage where the grapes of wrath are stored." He was leading the Union armies to a final conquest of sin and bondage.[9] In large parts of the North the moral issue of slavery, inter-mixed with divine will and national destiny, was so intensely felt and widely agitated during the war that racial reform for once leaped ahead before hostilities ended. Northern black spokesmen such as Frederick Douglass were able to press for immediate emancipation while pointing proudly to the very large proportion of black males who were serving in the Union armies. Then Lincoln's Emancipation Proclamation in 1863 made inevitable the complete termination of slavery by means of the Thirteenth Amendment (1865). In states and cities influenced by southern mores, Jim Crow laws were reduced or repealed.[10]

Breathtaking advances in race relations came almost immediately after the Civil War ended, in contrast to a slower climax of reform following the Revolution and World War II. Millions of African Americans were now free to choose their own work and residence, subject only to the constraints of a general impoverishment. Their exuberant political meetings and those of their northern allies resounded with invocations of the Declaration of Independence.

Within months, white southerners set out to restore a racial oligarchy, bulwarked by the notorious "Black Codes" that substituted labor contracts for ownership. Crying treason, the radical leadership of the Republican Party reacted by pushing beyond mere abolition. Public outrage demanded strong federal protection of freedmen's rights, and the Radicals were ready to supply it. Nothing less could ensure a "new birth of freedom" that would justify the enormous sacrifices of the war. This was the purpose of the Fourteenth Amendment.

But preserving civil rights would require a further extension of federal power, specifically to guarantee sympathetic local and state governments. In the face of insurrectionary resistance in the South and widespread disapproval in the North, Congress imposed temporary military rule in the South, created genuinely interracial governments there, and secured ratification in 1870 of a fifteenth amendment granting full voting rights to black males in North and South alike. Nowhere else in the Western world was the transition from slavery to full citizenship so swift and unmediated.[11]

It was the task of the Third Reconstruction to reestablish the full panoply of political and civil rights gained in the Second Reconstruction but lost or weakened in a great reversal at the end of the nineteenth century, when southern legislators and white mobs legalized and deepened black subordination. Beyond restoring first-class citizenship, the Third Reconstruction aimed at a wider goal. It sought an equality of social respect and economic opportunity for all Americans. It reached the first goal, but only part of the second. Instead, the Third Reconstruction encountered the same cyclical changes that earlier surges of racial reform had undergone. After a slow prewar rise, black discontent accumulated during the war years, gained its first major victories soon thereafter, reached a climax from 1963 to 1968, then underwent a lingering demise. An understanding of that last phase should tell us a good deal about the vulnerabilities of progress in America.

In all three episodes the shift from commitment to retrogression was sufficiently gradual to suggest at the outset a simple waning of idealistic nationalism and moral fervor. At the very beginning of the nineteenth century the antislavery societies that had sprung up after the Revolution showed signs of enfeeblement. As the Revolution receded into the past, its broad enthusiasm for human rights dwindled into a narrower preoccupation with the right to property. Simultaneously, the migration of freed people to a few urban centers created dense neighborhoods and congested alleys where blacks were no longer under the close observation of their employers. Fears of unrest palsied reformers—especially after the turn of the century, when atrocities and racial uprisings on French islands in the Caribbean aroused lurid suspicions of black conspiracies on the American mainland. After 1800, slave codes in the South were tightened, while traditional constraints on free blacks—on their right to vote, for example, and to live where they pleased—revived. A hedge of restrictive, discriminatory legislation rose around the black communities of the North and the vast slave population of the South. Manumission was severely restricted; migration was closely controlled.[12]

The sharpening of fear and discrimination at the beginning of the nineteenth century suggests a loss of adhesiveness, a loosening of national idealism, that was more dramatically evident in the waning of the Second and Third Reconstructions. There, too, a fear of blacks, with accompanying deterioration of communication and concern, marked the end of racial reform.

From 1865 to 1867, and again exactly one hundred years later, a nationalizing euphoria and commitment seemed to sweep all obstacles aside. During those triumphant years bitterly racist resistance in the South only intensified the will and strength of reformers to carry through what they called the equal rights revolution. In 1868 white southern resistance to the revolution continued unabated. In 1968 or thereabouts it was broken. Nevertheless, in the late sixties of both centuries many were tiring of strife. Ulysses S. Grant won the presidency with the slogan "Let us have peace." One hundred years later Richard Nixon talked the same language. By the seventies, public interest in great moral issues was declining.[13] Liberal nationalism was running out of steam. In the midst of turmoil, locally rooted racism proved—at least in the short run—more tenacious than an inclusive, democratic spirit.

When national idealism was already on the defensive, a second factor dealt a further setback to all three reconstructions. In each case an already flagging movement for racial reform ended when the economic environment turned decisively unfavorable. This brings into sight once again the significance of the postwar moment. From the eighteenth century to the twentieth, the big advances in race relations have been borne on a flood of postwar prosperity. Twenty years after the adoption of the Constitution, twenty years after the Emancipation Proclamation, and thirty years after World War II, a long postwar boom faltered or collapsed. Each of these eras of prosperity and progress opened space in people's lives for altruism; each sustained a glowing vision of the nation's future. When the boom subsided, self-interest crowded to the fore, perhaps as much among blacks as among whites. Indifference at the top of the social scale and bare-knuckled antagonism down below again widened the racial chasm.

In the First Reconstruction, Congress's prohibition of the African slave trade in 1808 was the last antislavery legislation of any note. A year earlier the Jeffersonian embargo, prohibiting commerce with any foreign nation, interrupted the great economic boom that followed the Revolution. A period of instability turned in 1819 into a sharp, lingering depression. In eastern cities the resulting downward pressure on the already meager wages of African Americans aroused intense hostility in the white working class. Also during this era of economic uncertainties, new ideas of irreducible inequality between races largely superseded the revolutionary generation's confidence in universal natural rights.[14]

The Second Reconstruction terminated in a similar way. In the 1850s, and especially in the years immediately following the Civil War, the North and West enjoyed dazzling economic growth with rising levels of real wages. The depression that began in 1873, however, created deep distress in the cities and reduced many farmers to tenancy. Contemporaries regarded it as the most severe depression in American history. Politicians turned their attention from moral issues to economic remedies and nostrums such as currency, tariffs, and strikebreaking. The Democratic Party—the party of white supremacy—recovered from the obloquy it had suffered during the war and postwar years.[15] A century later, in 1973, the parties had reversed their positions, but the sequence of events was familiar.

The parallels between the periods of racial reform are plain to see. In all three cases dissatisfaction with the status quo had grown slowly among morally engaged minorities before intersecting with a major challenge to the nation. At that point a great surge of national idealism, abounding prosperity, a common enemy, and, it must now be added, a spirit of collaboration between whites and blacks brought the most dazzling advances of equality in American history.

So much for parallels. There is also a striking difference in the three episodes beyond their obvious contrasts of scale and aspiration. Although the First Reconstruction demonstrated a yearning for freedom among the slaves, a black elite who could play an active role in shaping events hardly existed. Moreover, virtually no whites could as yet imagine a harmonious interracial society. Black participation in making change was therefore neither expected nor sought. The First Reconstruction was in some measure *for* African Americans but not *by* them.

The Second Reconstruction brought them more fully into the historical process. William Lloyd Garrison and other nineteenth-century abolitionists had welcomed blacks as coequal disturbers of the peace. Their eager involvement in the antislavery movement and in contests over the suffrage in northern states dramatized the meaning of freedom. Their participation in southern public life beginning in 1867 was essential, extensive, and moderately progressive. They were junior partners in Reconstruction governments, heavily obligated to white allies and not always ready for the responsibilities they held; but altogether they were men of varied abilities and backgrounds who gave ample proof that hundreds of former slaves could handle the business of government.[16]

The Third Reconstruction presents a major contrast in leadership. Now the initiative for and direction of change in the ascending phases was primarily in the hands of African Americans. The First Reconstruction had been the work of a governing elite of whites. The Second reflected and contributed to the democratization of American society in the mid-nineteenth century. Although it too was led by a white elite, its execution depended on broad approval in public opinion (both white and black) and on active support from the newly enfranchised black masses. In the Third Reconstruction, blacks predominated. They made the crucial decisions. They also bore the heaviest burdens. Yet the participation, validation, and power of whites remained indispensable.

How critical, then, was close, active collaboration between the races in the making of the Third Reconstruction? Earlier American history yields no precise comparison. But the trend it presents is suggestive, and the evidence of interracial cooperation in racial reform from the 1920s to the

1960s leaves little room to doubt that the Third Reconstruction was heavily dependent on a partnership between blacks and an influential segment of the white population. I find inescapable, therefore, the conclusion that the division that opened in the civil rights movement in 1965 with the rise of Black Power—and the antiwhite legacy it left—was a significantly contributing cause of the movement's decline.[17]

As we look forward to the preconditions for a fourth reconstruction in the twenty-first century, history seems to tell us that a restoration of cooperation and trust between leaders on the two sides will have to rank high. Those on each side will need to risk unpopularity while holding firmly to a popular following. The leaders must have a flexible, loosely bounded identity, undefensive and therefore willing to incorporate something of the "other" who is different from oneself. The great example, surely, must be Martin Luther King, Jr., who was able to stand firm against the massed power of southern white society without demonizing whites or losing his vision of an interracial future. But something also should be said of Harry Truman's willingness to gamble his presidency in 1948 on the possibility that new black voters in a few northern states could (as they did) save him from a racist backlash in the impending election.

These qualities will not be available unless both avant-gardes participate in some larger identity, some greater loyalty, that connects them without threatening their separate qualities and needs. Their wider solidarity will have to draw on the liberal nationalism that was forged in a Christianized Enlightenment and in the twentieth century renamed the American Creed. That is what has driven each of the advances toward racial equality thus far.

To recapture that spirit, will the country have to wait for another major war? What might serve as a moral equivalent? Since history may not again repeat itself, these troubling questions may not have to be faced. Some pundits tell us that racial differences are gradually losing depth and intensity as a miscegenated heterogeneity of style and appearance spreads through American life.[18] In the quarter-century since the breakdown of the civil rights movement, the reaction against it has been much shallower than the reaction against its predecessors. On the whole, the black middle class retains the great gains it made, and in many kind of settings acceptance is coming more easily. These tendencies owe much to the globalization of communications, travel, and migration since World War II. More and more, Americans seem to realize that no boundaries are impermeable.

Still, a nation surely cannot rely on global forces to solve its problems. In the best as well as the worst scenarios, America's own history will come into play. I suggest that the prospect before us may look less bleak if the past appears less dismal. The fashionable cynicism of our time stigmatizes the entire record of American race relations. The civil rights movement of the mid-twentieth century is generally regarded as a "tragic failure," and so, too, its predecessors.[19] In truth, none of them was a failure; they were simply incomplete. For many black people, each surge reached some objectives, and the advances were never entirely lost in the reversals that followed.

After the First Reconstruction, some blacks in the North retained the right to vote, and some in the South preserved a substantial personal status. After the Second Reconstruction there were greater gains. Personal servitude was never reimposed, nor was the ability to move or migrate denied. Robert Wiebe has pointed out that African American rights in northern states expanded slowly in the late nineteenth century and that the notorious segregationist doctrine of "separate but equal" represented a concession to black demands for decent treatment. Moreover, blacks helped themselves. Their own mutual aid societies did much to raise blacks' per capita income, while legions of black teachers reduced illiteracy among blacks in the South from 80 percent in the 1860s to 45 percent in 1910.[20]

When the Third Reconstruction created a cornucopia of opportunities, along with bitter disappointments, it was repeating on an upward gradient the experience of its predecessors. Historians have been unable to see these events together, related within a long-term pattern, because their attention has been riveted on failure and defeat, with scant allowance for success and victory. Since the vaulting expectations of the 1960s collapsed, a "culture of defeat" has infected attitudes toward national projects among academics, much of the black middle class, and even the public at large.[21] The American Creed lives on, but only one of its three pillars—the idea of human freedom—remains essentially unchallenged. Cynicism has ravaged belief in an inclusive national community and its reach toward a better world. Until schools and churches and other opinion makers repair the damage to national identity and to faith in human possibility, how can race relations rise much above the level of rancorous bargaining among unequal interest groups? It is time for Americans to make richer use of their deeply divided but nonetheless inspiring heritage.

PART III

Turning Points

Originally presented as the first of four Commonwealth Fund Lectures on "American culture in the Victorian age" at the University of London in 1968, this essay is less an argument over particulars than a visionary narrative aimed at capturing the shifting zeitgeist of the dozen years just before the Civil War. Taking in literature, politics, religion, and class relations and drawing on materials ranging from penmanship guides to funeral orations, Higham argues that the United States changed during these years from a nation of openness and vaulting ambitions to one of corporate order and limits.

Something like Higham's thesis had been afloat for quite a while—indeed, a tendency toward consolidation was obvious even to nineteenth-century thinkers like Henry George, Herbert Spencer, and Henry Adams. Many of the transitions that Higham sketches were already the objects of tillage in various fields. In literature, the nineteenth-century shift from romanticism to realism was a textbook staple; in politics, so was the shift from Jacksonian democracy to Gilded Age hierarchy; in intellectual history, George Fredrickson's *The Inner Civil War* (1963) had just appeared to explain the shift from humanitarianism to fatalism. Higham's accomplishment was twofold: first, he brought these disparate phenomena together and made an idealist argument for their relation to each other through the "spirit of the age," and, second, he pushed back the cultural watershed to the dozen years preceding the Civil War. The war itself had been the conventional dividing point of nineteenth-century American history.

Higham's essay came to occupy the same sort of historical cusp that he undertook to describe. In the conservative years of the early 1960s he had begun research for a book on the Gilded Age with his own experience during and after World War II in mind. To his surprise, his research revealed that the shape of the new era, which historians attributed to the Civil War and its aftermath, had emerged in the 1850s, just when western Europe was being molded by similar forces. But what really upset Higham's supposed analogy between the psychic aftermath of the Civil War and that of World War II was the almost unchallenged persistence of the first and the sudden breakdown of the second—a breakdown already under way while he was speaking in London. By the time the essay was published in 1969, assassinations, campus riots, and counter-cultural experimentation had created exuberant anti-institutionalism all around. It was hardly a propitious time for a study of consolidation. Higham thereupon moved away from grand analogies between past and present.

In any case, the search for zeitgeists—a common approach as late as 1965, as revealed in such titles as *Age of Reform* and *Age of Excess*—was falling out of methodological favor. Historians of the subsequent generation tended to embrace materialist arguments and to regard large generalizations with suspicion.

Despite the turn in intellectual fashion, this essay has continued to lead a kind of underground existence among teachers trying to make sense of the sprawling nineteenth century (it was available for many years in a twenty-five-cent reprint edition). Historians of an idealist bent, such as Robert Wiebe and Wilfred M. McClay, have acknowledged its influence. And even in the most materialist of recent social histories, we can glimpse the faint outlines of Higham's thesis as diverse, energetic working-class cultures give way to "incorporation," the "progressive society," or the "visible hand" of managerial capitalism.

Stuart McConnell
Pitzer College

9

From Boundlessness to Consolidation

The Transformation of American Culture, 1848–1860

[1969]

. . . better to sink in boundless deeps than float on vulgar shoals; and give me, ye gods, an utter wreck, if wreck I do.

HERMAN MELVILLE, *Mardi, 1849*

I would consent to any GREAT *evil, to avoid a* GREATER *one.*

ABRAHAM LINCOLN, Speech at Peoria, 1854

During the course of the 1850s an obscure, self-taught midwesterner, Platt Rogers Spencer, made a phenomenal success as a teacher of penmanship. First in his own business school in Pittsburgh, then as superintendent of penmanship in the new Bryant and Stratton chain of commercial colleges, and finally through a series of textbooks, Spencer fervently promoted what his admirers called "the first philosophical system" of handwriting. Like so much of Victorian culture, it was a compromise, adapted both to the practical needs of business and to the tasteful elegance of social life. The Spencerian style was thought to offer a middle way between the labored fullness of the "round hand" and the cramped angularities of the "running hand." Its great feature, according to Spencer, was the elliptical curve—"the form which nature most delights to employ." He loved to credit nature itself with inspiring his art—an art he claimed to have developed as a boy communing with the elements on Lake Erie's "wild and woody shore."

> I seized the forms I loved so well,
>   Compounded them as meaning signs,
> And to the music of the swell,
>   Blent them with undulating vines.[1]

To the historian, the relation of Spencerian handwriting to primeval nature must seem less intimate. Disseminated initially through business schools, Spencer's oval line won popularity at a time of rapid urbanization. Moreover, it reflected an international fashion. The same line framed Victorian portraits; it defined the contours of Belter furniture; it rounded the corners of Italianate villas; it permeated the floral designs on carpets and shawls. Everywhere these undulating vines suggested the fullness, the ripe abundance, of the natural world. But they also domesticated nature. They subdued its vitality.

In some important ways nature was becoming less inspiriting—less accessible to the American imagination—at the very time Spencer's copybook imitations were taking hold. Around the middle of the century, Henry Nash Smith tells us, the theme of human communion with nature began to fade from the popular western story. Instead of drawing spiritual guidance from the wilderness, as the early western heroes had, the Kit Carsons and the Deadwood Dicks developed into self-sufficient adventurers loose in a hostile or indifferent environment.[2] The same might be said of the protagonists in Francis Parkman's epic of the wilderness. Nature offered nothing but flinty resistance to the human spirit in the historical series that Parkman launched in 1851 with the publication of *The Conspiracy of Pontiac*. In that year Herman Melville published the greatest of the American romances of the sea; it was also the most ambiguous and virtually the last. Melville's next book, *Pierre*, moved from the natural world into the city. Henry Thoreau, on the other hand, maintained a lifelong absorption in nature, and surely no American has ever taken it more seriously. Nevertheless, in the 1850s he, too, lost touch with its transcendental dimension. His vision contracted to an objective observation of external detail. American landscape painting, beginning with the work of Frederick Church in the late 1850s, underwent a similar evolution from moral allegory to impersonal reality. Whether nature wore the grim aspect of Parkman's scene or the tameness of most painters', it was ceasing to convey to Americans a spontaneous, spiritual message well before they heard of Charles Darwin.[3]

Under these circumstances, what inferences can we draw from the rapid spread of a style of handwriting supposedly shaped to nature's specifications? It may not be altogether fanciful to suggest that the doctrines of another Spencer, one far better remembered than our professor of penmanship, contain a clue. Herbert Spencer began to reach a few Americans in the late 1850s; the readiness of their response was striking. No less a champion of Calvinist orthodoxy than the *Princeton Review* devoted a lead article to Spencer because, for all of his "infidel and materialistic drift," he "powerfully illuminates whatever pertains to the physical side of humanity."[4] The extraordinary growth of his reputation in America during the next two or three decades is too well known to need elaboration. In accounting for that reputation, it is a crude misconception to suppose that Americans adopted Herbert Spencer as their favorite philosopher simply because he preached laissez-faire individualism to a business society. Most characteristically, his admirers belonged not among the embattled ranks of businessmen but in such technical and professional occupations as teaching, law, journalism, and engineering.[5] One of the principal attractions of Spencer to such men inhered in his reaffirmation of the old Enlightenment belief in a beneficent order of nature underlying the conflicts, the confusion, the cross-purposes of a competitive way of life. Americans, in rejecting the authority of history, had turned in part to the authority of nature; and now that a sense of intimacy with that tutelary presence was dissolving in an urban milieu, Spencer translated the old assurance into terms relevant to a complex society. By conforming to the methods of nature, he insisted, human beings were evolving a more and more coherent, rational civilization. In short, Spencer succeeded where the romantics had failed: he reconciled the ideas of nature and civilization.

Platt Rogers Spencer was also—after a fashion—a philosopher of nature and a servant of civilization. He, too, gave his best efforts to working out an elaborate formal system, supposedly derived from external reality, well suited for utilitarian purposes, based on a few simple principles, and containing within one harmonious scheme a wonderful variety of permutations. Without pushing a risky analogy too far, it may be suggested that both systems—Spencerian philosophy and Spencerian penmanship—represented a quest for order. Each enclosed the freedom, movement, and diversity Americans had associated with nature within an intricate but fundamentally stable pattern. In that sense each of them illustrates a major development in American culture in the third quarter of the nineteenth century.

For a first approximate statement of the character of that development let us look at the basic proposition on which Herbert Spencer erected his vast system. Throughout the universe, Spencer argued, from stars to embryos and through all human endeavor, a dual movement runs. All things tend from a diffuse to a concentrated state, and this integration brings with it a progressive differentiation of wholes into more and more highly articulated parts. "Everywhere the change [is] from a confused simplicity to a distinct complexity . . . from a relatively diffused, uniform and indeterminate arrangement, to a relatively concentrated, multiform, and determinate arrangement." Having begun his career as an engineer, Spencer may have been drawn to this formula partly by reflecting on technological change and the industrial division of labor. But whatever his original inspiration, Spencer summarized as a universal law of nature an important shift in the culture of his time. In the United States more than anywhere else that shift followed the Spencerian formula, a circumstance that doubtless had something to do with Spencer's great prestige here.[6]

Leaving aside the anomalous features of the Old South, the culture of the United States in the Jacksonian era—the culture that Alexis de Tocqueville observed—might be described (in Spencer's words) as relatively diffused, uniform and indeterminate. In less pretentious terminology it was a culture with a very indistinct sense of limits, a culture characterized by a spirit of boundlessness. By that I mean partly what Daniel Boorstin has called the healthy vagueness of pre–Civil War America: the lack of sharp boundaries or rigid categories, which made possible much fluidity and adaptability and, in many institutions, a conglomerate mixture of purposes. I also mean what Stanley Elkins and David Donald have described as a disastrous loss of cohesion and erosion of institutional authority.[7] Both of these insights catch a prominent aspect of Jacksonian America, but one of them is too sympathetic and the other too critical to do justice to the whole. Beneath the vagueness and the anti-institutionalism of the age lay a common quality of boundlessness. William Ellery Channing, the most respected preacher in New England, grasped it in a lecture in 1841:

> In looking at our age I am struck immediately with one commanding characteristic, and that is the tendency in all its movements to expansion, to diffusion, to universality. . . . This tendency is directly opposed to the spirit of exclusiveness, restriction, narrowness, monopoly, which has prevailed in past ages. Human action is now freer, more unconfined. . . . Thought frees the old bounds to which men used to confine themselves. . . . Undoubtedly this is a perilous tendency. Men forget the limits of their powers. They question the infinite, the unsearchable, with an audacious self-reliance. . . . Still, in this dangerous wildness we see what I am stating, the tendency to expansion in the movements of thought.[8]

That expansiveness culminated in transcendentalism and in the early poetry of Walt Whitman, whose loose, antiformalist style pushed to an unendurable extreme the tendency that Channing noticed. Thus the famous declaration of the "Song of the Open Road," delivered in 1856 when the tide was already turning in another direction:

> From this hour I ordain myself loos'd of limits and imaginary lines,
> Going where I list, my own master total and absolute.
> ....
> I inhale great draughts of space,
> The east and the west are mine, and the north and the south are mine.
> I am larger, better than I thought.[9]

It was only in Whitman's time that the tendency he acclaimed began to flag, and the culture turned decisively in the direction Spencer was charting—toward concentration and specialization. From the seventeenth century until some time in the middle of the nineteenth, Americans moved steadily away from a closed, formal model of the good life; they moved toward an increasingly open model. The American Revolution accelerated the movement. Yet certain crucial limits on human aspirations remained normative until the beginning of the nineteenth century. For one, a habit of deference toward one's betters restricted the mobility drive. Even so unusual a careerist as Benjamin Franklin took pains to conceal his ambition and to pay tribute to superior rank. Second, a cyclical view of history, grounded in a reverence for antiquity, warned eighteenth-century Americans of the unlikelihood of surpassing the achievements of the distant past. This check on the idea of progress connected with a neoclassical respect for reason as a principle of restraint—reason as a curb on wayward, anarchic impulse.[10] Reinforcing the limits of deference, of the past, and of reason was a Calvinist skepticism about human nature, a dour conviction of an innate propensity to sin. Finally, a static world picture persisted in some considerable degree well into the eighteenth century. It showed the fixity and completeness of the whole natural environment within which the human story was enacted.[11]

After 1815 most of the limits that Americans had assumed would forever enclose the scope of their endeavors seemed to melt away. The limits of ascribed status yielded to an egalitarian celebration of the self-made man.[12] The limits of history dissolved in an ecstatic dedication to the future. The limits of reason were metamorphosed into the infinite possibilities of knowledge and the intuitive truths of the heart. The limits of human nature faded before a glowing promise of liberation from sin and social iniquity. The limits of nature itself receded in a new dynamic world picture overflowing with vitality and undergoing endless growth. It would be absurd to suppose that these expansive sentiments and ideas ever overwhelmed more cautious and traditionalist views. The point is rather that their explosive thrust defined the great issues of the age.

The reasons for so vigorous an assault on limits can be briefly put. It drew strength and assurance from a new sense of national security that followed the War of 1812 and the end of the Napoleonic era. After 1815 the Republican experiment no longer seemed in jeopardy. The Old World no longer threatened seriously the prospects of the New, due partly to the command of the seas by the British navy and partly to the absorption of the European powers in their own balance of power system.[13] Meanwhile an enormous widening of horizons resulted from technological changes—steamboats, railroads, factory machinery, and agricultural implements—which proliferated in a cumulative way and thus transformed the whole pace and scale of life, encouraging ordinary people to move great distances, to accept a continual renovation of their surroundings, to take advantage of innovation. The spirit of boundlessness fed also, of course, on the democratization of American politics that came with the development of mass parties and the excitement of almost annual elections. It derived a powerful emotional energy from evangelical Christianity, as the great revivals of the early nineteenth century roused a crusading spirit and summoned people to an epic victory over themselves. Finally, the spirit of boundlessness acquired an intellectual rationale through a selective importation of aspects of European romanticism—above all, from the romantic striving to encompass the infinite and from the romantic awe of nature's organic growth.[14]

To review all the consequences or manifestations of this state of mind would require nothing less than an examination of the entire history and civilization of the United States in the second quarter of the nineteenth century. For our purposes it will be sufficient to call attention to four prominent types of belief and behavior. One was the extraordinary popular restlessness and aggressiveness of the period; another its perfectionist conception of reform as a total eradication of evil; a third its heavy reliance on a moral law implanted in every heart; a fourth the intellectual sterility of the northern conservatives who sought to restrict the spirit of boundlessness. These cultural traits were all interrelated.

The restlessness and aggressiveness of the period appeared, on perhaps the most fundamental level, in the intense migratory impulse that seized most of the American people in the early decades of the nineteenth century, turning the United States (in the words of one observer) into "a bivouac rather than a nation, a grand army moving from the Atlantic to the

Pacific, and pitching tents along the way."[15] Although we have no statistics to prove that a greater proportion of the Americans moved then than before or since, there is no doubt that some very strong political and psychological resistances to the dispersion of population into the great interior broke down in the early nineteenth century, so that the decades from 1815 to 1850, when a new state entered the Union about every two and a half years, will always stand as the classic age of the frontier.[16] Whoever today tries to understand the frame of mind in which multitudes of ordinary Americans in the early nineteenth century cast themselves into the vast spaces of a West inhabited only by warlike Indians will be baffled unless he or she takes account of the spirit of boundlessness.

Aggressiveness displayed itself further in what historians like to call the social "ferment" of the era. It was a time of passionate crusades on the one hand and of vicious riots on the other. The crusading mentality, evident in tract and missionary societies, in cold-water armies, in frenzied denunciations of the "Monster Bank," was a fighting mentality. So was that of the mobs who rioted against Negroes, against abolitionists, against Catholics, Mormons, landlords, the price of bread, and even on one especially bloody occasion against a famous English actor.[17] The first half of the nineteenth century has had no monopoly on violence in American history. But what distinguished the tumult of that period from earlier ones was the swagger that accompanied it—the soaring, inflated, even boundless character of its affirmations. Whereas the Revolutionary era preferred a heavy satire that punctured pretensions, American humor and rhetoric now shifted into hyperbole. Out of the West came the tall tale, proclaiming the mythic feats of Mike Fink and Davy Crockett. Out of the East came fabulous newspaper hoaxes, the grandiose showmanship of P. T. Barnum, the spontaneous, tempestuous style of acting popularized by Edwin Forrest, and a new kind of advertising, which promoted patent medicines and other shams in such high-flown language that honest competitors (it was said) "must resort to the basest bombast to keep pace."[18] "What orator," asked a Kentuckian, "can deign to restrain his imagination within a vulgar and sterile state of facts?"

In political life this assertive temperament reached a crest in the expansionism of the 1840s. Indeed, one might speak of the politics of boundlessness as beginning in the War of 1812 and culminating in the War with Mexico. In general, Jacksonian Democrats adopted a more belligerent posture than the Jeffersonians, on whose ideas they otherwise relied. The Jacksonian attack on "aristocratic" privilege, after losing its usefulness in domestic affairs, passed into a crusade to extend democracy abroad, not merely by the static force of example but also by appropriation and conquest. Jacksonians denied that any natural limits confined the area within which American institutions would work. Some of them pressed for the absorption of all of Mexico. Others looked forward to effacing all "artificial boundaries" throughout the continent or the hemisphere.

In his inaugural address on assuming the presidency in 1853, the expansionist Democrat Franklin Pierce captured perfectly the idiom of his party and his age. "It is not your privilege as a nation," Pierce told the American people, "to speak of a distant past. The striking incidents of your history, replete with instruction and furnishing abundant grounds for hopeful confidence, are comprised in a period comparatively brief. But if your past is limited, your future is boundless."[19]

Most of the moral reformers of the period were Whigs and thus opposed to nationalistic expansionism. Their sense of national destiny was on the whole centripetal rather than centrifugal. While Jacksonian Democrats sought to diffuse power and to push outward the spatial limits of freedom, Whig reformers sought to cleanse and purify human relationships. They concentrated, therefore, on uplifting the downtrodden, developing a common school system, calling their fellow men away from the grogshop and the gutter, abolishing war, and stimulating cooperative enterprise. Their participation in the spirit of boundlessness took the form of an assault on the bonds of sin, ignorance, and appetite.[20]

The characteristic accent of the age sounded in the apocalyptic note the reformers struck over and over again. Fired by perfectionist and millennialist ideas, they tended to feel that the last days of the unrighteous had arrived: the triumph of perfect love was imminent. Accordingly they shrank from any compromise with evil. A horror of expediency encouraged a general abstractness of mind and a disinterest in making practical arrangements for an imperfect world. As Frank Thistlethwaite has pointed out, American moral reform acquired a sweeping, denunciatory vehemence unknown among the more cautious, utilitarian reformers in England.[21] It was easier to be a visionary in America's Age of Boundlessness than it was to be either an expert or a planner.

Yet the typical reformers, for all of their uncompromising spirit, were no more alienated—no more truly rebellious—than the typical democrats. American institutions seemed so fluid, so incapable of withstanding the great good changes that were coming, that reformers might sound radical while nevertheless associating themselves with the fundamental principles and underlying tendencies of America. In fact, the limits and restraints that were dropping away were conceived to be extrinsic both to nature and to America's true, inner culture. Far from casting off all inhibitions, nineteenth-century Americans ordinarily sought release only from the material and institutional confinements that bound them to a fixed place or a given social role. In proportion as those external ties relaxed, the internalized restraints of conscience and public opinion tightened. Thus the Age of Boundlessness combined a passion for freedom with an exceptionally strict moral code.

Yet conservatives could put no great trust in so intangible a check upon the turbulence of the period. For them it was (as William R. Taylor has suggested) an age of anxiety. The country seemed to be caught in a maelstrom of excitement. Agitation and instability were spreading everywhere. A general breakup of established modes of thought was occurring, many suspected. Had not the leading minds of New England, "bewildered amidst the deep and awful shadows of the transcendental labyrinth . . . been led off into the most absurd and foolish vagaries"? It was difficult for critics to say where the seat of such vague and protean troubles lay. Some feared that the disease was endemic to American culture, that it stemmed from "that principle of disintegration which is so strongly infused into the whole spirit of our constitution, and the character of our people. . . . that centrifugal bias which impels with a strong divergence states and individuals."[22]

Confronted by that alarming possibility, conservative intellectuals in the North had difficulty establishing a constructive relation to their own time. They might, on the one hand, throw anxiety to the winds and—like Daniel Webster—celebrate the "miracles of enterprise" that Americans were achieving; or they might, on the other, reassert a Burkean reliance on traditional institutions—family, state, and church—as the best preservers of stability in a disintegrating society. But the first strategy merely acquiesced in the spirit of boundlessness, while the second was nostalgic and negativistic. With very few exceptions, the conservative mentality was either slack or musty. The best thought of the period ran toward the aphoristic and the prophetic. The age was uncongenial to analytical or systematic thinking.

Much of what I have described became a permanent part of the American character and has reappeared in disturbing and exciting ways in our own day. But a time came when the predominant direction changed, when the emphasis in American culture shifted significantly from diffusion to concentration, from spontaneity to order. This should be remembered as one of the truly great turning points in our history, so we should know when it occurred. George Fredrickson has offered some compelling new reasons for associating it with the Civil War, and his argument agreeably reinforces the extraordinary hold the Civil War exercises over our historical imagination.[23] But the epic character of that war has long obscured a great deal that was happening in the United States in the immediately preceding years. Moreover, the uniqueness of the sectional conflict from which the war derived has long obstructed our view of the common threads interlacing western Europe and the United States in the mid-nineteenth century.

In the remainder of this essay I propose to call attention to certain crucial changes in American culture that were already clearly visible in the 1850s—changes that mark the emergence of a pattern of consolidation. In the United States, as well as England and much of Europe, the 1850s witnessed a subsidence of the radical hopes and reactionary fears of the early nineteenth century and the formation of a more stable, more disciplined, less adventurous culture. For European historians the transition is distinctly marked by the failure of the Revolutions of 1848. America, of course, had no revolution that year; nor had it even a Chartist movement. Nevertheless, the Americans felt the impact of those events far more deeply than we have suspected.

When the news of the overthrow of King Louis Philippe spread through the United States in late March and April of 1848, it set off frenzies of jubilation. Great mass meetings and torchlight processions acclaimed the final emancipation of Europe. Inevitably "the swelling tide of Revolution" would sweep all before it; the "regeneration of man by self-government" seemed assured. To the great majority of Americans the idea of revolution still meant the spirit of '76, the triumph of republicanism over monarchy and aristocracy. To judge from the newspapers of the day, most Americans, in spite of the unhappy excesses of the first French Revolution, expected that Europe would now follow the path the United States had blazed.[24]

Gradually, during the ensuing months and years, it became apparent that the political millennium had not arrived. The revolutions, turning into bitter class struggles, produced socialist uprisings and ended in military repression. Instead of creating broadly based constitutional republics on the American model, European liberals almost everywhere lost control of events. In spite of the enthusiasm that Louis Kossuth awakened on his visit to the United States in 1851, and in spite of the efforts of the Young America group in the early 1850s, confidence in the rapid spread of an American style of democracy rang increasingly hollow. Indeed, the very idea of revolution lost much of its luster. No longer associated primarily with the overthrow of aristocracy, after 1848 it came to signify the threat of socialism. Therein lay the seed of a profound change in the relation of the United States to the European political system.

The disillusion with contemporary revolutionary movements paralleled a shift of attitude toward America's own revolutionary past. In the Age of Boundlessness most Americans conceived of theirs as a young, new country, still bathed in the morning light of the American Revolution. This sense of the Adamic youthfulness of American culture survived the passing of Thomas Jefferson and John Adams in 1826. It was, in fact, reenacted by their obsequies and by a reading of the Declaration of Independence on each Fourth of July. But by 1848, when John Quincy Adams—"the last venerated survivor of the chief magistrates of our revolutionary era"—was struck down in the House of Representatives, Americans felt they were losing touch with the spirit of their revolutionary sires.[25] As Dolley Madison, Harrison Gray Otis, and other "Living Relics of the Revolution" followed Adams to his grave, editors repeated the same sad refrain: "in a very few years more not a link will remain of that magic chain which connects the present with the past era of our country."[26] Moreover, the Fourth of July was losing much of its significance as a reenactment of the republican faith; it was becoming a mere occasion for recreation and entertainment.[27]

Thus a disturbing sense of remoteness from the heroic age of the Revolution infiltrated American minds in the middle of the nineteenth century. To counteract the malaise and rebuild continuity with the past, a movement got under way for preserving and creating historic landmarks. In 1848 the cornerstone of the Washington National Monument was laid, and two years later New York State acquired the Hasbrouck House in Newburgh because of its Washington associations. In the mid-fifties the Mount Vernon Ladies Association rescued Washington's home from neglect, while Philadelphians began the restoration of Independence Hall.[28] Were not these and other early attempts at conserving a national heritage symptoms of a loss of youthfulness in American culture?

At any rate, it is suggestive that these preservationist efforts coincided with a certain deflation of the raucous national assertiveness so many Americans had vented in the Age of Boundlessness. The characteristic strut of American democrats was, after 1848, a little less cocksure. They could no longer so confidently suppose (as one did in 1842) that "the rotten and antiquated foundations of every despotic and exclusive institution of the Old World . . . only await a coming shock to crumble into ruin."[29] A good deal of nationalistic expansionism persisted into the fifties. For some a "manifest destiny" still beckoned the United States to extend itself in every direction. But the idea was increasingly discredited through its association with the spread of slavery rather than the spread of democracy. Outside proslavery circles it was commonly assumed by the late 1850s that the Union was complete.

Moreover, the spread-eagle rhetoric that accompanied the expansionism of the 1830s and 1840s became something of a national embarrassment. Demagogues and fire-eaters still engaged, of course, in the usual gasconade. Yet a new sense of limits appeared in the plain speaking of Abraham Lincoln and the skeptical, matter-of-fact humor of Artemus Ward, whose dry wit Lincoln enjoyed quoting.[30] Others were asking: "Is it wise and judicious for us, as a people, to feed our vanity so greedily on bombast? . . . Is it in the best taste for our statesmen and generals to be so often on stilts, looking down with pity upon the 'down-trodden,' miserable people of Europe, and pharisaically congratulating ourselves that we are not as other people?"[31]

Perhaps the best single indication of a reduction in grandiose pretensions came from the literary critics. In the 1840s the principal school of literary critics—the Young Americans, as they liked to call themselves—had demanded the immediate creation of a distinctive national literature imbued with the spirit of democracy. It would have to be "a New Literature to fit the New Man in the New Age." Nothing seemed more reprehensible than a servile imitation of English writers or dependence on foreign themes. To put down such craven tendencies Evert and George Duyckinck launched in 1847 the leading literary review of the decade, the *Literary World.* The weight of critical opinion, however, soon swung toward the more conservative and cosmopolitan position that James Russell Lowell spelled out in 1849. Writing in the *North American Review,* he described literary nationalism as "a less narrow form of provincialism, a sublimer sort of clownishness and ill manners." By then a transformation had overcome the *Literary World.* It abandoned the crusade for a democratic, new-fledged literature. Instead, the editors now warned Americans to beware of "the dreams of the theorist and the charlatan" and to put their trust in traditional institutions. Without adopting so conservative a stance in politics, the leading literary magazine of the 1850s, *Putnam's Monthly,* went further in the direction of international sophistication by printing regular reports on the current literature of England, France, and Germany.[32]

How much the failure of the Revolutions of 1848 may have contributed to the sobriety and restraint that descended like a pall on many of the enthusiasms of the forties no one can say. The resurgence of despotism on the European continent certainly deflated hopes of a speedy Americanization of the world, and the social radicalism unleashed in the revolutionary outburst gave pause to some American reformers. Nevertheless, other factors must account for much of the contrast between the 1840s and the 1850s both in Europe and in the United States. A conservative shift toward order and stability was not confined to the immediate aftermath of 1848. Drawing on many sources, it gathered momentum through the following decade and beyond.

The rising tide of the antislavery movement in the 1850s has obscured the concurrent decline of most of the other crusades of the Age of Boundlessness. Religious benevolence of the kind embodied in Bible and tract and missionary societies showed no falling off in absolute terms, but it was becoming institutionalized—a regular mode of Protestant activity rather than a shortcut to the millennium. The peace movement reached a high point in opposing the war with Mexico. Thereafter it declined, and by the mid-fifties it was moribund. The movement for more humanitarian administration of penitentiaries also peaked in the mid-forties. After Louis Dwight's death in 1854 the once powerful Prison Discipline Society quickly collapsed. The movement to abolish capital punishment won its chief victories between 1846 and 1852; then uneasiness about the prevalence of crime gave the advantage once more to the sterner apostles of law and order. A similar loss of confidence in the curability of the insane checked the impressive progress that psychiatry made in the years when Dorothea Dix roused the conscience of the North. Fourierite socialism was diluted into a cooperative store movement, which in turn petered out in the mid-fifties; and what remained of a labor movement spurned all varieties of reform to concentrate on "pure and simple" unionism.[33] Meanwhile, Sylvester Graham's dietary reform—food should be simple, plain, and natural—had aroused more extreme programs of self-denial. By the 1850s a rebound toward complete self-indulgence was building the ample bodies of the Gilded Age.[34]

Probably the most extensive of all of these endeavors was the great temperance crusade. Its growth phase persisted longer than the others', perhaps because the idea of prohibition, coming to the fore in the late forties, was congenial to the new search for order. Sparked by the famous Maine Law of 1851, prohibitory legislation spread across New England, the upper Middle West, and some of the mid-Atlantic states. But the wave broke in 1856 with the repeal of the original Maine Law. By the end of the decade only Michigan and some of the New England states remained technically dry.[35]

A parallel slackening of creative energy and intellectual daring may be observed among the great American writers, for whom the 1850s were both a culmination and the beginning of a descent into tame respectability. Ralph Waldo Emerson was the first to go. Already in the 1840s he was retreating from the radical individualism of his early manifestoes and emphasizing the necessary harmonies of evolution. As his views softened, his reputation soared. The august *North American Review* as late as 1847 denounced Emerson as a "chartered libertine"; but three years later the *Knickerbocker Magazine,* admitting that it was "attempting a somewhat thankless task in defending Emerson," assured its readers that he had put aside his earlier skepticism and had acquired "a deeper, more earnest tone." James Russell Lowell and John Greenleaf Whittier were also acquiring a deeper (i.e., more aquiescent) tone.[36] Herman Melville, who was a critic as well as a practitioner of boundlessness, lapsed into cynicism and then silence. The last fine frenzy of a passing era came to expression in Walt Whitman's *Leaves of Grass.* But even Whitman began to tone down the intensity and exhilaration of his work when he published a revised edition in 1860.

When historians have noticed the prewar declension of romantic reform, they have ordinarily seen it simply as a change of priorities—a shift of energy from the many goals of the 1840s to a single, overwhelming focus on slavery. The antislavery crusade, it is said, swallowed up all the others. But why should one idealistic cause, so intimately allied with many others in the 1830s and 1840s, have hurt them in the 1850s? Why should they not have gained from its triumphs and basked in its radiance?[37] The standard explanation, apart from its dubious psychology, fails to account for the increasingly conservative worldview of leading intellectuals—of Emerson, Lowell, Whittier, Harriet Beecher Stowe, Henry Ward Beecher, Charles A. Dana, Horace Greeley, and many others who had antislavery sympathies. Is it possible that the antislavery movement itself turned in the 1850s in a conservative direction?

Certainly antislavery agitation in the decade before the Civil War produced a rising level of violence and of disunionist feeling that looks radical in the extreme. Yet the abolitionists—true radicals who were sharply distinguished at the time from the mass of Free-Soilers—remained a tiny, ineffectual minority, their moral absolutism largely engulfed by a genuinely widespread, conservative desire to keep slavery where it was. In effect, northern opinion after 1848 split into two types of conservatism. One sought to maintain the status quo by avoiding further discussion of slavery, the other by stopping its expansion. By the late 1850s the great bulk of the intellectual and professional classes took the second view. They determined to set limits on slavery not primarily for humanitarian reasons but rather (so they thought) to preserve the American republic. As the spirit of boundlessness subsided, more and more northerners became convinced that a far-flung oligarchy, the Slave Power, was accumulating political and economic control over every aspect of national life. By resisting the aggressions of the Slave Power most Republicans cast themselves in the role of defending existing institutions.

To describe the broadening antislavery movement of the 1850s in such terms does not fully explain it. Nevertheless, an appreciation of the new drive for order that was advancing on the eve of the Civil War helps us understand both the failures and the successes of that epic struggle. We can see that the stunning triumph of the young Republican Party was not due simply to moral outrage on the one hand or to pragmatic leadership on the other, or even to a combination of the two, although these were important ingredients of its appeal. The Republicans came to power in 1860 primarily because they effected a temporary fusion between opposing ideological currents. For a few crucial, transitional years they married the crusading idealism of an older America with a rising conservatism that looked forward to a more stable and cohesive society. They stood at one and the same time for the assertion of freedom and the acceptance of limits. No one embraced and contained the contradictory implications of that position more sensitively than Abraham Lincoln. He was the spiritual center of nineteenth-century America, for he felt with equal intensity the infinite hopes of the Age of Boundlessness and that growing sense of human finitude that would haunt the coming decades of consolidation.

Not only the Republican leadership but also the outcome of the Civil War itself was shaped by the increasing emphasis in midcentury culture on limits and boundaries. It helps to explain why blacks gained only a partial freedom, why a genuinely radical kind of reconstruction was brief, why the war eventuated in a far clearer victory for national unity than for personal freedom, and why it gave democracy on the whole a setback. The results of the war might have been very different if a strong movement toward cultural consolidation had not already set in before the first shot was fired. The conduct of the war required a major shift in priorities. It engendered respect for institutions, for discipline, for the principles of loyalty and authority. Yet that respect might not have lasted into the postwar decades if the war had not simply accelerated an ongoing trend.

To grasp the full extent and the underlying causes of the transition that was only beginning in the 1850s we shall have to look beyond the familiar figures on the antebellum scene—beyond the romantic reformers, the transcendentalists, the Jacksonian expansionists, the revivalists, all of whom were retiring into the background—and notice the entrance of other players with different roles. Midcentury America gave new scope to prophets and pioneers of administrative rationalization like Henry Varnum Poor, to planners and organizers like Frederic Law Olmsted, to positivistic thinkers like Henry C. Carey, to scientists and literary realists like Oliver Wendell Holmes. On the eve of the Civil War, these and many other Americans whose importance historians have long overlooked were experimenting in many small, often fumbling, always imperfect ways with social control. They were exploring new possibilities for organizing and disciplining a culture of rampant individualism.[38] Continuing through the war and postwar years, the elaboration of a framework of order within and—so to speak—around American individualism tended to define Victorian culture in the United States.

In all likelihood, the principal reason for the trend toward consolidation will be found in the convergence of industrialization and urbanization in the middle decades of the nineteenth century. Certainly the need for a stabler, more distinctly organized environment first arose in the cities. It was there that the shock of mass immigration in the 1840s and 1850s created intense alarm over the breakdown of ethnic homogeneity. It was in those chaotically growing centers of population also that the necessity for new public initiatives in sanitation, public health, education, and law enforcement was first felt. In the foremost eastern cities, for example, professional police forces under a hierarchy of officers were compelled in the early 1850s to wear uniforms and badges; and more or less simultaneously the creation of citywide superintendents was a major step in the standardization and integration of big-city school systems.[39] There, too, in the 1840s and 1850s philanthropists tried out new techniques for systematizing charity and for coping rationally with poverty and unemployment.[40] That these techniques seem from the point of view of the modern welfare state neither bold nor altogether wise may partly account for a persistent neglect of their historical significance.

The increasing importance of formal structures and definitions affected other aspects of American life as well. The founding of national professional societies—notably the American Medical Association (1847) and the American Society of Civil Engineers (1852)—sparked a revival of professional consciousness, with the object of controlling what a leading physician in 1851 called the "dishonourable competition, which an uninterrupted individualism is so apt to engender." In the Protestant churches the growth of professionalism not only discouraged "dishonourable competition." It also produced a more highly trained ministry, greater concern with the liturgical side of religion, and a decline of the crusading fervor of an earlier day. A stiffening formality was still more apparent in middle-class manners, as evidenced by the elaboration of rituals and rules in popular etiquette books.[41]

I have touched all too briefly on some of the ways Americans before the Civil War were already demonstrating on the level of culture what Herbert Spencer mistook for a cosmic process. In the postwar decades these tendencies became much more obvious; and their imaginative impact was reinforced both by scientific materialism and by the tightening mesh of industrial technology. It is little wonder that the magazine *Science,* commenting in 1886 on a new plan of astronomical research, declared: "Like all the schemes of this day, Professor Pickering's is one of consolidation."[42]

Institutionally, the process of consolidation has proved irreversible. Spiritually, it has never satisfied. A time would arrive when initiative would revert to rebellious people longing to break out of the closed, stifling atmosphere of late nineteenth-century culture. The rebels would invoke again the open, spontaneous spirit of boundlessness. At that point, we stand on the threshold of our own time. A renewed assault on boundaries—a fresh impatience with closed space, fixed principles, and formal manners—signaled the passing of the Victorian age. And has not this same impatience, erupting time and again, become one of the hallmarks of American culture in the twentieth century?

An essay review of *Alternative America* (1983), John L. Thomas's collective biography of Henry George, Henry Demarest Lloyd, and Edward Bellamy, provided an opportunity for Higham to assess American radicalism. These three American utopians of the latter nineteenth century dramatized the evils of corporate industrialism in best-selling books. The panaceas they proposed—George's single tax, Lloyd's labor politics, and Bellamy's nationalized industry—proved much less compelling than their diagnoses, and by the century's end their political crusades had disbanded in defeat. Higham seems to endorse Thomas's contention that these visionaries failed because their idea of a "pure and loving community" was made obsolete by the growing power of interest groups with reformist agendas. Thus the utopians could be seen as victims of the shift from boundless aspirations to pragmatic, institutional change that had begun a generation before them and culminated in the Progressive era that succeeded them. Even in their failure, however, these social prophets demonstrated that the moral conscience and millennial dreams of nineteenth-century Protestantism prepared the way for Progressive reform among those whom the historian Daniel Aaron calls "men of good hope."

Although Higham clearly admires the utopians, he takes issue with Thomas's sweeping claim that they were the founding fathers of a radical American "adversary tradition" that charted a middle path between capitalism and socialism. Higham suggests a counterinterpretation: that a truly radical adversary tradition never crystallized in America owing partly to the nineteenth-century utopians themselves. Because they sought the restoration of such traditional American ideals as respect for the "producing classes," they behaved as reformers, not genuine radicals. After 1900 the American Socialist party under Eugene Debs introduced a more modern, tough-minded social critique derived from Marx. By then, however, it was perhaps too late for a socialist party in this country to build a durable popular base. In the 1880s and 1890s, while social-democratic parties in Europe were doing just that, the utopian prophets obstructed the path to an American socialism: they diverted its natural constituency toward rival versions of the American dream.

In Higham's review, however, one may sense more confidence than disappointment. His deft inversion of Thomas's thesis reflects, through the prism of irony, his conviction that an elastic and resilient American dream has made the nation's social experience exceptional.

Richard A. Gerber
Southern Connecticut State University

10

America's Utopian Prophets
[1984]

One of the great tasks of intellectual leadership has been the definition of injustice. When a new injustice, or complex of injustices, first emerges fully into view, the intellectuals who grasp and report its meaning can make a critical difference in the history of the next half-century or more. That is why Henry George, Henry Demarest Lloyd, and Edward Bellamy are fascinating and important. Between 1879 and 1894 each of them published an extraordinary book that dramatized and interpreted in a new way the economic injustice of an urban, industrial society. Their books stirred the American conscience like nothing since *Uncle Tom's Cabin.*

All three authors were journalists. The next generation of social theorists would dwell for the most part in the groves of academe. Social analysis would become less apocalyptic, less grandiose, less personal. But the first burning perceptions of what had gone terribly wrong in the great cities of America and how the wrong could be righted came from writers who were self-taught and self-directed and who risked their jobs to discover the truth of their times. In *Alternative America: Henry George, Edward Bellamy, Henry Demarest Lloyd and the Adversary Tradition* (1983), John L. Thomas has woven together into a single compelling narrative the story of the three men's lives, their ideas, and their place in history.

Different though their backgrounds were in some ways, all three were shaped by a Protestant heritage of vocation and moral accountability, which in a simpler era had flowered in the antislavery movement. George's impecunious father ran a religious bookshop until it failed. Lloyd and Bellamy were sons of clergymen. In the flamboyant secularism of the Gilded Age, none of the sons held on to their parents' orthodoxy. But all of them felt an essentially religious yearning to discover or restore a true community, and all of them underwent something like a religious conversion when the scales dropped from their eyes and the possibility of a new civic religion opened before them.

George, the oldest of the three, had his moment of illumination around 1870 while horseback riding in the hills behind Oakland. The land about him was empty, but the teeming city of San Francisco straddled the horizon. George was already haunted by the extremes of wealth and poverty developing in his young state and by the expectation that the coming of the transcontinental railroad would further extend the power of capital while depressing the level of wages. Pausing a moment, George learned from a passing teamster that one local landowner was asking a thousand dollars an acre for this unused real estate. Suddenly an intuition dawned. Poverty and wealth were increasing simultaneously because the value of land goes up with the growth of population, and the "true producers"—the venturesome capitalist and the honest worker—must pay more and more to the grasping landlord. Let the state expropriate these unearned rents, and the imagined harmony of a bucolic America could be restored to a nation of cities. Elaborately developed and passionately argued, this revision of classical economics became George's great tract, *Progress and Poverty* (1879).

While George shifted restlessly from one unsuccessful California paper to another, Lloyd fretted at his lack of independence as a junior editor of the mighty *Chicago Tribune.* There, while writing financial commentaries of impeccable respectability, he came up against the great railroad strike of 1877. The news of pitched battles between strikers and state militia in several cities, the scenes of mobs burning railroad yards and looting storehouses, produced in Lloyd a conversion similar to that which the vision of land monopoly had inspired in George. Both glimpsed an approaching breakup of modern society if the conflicts within it were not resolved.

Lloyd found a new conceptual framework not by reformulating Manchesterian liberalism, as George did, but by rejecting it. A new respect for the state as a regulatory power incarnating the conscience of a people was becoming available in the writings of German and English economists and political theorists. Seizing upon it, Lloyd launched a campaign of outraged social criticism in magazine articles. These culminated in *Wealth Against Commonwealth,* a six-hundred-page indictment of Standard Oil, set in a panoramic moral history of the rise and impending decline of an acquisitive way of life.

The great railroad strike left Edward Bellamy depressed and pessimistic about the future. Social evils, he was convinced, could not be corrected by invading the rights of property or trusting in self-interested reformers. Bellamy was an unworldly recluse—neurotic, inhibited, and sickly. After spurning his parents' religion, he could not leave the shelter of their home but spent much of his time dreaming of a religion of universal solidarity that might replace the faith he had discarded. Bellamy's salvation was internal. It came gradually in the 1880s as he became capable of forging new human ties, through marriage and children, thus building a tenuous bridge between his private fantasies and a living community. The sense of connectedness and involvement that fatherhood gave him made the world seem redeemable. A book that Bellamy started to write as an escapist fable of an earthly paradise turned into a blueprint for an attainable transformation. The result was *Looking Backward* (1888). In this runaway best-seller the utopian anticipation of an approaching millennium, which all three writers felt, reached its fullest expression.

To many present-day readers, these late nineteenth-century classics of social protest are more familiar than are the careers of agitation into which their authors were drawn. For each writer, the grand theory became a rallying cry for a cause more dear than life itself. Henry George began lecturing on land reform in California before his book was completed. After its publication, he took off for New York, leaving wife and family behind, to be his own missionary. His first allies were Irish nationalists, then locked in a bitter struggle with England over oppression by alien landlords. Sent abroad as the correspondent for a leading Irish-American newspaper, George gathered an enthusiastic following among Irish-American workingmen. This in turn led him into the Knights of Labor and a wider concern with modern social problems. Academic economists gave George no quarter, dismissing him as a simpleminded moralist dabbling in a science beyond his grasp; but the adulation of the people fed his unshakable convictions. Between tours of Britain, Australia, and New Zealand, he fought two frenzied campaigns to be mayor of New York. In the second he had no chance. His doctors warned him that the effort would probably be fatal. But George courted death, and it came to him on a grueling day a week before the election.

Like George, Henry Demarest Lloyd discerned in the organization of labor a cooperative principle that might be broadly applied to the reconstruction of society. Lloyd took up the role of adviser to and spokesman for the American labor movement at a time of bitter class divisions, when unions tended to think of themselves as the seeds of a new order, and a middle-class intellectual like Lloyd who tried to bridge the gulf between classes was seen as a dangerous enemy of civilization. (He was in fact disinherited by his wealthy father-in-law.) Lloyd took heart, however, from the eminently respectable character of Fabian socialism in England. As an activist in Chicago, he busied himself spreading word of municipal experiments elsewhere, helped organize the World's Labor Congress at the Chicago World's Fair, and strove above all to turn the People's party into a farmer-labor coalition. Few were ready for that. In 1896 the Populist remnant repudiated Lloyd, then faded into oblivion itself.

The most amazing emergence into activism was Bellamy's. His lack of interest in politics, his distaste for power, and his personal isolation kept him aloof from any reform activity until the readers of *Looking Backward* spontaneously formed clubs to discuss the ideas in the book. Arguments over the specifications of his blueprint mounted. Soon this growing community of discourse persuaded Bellamy that choice, commitment, and struggle are inescapable. He had been wrong to rely on an inevitable process of consolidation to bring the new commonwealth into being. He had been equally wrong to entrust his collectivized future to an industrial army laboring obediently under a council of disinterested patriarchs. Politics and the struggle for reform could not be avoided. Leaving the seclusion of his home in Chicopee Falls, Massachusetts, Bellamy launched a national newspaper in Boston and, like Lloyd, embraced the Populist cause. For the next two years Bellamy poured all of his overtaxed energy into a campaign to make Nationalism (his own collectivist program) the ideological spearhead of the Populist movement. He spoke at rallies, ran for office, hobnobbed cheerfully with Boston journalists, and fired off advice in every direction. In 1893, Bellamy's energy gave out and he took to bed. He lived only long enough to complete a more democratic sequel to *Looking Backward,* entitled significantly *Equality.*

The appealing human qualities of John L. Thomas's three heroes blend in his book with a detailed assessment of their ideas. The sources of those ideas differed somewhat in the three instances, but essentially Thomas locates them in the native soil of the early American republic. The millennial and reformist strains in evangelical Protestantism joined in the middle decades of the nineteenth century with a heritage of Jacksonian working-class values that Thomas calls producerism. The latter was a dissenting tradition that reached back to seventeenth-century England; it played an important role in the American Revolution and throughout the nineteenth century animated the protests of farmers and workers against capitalistic monopolies. Producerism taught that the "producing classes" were victimized by parasitic idlers who controlled the government. When this social theory was mixed with the religious quest for a new birth of freedom, the two formed a potent creed.

Why, then, was it so roundly defeated? Why did the Populists fail to gain a following in the cities? Why did their challenge to corporate America fade so quickly in all parts of the country? Why did the Nationalist clubs fold after a season or two? Why did George become narrow and increasingly doctrinaire in his later years? Thomas suggests that the three prophets and the ideas they expressed were overwhelmed by "modernism," which is a way of saying that they were out of date. By the end of the century the utopian anticipation of a pure and loving community just beyond the horizon was giving way to a more pragmatic, secular worldview, and already tough-minded interest groups like the American Federation of Labor had demonstrated the uselessness of the quaint conception of a union of all producers.

Yet Thomas is unwilling to end on an elegiac note. The nineteenth-century utopians, he believes, opened a middle way between modern capitalism and modern socialism, which men of goodwill may still tread. Here the argument becomes very sketchy indeed. Thomas emphasizes that both Lloyd and Bellamy in their later work became more and more fascinated with local cooperatives, garden cities, and decentralized authority. This is a legacy that Lewis Mumford, Frank Lloyd Wright, and various regionalists and planners have fruitfully drawn upon. To call it the "adversary tradition," however, implies an ideological coherence, a continuity, a breadth of support, and a social polarization that twentieth-century America has simply not experienced.

A more persuasive conclusion might be that an adversary tradition has never crystallized in America, if by that phrase we mean a *radical* tradition, and that the three prophets discussed here bear some of the responsibility. Instead of stressing, as Thomas does, their common endeavor to adapt early American ideas to new social conditions, one might dwell more heavily on the confusions into which their redemptive visions led. Because the late nineteenth-century prophets saw themselves as restoring perennial truths that an unprincipled minority was betraying, they usually thought and acted as reformers rather than radicals. Confronted by new problems of bigness and impersonal organization, the three prophets gave uncertain answers to questions about the allocation of power. Their ideas were a shifting mélange of modern perceptions and old-fashioned attitudes.

An enduring adversary tradition would seem more likely to have taken root under the auspices of Marxian socialism. After 1900 the American Socialist Party gave a more consistent, up-to-date, and radical expression to the strains of discontent the utopian prophets had articulated during the two preceding decades. Socialists like Eugene Debs were the truest inheritors of the torch that Bellamy, Lloyd, and the Populists tried to light. But the Debsian Socialists had all too brief a time, before the great reaction of the 1920s set in, to make their movement a familiar American institution. During the late nineteenth century, when socialism was domesticating itself in western Europe and establishing permanent bases there, its penetration of native American opinion was blocked by the commanding presence of the utopian prophets. Instead of creating an adversary tradition, they renewed an American dream, which absorbed and dissipated the kind of support that socialists were rallying elsewhere. Quite unintentionally, the gallant crusaders who live again in Thomas's stirring book may have placed an alternative America out of reach.

First published in 1965, this essay became the last of four Commonwealth Fund Lectures that Higham delivered at the University of London in 1968. Serving as the bookend piece opposite "From Boundlessness to Consolidation" (Chapter 9), "The Reorientation of American Culture" describes the 1890s as a watershed decade, when the consolidating impulse of the Victorian era received a major setback. Here, more explicitly than in the earlier essay, Higham makes the case that the task of cultural history is to define the "spirit of an age" and discover underlying shifts from one cultural pattern to the next. Here, too, is further evidence for the suggestion, hinted in the final sentence of "Boundlessness," that American culture has developed cyclically over time. The recurring periods of consolidation and release proposed by Higham are reminiscent of other cyclical theories of American history, such as Arthur M. Schlesinger's notion that American political culture reflects periodic swings between conservative and liberal moods.

Higham argues that the 1890s produced a psychic upheaval. During the Gilded Age, Americans had accepted industrialization and its controls, adapting with relative ease to domesticated nature, an organized economy, cramped and cluttered homes, a genteel code of behavior, and formalistic modes of thought. In the 1890s, however, middle-class Americans turned restive. Some became pessimistic, succumbing to fin de siècle fatalism or, as Higham showed in Chapter 5, retreating to racial exclusivism. Others, more characteristically American, opted for a strenuous life of imperial crusades, combative sports, lively music, exercise in unbridled nature, and activist reform. The psychic revolt that underlay the new activism found its way into Progressive crusades and also infused a continuing discontent with organized life.

Written at a time when most historians assumed that the American experience was exceptional, Higham's essay was notable for its thoughtful examination of common trends in Western culture, but with the Americans' particular national variations foregrounded. As Higham ranged through the precincts of high and popular culture, he hoped that his synthesis would serve as a model for a type of cultural history that could unite international themes and national variations, intellectual and social history, consensus and conflict, into an organic whole.

In capturing the conflicting values at play in the 1890s, Higham's essay dramatized an emerging set of attitudes that would reverberate through the twentieth century and come especially to the fore in the cultural revolutions of the 1960s.

Those revolutions, ironically enough, shook up the enterprise of cultural history as Higham defined it. By the 1970s the attack on consensus history that Higham had helped to initiate more than a decade earlier escalated to the point of questioning any unitary description of American culture. Preoccupied with issues of class and racial strife, historians of the next generation did not heed Higham's model for an organic style of cultural history. Nevertheless, many historians working on imperialism, Progressivism, women's and men's gender history, intellectual history, sports history, and the history of music and entertainment utilized Higham's insights about the 1890s and the transition to modern life, making his essay an enormously influential one in American historiography.

Lewis A. Erenberg
Loyola University
Chicago

11

The Reorientation of American Culture in the 1890s
[1965]

Not long after World War II, Henry Steele Commager ventured an arresting hypothesis. The 1890s, Commager declared, formed the "watershed of American history."[1] His argument attracted much notice, falling in as it did with a general pedagogical tendency to conceive of recent American history as beginning about that time. Many, however, remain unconvinced. If a truly fundamental alteration in the course of things occurred around the end of the nineteenth century, on what experience did it center? No single event, such as a major war or a drastic social upheaval, offered an obvious answer. By surveying a varied and miscellaneous array of items, Commager depicted a multitude of particular transitions rather than an integral change; the decade looked more like a concourse than a watershed. In some respects it was not a decade at all. In considering intellectual movements Commager ranged across a much longer span of time and emphasized innovations in political, religious, and scientific thinking that can be located perhaps more exactly in the seventies and eighties than in the nineties.

After Commager's study appeared, the whole notion of searching out basic discontinuities in the course of American history fell for a time into some discredit. Marcus Cunliffe, for example, suggested that American historians strain to find watersheds because their own history has flowed so smoothly and continuously forward.[2] Yet history, as a coherent body of knowledge, cannot do very well without some principle of periodization that takes advantage of changes in tempo and direction. If we dispense with the metaphor of watersheds and flatten the concept of revolution, we will perforce fall back before long on such good old standbys as the turning point and the crisis. It is therefore instructive for students of American history to observe that leading authorities on European intellectual history have been discovering a major crisis or turning point at the end of the nineteenth century, and discovering it just when Americans seem most inclined to deny any comparable transformation on this side of the Atlantic.[3] If European culture was indeed undergoing an upheaval, we have here an admirable opportunity for testing the vaunted continuity of American culture. Assuming that momentous changes were occurring in Europe, how much did Americans participate in them?

The question might be formulated in different ways. It would be possible to choose certain major events or institutions of the late nineteenth century, such as the rise of imperialism or the growth of bureaucracy, and ask how Americans responded or contributed. Alternatively, one might examine in depth one or more major ideas as they emerged in a European and in an American setting, ideas such as socialism or liberalism, or the images and feelings embedded in an international art movement like Art Nouveau. A third approach is that of the cultural historian. That perspective cannot afford to exclude the other two. The cultural historian cannot ignore the substantial instruments of power that concern the institutional historian nor overlook the developed systems of thought that occupy the historian of ideas. But the cultural historian's special interest centers on the configurations of attitude and habit that connect these different levels of experience at a given point in time.

Although cultural history seeks a unifying vision, it cannot do everything. It does not lend itself very well to locating the source of change. It lacks the specificity—it does not have the narrative thrust—that enables us to follow a path of sequential activity and call it cause and effect. Cultural history also tends to sacrifice some of the delicacy and precision that distinguish the history of ideas at its best. Cultural historians' delineation of characteristic or pervasive modes of experience prevents them from doing full justice to the singular quality or complexity of any one perception of the world. On the other hand, cultural history excels in indicating the range or scope of historical phenomena. It comes into play in an effort to draw the outlines of national character or to define the spirit of an age. Its utility for coping with problems of periodization is unmatched, for historians, in order to distinguish one era from another, must either arbitrarily assign a preponderating influence of one level of experience, such as economics or foreign policy, or they must discern an underlying shift in the cultural pattern.

If such a shift got under way about the end of the nineteenth century, it was manifest then only in an emergent and formative stage. One must look for a set of attitudes that became prominent at that time but developed much more fully in the twentieth century. Phenomena unique to a particular decade can easily mislead cultural historians in search of underlying trends. The nineties were—as every student knows—an unusually troubled decade, memorable as a time of economic crisis, industrial strife, and ethnic turmoil. It would be well, however, to put aside for the moment our usual preoccupation with angry Populists and striking workers, in order to detect in the broad reaches of middle-class life less dramatic but more enduring symptoms of cultural change. There one is struck by the appearance of a temper of mind that may also illuminate the rhetoric of agrarian and proletarian unrest, if not its substance.

Our inquiry may begin on the campuses of American colleges and universities. The great reconstruction of American higher education had already occurred in the 1870s and 1880s. In the 1890s the structure of the modern university solidified. Within that structure, however, the life of the undergraduate now acquired its own glamor and took on a significance quite distinct from the official goals of the institution. The twentieth century was to put a special premium on youth, a period of life that became differentiated from the dependence of childhood on one side and from the sober responsibilities of later adulthood on the other; and it was in a college setting about the end of the nineteenth century that the model of a youth culture came into being.[4] Clark University's president, G. Stanley Hall, published in 1904 an epochal study, *Adolescence,* summing up ideas he had been formulating since the 1880s, which gave the sanction of academic psychology to a phase of life supposedly characterized by a maximum of spontaneity, freedom, and vital energy. But already the avid fans of Frank Merriwell knew something of what Hall was writing about. Invented by a pulp magazine writer in 1896, Merriwell, the carefree champion of every sport at Yale, was the first great hero of American popular culture whose exploits took place on a college playing field.[5]

In 1894 a group of Dartmouth alumni asked Richard Hovey, a young and dedicated poet, to write a new college song for his alma mater. Dartmouth's heritage of Puritan piety had faded; its rural isolation no longer seemed an asset; the school needed a fresh, up-to-date public image. This Hovey obligingly supplied in the rousingly successful "Men of Dartmouth":

> They have the still North in their hearts,
> The hill-winds in their veins,
> And the granite of New Hampshire
> In their muscles and their brains.[6]

This chilly, rockbound portrait, naive as it may sound today in its unconscious anti-intellectualism, exactly suited the emerging, collegiate spirit of the nineties. Hovey's song not only subordinated mind to muscle; it also associated both of these with the ruggedness of nature rather than the refinements of culture. In doing so, it turned the disadvantage of Dartmouth's location into an asset: it suggested to the men of Dartmouth their particular claim to the virility that college men throughout the country eagerly desired.

A rage for competitive athletics and for outdoor activities of all kinds was sweeping the campuses of the nation. A combative team spirit became virtually synonymous with college spirit; and athletic prowess became a major determinant of institutional status. Football made the greatest impact. Sedulously cultivated by Yale in the 1880s, it expanded into a big business after Walter Camp in 1889 named the first all-American team. While football dominated the autumn, older sports such as baseball and track flourished in the spring. To fill the winter gap and to arrest the flight of students from the confines of the gymnasium, a YMCA teacher invented basketball in 1891. It was taken up almost at once. Intercollegiate wrestling matches soon followed.[7] Dartmouth, following Hovey's lead, learned to feature skiing and winter carnivals.

The transformation of the colleges into theaters of organized physical combat illustrates a master impulse that seized the American people in the 1890s and reshaped their history in the ensuing decades. Theodore Roosevelt articulated that impulse in a famous speech delivered in 1899, "The Strenuous Life." Denouncing "the soft spirit of the cloistered life" and "the base spirit of gain," Roosevelt told his listeners to "boldly face the life of strife . . . for it is only through strife, through hard and dangerous endeavor, that we shall ultimately win the goal of true national greatness."[8] If these words struck the keynote of Roosevelt's own career, they also sounded the tocsin of a new era. Countless others, in their various ways, expressed similar feelings. John Jay Chapman, a leading cultural critic, flayed the tepid conformity, the pervasive desire to please, the shuffling and circumspection, the "lack of passion in the American." Even Henry James—although in most respects he was a paragon of the older culture that valued restraint—put into the mouths of his emotionally starved protagonists a choked cry for vivifying experience. "Don't forget that you're young," Strether tells little Bilham in *The Ambassadors*. "Live all you can; it's a mistake not to. It doesn't so much matter what you do in particular, so long as you have your life."[9] Common folk felt much the same way. A whole range of newly minted epithets gained currency in the 1890s: sissy, pussyfoot, cold feet, stuffed shirt.[10] All of these bespoke an impatience with the more civilized vices, the vices of gentility.

From the middle of the nineteenth century until about 1890, Americans on the whole submitted docilely enough to the gathering restrictions of a highly industrialized society. They learned to live in cities, to sit in rooms cluttered with bric-a-brac, to limit the size of their families, to accept the authority of professional elites, to mask their aggressions behind a thickening facade of respectability, and to comfort themselves with a faith in automatic material progress. Above all, Americans learned to conform to the discipline of machinery. The time clock, introduced into offices and factories in the early 1890s, signaled an advanced stage in the mechanization of life.[11]

By that time, a profound spiritual reaction was developing. It took many forms, but it was everywhere a hunger to break out of the frustrations, the routine, and the sheer dullness of an urban-industrial culture. It was everywhere an urge to be young, masculine, and adventurous. In the 1890s the new, activist mood was only beginning to challenge the restraint and decorum of the Gilded Age. Only after 1897, when the oppressive weight of a long, grim economic depression lifted, did a demand for vivid and masterful experience dominate American politics. Yet the dynamism that characterized the whole political and social scene from the turn of the century through World War I emerged during the 1890s in large areas of popular culture. To some of these areas historians have not yet paid enough attention to appreciate the extent and nature of the change that was occurring. We are well aware of the aggressive nationalism that sprang up after 1890. We do not so often notice analogous ferment in other spheres: a boom in sports and recreation; a revitalized interest in untamed nature; a quickening of popular music; an unsettling of the condition of women.

The sports revolution in the colleges was part of a much broader upsurge of enthusiasm for outdoor recreation and physical culture in the American public. The growing zest for both spectator and participant sports amazed contemporary observers in the early nineties. The most universal sport was bicycling, one of the great crazes of the decade. Primarily social and recreational rather than a means of necessary transportation, bicycles reached a total of one million in 1893, ten million in 1900. Bicycle clubs and championship races excited enormous interest. Among games, baseball retained its primacy at both the professional and sandlot levels.[12] It did not, however, enjoy the sensational growth of other sports that catered more directly to a taste for speed or a taste for violence. Racing of various kinds, to say nothing of basketball, satisfied one taste; football and boxing fulfilled the other. Only boxing, among the spectacles of the nineties, grew as rapidly as football in public appeal. Most states of the Union still outlawed professional prizefighting as a relic of barbarism. Nevertheless, it began to lose its unsavory reputation after 1892, when padded gloves replaced bare fists and "Gentleman Jim" Corbett displayed an artful technique in defeating John L. Sullivan.[13] Henceforth heavyweight champions loomed large among American folk heroes.

An accompanying gospel of health through rugged exercise spread literally by leaps and bounds. Of the many shamans who arose to lead the cult, Bernarr Macfadden was the most successful. His career began at the World's Fair in Chicago in 1893, where he demonstrated the muscular attractions of an exerciser. He advanced through health clubs and lectures and won a national audience as publisher of the magazine *Physical Culture*. The first issue, appearing in 1899, flaunted his slogan: "Weakness Is a Crime."[14]

Closely linked with the boom in sports and health came an enthusiasm for the tonic freshness and openness of nature. This, too, had both a participant and a spectatorial aspect. At its mildest, participation meant escaping to the country astride a bicycle, taking up the newly imported game of golf, or going to the innumerable vacation resorts that emphasized their outdoor facilities. Somewhat more strenuously, it meant hiking and camping. In 1889 nature lovers launched a campaign on behalf of California's redwood forests, and the following year Congress created Yosemite, Sequoia, and General Grant National Parks. Here was the beginning of a sustained movement to preserve the American wilderness from the encroachments of civilization. During the ensuing decade hundreds of nature-study clubs formed to encourage amateur naturalists. At least fifty-two periodicals devoted to wildlife began publication.[15] In fact, the flood of nature writing, based on intimate knowledge and vivid observation, registered a major shift in popular interests. Only the leading novelists exceeded the popularity of some of the nature writers, such as John Muir and Ernest Thompson Seton, whose first books appeared in 1894 and 1898, respectively.[16]

Although the outdoor movement clearly drew upon a traditional American distrust of the city, it also ministered to the more general psychological discontents of the 1890s. Among the values that middle-class Americans were rediscovering in nature, two stand out. For one, the great outdoors signified spaciousness—an imaginative release from the institutional restraints and confinements that Americans had accepted since the Civil War. It is suggestive that one of the features of the return to nature was a passion for bird-watching. In a six-year period New York and Boston publishers sold more than seventy thousand textbooks on birds, while a children's magazine, *Birds*, reached a circulation of forty thousand in its first year of publication.[17] Congress had chosen a great soaring bird as the national emblem over a century before, and a bird on the wing continued to symbolize for Americans the boundless space they wished to inhabit.

Second, nature meant—as Hovey's description of Dartmouth men indicated—virility. It represented that masculine hardiness and power that suddenly seemed an absolutely indispensable remedy for the artificiality and effeteness of late nineteenth-century urban life. Nothing revealed the craving for nature's untamed strength so well as the best-selling fiction of the late nineties. For decades the popular novel had concentrated on domestic or rococo subjects rather than wilderness adventures. Above the level of the dime novel, the Wild West had played very little part in fiction since the 1850s. Now it came back with a rush in a best-selling Canadian thriller, Ralph Connor's *Black Rock* (1898), in Jack London's red-blooded stories of the Klondike, and in Owen Wister's classic cowboy tale, *The Virginian* (1902). In effect, these and other writers were answering James Lane Allen's plea of 1897 for a reassertion of the masculine principle of virility and instinctive action in a literature too much dominated by the feminine principle of refinement and delicacy.[18]

A similarly muscular spirit invaded popular verse and music. The conventional style of song in the late nineteenth century was mournful and nostalgic. It projected a life heavy with disappointment and regrets, a life girt with limitations, a life drenched in tears. The fascination with death in such poems as Eugene Field's "Little Boy Blue" and with parting in such hit tunes as "After the Ball" betrayed a loss of youthfulness in American popular culture. Against this drowsy mood, a new generation of high-spirited poets and musicians affirmed Allen's masculine principle. Richard

Hovey won a great popular success as coauthor of *Songs from Vagabondia* (1894), which perfectly expressed the fresh out-of-doors spirit. Like no poems since Whitman's, these combined the love of nature, the freedom of the open road, the rollicking comradeship of men, and the tang of vivid experience.[19]

Meanwhile, cheerful energetic tunes spread from the midways and outdoor amusement parks that were themselves symptoms of a new era. "Ta-ra-ra-boom-der-e," first published in 1891, struck a new, rhythmically vital note. Thereafter itinerant black pianists taught the white public the excitement of ragtime, a form of syncopation applied against a steady bass rhythm. A high-kicking dance step called the cakewalk spread along with the ragtime craze. In vain, custodians of white respectability denounced this "nigger music" and the "vulgar," "filthy" prancing that went with it.[20]

Both the new music and the new athleticism were connected with the emergence of the New Woman. Her salient traits were boldness and radiant vigor. She shed the Victorian languor that had turned American middle-class society—as William Dean Howells noted in 1872—into a hospital for invalid females. Women took to the open road in tremendous numbers on bicycles suitably altered by an American inventor. They sat for portraits clutching tennis rackets; they might be seen at the new golf clubs or at the race tracks smoking cigarettes. In 1901 they could learn from Bernarr Macfadden's book, *The Power and Beauty of Superb Womanhood,* that vigorous exercise "will enable a woman to develop in every instance muscular strength almost to an equal degree with man."[21]

> Running, jumping, and natation, navigation, ambulation—
> So she seeks for recreation in a whirl.
> She's a highly energetic, undissuadable, magnetic,
> Peripatetic, athletic kind of girl![22]

The New Woman was "masculine" also in her demand for political power. The women's suffrage movement had been crotchety and unpopular; now it blossomed into a great nationwide middle-class force.[23]

While women became more "manly," men became more martial. By 1890 the sorrow and weariness left by the Civil War had passed; jingoism and a deliberate cultivation of military values ensued. The United States picked quarrels with Italy, Chile, and Great Britain before it found a satisfactory target in the liberation of Cuba. A steady buildup of naval power accompanied these crises. The rising respect for military prowess also manifested itself in a remarkable cult of Napoleon. The first two installments of

Ida Tarbell's biography of Napoleon in *McClure's Magazine* doubled its paid circulation; and hers was only one of twenty-eight books about the Corsican general published in the United States in the three years from 1894 to 1896. For a collective symbol of the strenuous life, mythmakers depended heavily on the Anglo-Saxon "race," which they endowed with unprecedented ferocity. A Kansas senator, for example, proudly described his "race" as "the most arrogant and rapacious, the most exclusive and indomitable in history."[24]

Meanwhile, flag ceremonies, such as the newly contrived Pledge of Allegiance, entered the schoolhouses of the land. Patriotic societies multiplied as never before. In function they resembled the cheerleaders who were becoming so prominent a part of the big football spectacles and who lifted the massed ranks of students into collective glory. The link between the new athleticism and the new jingoism was especially evident in the yellow press: William Randolph Hearst's *New York Journal* created the modern sports page in 1896, just when its front page filled with atrocity stories of the bloody debauchery of Spanish brutes in Cuba.[25] At the same time the new music produced such martial airs as John Philip Sousa's masterpiece of patriotic fervor, "Stars and Stripes Forever" (1897), and "A Hot Time in the Old Town" (1896), which Theodore Roosevelt adopted as the official song of his Rough Riders. Indeed, Roosevelt was the outstanding fugleman of the whole gladiatorial spirit. He loved the great outdoors, the challenge of sports, the zest of political combat, the danger of war. He exhorted women to greater fecundity. He brought boxing into the White House and contributed immensely to its respectability.[26]

The change in temper that I have been describing did not occur in the United States alone. It swept over much of western Europe about the same time. Its most obvious manifestations appeared in the navalism and jingoism of the time: the various national defense societies, the Pan-German League, the bombast of William II, the sensational journalism of the Harmsworth brothers, the emotions that swirled around General Boulanger and Captain Dreyfus. Europe was more receptive than America to the militaristic aspects of the new mood. Two Englishmen, H. Rider Haggard and Rudyard Kipling, popularized the martial and masculine adventure story before respectable American authors turned to that genre; and the Americans did not insist, as did Kipling and the German youth movement, on the values of discipline and obedience. In other respects, however, America may have some claim to priority and leadership. The outdoors movement may have started in America, although England and Germany

were not far behind.[27] The New Woman, together with her bicycle, materialized in England and in America about the same time. Demands for a
freer sexual morality got an earlier hearing in England, but the achievement
of political rights and economic independence came more easily in this
country than anywhere in Europe. The very phrase "New Woman" may
have originated in the talk of an American character in an English novel that
had its greatest success in the United States. Sarah Grand's *The Heavenly
Twins*, published in 1893, expounded feminist ideas in a glamorous setting
and sold five times as many copies in America as in England.[28]

In the sports revival, which also affected both continents, Americans
seized a commanding lead. No people except the British loved athletic
contests so much; and the Americans clearly excelled in ferocity. They won
most of the events in the early Olympic Games, nine out of fourteen at
Athens in 1896 and fourteen out of twenty at Paris in 1900. They racked up
a disproportionate number of "world records."[29] They so dominated professional boxing that the championship of the United States became, from
1892 onward, identical with that of the world. A French observer, bemused
by the American taste for pugilism, concluded that it was "too brutal a sight
for a Frenchman of the nineteenth century."[30]

On the other hand, Europeans found the energy of American music
much to their liking. "Ta-ra-ra-boom-der-e" spread through Britain and
beyond like an epidemic. "No other song ever took a people in quite the
same way," an English historian tells us. "It would seem to have been the
absurd *ça ira* of a generation bent upon kicking over the traces."[31] Translated into French as "Tha-mara-buom-di-hé," the song proved a great hit in
the leading Parisian cabarets. Across the Atlantic went the cakewalk, too,
dazzling audiences in the music halls of London and Paris, and Sousa's
band, giving Europe its first taste of ragtime.[32] The taste suited. In 1908,
Claude Debussy used this American idiom for *The Golliwog's Cakewalk*.
Altogether, the United States exercised initiative only within some aspects
of the burgeoning activism of the 1890s. Nevertheless, American influences were widely felt. Europeans who feared the threat that the new spirit
posed to traditional values sometimes called it Americanism.[33]

To say that Americans took part in a far-reaching reaction against the
constrictions of a routinized society does not explain why the reaction
occurred. Historians have no satisfactory answer to such large problems.
Recognition that we are dealing with an international movement—with a
change of phase evident throughout the Western world—makes quixotic

any effort to explain the change in its American context alone. Yet the mentality I have been describing did have undeniable American roots. Not wholly new, it was to some extent the reawakening of a spirit present in American life virtually from the beginning. Since the Antinomian outbreak that Anne Hutchinson led in 1636, an exuberant libertarian aggressiveness, impatient of restraint and tradition, had ebbed and flowed in America. It reached a crest in the transcendental ecstasies of Emerson, Garrison, and Whitman and was then submerged during the Civil War and the decades that followed.

Some evidence for suspecting that the strenuous life in the late nineteenth century was partly a revival of buried impulses emerges in its rhetoric. Apostles of strenuosity repeatedly lamented the excessive refinement and the enervating tendencies of modern civilization; they saw themselves as revitalizing primitive virtues. Sports enthusiasts declared that "this vaunted age" needed "a saving touch of honest, old-fashioned barbarism, that when we come to die, we shall die leaving men behind us, and not a race of eminently respectable female saints."[34] Imperialists warned of the exhaustion that might overtake an effete society, confined within fixed geographical limits; they called for a resumption of the vigorous outward push of the frontier. The chief ideologists for the New Woman harked back to a primitive era of strong females, before men enslaved them in the home.[35] In many such instances the activists' rhetoric affirmed a continuity with an older, premodern culture.

It is possible to locate the social sources of the continuity to some extent. The new élan of the nineties sought particularly to loosen the constraints and conformities binding urban, middle-class life. This activism had a base in other groups who had never submitted completely to Victorian gentility because they were outside its range. Activists were impatient with what one of them described as "the bourgeois spirit [of] that element which dares not use slang, shrinks from audacity, rarely utters a bold sentiment and as rarely feels one. It is as correct as Sunday clothes and as innocuous as sterilized milk, *but it is not aristocratic.*"[36] Nor was it plebeian. The strenuous life invoked values that had persisted both above and below the great American middle class. Each of the manifestations of the new activism that I have described thus far was already a part of patrician experience on the one hand and of the life of the poor on the other.

Consider, for instance, the sports revolution and the accompanying return to nature. Rough outdoor sports were habitual pleasures of rural gentry and small-town loafers before they became respectable in the cities. Bloody, bare-knuckle prizefighting gladdened the hearts of miners, saloon keepers, and their rowdy patrons throughout the decades of civic opprobrium, while the "science of boxing" according to the Queensberry rules first took hold in elite athletic clubs. Baseball too was initially played by gentlemen's clubs, like the Knickerbockers in New York; football originated as an Ivy League sport.[37] The open spaces of the West always appealed, of course, to the pioneer type. Moreover, the western adventure story enjoyed a continuous vogue among the uncultivated readers of the dime novel during the era when respectable publishers concentrated on the idylls of domesticity.

Other strands in the activism of the nineties also combined patrician with plebeian lifestyles and brought them to bear on middle-class culture. The novelty of the New Woman was in part her middle-class status. The daughters of the poor had never been immobilized within a strictly domestic existence, and such patrician ladies as Josephine Shaw Lowell and Julia Ward Howe had enjoyed a wide sphere of authority during the post–Civil War decades. Ragtime music evolved from the vigorous folk melodies of the black peasantry of the Deep South; and among its early supporters were society leaders in Chicago, New York, and Newport.[38] Finally, the belligerent nationalism of the nineties can be traced back to a persistent jingoism among the underprivileged masses, aided by an imperialist elite. Both groups despised the timidity of what Roosevelt called the moneyed and semi-cultivated classes.[39] In short, the new vitality may be understood as an infusion of lower-class and upper-class aggressiveness into the middle-class world.

Still, it was in some sense a new phase in American cultural history that was coming into being, not a mere revival of pre-Victorian values. Even as a movement of revitalization, the activism of the nineties received from its context a character very different from the early American ebullience. *That* had flowered in a time when many traditional institutions were losing authority; the outward reach into open space was a common fact as well as an ideal. *This* was occurring within the confines of an increasingly organized society.[40] The steady growth of rational structures, making for an ever more integrated, impersonal way of life, was irreversible. The new activism could do little more than reform those structures or cultivate the life of impulse within them. Consequently, the emergent culture of the Strenuous Age had an ambiguous relation to its institutional matrix. In some measure a rebellion against the constraints of a highly organized society, it was also an accommodation to those constraints, a way of coming to terms with them.

The degree of innovation that a cultural change releases appears more clearly if we look not just at the thrust of mass movements but also at what the most creative minds were doing. It remains, therefore, to ask if American intellectuals underwent an awakening comparable to the upheaval in popular feelings. How much were intellectuals involved in the psychic turbulence of the 1890s? The Americans did not unleash as direct an assault on genteel culture as some of their European contemporaries mounted. Yet a change of mood among intellectuals on both continents paralleled the shift in middle-class attitudes.

The reorientation among intellectuals followed upon the dominion that a materialistic outlook had won during the immediately preceding decades. From the 1860s through the 1880s, in Europe and America alike, the combined prestige of science and business enterprise shaped the direction of thought. During these years romantic idealism declined. So did religious vitality in the face of a sweeping secularization of values. Ornateness and a certain heaviness of style prevailed. All encompassing, monistic systems of thought were in favor: Spencerian and Hegelian systems contended in America; Comtean positivism and Marxian socialism loomed large in Europe. A triumphant belief in evolutionary progress, although much stronger in America than in Europe, everywhere blunted moral sensitivity.

By 1890 this vesture of assurance and complacency was wearing through. It failed to cover the emotional and material needs of the laboring classes; it did not entirely smother the conscience of the middle class; and it was too tight a fit for many intellectuals. For the last, the cult of progress, stability, and materialism was becoming oppressive and suffocating. It brought restraint and uniformity into the world of thought without resolving the increasing conflicts in society.

The first response of intellectuals to the obvious social dislocations of an urban, industrial age was an attempt to strengthen the framework of order and to reinterpret the path of progress. The equipment of liberalism with a collective social ethic constituted the principal achievement of social thought both in England and in America in the 1880s—a work accomplished in one by Thomas Hill Green and the Fabians, and in the other by Henry George, Lester F. Ward, William Dean Howells, and a variety of historical economists. But these ideas made only modest headway in the following decade, while the problems they addressed grew much more acute. The special significance of the 1890s lay in a change of mood that swept many intellectuals beyond the earnest sobriety of the seventies and eighties. A readjustment of rational principles in the light of existing facts seemed in itself ineffective and uninteresting.

Two other strategies were possible; and the clash between them pervaded intellectual life. One might, in contempt or despair, spurn the trust in progress and find solace in contemplating the decline of a moribund civilization. Or one might look beyond the conventional framework of thought for access to fresh sources of energy. The first alternative was the counsel of defeat; the second was a call to liberation. One way led to pessimism, decadence, and withdrawal into art for art's sake. The other pointed to a heightened activity and an exuberant sense of power. Both alternatives broke sharply with the complacent faith in material progress and human rationality that had ruled the Western world for two generations. Both the pessimists and the activists of the 1890s felt that the rational schemata of their time had become closed systems, imprisoning the human spirit. Pessimists accepted the denial of responsibility and purpose. Activists, on the other hand, attacked closed systems and created meanings from the flux of experience.

The acid of defeat and the elixir of liberation mingled in the intellectual ferment of the decade. A good many Americans as well as Europeans tasted both, with lasting effect. In general, however, one may say that the elixir proved an effective antidote to the acid. The strenuous spirit so prominent in popular culture quite generally overcame a defeatist spirit among intellectuals. The melancholy of the fin de siècle belied its name: it lifted before the end of the century.

This was especially the case in the United States, where a pessimistic outlook had only recently taken root in a serious way. Worldly pessimism had composed an important strain in European thought since the Enlightenment. Americans, however, had derived their sense of evil from the bracing doctrines of Calvinism, and they encountered the world determined to resist it. Neither the terrors of personal frustration as in Poe nor the transcendental doubts of Melville had resulted in a pessimistic philosophy of life. The emergence of such an outlook was therefore a milestone in American intellectual history.

The melancholy and the ennui that invaded certain fastidious American minds in the late eighties and early nineties bore the direct imprint of European decadence. Schopenhauer together with Spinoza and Lucretius provided the basic philosophical structure for most of the poetry that George Santayana wrote in the nineties. Leopardi, Swinburne, and the English aesthetes supplied additional models for the circle of Harvard poets that formed around Santayana in those years. In New York, Edgar Saltus, who also began from Schopenhauer, published delicately scandalous novels resembling those of Oscar Wilde in their knowing insolence and perverse wit. Others were reading Ernest Renan appreciatively. Renan instructed Henry Adams in the artistic uses of a spiritually exhausted religion as Adams drifted from the South Seas to the cathedrals of France.[41] The same lesson reached a wide public through Harold Frederic's bestselling novel, *The Damnation of Theron Ware* (1896). Here an ultracivilized, skeptical Catholic priest reveals to a simpleminded Methodist clergyman the world-weary elegance of a religion of art. "The truth is always relative, Mr. Ware," Father Forbes concludes.[42]

Other writers, untouched by European aestheticism, arrived at a grimmer sort of pessimism. There was, for example, the savage irony of the San Francisco journalist Ambrose Bierce, whose first book of short stories, *Tales of Soldiers and Civilians* (1891), depicted a pointless, mocking destiny. There was Henry Adams's brother, Brooks, whose *Law of Civilization and Decay* (1895) diagnosed the decline of Western civilization since the defeat of Napoleon and warned of its impending dissolution. This powerful, serious book was perhaps the first modern formulation of a cyclical theory of history. It was certainly the first full-length American critique of the conception of history as progress. More informally, Mark Twain was reaching the same conclusion. His laughter turned increasingly into bitterness; visions of destruction welled up at the end of *A Connecticut Yankee in King Arthur's Court* (1889), and by the late nineties an explicit fatalism convinced Twain that history was an endless cycle of cruelty and corruption, "a barren and meaningless process."[43] E. L. Godkin, too, was giving up hope for the future of American civilization. The toughest minded of all of the nation's social philosophers, William Graham Sumner, was warning his compatriots that the utmost they could do was "to note and record their course as they are carried along" in the great stream of time.[44]

Such attitudes exemplified the naturalistic determinism that originated with Darwin and Spencer and became increasingly oppressive as the century waned. Until the 1890s American intellectuals had tempered the naturalistic creed with a supreme confidence in their own destiny. In Europe evolutionary thought slipped more easily into a dark vision of a blind and purposeless universe. Thus the naturalistic novel, in which the human being appears as the hapless plaything of great impersonal forces, was well established in France and England before Stephen Crane in 1893 published *Maggie*, the first American example of the genre. Pessimism seems to have invaded American minds only after the actual course of social change clearly refuted the liberating significance that Americans had imputed to the evolutionary process. By 1890 the consolidation of big organizations, the massing of population, and the growing intensity of class conflict were inescapably apparent. These trends did not at all correspond to the individualizing movement that Herbert Spencer had confidently envisioned. Instead of an inevitable development from an "incoherent homogeneity to a definite, coherent heterogeneity," Brooks Adams observed a steady centralization and a loss of vital energy, which would result in anarchy. Henry Adams refined the theory into one of a general degradation and dispersion of energy.[45] Many felt an erosion of their own independent station in society. Clearly, the survival of the fittest was not synonymous, as Darwinians had formerly supposed, with the survival of the best. Nor did the course of events conform to the ancient belief in America's uniqueness, confidence in which had always provided an ultimate bulwark of the national faith in progress. "We are the first Americans," Woodrow Wilson gravely warned, "to entertain any serious doubts about the superiority of our own institutions as compared with the systems of Europe."[46]

A signal indication of the intensity of concern over these defeatist attitudes was the feverish discussion provoked by Max Nordau's book *Degeneration*. I believe that no other European book of any kind published during the entire decade aroused so much comment in the American press. Even before its translation into English in 1895, the book received a long review in the *Critic*.[47] Soon the Sunday supplements and the daily papers were trumpeting its charges. Much of this attention resulted from the sheer sensationalism of Nordau's argument that the eminent artists and writers of the day were suffering from mental deterioration. Many, perhaps most, commentators regarded Nordau as at least as degenerate as the people he attacked. But his fundamental charge that the age was suffering from "a compound of feverish restlessness and blunted discouragement, of . . . vague qualms of a Dusk of Nations," touched a sensitive nerve.

When all this is said, the fact remains that pessimism became in America neither general nor profound. Sourness and irony Americans could sometimes stomach; they had little taste for despair. Even Henry Adams never ceased to struggle against despair, and Santayana transmuted it into a flawless serenity. Most American intellectuals resisted pessimism. Philosophers (with the partial exception of Santayana) rallied against it; literary critics denounced it; social scientists were challenged rather than overcome by it. Accordingly, the voices of negation rose from rather special quarters: from people who were being left behind. The most somber temperaments belonged, on the one hand, to old men like Twain and Sumner, who had fought the good fight through the seventies and eighties and who now lost heart; or they belonged, on the other hand, to men of patrician background like Adams, Saltus, and the Harvard poets, scions of old and cultivated families who felt displaced in a pushing, competitive, bourgeois world.

The naturalistic novelists cannot be included among either the old men or the patricians. They were young, and they came from middle-class homes. But it requires no close inspection to discover that Norris, Crane, London, and even Dreiser were only partly fatalistic. Unlike many European naturalists, they expressed the affirmative as well as the negative possibilities of their age. The American naturalists gloried in identifying themselves with the triumphant strength of nature or with the struggles of embattled man. Instead of observing life clinically, they celebrated power. "The world," intoned Frank Norris, "wants men, great, strong, harsh, brutal men—men with purpose who let nothing, nothing, nothing stand in their way."[48] Dreiser and London shared Norris's fascination with the ruthless pursuit of success. Crane spent his volatile life imagining and seeking war. Here, as Van Wyck Brooks has pointed out, began the cave-man tendency in modern American literature.[49] In the fierce joy of conflict these writers discovered the activist reply to the specter of an indifferent universe.

No one better reveals the instability of the pessimism of the nineties than its most systematic exponent, Brooks Adams. Younger and less cosmopolitan than his brother Henry, who remained generally defeatist, Brooks underwent a great conversion around 1898. He decided that the Spanish-American War disproved his theory of history. Evidently centralization was leading not to a degradation but to a revival of national energy. Only Europe, not America, is decaying, Brooks chortled. "I am for the new world— the new America, the new empire . . . we are the people of destiny."[50] And he became henceforth an activist, who bombarded his fellow countrymen with advice on geopolitical strategy and public administration.

Thus Brooks Adams illustrates two of the spheres in which the strenuous life came to intellectual fruition. The escape from pessimism flung him into reform as well as imperialism. Since imperialism proved after a short while an unattractive outlet for American effort, his attention turned increasingly in the early twentieth century to the uses of power in domestic affairs. This happened to a great many American intellectuals. We know that imperialism and Progressivism were closely related crusades, and it seems clear that together they largely banished gloom and anxiety in favor of an optimistic, adventurous engagement in social change.[51] The activism of the nineties contributed, therefore, to the hearty interest that progressive intellectuals showed in *doing* things, in closing with immediate practical realities, in concentrating on techniques rather than sweeping theories. The early twentieth century was not a very congenial period in America for the speculative thinker with interests remote from the facts of contemporary life. It was a time of administrative energy and functional thought.

Must we then conclude that the new activism was generally antiintellectual and had little constructive impact on other areas of thought, beyond concrete social issues? Were its positive achievements only visceral and practical? Or did the shattering of closed systems and the relief of pessimism also enlarge the imaginative resources of American intellectuals? These questions do not admit of any final answer. But a brief comparison of three major intellectuals who participated in the cultural reorientation of the 1890s may suggest how stimulating it could be in very diverse fields.[52]

William James was neither the first of the American pragmatists nor in every respect the greatest, but he was surely the most passionately concerned with emancipating his fellow human beings from tradition, apathy, and routine. His predecessor Charles S. Peirce was preoccupied with traditional metaphysical and logical problems; his successor John Dewey with gaining rational control of experience. James, standing between them, was the arch foe of all intellectual systems, less concerned with organizing thought or experience than with validating their manifold possibilities. Although each of the major pragmatists took part in the intellectual life of the 1890s, James belongs to that decade in a very special sense. Having anticipated much earlier its revolt against pessimism and fatalism, James applied himself intensively to its spiritual needs. His *Principles of Psychology* came out in 1890. Thereafter he grew beyond his first career as a psychologist, greatly enlarged his interests and sympathies, and launched pragmatism as a broad philosophical movement.

For James the nineties were years of fulfillment and fame. For two young men born in the 1860s—Frederick Jackson Turner and Frank Lloyd Wright—this was the crucially formative period, when the emancipation that James preached was taking effect. Turner received his Ph.D. at Johns Hopkins in 1890 and returned to Wisconsin to work out his own ideas about American history. In the next few years all of his major ideas emerged. The famous address of 1893 on the significance of the frontier announced his revolt against the eastern, European-oriented view of American history that then prevailed. In other work of the mid-nineties, Turner inaugurated a broadly economic interpretation of American history in terms of sectional cleavages.[53] Wright, a budding Chicago architect, also declared independence in 1893 by quitting his beloved master, Louis Sullivan, and opening his own office. During the course of the decade Wright developed his own personal, flexible style in opposition both to Sullivan's sentimentality and to the conventions of the European architectural tradition. Unknown to one another, James, Turner, and Wright were the great leavening and liberating figures in their respective disciplines at the turn of the century.

None of them engaged in the crude, swaggering bombast so prevalent in the popular activism of the period. Indeed, James roundly attacked people like Theodore Roosevelt who were arousing "the aboriginal capacity for murderous excitement which lies sleeping" in every bosom, and he once coolly remarked of his friend Oliver Wendell Holmes, Jr., that "Mere excitement is an immature ideal, unworthy of the Supreme Court's official endorsement."[54] Nevertheless, James, Turner, and Wright were in their own ways hardy, fighting men, full of zest for new experience, in love with novelty and experiment, eager to adapt philosophy, architecture, and history to the ever-changing needs of the present hour. James himself struck the distinctive note of the 1890s by interpreting all ideas as plans for action and by exalting the will.

All three men possessed exuberant, optimistic, restless personalities. Their brimming energies threatened continually to overflow any imposed discipline, so much so in the cases of James and Turner that neither succeeded in finishing the big, systematic book he wished to write. Neither in his intellectual habits was at all methodical. "Turner bubbled it out," one of his students remembers,[55] and the same could equally have been said of James. Wright had the strongest personality of the three. He ran away from home, scorned all formal education, and built within himself an oracular self-confidence touched with arrogance.[56] Only Wright wore his hair long to flaunt his independence, but James and Turner also enjoyed a poetic flair and a lilting heart.

Intellectually, their deepest affinity arose from a common opposition to all closed and static patterns of order. James's repugnance for a "block universe" is well known. "All 'classic,' clean, cut and dried, 'noble,' fixed, 'eternal' *Weltanschauungen* seem to me to violate the character with which life concretely comes and the expression which it bears of being, or at least involving, a muddle and a struggle."[57] This resembles Wright's hatred of the stiff classical and Renaissance traditions in architecture. A dynamic flow— an image of continual becoming—pervades Wright's buildings, and runs equally through James's philosophy. Similarly, Turner's history spoke always of people on the move, venturing westward, breaking the cake of custom, ever engaged in struggle and contradiction. Turner rebelled against the dominant mode of historical scholarship, which emphasized the stability and continuity embodied in the formal structure of institutions. He presented history not as a logical unfolding of constitutions but as a continual flux of experience. In breaking up American history into a balanced interplay of opposing sections,[58] Turner accomplished what James's pluralism achieved in philosophy and what Wright's juxtaposition of advancing and receding planes realized in architecture.

The revolt of these men against intellectual rigidities closely paralleled the assault in popular culture on a confined and circumscribed life. It is hardly a coincidence that Turner and Theodore Roosevelt made the frontiersman the heroic figure in American history just at the time when he was becoming the hero of best-selling novels. Nor is it happenstance that Wright did away with interior doors and widened windows just at the time when Edward Bok, editor of the *Ladies' Home Journal*, launched spectacularly successful campaigns to clear out the clutter from parlors and the ugly litter from cities.[59] Like so many other Americans, James, Turner, and Wright were reaching out into the open air.

All three quite literally and passionately loved the out-of-doors. James and Turner were never so happy as when they were camping in the wilderness, and Wright felt as keenly as they the moral strength to be derived from the earth. His prairie houses, stretching outward to embrace the land, attest his fidelity to his mother's injunction, "Keep close to the earth, boy: in that lies strength."[60] For each of these men, nature signified not just power but also the freedom of open space. By explaining American democracy as the product of "free land," Turner extracted a dimension of freedom from the realm of necessity; and this is what Wright did in constructing "the new reality that is *space* instead of matter."[61] Meanwhile, in philosophy, James argued against a restrictive materialism by emphasizing the incompleteness of visible nature and by calling attention to those natural facts of religious experience that suggest a vaster realm of spiritual freedom.[62] In a sense, he, too, converted matter into space.

In part, the open-air activists of the nineties were harking back to the old American values affirmed by Walt Whitman, the poet who most rapturously identified himself with boundless space.[63] Wright adored Whitman. Turner quoted him. James, the most discriminating of the three, put his finger exactly on Whitman's spaciousness: "Walt Whitman owes his importance in literature to the systematic expulsion from his writings of all contractile elements. The only sentiments he allowed himself to express were of the expansive order; and he expressed these in the first person, not as your mere monstrously conceived individual might so express them, but vicariously for all men, so that a passionate and mystic ontological emotion suffuses his words."[64]

Appropriately, Whitman's reputation was just then emerging powerfully from the distrustful and evasive gentility that had obscured it earlier. His flowing lines supplied the largeness and virility that more and more Americans wanted in order to overcome the contractile elements in late nineteenth-century culture. A biography of Whitman published in 1896 by the influential nature writer John Burroughs made this appeal explicit:

> Did one begin to see evil omen in this perpetual whittling away and sharpening and lightening of the American type,—grace without power, clearness without mass, intellect without character,—then take comfort from the volume and the rankness of Walt Whitman. Did one begin to fear that the decay of maternity and paternity in our older communities and the falling off in the native population presaged the drying up of the race in its very sources? Then welcome to the rank sexuality and to the athletic fatherhood and motherhood celebrated by Whitman. Did our skepticism, our headiness, our worldliness, threaten to eat us up like cancer? Did our hardness, our irreligiousness, and our passion for the genteel point to a fugitive, superficial race? Was our literature threatened with the artistic degeneration—running all to art and not at all to power? Were our communities invaded by a dry rot of culture? Were we fast becoming a delicate, indoor genteel race? Were our women sinking deeper and deeper into the

"incredible sloughs of fashion and all kinds of dyspeptic depletion,"—the antidote for all these ills is in Walt Whitman.[65]

Evidently the new appreciation of Whitman, the antiformalism of James, Wright, and Turner, and the various popular displays of a quasi-primitive vitality arose from a common antipathy toward confinement in life and thought. Evidently also this reaction sprang to a considerable extent from indigenous sources. In fact, the new activism was accompanied by a revulsion against European cultural leadership, and the principal innovators were markedly anti-European in their social and moral attitudes. As a young man, Wright refused a splendid opportunity to study architecture in Europe, all expenses paid. He felt, when he did so, that he was "only keeping faith" with America. James, oppressed by the weight of the past world in Europe, returned to the less tradition-laden atmosphere of Harvard, exclaiming, "Better fifty years of Cambridge than a cycle of Cathay."[66] Turner, who conceived of American history as a movement away from Europe, gave our past so native a hue that his successors for half a century treated it as a largely endogenous phenomenon. All of these men associated Europe with the constraint and decrepitude they abhorred. All of them associated America with the freshness and openness they sought to revive.

Nevertheless, their discontents paralleled a similar ferment in European thought and feeling, as we have already noticed in respect to popular culture. In Europe as well as America the balance shifted from a constricting pessimism to a regenerative activism. There, too, the change may be described broadly as a reaction against the stifling atmosphere of bourgeois materialism. Yet the strategy of the rebellion in European high culture had certain distinctive characteristics that may help us to understand the American experience.

A short way of putting the matter is to say that cultural discontent among European intellectuals was more drastic.[67] American intellectuals did not—any more than the American painters of the day—go in for strong colors. One cannot imagine among them a Vincent Van Gogh or a Georges Sorel. Hardly anyone in America directly and belligerently assailed conventional standards of morality. American intellectuals did not, like so many Europeans, feel profoundly alienated from their own society and culture. James, Turner, and Wright conceived of themselves as revitalizing values rooted in American life. Feeling that great reserves of energy lay all around them, they did not look so far afield as those Europeans who turned to primitive myth or to the international proletariat. Nor did they look so far beneath the surface as those Europeans who plunged into the depths of the private self.

Nothing seems more striking in comparative terms than the relative absence in the United States of the radical subjectivity that was entering European thought. In European literature the symbolists were creating an art of equivocality, distortion, and illusion. In philosophy Bergsonian irrationalism and the Nietzschean celebration of the Dionysian ego were beginning to be heard. In psychology Freud was probing the strange world of dreams. In history the leading German theoreticians were declaring their independence from scientific laws and insisting on the subjective basis of historical knowledge. In all these fields, European intellectuals were rending the fabric of external reality and discovering truth in the depths of subjective, personal experience. In America, William James, the most precocious and in some ways the most European of our intellectual leaders, was moving in the same direction. For the most part, however, on this side of the Atlantic literature remained realistic, philosophy empirical, psychology behavioral, history scientific. Yet on both continents intellectuals were seeking liberation from closed systems and formalistic abstractions.

The difference may be explained in terms of contrasting environments. America was a big country with a relatively fluid rather than a relatively stable society. In spite of the tightening mesh of institutions, America still offered elbowroom, physically and sociologically. Here restless intellectuals reached outward to the range, flux, and diversity of life around them. In Europe they were more likely to reach inward to the intense and often mystical feelings within themselves. Americans rebelled by extending the breadth of experience, Europeans by plumbing its depths. For Americans liberation meant variety, maneuverability, multiplication of the individual's relationships with the world. Accordingly, James—connoisseur though he was of the "sick soul"—stayed healthy by celebrating multiplicity and constructing an essentially eclectic philosophy. Turner widened the breadth of history in order to interrelate political, social, economic, and geographical changes. Wright swept away confining walls and opened up fluid space.

Unready for the heightened subjectivity of European thought, American intellectuals did not engage in the accompanying criticism of scientific ideas. In Europe objective reality lost some of its authority. Americans, however, resisted sharp segregation between various levels and types of thought: between facts and values, intellect and intuition, the scientific and the supra-scientific. "Something there is that doesn't love a wall,"

an American poet declared some years later; and the chief American philosophers—James, Dewey, and Peirce—wanted to do away with walls separating subjective values from objective facts. For Americans the external
world retained a promise of ultimate goodness and harmony.

Consequently, the broad and various reaches of nature symbolized for
the expansive Americans of the 1890s both the vitality they sought and a
spacious alternative to the European self-consciousness they shunned. A
genteel literary critic of the 1890s, Hamilton Wright Mabie, offers us a
final summation of the intellectual strategy that—for better or worse—
prevailed:

> nothing breeds doubt and despair so quickly as a constant and feverish self-
> consciousness, with inability to look at life and the world apart from
> our own interests, emotions, and temperament. This is, in an exceptional
> degree, an epoch of morbid egoism, of exaggerated and excessive self-
> consciousness; an egoism which does not always breed vanity, but which
> confirms the tendency to measure everything by its value to us, and to
> decide every question on the basis of our personal relation to it. It is always
> unwise to generalize too broadly and freely about contemporary condi-
> tions, but there are many facts to bear out the statement that at no previous
> period in the history of the world have so many men and women been
> keenly and painfully self-conscious; never a time when it has been so diffi-
> cult to look at things broadly and objectively. . . .
>
> From this heated atmosphere and from these representations of dis-
> ease, put forth as reproductions of normal life, we fly to Nature, and are led
> away from all thought of ourselves. We escape out of individual into univer-
> sal life; we bathe in the healing waters of an illimitable ocean of vitality. . . .
> To drain into ourselves the rivulets of power which flow through Nature,
> art, and experience, we must hold ourselves open on all sides; we must
> empty ourselves of ourselves in order to make room for the truth and
> power which come to us through knowledge and action; we must lose our
> abnormal self-consciousness in rich and free relations with the universal
> life around us.[68]

In keeping with his own gentility, Hamilton Wright Mabie softened the
outreaching strategy of American culture. For him and for many other
Americans it meant escape rather than engagement or rebellion. This was
not true, I think, of James or Turner or Wright. But they shared Mabie's
confidence in the openness that still redeemed the American situation.

The clear evidence of accommodation and continuity in American culture should not lead us to suppose that the reorientation of the 1890s was
unimportant. Even in America the great restlessness that seized the nations

of the West toward the end of the nineteenth century has not dissipated itself in dreams of natural harmony or in boasts of physical prowess. The underlying desires and discontents grew stronger in the twentieth century. If a cultural revolution did indeed begin in the 1890s, its developed proportions and its essential character have only in our own time become visible.

On the occasion of his Emeritus Lecture at the Johns Hopkins University in December 1989, Higham invoked the ethnically and politically charged environment of his high school years in New York City during the mid-1930s. The essay here, which expands that lecture, offers a fresh explanation for the extraordinary mobilization of class and ethnic energies known as the New Deal.

In the essay Higham addresses a much debated issue in American social history: the complex relations between class and ethnicity. By offering a comparison of these ordinarily distinct forms of social consciousness over the course of a century, he seeks to show why in the United States they ultimately combined in the 1930s as the political expression of the new immigrants from eastern and southern Europe and their descendants. The combination of their strong feelings of ethnic identity and deeply felt class grievances gave the New Deal much of the dynamism that produced an American welfare state.

Looking back beyond the immediate economic collapse of the 1930s, Higham adopts a *longue durée* approach toward social change. Historians have often noted the coexistence of ethnicity and class in American society—generally to the detriment of the latter category—and some, like Lizabeth Cohen (1990) and Thomas Göbel (1988), have looked specifically at their convergence in the thirties. Here Higham provides a long-term scenario to explain why such intense mobilization had not occurred before, what steps gradually led to it, and, in a concluding hint, why it so quickly dissolved in the face of postwar conservatism. The presence of an ethnic middle class in the nineteenth century and its virtual absence among the newer ethnic communities of the early twentieth are here underlined as significant for ethnic cohesion in the former period and for working-class consciousness in the latter.

A second distinctive feature of the essay lies in its grounding in immigration rather than working-class history. Accordingly, it gives more weight to the fluidities of process than to the rigidities of structure. (On the theoretical background, see Higham's "From Process to Structure: Formulations of American Immigration History," in *American Immigrants and Their Generations,* ed. Peter Kivisto and Dag Blanck [1990].) In the present essay, the emergence of class consciousness is correlated less with the structures of trade unionism, workplace culture, or economic exploitation than with the "new" Americans' pursuit of civic equality.

In forming the New Deal coalition, the immigrants and their children hastened their own incorporation into American society. It is no coincidence that the mobilization Higham describes here overlaps with the rise of the ideology of American "universalism," which he portrays in Chapter 13. The New Deal's celebration of the common people and its dilution of ethnicity created a foundation for the postwar expansion of universalism through liberalized immigration and civil rights legislation.

Even so, at both ends of the time span referred to in Higham's essay, race "sliced" through class and ethnic consciousness, making their convergence in the 1930s truly exceptional. Slavery and the Civil War weakened and preempted nonracial forms of social identification in the mid-nineteenth century, and the civil rights movement of the mid-twentieth century, despite its colorblind egalitarianism, had the effect of accentuating racial (and eventually ethnic and gender) identity politics.

Catherine Collomp
Université Paris VII

12

The Long Road to the New Deal

As the years of conservative government in the United States roll on, regardless of the party in power and with no end even faintly in sight, the New Deal of the 1930s seems more and more anomalous. Those of us who grew up in the 1930s used to think that power would shift back to liberal hands when the economy again revealed dramatic shortcomings. The economy obliged in 1973, coinciding moreover with a disgraceful war and a major scandal in the White House. The result was simply the substitution of a conservative Democrat for a conservative Republican, not a major change in domestic policies.

My suspicion that we need to look beyond the depression of the 1930s for an explanation of the New Deal is confirmed by a further observation. So far as I know, nowhere outside the United States, during that decade of rending hardships, was a democratic welfare state created at a national level. If the Depression was decisive in producing a politics of welfare, should it not have done the same somewhere else?

These speculations lead to questions about another feature of the political and cultural ferment of the 1930s. No one can doubt that a progressive tradition—abundantly examined in studies of the late nineteenth century and the Progressive era—contributed massively to the accomplishments of the New Deal.[1] Why then did liberal nationalism begin to lose force so soon after World War II *in every area except race?* And why was the liberal movement thereafter unable to advance in areas other than race in spite of an unexhausted agenda of urgent social issues? Without answering all of these questions, I suggest that they highlight a particular generation of immigrants and their children—an ethnic conglomerate who only gradually learned their special place on the American scene, then flamed with a commitment that for a few years changed the course of history, and finally, quietly, gave up the boundary-crossing identity that shaped their rendezvous with destiny.

My interest centers on what was distinctive about the two generations and on the 1930s as a dramatic turning point in their experience. I use the term "New Deal" loosely: not to specify policies or personalities, or even to allude to the immediate cultural setting that Lizabeth Cohen has described so perceptively, but simply as a shorthand designation for a social movement that altered the distribution of power in the United States at several levels.[2] Tracing back into the nineteenth century the intermittent engagement of the immigrants in a tradition of social protest may show us how they reached their rendezvous in the 1930s. Many historians in recent years have worked intensively on phases of this story. My project is to connect the experience of successive mobilizations in a way that makes sense of the emotional heights and historic achievement that the immigrants reached in the New Deal years.

The mass migration from Europe in the nineteenth and early twentieth centuries rose to a significant level in the 1830s and then climbed to two great peaks, the first in the 1850s, the second from 1900 to the First World War. The earlier of those peaks belonged to what historians used to call the Old Immigration. It derived from northwestern Europe and predominated until the 1890s. The second peak was a product of the so-called New Immigration from southern and eastern Europe. It got under way in the 1880s, rose more suddenly, and was largely cut off by U.S. restriction laws in the early 1920s. Historians now avoid this distinction between an older and a newer phase of nineteenth-century European immigration because it was formulated in a prejudicial way. For my purpose, however, the distinction helps to illuminate the special significance of southern and eastern Europeans in the protest movements that culminated in the New Deal.

My argument is that the differences between the old and the new phase of the great immigration made America more democratic than it had been or would have become without that experience. Many older Americans feared that the shift in origin was lowering the quality of the immigrants and diluting the common culture on which democracy depends. Looking back, however, we can see that the recurrent clamor of the immigrant masses stretched and flexed existing institutions and that the very needs of the new immigrants gave their demands a progressive thrust.

My approach is comparative. First, I compare successive political and social movements that swept across ethnic boundaries, joining ordinarily discrete minorities in common struggles. Then, on reaching in the 1930s the climax of this narrative history, we arrive at the big question that requires an international comparison. What was distinctive about the New Deal coalition that enabled it to survive World War II long enough to put a welfare state permanently in place?

In general, immigrants to America have rarely had either the will or the power to change the society that receives them. This is to be expected, since new settlers usually suffer two marked disadvantages. They are poor and therefore find themselves at a low class level. They are also alien in speech, culture, and appearance, which places them at an ethnic disadvantage. At times these liabilities can become assets, as when people mobilize in defense of their interests along either class or ethnic lines. Yet a single ethnic group seldom provides a broad enough basis for effective social action, and the huge variety of such groups in the United States commonly frustrates class solidarity. The best opportunity for minorities to amass sufficient power to attain collective goals arises when class and ethnic consciousness converge—that is, when a sense of one's dignity as a member of an aggrieved racial or national group seems compatible with a wider sense of sharing in the needs and hopes of an entire social class. When strong feelings of ethnic identity do coalesce with deeply felt class grievances, an unusually powerful force is created. Through most of American history only flickerings of this volatile mixture appear. During the era of mature industrialism, extending from the 1890s to the 1940s, it burned brightly. It was the fuel for the social movements that produced the New Deal upheaval.

Let us bear in mind that the great migration from Europe reached a substantial level much earlier, when industrialization was developing relatively slowly and undramatically. Manufacturing establishments remained scattered and generally small. Capital and labor were overwhelmingly engaged in the conquest of a vast interior. Drawn by the general expansion of the American economy, the Old Immigration came on the American scene before there was a widespread awareness of factory operatives as a class distinct from their employers. Instead of massing in factories, the newcomers from northern and western Europe in the mid-nineteenth century toiled in a great variety of occupations and situations—commonly in the poorest jobs but often in skilled and specialized work for which prior knowledge had qualified them. A study of 2,664 adult male Scottish

immigrants who came to the United States before 1855 showed, for instance, that before emigration about a third had earned their living from a
remarkable variety of skilled crafts. Others had been either farmers or ser-
vants and laborers.[3] This diversified work experience must have forestalled
any immediate inclination to identify, consistently or predominantly, with
one class or another. The newcomers' primary allegiance (beyond relatives
and neighbors) would have been to their fellow countrymen, especially to
those already established in America.

And, indeed, each of the ethnic groups who were drawn into the early
American factories and mines found in their new homeland compatriots
comfortably settled in business and the professions. The mass immigration
of the 1830s merely resumed the migration from northwestern Europe that
had begun early in the eighteenth century. Accordingly, Germans, English,
Scots, Irish, Welsh, and Jews had already made their presence and institutions felt in America in preindustrial settings. All of them had developed a
middle class that was able to exert influence and leadership across class
lines. In Philadelphia, for example, a largely assimilated Irish American
middle class controlled both the religious and the secular institutions that
molded the group consciousness of the peasants who came in such torren-
tial numbers after the Famine.[4] The Old Immigration would never become
so completely associated with an industrial working class as would the
newer groups who arrived in the late nineteenth century.

Along with the objective circumstances that separated ethnic consciousness from class consciousness in the early industrial era, immigrants
to the United States encountered a resident culture that made ethnic identities more meaningful than class identities. Native-born Americans rel-
ished national and racial stereotypes. The American habit of thinking about
others in terms of ethnocultural inequalities and differences undoubtedly
reinforced the stereotyping propensities that immigrants brought with
them. On the subject of class, however, American predilections were much
less supportive of attitudes formed in Europe. American culture discouraged overt displays of rank and privilege. Immigrants marveled that "no
kind of work is looked down upon here," that the poor did not have to
doff their caps to their betters, that farmers and artisans "have practically
the same manners" and "enjoy the same degree of respect as the merchant
and the official," that capitalists and workingmen march together in parades. "It is an American political creed to be one people," a happy Swedish
immigrant wrote home in 1848. "This elevates the lowly and brings down
the great."[5]

Still, workers' resentments sputtered in urban settings and might have built up strongly if ethnic divisions had not supervened. By the 1850s industrialization was transforming key cities and towns, turning artisans into wage workers and removing them almost completely from the genteel society of business and professional people. Yet brave attempts to organize citywide federations of unions, bringing native Americans and Irish together with German workers, came to naught.[6] Instead, the great crisis over slavery that convulsed the Union at midcentury brought on a vast ethnic polarization that sliced through all class lines. With New Englanders and their midwestern descendants gathering at one extreme and white southerners at the other, many in the mid-Atlantic states who cared little about slavery one way or another turned on the swarming Irish Catholic immigrants in their midst as an excellent alternative target for outraged national feelings.[7]

Accordingly, in the 1840s and 1850s the Irish underwent their baptism of fire in America in an essentially defensive (though sometimes quite aggressive) battle to protect their churches and children from Protestant prejudices and to drive free blacks from the rough lower-class jobs in northern cities that no one else wanted. This tangle of clashing identities in the Know-Nothing years—sectional, religious, and racial—left everyone discontented and no one much advantaged.[8] But the Irish, while railing at Protestant reformers, did gain access to the lower echelons of the Democratic party in numerous cities, and the connection served them well in years to come. German Catholics also found a foothold in the Democratic party, but were largely preoccupied with their own intragroup disagreements, their own parishes and style of worship, and their own German culture. The radical ideologies that some working-class Germans brought to America were to a great extent sealed in the cocoon of the German language.[9] Both Irish and Germans were guarding an inherited culture.

In the first half of the twentieth century the tendency of ethnic consciousness to undercut class consciousness diminished markedly. Instead, the two forms of assertive self-consciousness tended to converge, rising and falling together and eventually—in the 1930s—merging. An amalgam of class and ethnic feeling produced a new social formation for which we have no name: a multiethnic oppositional body that had its center of gravity in the immigrant working class.

The formation of this ethnic coalition was made possible by an apparent hardening of the American class structure. By the 1890s, according to one study, an assumption that industrialization "was producing a permanent working class and a class society according to the European model informed almost every contemporary analysis of economic development, regardless of the analyst's political sympathies."[10] Other scholarship also reveals a quantum increase in the spatial segregation of social classes as local communities lost cohesiveness and autonomy. The middle and upper classes retreated into exclusive neighborhoods or fled entirely from the cities, creating suburbs that firmly resisted metropolitan annexation. Simultaneously, huge factories gathered their work force into nearby, class-segregated districts. Further reinforcing the experiential boundary between middle and working classes was the development of country clubs, "service" clubs, vacation resorts, automobiles, private schools, and public high schools permeated by genteel values. A banker in William Dean Howells's novel *A Traveller from Altruria* summed up the resulting class awareness: "There is as absolute a division between the orders of men, and as little love, in this country as in any country on the globe. The severance of the man who works for his living with his hands from the man who does not work for his living with his hands is so complete, and apparently so final, that nobody even imagines else."[11]

Yet millions did imagine else, including Howells himself, and much of the history of the early twentieth century is about efforts to deal with these gaping rents in the social order. On one side of the division that Howells described, a native-born middle class, feeling squeezed between an oligarchy above and a restive lower class beneath, rallied to the broad political movement that called itself progressive. More directly relevant to the story of the immigrants was a simultaneous though largely separate mobilization of working people—a class-conscious movement to cope with a new class structure. A weak, tenuous federation of unions blossomed in the early twentieth century into a durable mass movement, particularly in certain basic industries where the American Federation of Labor's efforts to restrict unionization to skilled trades collapsed; and for almost the entire period 1901–1919 the number of strikes (relative to the number of non-agricultural employees) soared above anything recorded in the previous century.[12]

The institutionalization of class consciousness within an expanding labor movement provided a context in which ethnic fragmentation of the industrial work force was reduced. In some industries the unionizing struggles of the early twentieth century forged a remarkable class solidarity among different ethnic groups. In a study of the anthracite coal industry, Peter Roberts marveled in 1901 that the "foreigners" "have formed unions which are more compact and united than any which ever existed among the various English-speaking nationalities who first constituted these communities. It is conceded by men intimate with the situation throughout the coal fields during the last strike, that its universality was more due to the Sclav than to any other nationality."[13]

Admittedly "class" was in the air in the early twentieth century, challenging as never before the old American confidence in individual opportunity. But that alone cannot account for the solidarity, to say nothing of the communal passion, that immigrant communities now displayed during strikes in the coalfields and elsewhere. These uprisings expressed not only class assertiveness but also and simultaneously a newborn ethnic consciousness, especially among recent immigrants from southern and eastern Europe. Those newcomers became self-consciously ethnic in the very throes of discovering a wider class identity.

Peasants drawn to America from southern Italy, Hungary, and Slavic lands after 1880 came with scant awareness of a world outside their own villages. Identity for them was very parochial. The nation was an idea in the minds of educated elites, far beyond their ken. In America these immigrants formed little communities, restricted to an immediate neighborhood or even to people from a single village. Then, around the turn of the century, leaders of the little communities began to build wider networks of communication between them, invoking the ties of a common language, culture, and often religion. Some, who were labor activists or radical intellectuals fleeing from repression in the old country, stressed the solidarity of class. Necessarily, however, they organized along national lines and thus promoted awareness of a national as well as a class identity. Others, with middle-class goals, appealed directly to the idea of the nation as a great community struggling for realization. National fraternal societies and ethno-nationalist newspapers sprang up alongside the burgeoning labor organizations. While ethnic consciousness was gaining as a vehicle for class consciousness, it was also fueled by rivalry between the two.[14] Both impulses widened horizons, and many former peasants must have felt the enlargement of their identity as a single consciousness-raising experience.

If the new immigrants from southern and eastern Europe had found among their compatriots in America an entrenched middle class capable of guiding their acculturation, the ethnic bond would surely have impeded class consciousness. But no such elite was on hand.[15] Few southern and eastern Europeans had settled in the United States before the 1870s. Less than 5 percent of the total foreign-born population in 1880, they came in the next two decades almost without precursors.[16] In nineteenth-century immigrant communities—Germans, Irish, and others—the influence of a successful, Americanized middle and upper class had strongly counteracted class grievances. Within the new immigrant communities class and ethnic feelings could more easily spring up together as complementary foci of social consciousness.

To organize their local communities, the newcomers had to either create their own leaders or fall under the control of bosses, politicians, and priests who neither spoke their language nor shared their heritage. At the end of the nineteenth century, therefore, the New Immigration produced its own thin middle class of shop owners, saloon keepers, newspaper editors, priests, and officers of fraternal societies. A large proportion of such local leaders came from peasant stock. Sharing the sympathies and experiences of their neighbors and customers, they were close to the laboring masses. The dependence of this petite bourgeoisie on a vastly larger body of factory hands meant that the new ethnic communities in the early twentieth century belonged to a relatively undifferentiated working class.[17]

By the outbreak of World War I, the rising ethnic consciousness in the new immigrant communities was finding expression in nationalist as well as class programs. In the nineteenth century, only the Irish had supported a broad movement for liberation of their homeland. Beginning in 1914, however, movements to defend the homeland or free it from oppression spread through a dozen ethnic groups, each resonating to the others and all together awakening in the usually fatalistic immigrant masses a level of collective expectation that was unprecedented. Substantial numbers of Poles, Serbs, Czechs, Slovaks, and Jews who were not yet U.S. citizens returned to the Old World to fight for the nationalist cause. Except for German American publications, the foreign-language press thrived on the war; the number of non-German foreign-language papers increased about 20 percent between 1914 and 1918. Nationalist heroes like Ignace Paderewski, the famed Polish pianist, and Thomas Masaryk, the exiled philosopher-statesman of the Czechs, toured American cities. In Washington ethnic lobbying designed to influence the peace settlement became, for Jewish Zionists, Ukrainians, Yugoslavs, Italians, Greeks, Lithuanians, and others, a new style of politics.[18]

None of these mobilizations was more impressive than that of eastern European Jews in behalf of a Jewish homeland in Palestine. For almost two decades before World War I little Zionist societies had been helpless in the face of the Jewish immigrants' eagerness to be Americans. But the war created such enormous needs for relief, both in Palestine and in eastern Europe, that anxiety about divided loyalties was swept aside. Linked with the Wilsonian ideal of national self-determination, Zionism now received the fervent support of the Jewish immigrant masses, who began through Zionism to exercise a new influence in American Jewish affairs.[19]

Similarly, among African Americans the First World War transformed a previously inconsequential racial nationalism into a spectacular mass movement. Through Marcus Garvey the flickering vision of an African homeland suddenly became, in the black ghettoes of America, a palpable prospect. Like the socialist agitators who came in the same years from southern and eastern Europe, Garvey arrived in 1916 from the island of Jamaica to proselytize among West Indians in Harlem. His original project was a conservative racial improvement society he had founded in Jamaica. Only after observing the agitation of other nationalities in the streets of New York did Garvey comprehend the messianic power of the nationalist idea.[20] Before Garvey, the principal black protest movements had not reached much beyond an educated elite. It remained for this flamboyant Jamaican immigrant—attuned to the international scale of the ethnic ferment in American cities—to galvanize a million urban blacks into collective action.[21]

Compared to the other ethnic nationalisms of the era, Garvey's program had a fatal weakness. Garvey rallied blacks who were giving up on America. His followers embraced an African dream as an alternative to the promise of America. In contrast, the ethnic nationalisms of the European groups in this country rested on a genuinely hyphenated foundation. For Jews, Italians, Poles, and all the rest, identification with the best interests of the homeland seemed not only compatible but intimately connected with a fervent American nationalism. When the United States entered the war, the eastern European peoples in America could feel that their own liberation movements were a service to the American cause and attested to their own Americanness.[22]

Conceived in this way, one of the attractions of nationalist mobilization was the usually welcome visibility it gave to ethnic groups yearning for greater recognition on the crowded stage of American life. Rallying opinion and raising funds for overseas projects produced countless public demonstrations: receptions for representatives from the homeland, mass meetings to pass resolutions and secure pledges, musical festivals to display a cultural heritage, and, above all, parades. In reporting these events, general circulation newspapers were sometimes noticing for the first time the local presence of an entire community that had earlier been largely invisible.[23]

After the United States entered the war, government agencies worked to orchestrate the ethnic campaigns in the interest of a united war effort; that led to still greater visibility. When Liberty Loan officials in 1918 organized a monster Fourth of July parade up Fifth Avenue in New York, the notion of demonstrating the loyalty and affinity of every nationality to the American cause proved so popular that the original roster of forty-four participating groups expanded to sixty-four. A ten-hour procession, numbering 109,415 marchers and 158 bands, included American Indians, Haitians, Liberians, Japanese, Parsees, Russians, Carpathians, "Zionists for the Jewish Nation," and "Americans of German Origin." The Poles won first prize for floats, but the judges also commended the Assyrians, Bolivians, and Americans of German Origin.[24]

In the tumult of reverberating patriotisms, what scope was left for the mobilization of a working class along lines of economic self-interest? The standard view of American history, with its heavy emphasis on the repression of dissent during the war years, suggests that class action was sharply contained. It is true that the war brought governmental intervention and manipulation here, too; but any presumption that the organizing drive of labor was thereby vitiated is patently false. Whereas authorities scourged the socialists and syndicalists who opposed the war, the great majority of unions received unprecedented governmental support. After a pause on the eve of the war, the mobilization of immigrant labor resumed through unionization of war industries. The appointment of many labor leaders to governmental boards and commissions gave the labor movement a new kind of civic recognition, prompting some unions to claim (to the disgust of employers) that Uncle Sam was on their side.[25]

Even the sharpest ideological divisions seemed incapable of dampening the fervor of class mobilization. On an ideological level, a deadly enmity divided clerical nationalists from socialists in many ethnic groups. In opposing the war, the socialists appealed for proletarian solidarity among all the wretched of the earth. At an emotional rather than ideological level, however, the aroused class consciousness and militant national consciousness were symbiotic. They flowed together, for both were grounded in a tremendous, expectant yearning for a better life, here in America and through America's leadership in the Old World as well. An apocalyptic sense that the war signified the death throes of a brutal system of oppression was shared by antiwar radicals and prowar nationalists, which may explain the fact that Socialist candidates running on antiwar platforms made heavy gains in municipal elections in such cities as New York and

Chicago, where ethnic nationalisms were also strongly organized and visible. At a union meeting in Pennsylvania a Polish steelworker summed up his medley of commitments. "For why this war?" he asked. "For why we buy Liberty bonds? For the mills? No, for freedom and America—for everybody. . . . For eight-hour day."[26]

This was a new stage in the making of a multiethnic working class, not only because of the alignment of class and ethnic sentiment but also because of the direction in which the alignment pointed. The distinctively ethnic mobilizations of the nineteenth century, among both immigrants and natives, had been mostly defensive. People rallied to save their own traditions from the intrusions of outsiders—to protect especially their religion, language, and mores from proselytizers, public officials, and unwelcome neighbors. The early class mobilizations were also largely defensive in looking back to the imagined harmony of a producers' Eden before the coming of the factories and foreigners. For all such movements—ethnic and class alike—the points of reference were anterior to the polyglot reality of contemporary America. In the twentieth century, however, a basic urge to change the world infused both class and ethnic consciousness, connecting them through a common reference to a future that all could hope to share. In spite of clashing ideologies and divergent cultures, the immigrant working class was becoming aware of itself as a segment of America, marked partly by its disadvantage vis-à-vis the older strata but drawn together also by intuitions of a single destiny.

In the war experience we can discern one of the origins of an ethnic pluralism that sprang up almost unbidden, in practice rather than theory, in the midst of crudely intrusive efforts at Americanization. Through a tacit bargain combining pluralism with integration, national leaders and mass media testified to their respect for every descent group while receiving in return each group's acknowledgement of civic attachment, belonging, and obligation. Some government agencies took a repressive, 100 percent American approach, particularly against immigrant radicals, and did only harm. But others chose pluralistic integration. The U.S. army, for example, in dealing with half a million foreign-born recruits, learned from ethnic leaders and social scientists to let the immigrants speak for themselves, and was rewarded with a mingling of American patriotism and ethnic pride.[27]

Carried over into peacetime when the war suddenly ended, dreams of a brave new world of class solidarity and national liberation shattered. The most devastating blow to the New Immigrant groups fell early, in 1919, when they undertook against the huge United States Steel Company, and against the advice of conservative labor leaders, the largest strike in American history. It failed completely. During wartime labor shortages New Immigrant workers had gained access for the first time to the better-paying jobs; foremen suddenly treated them with respect. Now they confronted postwar inflation and were once again "Hunkies." Management refused to deal with the immigrants, some of the immigrants' own middle class deserted them, the older craft unions ignored their strike, and the labor movement shut them out. The result was an abiding mood of defeatism and apathy.[28]

Both working-class and ethnic consciousness thereupon underwent a precipitous decline. For a decade thereafter labor union membership and the number of strikes dwindled year by year.[29] Within the various ethnic groups radical organizations withered. Nationalistic agitation virtually collapsed. Even the Zionist movement, greatly shrunken, survived only by shelving its political agenda and concentrating on raising funds for humanitarian projects in Palestine. Demobilized and probably reluctant to aggravate the sharply nativist mood of the day, the immigrants put up only feeble resistance to the victorious immigration restriction movement. Their few friends in Congress received the definitive Johnson-Reed Act of 1924 with weary resignation.[30]

Historians have commonly attributed the postwar decline of radicalism to repression, while blaming "war-weariness" and factional quarrels for the fading of homeland issues.[31] But the simultaneous onset of demobilization on both nationalist and radical fronts points to a deeper common cause, abundantly visible and vividly symbolized in the literature and politics of the postwar decade: a general surrender of grandiose ideals. Like many other Americans, the immigrants were disillusioned.

But the Americanization of their ethnic identities continued. The 1920s turned out to be hardly more than an interlude in the consolidation of an ethnic American working class. Under the hammering of the Great Depression, the ethnic and class mobilizations that had begun to coalesce during and before World War I revived in a new, more integrated form. During the intervening years southern and eastern European groups had gradually acquired—through home ownership, naturalization, and education—a modicum of stability. The Old World had receded in importance. By the end of the 1920s a second generation, born in America, substantially outnumbered the immigrants themselves in most of the New Immigrant communities. Moving out of the narrower world of their parents, the second generation became the spearhead of the last and greatest mobilization of European immigrants. To use the language of the day, this was a mobilization of New Americans pushing for wider access and fuller acceptance in the only country they really had.[32] In place of the hyphenated nationalisms of World War I, the New Americans substituted an expanded American nationalism that could contain both a class protest and a residual demand for ethnic recognition, now delivered not in the name of what they had been—Polacks, Wops, Hunkies, and Sheenies—but in the name of what they were becoming: Americans All.

A special stimulus to this last mobilization arose from an experience no previous generation of European immigrants had undergone. The New Americans grew up in a country that had turned decisively against large-scale immigration, a country that no longer wanted any more of their kind. According to Louis Adamic, a leading interpreter of immigrant life at the time, the stigma of inferiority stung the American-born children of the immigrants more sharply than their parents, for the children were largely Americanized and felt little connection with an older heritage.[33] Thus the New Americans sought dignity and inclusion, and to a remarkable degree during the 1930s and 1940s they attained these goals. They succeeded because their own repressed anger converged with the economic discontent of other significant groups and because all of them were able to utilize the instrumentalities of earlier ethnic mobilizations, the Democratic party and the labor movement.

The shape and scale of the New Deal uprising are too familiar to require more than a brief reminder of the crucial importance of the ethnic factor in producing it. The first sign of a new order of things appeared with the presidential election of 1928. Alfred E. Smith, campaigning against prohibition, called forth in the industrial cities where New Americans clustered a huge outpouring of first-time voters who had been too apathetic or too young to participate earlier. In cities with a relatively low proportion of recent immigrants, the electorate increased only slightly and divided according to economic standing. Analysis of subsequent elections made clear that the biggest influence on the new Democratic voters was ethnic identity rather than class.[34]

What had first appeared as another cultural mobilization against "puritanical" government turned into a political upheaval, which in turn produced a major shift in economic power. Victory at the polls in 1932 awakened the ravaged unions and stirred in unorganized workers a fitful courage to test anew their collective strength. But a second and stronger demonstration of electoral might proved necessary before a major economic mobilization could come about. Not until Franklin D. Roosevelt's spectacular reelection in 1936, by majorities that reached from 70 to 80 percent in the most heavily ethnic cities, did the New Americans become fully conscious of their power.[35] During the following year the American labor movement made the greatest gains in its history.

Of course, the new peoples joined forces with many others who were also bent on reducing inequalities of power and origin. Yet the basic concern of the New Americans is clear enough. It was not equality. It was incorporation, and that is why the militant self-assertion that impelled their mobilization was infused with a passionate Americanism. Throughout the organizing drives of the Congress of Industrial Organizations, American flags fluttered, patriotic songs invoked visions of national fraternity, and even the Communists enthusiastically adopted the language of Americanism. Instead of affirming distinctive ethnic heritages or an exclusive class loyalty, the inclusive nationalism of the New Americans celebrated the heterogeneous origins and the (theoretically) democratic spirit of the American people. The Statue of Liberty became the central American icon. In popular culture the "common man" emerged as the authentic voice of "democracy," which in turn was now the essential label for the entire political and social system.[36]

In this extraordinary shift from the vigorous individualism of the 1920s to the quasi-collectivism of the 1930s, both an indigenous progressive tradition and a worldwide depression were obviously major factors. But could the shift have occurred without the third factor examined here? I do not think so, for the simple reason that other democratic societies with their own progressive traditions hardly changed at all during the Depression years.

Instead of calling forth new majorities to undertake bold social experiments, the Depression more often reinforced the status quo. Of the major Western countries only Nazi Germany and the United States moved decisively in a new direction; and in both cases a strong ethnic consciousness impelled the new departure. In many societies the Depression did galvanize radical minorities, but it also intimidated the great mass of people. It was so pervasive and frightening, so seemingly beyond human control, that people tended to rally around traditional institutions and familiar leaders.[37] Where democratic governments of the left were in power at the onset of the Depression, the economic slump was likely to discredit them, pro-ducing—as in Britain and Australia—a return to niggardly conservatism. A decisive swing to the left was not impossible during the Depression. But leaving the United States aside, solid left-liberal victories took place only in socially homogeneous countries where a social-democratic party had stead-ily evolved under the legitimizing aegis of a statist tradition. This was the case in Scandinavia and in New Zealand.[38]

The closest parallel to what happened in the United States was the victory in 1936 of the Popular Front in France. For the first time a Socialist took the helm in that large, heterogeneous, but basically conservative na-tion and organized a broad left-to-center coalition. Like the New Deal, the Popular Front sought to integrate an alienated working class into the na-tional community. As in the United States the same year, the electoral victory that gave France its first Socialist premier produced a huge wave of jubilant industrial strikes and a general sense of a significant shift in power. The great difference was that Léon Blum lasted hardly more than a year as premier and left few institutional changes.

Why did the Popular Front largely fail and the New Deal succeed? Some reasons have little to do with the two electorates. A parliamentary system of unstable coalitions denied French premiers the vigorous leader-ship that an American president with a strong popular majority could ex-ercise. Blum's dependence on the centrist Radical party, for example, was at least partly responsible for his entrapment in a disastrous monetary policy. Even here, however, the absence of a coherent agenda for social change is telling. Initially this incongruous alliance of center and left was inspired by fear of an aggressive fascism just across the Rhine and related right-wing nationalist movements in France itself. From its origins, there-fore, the Popular Front was, in the words of its historian, "a negative coalition; in this lay the seeds of its disintegration."[39] The Front's great rallying cry in the streets—"The Republic in Danger"—reflected this pri-marily defensive psychology.

Compared to the United States, France was a compartmentalized so-ciety, stratified by ideological barriers and class divisions, though united by a strong civic spirit. The barriers stood in the way of the kind of social dynamism that has emerged at times from the fluid discontents of Amer-ica's migratory groups. Blum had tried to break down barriers, but the Popular Front was never more than a temporary rapprochement. As John Garraty has suggested, Blum could not keep alive a popular feeling of

participation in a great national cause.[40] Rooseveltian government, however, seemed to authorize and legitimize the ongoing socioethnic revolution that made that government possible. Only in America, during the
Depression years, did a new regime ratify a major extension of the boundaries of the national community.

The social dynamics of the New Deal may be tested further by noting the absence of any comparable mobilization in the other principal
immigrant-receiving countries of the western hemisphere. Immigration to
Canada and to Argentina reached a crest just at the time when U.S. immigration was also peaking. During the first decade of the century the influx to both Canada and Argentina amounted to more than one-third of
their preexisting populations. This was a much higher level of immigration
than the United States received; here the total immigration of 1900–1909
equaled 11 percent of the population of 1900.[41] Even more than the United
States, therefore, Canada and Argentina had in the 1930s a restless immigrant population who might have demanded their place in the sun. Yet the
newcomers and their children did not in either country seriously challenge
the existing power structure. What explains the insurgency of ethnic newcomers in one milieu and their relative quiescence in these others?

The situation in Argentina was so different that the essential comparison with the United States must be between two sharply contrasting
social systems. Although the immigrant peoples in Argentina concentrated
(like those in the United States) in large cities, especially Buenos Aires,
they did not constitute a disadvantaged class. Instead, they were the middle
class—the professionals, the skilled workers, and the entrepreneurs. In the
great economic boom of the early twentieth century Italian and Spanish
immigrants had risen easily from entry-level jobs to every kind of commercial and technical employment. Buenos Aires, their creation and their possession, was an extension of Europe, and its nouveaux riches sent their
children back there for an education. Divided among themselves and inse-
cure in their relation to the rest of the country, these second-generation
Argentines felt both too comfortable and too vulnerable to initiate collective protest. Their middle-class parties were hopelessly fragmented. The
General Confederation of Labor was small and ineffectual. A landed oligarchy, which distrusted the immigrants and discouraged their naturalization,
continued to dominate the political system. At the other end of the social
spectrum, a resentful lower class of racially mixed peons piled up in the
slums surrounding the cities.[42] Thus the foreign stock in Argentina comprised a disunited middle stratum in a steeply hierarchical society. As Gen-

eral Juan Perón would demonstrate in the 1940s, the New Argentines were not waiting for an eclectic and egalitarian movement, like the American New Deal, but for a man on horseback.

Canada presents a more revealing comparison because so much is similar in the two North American countries. Not only have they shared common traditions, but the early twentieth-century immigrants who might have stood out in both countries as disturbingly foreign also came from similar backgrounds in southern and eastern Europe. Yet major contrasts in social structure make the comparison problematic.

First, there was a great disparity in the numbers and presence of the two migrations. Between 1901 and 1915 almost 80 percent of the people entering Canada came from familiar British, Irish, and U.S. sources. The remaining 19 percent were overwhelmingly from northern and western Europe. A mass migration from southern and eastern Europe got under way only when the U.S. quota law of 1924 diverted that stream northward to Canada.[43] During the 1920s, when a second generation of southern and eastern Europeans was coming to the fore in the United States, in Canada they were still getting born.

Moreover, the New Canadians lacked the locational advantage the same groups enjoyed in the United States. In this country the new peoples formed the bulk of an industrial working class gathered at the centers of social action: the cities of the North and West. They could make a decisive difference in elections. In Canada's less developed economy a more dispersed pattern of employment impeded mobilization. Arriving as unskilled workers and peasants, and usually with no desire to stay for long, the newcomers found themselves caught up in seasonal labor and hurried off to railroads under construction, mines, and logging camps deep in the interior. In the 1930s, the New Americans were capturing public offices in U.S. cities. In Canada they were just beginning to develop a stable community life. No major city in this country was as British in its population mix as Toronto.[44]

Industrial unions sprang up readily enough in Canada, as the CIO's great surge in 1937 spread from Michigan to Ontario. But holding those gains proved hopeless. Canada had nothing like the Wagner Act. Conservative premiers won widespread approval in breaking several organizing drives. The CIO collapsed within a year's time.[45]

Beneath these differences in numerical strength and stage of development of the newer immigrant groups, there was also at work a larger contrast between the two nations. Resisting the level of national integration

the United States had reached, the entire structure of Canada as a nation
served to contain mass movements of any kind. The primacy of traditional
loyalties rooted in very distinct regions tended to confine protest movements to individual provinces. Neither of Canada's two national political
parties had the flexibility that allowed a major party in the United States to
accommodate new claimants for power. The non-British ethnic groups
tended to support the Liberal party because of its tolerance of social diversity; but the Liberals' careful respect for regional interests made them
extremely reluctant to assume national responsibility for the problems the
American New Deal addressed.[46] The Liberals' unresponsiveness to social
change forced protest into third parties, where regional and social separateness once again obstructed nationwide organization. The most promising of the third-party ventures, the Cooperative Commonwealth Federation, failed to take hold in more than two or three provinces. Moreover, its
leadership and style were so markedly British that neither the New Canadians nor the French Canadians could identify with it.[47] Canada was not
ready for the politics of incorporation.

The inability of Canadian political parties and labor unions to accomplish the kind of mobilization that occurred in the United States makes
clear how essentially the victories of the New Americans were built on a
long history of earlier ethnic struggles. Canada is a younger nation than the
United States, and it has not been so continually subjected to the stresses of
large-scale immigration. For a generation after the mid-nineteenth century, while immigration was at a low ebb, English Canada hardened and
consolidated, as French Canada had done in the eighteenth century.[48]

It is true that American localism has also, like Canadian traditionalism,
obstructed collective protest by decentralizing power. But the experience
of recurrent waves of ethnic conflict gradually made the American political
system more flexible and responsive than that of Canada. In the cultural
mobilizations of the nineteenth century the Democratic party gave urban
immigrants a voice, and between major waves of ethnic militancy its city
machines provided continuity in the representation of immigrant voters.
Veteran politicians were therefore well positioned to organize the new
insurgency when it erupted in the late 1920s.

Yet the comparison with France and Canada leaves us finally with a
poignant irony. After World War II both of those conservative countries
constructed more far-reaching welfare states than the United States created in the midst of the Great Depression, or has yet developed. While
Canada and France were moving toward greater social integration under

conservative leadership, the class and ethnic consciousness that empowered the New Deal was melting away. Class polarization in voting lessened greatly, as did the vigor of the labor unions. What is more, nearly all of the local institutions that sustained traditional ethnic and class identities—lodges, taverns, national parishes, and political machines—were gravely weakened. The immigrant working class lost its identity in the course of attaining the incorporation it had sought for so long.

In the end the hunger of the New Americans for incorporation was too strong to sustain the dual identities that the labor movement and the whole society needed so badly. In becoming indistinguishable from many other Americans, the children of the immigrants gave up the difficult struggle toward racial democracy that had distinguished the CIO during its best years.

PART IV

Prospects

Starting out as a call for multicultural education in the 1970s, the movement that became known as multiculturalism expanded in the next decade into a widespread assault on the assimilationist tradition. Multiculturalist scholars celebrated diversity and championed the preservation of ethnic and racial boundaries. Some denied the claims of a common American culture, and others went so far as to question the existence of universal standards and values. As the "culture wars" between multiculturalists and their enemies heated up, Higham decided out of "sheer impatience with obfuscation" to "make audible again a liberal alternative." To test his case against lively opposition, he wrote this essay to be the centerpiece of a symposium in the *American Quarterly,* knowing that the sponsoring American Studies Association had committed itself deeply to views on race, gender, and ethnicity that considered any "master narrative" of American history inherently oppressive.

Higham's sweeping essay promotes the tradition of American universalism—an "oxymoron," as he wryly puts it—that he hopes will persuade the doubtful that Americans can have many identities and still be linked to a common center of shared values and vision. Returning to such relatively neglected subjects as class, religion, region, and nation will make it clear, Higham contends, that Americans have always relied on belief systems that cut across group boundaries. In particular, the various declarations of equality and human rights that are embodied in our civic documents and debates represent a rich, though not always honored, heritage of universalism for Americans of all kinds to draw on as they assert their claims and also acknowledge their interdependence.

Gerald Early, director of the Black Studies program at Washington University, spoke for the majority of Higham's respondents in the *American Quarterly* when he contrasted multiculturalism's exciting open-endedness with the failed teleology of universalism. Rebutting Higham's charge that the multiculturalist movement had no vision of goals, Early asserted that it proposed to do away with universal creeds and to create "an America of endless multiplicity." Other critics charged that Higham had painted far too rosy a picture of American universalism, neglecting the racist and reactionary causes that had posed, even in the allegedly liberal twentieth century, as true defenders of American ideals.

Since the *American Quarterly* encounter, multiculturalism has widened its scope and drawn new critics. Opposition to standards has been stiffened by invoking the concept of "whiteness" as a way to describe past ideals as the ideological reflection of race and caste privilege. From the right, advocates of Americanization have taken the offensive, pressing to end bilingual education, to strengthen barriers to immigration, and even to revoke for children of illegal aliens the constitutional provision of citizenship. Leftist critics, in contrast, have scolded multiculturalists for neglecting to root their resistance to assimilation in issues of class and the distribution of economic and political power.

From Higham's perspective, the polarized situation calls for historians to rise above specialization and partisanship in order to discern the larger story of overlapping American fates. Only after all groups attempt to grasp approaches and circumstances other than their own can the hard work of describing the complex connections between the one and the many in the American past come to fruition. And only then can the essential task of rebuilding a persuasive new version of American universalism begin.

Alan Lawson
Boston College

13

Multiculturalism and Universalism
A History and Critique
[1993]

People, I just want to say, you know, can we all get along? Can we get along? Can we stop making it, making it horrible for the older people and the kids? . . . We'll, we'll get our justice. . . . We all can get along. I mean, we're all stuck here for a while. Let's try to work it out. Let's try to beat it. Let's try to work it out.

STATEMENT BY RODNEY G. KING, MAY 1, 1992, URGING
AN END TO THE RIOTS PROVOKED IN LOS ANGELES BY A
COURT'S EXONERATION OF HIS TORMENTERS.
New York Times, May 2, 1992

Two distinct demands for greater equality run through the history of the Western world in the twentieth century. One opposes discrimination against people on grounds of race, ethnicity, gender, or physical condition. These inescapably given traits are commonly understood as personal, as internal, as part of the very substance of who we are. To use them as devices or reasons for subordinating outgroups affronts our sense of equal justice. Recognition of a moral equivalence of endowment is therefore a fundamental objective in modern society.

A second egalitarian force pushes against the disadvantages of external condition, the burdens of class. Here the distribution of tangible resources—a nexus of property, skill, and political power—constitutes a more generalized structure of inequality. To reduce such external disadvantages, people of all kinds demand equality of opportunity; some claim equality of condition as well. My interest is in the pursuit of equality along the first path, that is, between groups defined by their cultural or biological inheritances. But the second path also runs through this story. Our current preoccupation with an egalitarian understanding of collective endowments too often lacks a full historical context, in which struggles to equalize society-wide relations between classes play a significant part.

Rising and falling, entwining and separating, these two great modern movements against unacceptable inequities have always interacted. Occasionally, the discontents of underprivileged races or ethnic groups converge with those of underprivileged classes. When that occurs, as in the United States in the 1930s, equality makes a mighty leap forward. Only infrequently, however, can such a coalition of the disinherited come together, much less prevail. Class typically cuts across ethnicity and gender, since endowment groups generally occupy more than one class level. Altogether, inequalities lace modern society in so many crosscutting directions that movements to level one citadel of privilege usually reinforce others, intentionally or unwittingly.

When distinct ethnic segments join forces, either with one another or with a discontented class, their alliance requires a guiding ideology to define a common plight and inspire hopes of a common redemption. The United States has had such a belief system from its beginnings as a nation; during the first half of the twentieth century egalitarian movements drew on it more freely and comprehensively than at any time before or since. Channeled by this deeply rooted ideology, the outcries of excluded races and ethnic groups flowed together and mingled simultaneously with the energies of class protest.[1]

At the time of its greatest power, Gunnar Myrdal labeled this familiar bundle of beliefs the "American Creed."[2] Today many scornfully call it "American exceptionalism."[3] I shall try to avoid both the piety and the scorn by resorting to a neutral oxymoron. Let us name our egalitarian ideology "American universalism." Molded by the Enlightenment and forged in the Revolution, American universalism has been simultaneously a civic credo, a social vision, and a definition of nationhood.

As a civic credo, it is universal in grounding public life and institutions not on an exclusive heritage but on natural rights—that is, on rational principles, supposedly valid everywhere, that grant all citizens equality in public life and encourage all residents to claim a common citizenship. These principles not only legitimize American governments but should also ultimately spread around the world and win universal approval by protecting everyone's basic rights. American universalists expected, in the words of Thomas Jefferson, that "a just and solid republican government maintained here . . . will be a standing monument & example for . . . a great portion of the globe."[4] The civic credo was exceptionalist in what it stood for, but universal in what it could become.

At this level, as an official proclamation of human rights, American universalism remains sturdy and intact. As a social vision, it endures but has lost its early buoyancy. Originally, it was a message of hope, holding out to individuals a promise of overcoming all social barriers external to the self. It celebrated the mobility, renewal, and self-transformation that the pioneer, the immigrant, and the self-made man symbolized; its special animus was against the privileges of entrenched social classes. Classes, in this parochially universalist view, were unnatural: the artificial creation of bad laws in a corrupt Old World. Any tendency to import them here, and thus to harden existing lines of privilege, must be opposed. In conservative times, Americans liked to boast of their nation's exemption from the sharp class divisions of Europe. In times of stress and challenge, however, class conflict exploded in the form of broadly popular uprisings against privileged minorities. In short, American universalism either denied that class inequalities had taken root in America or struggled to extirpate them.

Inequalities of endowment presented a knottier conceptual problem. Unlike class, distinctions in endowment were generally seen to have a certain fixity in nature. These supposedly "natural" inequalities authorized the "herrenvolk" definitions of American nationality that developed in the nineteenth century.[5] Nevertheless, a universalist point of view lives on. It insists that the task of nation-building is to be as inclusive and as egalitarian as possible.

We come to the crux of American universalism in recognizing that it embodies an invigorating paradox. Supposedly universal rights became institutionally and socially operative through the collective efforts of people who used them to create a bounded community of their own to the disadvantage of others. What was theoretically and potentially universal was soon understood, therefore, as the sacred possession—the very linchpin of identity—of a peculiar people. The Americans stand out, said James Fenimore Cooper, for having "dared the war of their independence in the maintenance of a perfectly abstract principle, for no one pretends that the taxation of England was oppressive in fact." More loftily still, Henry James the elder contrasted the insularity of the English with the unbounded identity of Americans: "We are no mere civil polity. We are at bottom nothing more than a broad human society or brotherhood, of which every man is in full membership by right of manhood alone."[6]

Such expansive affirmations, ritualized on every Fourth of July, provided the connective tissue that was vital for a new nation with a loose-knit
social fabric, an extraordinarily decentralized political system, and a highly
rhetorical religion. At the same time, the celebration of human rights as the
distinguishing feature of a singular nation—however fallacious that may
appear in retrospect—gave an impetus to wider humane concerns. In the
early republic, sympathy for the suffering of humanity everywhere was
readily experienced as a natural extension of patriotic feelings. Nationalism
and a proto-universalism fertilized one another, their symbiosis represented in the classical goddess of liberty whom Congress in 1792 designated as the obligatory female symbol complementing the masculine eagle
on all American coins.[7]

The coupling, in many national icons, of a distinctively American bird
of prey with a transnational symbol of freedom cannot be fully understood
as a smokescreen or a delusion. It reflects the inescapable locatedness
of any universalistic perspective. More specifically, it displays the enduring tension, in what I have called American universalism, between closure
and openness, between separateness and inclusion.[8] From the time of the
American Revolution onward, a principal way of managing this tension has
been to extend the circle of those who are acknowledged as makers of an
American nationality and to project each incremental addition as a promise
of still wider inclusiveness.

Thomas Paine took an early step by arguing in 1776 that Americans
owed the cosmopolitan breadth of their social sympathies to the freedom-
loving refugees who had flocked to the New World "from *every part* of
Europe," not just from "the narrow limits" of little England. By the middle
of the nineteenth century, the idea was widespread that a mixed population
is more vigorous, and more variously endowed, than any single ethnic
strain. Immigrant groups, especially the Germans, eagerly adopted the
claim that they were making important contributions to an American character.[9] Often these hyphenates constructed an ethnic identity and a new
American identity concurrently. Generation after generation, they came
from more and more homelands, and their infusion into the host society
gave increasing substance and visibility to its cosmopolitan bent. Admittedly, European ethnic groups generally shrank from drawing interracial
implications from their own ongoing assimilation; but African Americans
and radical Republican intellectuals took the idea of fusion all the way. "My
idea of American nationality," declared Wendell Phillips in a great Lyceum
lecture, "makes it the last best growth of the thoughtful mind of the cen-

tury, treading underfoot sex and race, caste and condition, and collecting on the broad bosom of what deserves the name of an empire, under the shelter of noble, just, and equal laws, all races, all customs, all religions, all languages, all literature, and all ideas."[10]

To be sure, a defensive, ethnically based national consciousness, gathering strength in the mid-nineteenth century and after, persistently obstructed the advance of American universalism.[11] Even now, a presumption that white males of European descent should remain the solid core of American society is weakening only haltingly. Yet the pursuit of equality quickened greatly in the twentieth century. For a while, it reached across the gulf between excluded races and a largely white working class.

By the opening of the new century, unanticipated dangers to equal rights were becoming too visible and menacing to ignore. The self-segregation of middle and upper classes in exclusive neighborhoods, suburban enclaves, country clubs, and automobiles accompanied the elaboration of corporate bureaucracies and the concentration of an industrial work force in factory-dominated districts. Although the anger and bewilderment of native white Americans at the hardening of social categories released a storm of racism, the revitalizing movement that called itself Progressive simultaneously produced a new egalitarianism. The agencies of revitalization were numerous and powerful. They included the Democratic party, industrial and interracial labor unions, churches infused with a social gospel and an ecumenical spirit, universities and public schools, and a multiethnic popular-culture industry.

The revival of American universalism between the 1910s and the 1950s was fired also by a new intellectual class, which significantly modernized the terms of the national ideology. These modernizers introduced a more realistic, critical, and historically contextualized understanding of human rights and social processes. They also identified personally with, and in many cases emerged from, ethnic groups that had never before had such influential and creative spokespersons. John Dewey, Jane Addams, W. E. B. Du Bois, and Thorstein Veblen variously exemplify the new intellectual class. In making American universalism more truly cosmopolitan and more responsive to the aspirations of ethnic minorities and underprivileged classes, they infused into the promise of America a concrete sense of the common good. This social-democratic perspective virtually took possession of the social sciences and of the literary intelligentsia between the two world wars.[12]

By the early 1960s, the renewal of American democracy had made impressive headway. European and Asian immigrant groups had emerged from the shadow of racism. The urban working class, moving to the suburbs, was blurring distinctions between itself and an amorphous middle class. The desegregation of public space and the integration of public schools and the political process were progressing with surprising speed. Among young people, appreciation of African American culture was no longer condescending, but was hearty and widespread. In important ways, however, the movement was running out of steam.

One ominous sign was Martin Luther King, Jr.'s failure in 1966 and 1967 to turn his civil rights crusade into a broader class coalition. King realized that without a common front of underprivileged people—white and black—committed to a broad redistribution of wealth, the problems of northern ghettoes would remain intractable. At first he won some union support; then riots intruded. King's assassination soon followed.[13]

Indeed, this last dream of Martin Luther King, Jr., so deeply imbued with American universalism, was already foreclosed. A new style of black leadership, speaking the language of racial power rather than the ideal of universal rights, was on the march. In truth, the era had already passed when claims for racial and for class equality could buttress one another. In the late 1950s labor unions, having lost their militancy, entered a long decline that has continued almost to this day. A sad observer, looking back across his lifetime, remarked in 1992: "The hopes of the Thirties, the complacencies of the Fifties, and the slumbers of the Seventies are gone past recall for industrial labor. Nothing remains but the breaking of hearts."[14]

Meanwhile, suburbanization and economic advancement were draining from white ethnics the class resentments that the Democratic party had mobilized. In Washington, policy debates narrowed from broadly social issues to fiscal policies and interest-group politics.[15] Altogether, the alarm that had awakened Americans in the first half of the twentieth century—the danger of impending entrapment in an increasingly stratified society—gave way among the majority of whites to a consumer-oriented spirit of expansiveness and self-indulgence.

The people who were being left furthest behind were not an entire social class but were the poorly organized segments of certain endowment groups, notably lower-class blacks, middle-class women, and uncared-for children. This was the context in which an outpouring of rage in black America, in the 1960s, sent shudders of guilt and anxiety through the affluent classes of white America, and the mixture of rage and guilt sparked an educational reform movement. The reformers proposed to make education more accessible and supportive to minorities by infusing both the curriculum and the entire educational environment with recognition and respect for "ethnic diversity." The schools could thereby nourish ethnic pride and, at the same time, assuage a fearsome anger. At first, in the 1970s, the reform movement was known as multiethnic education, or occasionally as multicultural education.[16] (Only since the mid-1980s has the latter name gained a provocative notoriety.) Regardless of nomenclature, however, the multicultural movement has tried to carry forward the great campaigns of the mid-twentieth century against racial and ethnic inequalities without reviving the wider outcry of that earlier era against class inequalities.

To sum up the breadth that the project gradually attained, multiculturalism fosters cultures of endowment while drawing a veil over the cultures of class. The new curricula have made a fetish of diversity. Only an occasional rhetorical flourish, however, hints that different social classes— with all their complications of region and religion—have had subcultures just as distinct from one another (and just as overlapping) as those of racial or ethnic groups.[17]

Officially, invocations of class are obligatory in defining programs and objectives, since the academic leaders of the multicultural movement cluster on the left. Thus Paul Lauter, an influential proponent of overhauling the teaching of American Studies, notes that a "loosely constituted 'Left' comprised of feminists, black scholars, gay and lesbian academics, educational progressives, and cultural radicals, wishes to reconstitute curricula around the central perception of difference—especially of race, gender, class, and sexual orientation—and to open colleges to more democratic decision-making."[18] In 1988, the American Studies Association took up the cry. For the first time the association chose "Cultures of Gender, Race, Ethnicity, and Class" as the theme of its annual meeting. Since then, American Studies programs around the country have increasingly redesigned themselves as multicultural alliances, "worshipping"—in the words of one enthusiastic participant—"the 'holy trinity' of race, class and gender."[19]

In practice, however, class is among the absentees from the celebration of diversity. Multiculturalists care little more about class as a fully elaborated identity—bearing its own meanings, associations, and vulnerabilities—than they do about differences between religions, regions, and nations. Fresh scholarship on the structure and mentality of all of these groups continues to instruct us but owes little or nothing to multicultural auspices.[20] To its academic apostles, multiculturalism signifies a preoccupation with race and gender—a preoccupation that allows just a whiff of class consciousness to sharpen the pungent odor of subjugation and resistance.

How shall we construe this extraordinary dissociation in American academic culture between two great structures of inequality, which (in the same academic culture) are generally assumed to reinforce one other? Is the deflection of attention from broad disadvantages of class to specific disabilities of endowment simply an expediential mimicry of practical politics? Is the academic left simply acknowledging that supporters of "endowment" issues—such as racism, sexism, abortion, gay rights, defense of Israel, and protection of the environment—have won significant victories in recent years, whereas class-oriented demands have only stiffened resistance to change?[21]

Or is this shift in national priorities from class to endowment, and the accompanying response of multiculturalists, explicable from a larger perspective as a reversion to a traditional politics of race? After a period when class and race were seen as jointly responsible for violating the "American Dream," an older diversionary pattern—going back to the country's earliest experience—has reappeared. Again, as in the eighteenth and nineteenth centuries, racial antipathies submerge and suppress class identities. The troubling contradiction between the ideal of a classless society and the realities of racial enslavement and degradation has long tempted Americans to use race as an antidote to class divisions. Mostly this practice has meant diverting onto endowment groups an anger aroused by class injustice. Now, in a variant of that pattern, multiculturalism cultivates the anger of unequal endowment groups as an alternative to class consciousness. Class has ceased to excite us, but the politics of race live on. In David Brion Davis's words: "We seem . . . to have entered another period when race has preempted class."[22]

If multicultural education unwittingly defeats its own egalitarian purpose by absolutizing racial differences while obscuring the broader inequalities of class, some changes in its instructional aims would seem to be in order. Young Americans need to learn what anthropologists have known all along: that race and ethnicity do not always confer desirable identities, nor are these identities unalterable, uncontested, or monolithic. They are surprisingly fluid, at least in America. In changing circumstances, individuals continually reinvent their ethnic identities. They renegotiate the loyalties they must choose among, or alter the dimensions of a predominant identity that begins to pinch.[23] An effective civic education should widen, not narrow, the options that people can entertain. It must not allow race and ethnicity to seem intractable or class to remain invisible.

The contrast between the boundless diversity that multiculturalism appears to espouse and the focused agenda it actually pursues is only one of the confusions that have made it a subject of angry controversy. On other problems of civic education, which have nothing directly to do with the issue of class, multiculturalism offers very unclear guidance. To understand why this is so, we will need to explore its teachings and its recent history more closely.

The truth is that multiculturalism has remained a stubbornly practical enterprise, justified by immediate demands rather than long-range goals: a movement without an overall theory. Understandably, the multicultural strategies of academic intellectuals and educators began as ad hoc responses to the outcries of minorities in a crisis situation. The schools were failing; the streets were burning. Something had to be done for ghetto children—something to raise their self-esteem and engage their energy and attention. Still, it is troubling that, twenty years after those convulsive beginnings, multiculturalism suddenly became a policy issue in America's colleges, universities, and secondary schools without yet proposing a vision of the kind of society it wants. In view of the indistinctness of multicultural goals, it is hardly surprising that no independent assessment of what it is accomplishing has yet appeared.

Sorting out the confusions that have sprung up in the absence of a multicultural theory of society takes us back to the intellectual origins of the movement. The seeds of the present disarray were sown in the intellectual ferment of the early twentieth century, above all in the haunting, ambiguous visions of a more inclusive America that era has left us. Those rival visions, so innocent and far away, led circuitously to the angry disputes that have exploded throughout the educational system in the last few years.

The great reconstruction of American universalism in the Progressive era produced the first systematic studies of ethnic processes and the first college courses on race relations. As never before, the actual diversity in the American population was documented and dissected.[24] Nevertheless, most of the revisionists clung to a traditional reliance on assimilation as the path to equality. They believed that the cauldron of the modern city, aided by intermarriage, would gradually meld the country's various ancestral strains into a single people. In the spirit of Robert E. Park, the outstanding pioneer of race relations research, they foresaw an irreversible (if some-times painful) process of assimilation. But a daring handful of social proph-ets went further. These cultural pluralists, as they were soon called, de-clared that ethnic minorities in the United States were proving so tenacious of their own identities that no distinctively American culture existed or could be expected. Not an ultimate homogeneity, said Randolph Bourne, but a mutually invigorating, egalitarian pluralism is the incomparable dis-tinction of America, "the first international nation . . . the world-federation in miniature."[25]

The new perspective was an intellectually intriguing deviation from the mainstream of liberal thought. As a philosophy of minority rights, it con-ceived of America as a federation of minorities in which one (the Anglo-Saxon ruling class) had usurped hegemony.[26] The predominant version of American universalism, on the other hand, remained distrustful of the danger that accentuation of group differences posed to equal rights. Most universalists were concerned less with the cohesiveness of groups than with the freedom of individuals to move beyond their origins and make them-selves over. Until the 1960s, however, the disagreement was of little con-sequence. Pluralists and assimilationists alike looked forward to a great community, both national and transnational, in which law and voluntary cooperation could increasingly soften group differences.[27]

Then, suddenly, accommodation and inclusiveness lost credibility. In a revolution of rising expectations amid a disintegrating national consensus, Black Power introduced themes of anger, enmity, and intimidation toward whites. Other minorities soon moved in the same direction. For them, too, conflict became an imperative. Thus a harsher form of pluralism emerged in the 1970s to demand that the schools recognize the power of ethnic and racial minorities, not just the value of their cultures. The term "cultural plu-ralism" acquired an ever-wider popularity, while its meaning for society as a whole became more difficult to define. Some radical multiculturalists still invoke cultural pluralism as their founding principle, but their indignant opponents often describe multiculturalism as an abandonment and be-trayal of pluralism, and middle-of-the-road educators represent pluralism as a strain within multiculturalism, balanced by assimilation.[28] Lurking in this verbal confusion is a good deal of the old commitment to universal prin-ciples, to a common culture, and to a long-term process of acculturation. But those ideas all seem somehow on the defensive. What had happened?

Essentially, universalism largely lost its link to any great community, especially to the American nation. In earlier times, Americans had felt connected to one another through the ideological origins that enabled their country more than any other to unite heterogeneous peoples. On that common ground, down to the 1950s, both cultural pluralists and assimilationists stood. Both planted themselves on what they regarded as the "American Idea."[29] Their confidence in the possibility of building "a house for all peoples" was reinforced, moreover, by a belief in progress as the overall course of modern history.

The loosening of this sturdy civil culture did not begin in the 1960s. After the nationalistic excesses of World War I and the technological impersonality of postwar society, patriotism and urban boosterism never fully regained their earlier adhesive power. By the 1940s the acids of modernity were also corroding popular faith in social or moral progress. Not until the upheavals of the 1960s, however, did the tendency of cultural pluralists to emphasize the separateness of ethnic cultures in this country take on a darker, anti-American meaning. Now any claim for centeredness, any affirmation of a unifying national culture, became ipso facto oppressive. By the early 1970s popular television serials displayed a society without shared ideals or respected institutions.[30] All in all, a cynical state of mind made it difficult to discuss, and impossible to clarify, common loyalties and responsibilities within a population as diverse as that of the United States.[31]

Nevertheless, the sense of crisis that launched the present era in ethnic studies eased. From the early 1970s through most of the 1980s, polemical posturing subsided. The rhetoric of black nationalism collapsed,[32] while cumulative improvements in race relations—often modest but sometimes dramatic—went steadily forward. Moderate black politicians increasingly won elections, not just because they were moderates but also because young white voters gave them record levels of support. With little complaint, whites also accepted new voting-rights legislation designed to create safe electoral districts for minority candidates. Intermarriage rates rose because opposition to intermarriage on the part of whites gradually weakened. The black middle class, expanding and prospering, gained sometimes grudging but substantial respect. Overall, through the recession of the 1970s and onward to the most recent statistics, racial differences in education and median household income have persistently diminished.[33]

The scale of these changes went largely unnoticed. Most whites grew weary of racial issues in the 1970s, while a continuing bitterness and fear of the future kept many blacks edgy and defensive. Neither side could fully appreciate that a great, incomplete, but irreversible social transformation was under way. In the midst of large, continuing disparities of income and education, deep and persisting segregation, and the degradation of urban ghettoes, many blacks and whites were learning that accommodation is a beneficial, reciprocal process.

Alan Peshkin has reported in depth on a multiethnic public high school in California, in which teachers give no special attention to ethnicity and hold all students to a common standard. Without rejecting their own identities, the students interact positively and unselfconsciously across ethnic lines. Although such a school is unusual today, it exemplifies the possibility of a more egalitarian future.[34] Some recent polling data have sent a similar signal. A cross section of adults were asked in 1990 which ethnic groups in America should have more power. Forty-seven percent of the respondents said blacks should have more power; 46 percent said Hispanic Americans; 6 percent said whites.[35]

This is the puzzling context in which a new eruption of ethnic tensions has shaken us. It began around 1986 in universities, secondary schools, and fear-ridden urban neighborhoods. The street incidents were deadly criminal encounters between black and nonblack individuals. Self-anointed black spokesmen inflamed the incidents into dramatic protests against an allegedly oppressive and conspiratorial power structure. The fuel for these often self-destructive but intimidating protests came from the angry misery of ghetto dwellers who found themselves more and more trapped and abandoned as middle-class black neighbors fled to safer areas.[36]

About the same time, similar themes of outrage, isolation, and demagoguery were played out on college campuses without the personal violence. Here the provocation was verbal harassment by white students, many of whom had grown up in escapist suburbs with no knowledge or appreciation of the civil rights movement. Crass racial humor in student newspapers and in fraternity high jinks, along with worse slurs in anonymous graffiti, were shocking to faculty and administrators. To black and Hispanic students, who often felt out of place even in polite campus settings, these incidents were searing. Minority students responded by demanding more university support for their own campus centers and organizations. That, in turn, resulted in a sharper splintering of the student body into separate racial blocs.[37]

Another strategy, pushed especially by multicultural activists in the faculty, requires every student to take a course in ethnic studies. Such courses, it was hoped, would teach the delights of diversity and puncture provincial stereotypes. (They would also most certainly create new faculty positions for minority teachers.) Again, anxious authorities rushed to oblige. The requirement became common in the larger universities.[38]

These new demands and confrontations are the setting in which multiculturalism has become a buzzword, a crusade, and a gigantic mystification. Some teachers, equating multiculturalism with global inclusiveness, point out that social studies curricula have developed strongly in that direction since the 1960s. Leading the way, the state of California adopted in 1987 a new curriculum that provides a working balance between American and world history. Diane Ravitch, a coauthor of the curriculum, says that "the United States has a common culture that is multicultural." In her view, radical multiculturalists have pushed a sound principle to a pernicious extreme. They have turned the pluralist impulse into a virulently explicit assault on the European heritage that undergirds American education.[39]

The critics of the California plan, however, see it as just another instrument of cultural imperialism. America has no common history. To escape intellectual oppression, every race has to center its children in its own distinctive culture and its own proud history. From the critics' perspective, pluralism merely "disguises the perpetuation of exclusion." Mainstream pluralists such as Ravitch are purveying a "white self-esteem curriculum" that kills the mind and spirit of nonwhite children.[40]

In this polarization between a rebellious sense of exclusion and an inclusiveness built on European foundations, the two versions of multiculturalism are locked in defensive suspicion of one another. Between them, left-of-center academics have tried to stake out a middle ground. "I am baffled why we cannot be students of Western culture and of multiculturalism at the same time," Catharine R. Stimpson declared in her presidential address to the Modern Languages Association. "Surely some Western texts," she continued, "are also multicultural."[41] Unfortunately, her phrasing betrays a widespread presupposition that what is multicultural stands outside a common arena. Typically, it has to do with marginal groups and oppositional attitudes, not with a standard human condition.

Conceivably, the concept of multiculturalism can find a center of gravity in a centerless space where outsiders resist and simultaneously enrich an overall national culture. As it stands, however, the multicultural idea is shaped by its explosive emergence from clashing ethnocentric demands and antagonisms: Afrocentric, Eurocentric, phallocentric, and so on. Among alienated, postmodern intellectuals this oppositional thrust has released a rejuvenating rhetoric. By the late 1980s the older language of cultural pluralism, from which multiculturalism stems, sounded too soft and tame to articulate a radical critique of America.

Yet an easing of current ethnic hostilities will not by itself resolve the problems of multiculturalism. As the legatee of cultural pluralism, it will still contain the limitations, and reflect the incompleteness, that the pluralist perspective has never lost. America is more than a federation of minorities. It encompasses many millions who will never conceive of themselves in those terms. Americans are a people, molded by processes of assimilation. An adequate theory of American culture will have to address the reality of assimilation as well as the persistence of differences.[42]

In brief, the present disarray in multicultural education leads us back before the angry disputes of the 1990s, and also before the immediate sources of those disputes in the cultural divisions of the 1960s. Embedded in cultural pluralism from its beginnings are underlying dilemmas with which a constructive educational policy will have to deal. There are no easy answers for these dilemmas, but teachers and scholars who aspire to be in some sense multiculturally responsible can find guidance from them.

One dilemma is methodological. It concerns how teachers and scholars structure their work in the most general sense. Should we analyze problems or hold celebrations? Since few will admit to being unabashedly celebratory, the right answer might seem clear-cut, at least for high school and college classes. At mature levels, education tackles problems. But appreciation and advocacy (to substitute less inflammatory words in place of celebration) are unavoidable in any institutionally established study of the sponsor's culture and heritage. How is it possible for any program created in the interest of a particular constituency *not* to be a vehicle of sympathy and support, unless that constituency becomes alienated from itself?[43] Moreover, this practical reality is by no means deplorable. People who are conscious of unequal antecedents need to feel some collective affirmation of their rightful membership in a heterogeneous community. At the same time, scholars betray their professional code if they fail to maintain a critical distance from people who engage their own personal loyalties. Appreciation is merely provincial if not grounded in knowledge and values that bring into judgment a range of humanity far wider than the people who are immediately at issue.

Every inquiry in the humanities must wrestle with the dilemma of celebration versus analysis. But multicultural studies pose it in a particularly acute way because they compel scholars to problematize overlapping and conflicting identities. However much one may wish to represent sympathetically more than a single ethnic or sexual identity, empathy tends to slide from the "multi" to the "mono," from diversity to specialty. Logically, all the cultures in a multicultural situation deserve what each desires alone.

In this connection, we need more awareness of how rapidly fashions in the distribution of empathy can change and of how vulnerable to the careless winds of history our own passionate sympathies may become. Fifty years ago, when historians and literary critics were still largely untouched by cultural pluralism, the paramount object of appreciation in American Studies was what is now called "mainstream" culture, and the icon of celebration was the famous American melting pot. History textbooks took note of ethnic problems but viewed them in the light of specific stereotypes and disadvantages of particular groups. There was a Negro problem, an Indian problem, and an immigration problem, and each inflected inequalities that the melting pot could ultimately dissolve. Then, in the 1960s, the relation between problems and celebrations turned upside down. The ethnic groups now got the celebrations; the melting pot became the problem.[44]

Today the distribution of empathy is shifting again. Some European ethnic groups, such as Jews and Italians, are losing the benefit of being considered minorities. Not long ago, an ethnic scholar who was widely influential in the 1970s and early 1980s is said to have remarked, "I feel as if I have been abolished." In a good many ethnic studies programs the multicultural faculty seems to exclude professors who are identified in any way with European antecedents. Ethnicity is equated with race, and all whites are lumped together.[45] Recently, for example, a stalwart scholar of European descent, long established in comparative ethnic studies, was forced out of a statewide conference he had organized. The steering committee insisted that only "people of color" qualified as ethnic.[46]

Less striking but surely unsettling to multiculturalists is the emergence of a scholarly literature that applies sympathetic ethnic perspectives to numerous subgroups within the old-stock white population or even to the larger (but always conflicted) experience of becoming American. The New England Puritans now stand forth as paradigmatic exemplars of the anguish of emigration and of the immigrant's struggle for cultural survival.[47] One recent monograph brings out a hitherto neglected civic consciousness among rank-and-file members of the Ku Klux Klan of the 1920s. Another illuminates a special sense of identity among the Civil War veterans who formed the Grand Army of the Republic.[48] On a popular level, but supported by heavy academic credentials, Ken Burns's powerful television

series, *The Civil War,* taught contemporary audiences a lesson in grief for
the hundreds of thousands of young men who suffered and died in that
terrible struggle.[49] These extensions of scholarly empathy to people who
lived within the dominant American culture would not have been possible
a decade ago. They suggest that without a universal standard the reservoirs
of academic empathy can flow in unforeseeable directions that may leave
some minorities more vulnerable than ever.

The dilemmas of empathy—who deserves it and how much should they
have—are at least familiar. Other underlying dilemmas, springing from the
special aims of multicultural studies, may be more damaging because they
are systematically ignored. Multiculturalists, in fact, have nothing to say
about goals as we usually understand that term. Instead, they dwell on
needs: the needs of victims for greater self-esteem, more ethnic recognition, compensatory assistance, and role models of their own kind. Needs
are subjective and difficult to measure. To question them is to challenge
the complainant's inner strength. Goals are public and therefore more
open to challenge and to critical assessment. Needs are a present hunger,
not a direction. Goals imply change over time and the importance of purpose in shaping growth. Shifting from needs to goals brings us up against
policy dilemmas that multiculturalism has been unwilling to address. Here
are some of those unspoken dilemmas.

Arousal or Restraint? Should scholarship and teaching arouse or subdue ethnicity as a social force? If we wish to strengthen feelings of attachment, loyalty, and pride in one's own group (or in a particular group we
happen to favor), we do so to enhance the power of that group in dealing
with others. At the same time, we want to build self-esteem in members of
the group who have been damaged by its poor reputation. Whether inner
confidence—rather than aggressive egotism—can be produced by school
lessons that teach the good news about one's own group and the bad news
about others seems highly doubtful.[50] In today's world, ego strength means
incorporating contrarities within the self. There is little doubt, of course,
that a *group* is strengthened politically by teachings that mobilize it for encounters with opponents. The problem is that ethnic mobilization rapidly
spreads to other groups, creating situations full of danger for all of them.

Shall we then seek to subdue ethnicity, either by harnessing it to other
social forces or by tempering its impact? The goal of harnessing ethnicity is
mostly pursued by scholars on the left, for whom ethnic and other cultural
discontents offer a substitute for class as a basis for building coalitions to

challenge capitalist society. For example, a radical faction in Brookline, Massachusetts, temporarily succeeded in revamping the high school curriculum along supposedly multicultural lines. In reality, it was a Third World curriculum in anticolonialism. European history disappeared from the required sequence. The breakup of the Soviet Union went unmentioned, and a new required course, "World in Crisis," focused on Northern Ireland, Vietnam, and Israel.[51]

A better way to subdue ethnicity is to temper the presentation of group differences and conflicts by rendering the experience of minorities and majorities as a scene of lights and shadows, of satisfactions as well as failures, all the while questioning the sharpness of the social boundaries separating groups from one another. This can have a wide appeal. It does not, however, produce a deep and burning commitment. It cannot satisfy the core constituencies for ethnic studies, those who want affirmations of their importance and autonomy. Anyone who seeks to temper the claims of ethnic groups is therefore easily charged with rationalizing a conservative complacency. So the dilemma between arousal and containment remains.

Convergence or Divergence? Should multicultural studies anticipate or seek a future of greater or reduced separateness and autonomy between ethnic groups? Should they promote convergence or divergence in group identities? In spite of all the slogans about diversity, this fundamental question is never posed in the present controversy or in the scholarship accompanying it.

In pursuit of an answer I have studied the "platforms" that candidates for office in the American Studies Association write for the guidance of those who must elect them. In 1992, the twelve candidates who ran for the top offices sounded very much alike in their ardent espousal of diversity. Eight of them explicitly championed multiculturalism. Another urged an examination of "our culture not as a totality but . . . as a structure of diversity," while another denounced any "kind of . . . homogenizing, consensual 'we.'" The eleventh spoke ambiguously of mapping "the interface of class, race, gender, and aesthetics," but failed to be elected. That left only one candidate to strike a genuinely different note. Recommending a "continuing internationalization of American Studies" and a "more *integrated* understanding of the culture of the United States," he, too, was defeated. In this massive multicultural unanimity, however, I could find no clue to whether the future leaders of the ASA want to foster greater diversity or simply bring out what they fervently believe is already there.[52]

This is curious, since the whole multicultural movement—if my account of it is correct—stems from the long striving in America for greater equality. On the surface, one would think that the goal of equality would not be well served by highlighting or increasing differences among people. At the least, we are entitled to some explanation of how an emphasis on differences of endowment will advance equality. To my knowledge none has been suggested by our multiculturalists. Between divergence and convergence they leave us guessing.[53]

Preserving or Creating? A third dilemma that multiculturalists steadfastly ignore betrays acutely the absence of any long-term historical perspective from pluralist thought since the 1960s. In championing group identities, should ethnic studies be prospective or retrospective? Should they look to the past to save what is being lost or to the future to gain something new? How can these two desirable goals be reconciled or accommodated?

Within individual minority groups, these questions arise obsessively. Every group has its fundamentalists, who jealously guard the ancient ways; its reformers, ready to adopt new ways; and its equivocal mainstream. The balance between them varies from group to group and shifts as the specific history and dynamics of each group change. Fundamentally, ethnicity is a conservative force. It stresses continuity, survival, and the links between generations. At certain historical junctures, however, it has a revolutionary potential. Briefly, that was the case with black nationalism at the end of the 1960s. Today revolutionary nationalists are little heard from, but the differences between racialist conservatives and flexible reformers are great. While Afrocentric fundamentalists reinvent an ancient racial heritage, reformers argue "that race and history and metaphysics do not enforce an identity; that we [blacks] can choose within broad limits . . . what it will mean to be African in the coming years."[54]

An unequivocal concern with building new identities is clearly uppermost among other dissident minorities who associate themselves with multiculturalism. Feminists, for example, are not looking for roots. They may search the past for clues to women's underrecognized potentialities, but their object is to reshape the traditional woman. The issue of preserving, as opposed to creating, identities arises in such different ways in the circumstances of individual groups that no truly multicultural agenda can address it.

All three of these unexamined dilemmas have a common source. Multiculturalism is silent on problems of arousal, divergence, and direction because, like so much else in American life today, it lacks a vision of what it wants the country to become. For young people in search of some common purpose beyond the confines of their own endowment, multiculturalism offers no nourishing center or beckoning horizon.

Nevertheless, an indispensable heritage of equality lives on amid the contradictions of the multicultural movement. Although truncated and fragmented, this heritage awaits a wider understanding and employment. If multiculturalism can shake off a fixation on diversity, autonomy, and otherness, the vision that American universalism sustained and enlarged through two centuries can be renewed. It can teach us that we are all multicultural and increasingly transnational—that minority and majority cultures alike are becoming more and more interconnected, interpenetrated, and even indistinguishable.

To adopt the fashionable language of multiculturalism, we are all "others" to others. But otherness is only relatively so, and diminishes as the bounds of "our" own identities expand, overlap, and combine. On that basis, Rodney King's distraught appeal to the consensual "we" whom multiculturalists scorn might be heard. We can work it out. Unless we have grown too cynical or self-enclosed, an American universalism can be rebuilt.

From the beginning of his career, John Higham has written about the history of history writing. His first substantial scholarly article, "The Rise of American Intellectual History" (*American Historical Review*, 1951), was in this genre. At one point his historiographical writing overflowed into a book, *History: Humanistic Scholarship in America* (1965), which is still used in graduate programs. He has illuminated changes within the discipline for nearly half a century.

Sometimes a critical bent has drawn him into swirls of controversy. His article "Beyond Consensus: The Historian as Moral Critic" (*AHR*, 1962) put him in the forefront of the reaction against the consensus school of the 1940s and 1950s. Yet his books and comments, if sometimes polemical, were never simplistic. His appreciation of the complexity and subtlety of human experience enabled him to see even the histories with which he disagreed not as two-dimensional caricatures but in the round.

Concerned about the future of historical thinking as well as its past and present, Higham has urged colleagues and students to be ever conscious of their own involvement in a collective endeavor with consequences that extend beyond their lifetimes. This theme is especially strong in Higham's article, "The Future of American History." Here his attachment to those who have gone before him is evident in the quality of his criticism as well as his praise. Whatever their limitations, Henry Adams, Frederick Jackson Turner, and Charles Beard were all passionately engaged in the project of writing American history, and the example of their commitment has resonated just as fully as has the influence of their interpretations.

Historians need to be very cautious about predicting the future. Here Higham does not so much predict as encourage young scholars of U.S. history to discover opportunities in the new relations that are developing between local sites and transnational vistas. Both the transnational and the local can gain, he suggests, if we reimagine the nation as a link between them. At the same time, a view of national culture that is enriched through transnational comparisons and regional studies can help explain how the "great amorphous form of America" holds together.

Kathryn Kish Sklar
State University of New York at Binghamton

14

The Future of American History
[1994]

No one can predict what kinds of history Americans will be writing in the twenty-first century. It is reasonable to ask, however, what sorts of history Americans are likely to need and what goals might enable the next generation of scholars to address those needs. Should the history of the United States continue to enjoy a high priority? If so, in what form? Must it obstruct the fullest possible development of supranational or world history? How should the national and the supranational levels of history be related? What can be done to connect them?

Any response to these questions depends, of course, on value judgments, together with a sense of what is malleable and what may be fixed in the present situation. I take my starting point from a conviction that the nation-state will remain for a long time the strongest political structure in the world. It will also remain the seat of one or more nations, which in much of the world are preeminently encompassing and coercive communities. Nevertheless, in the late twentieth century the state is under siege. In western Europe and North America, the abounding trust it once enjoyed is eroding. Everywhere nations and states are becoming, on the one hand, less capable of dominating the subgroups within their boundaries and, on the other hand, more vulnerable to markets, technologies, and ecological forces that spread wildly across national borders. At the same time new nations are clamoring for self-determination, and old elites are uncertain about how to limit it.[1]

To date, historians of the United States have done very little to understand these invasive challenges to national identity or to gain some intellectual control over them. The present training of those of us who study

American history fails to encourage outreach from local or national experience to transnational patterns. Professors and students alike know that early specialization within American history will bring the best jobs, the easiest teaching, and the quickest advancement. Whatever language or course requirements graduate students must fulfill outside this central preoccupation are more or less casually chosen and infrequently used in later life.

The permissiveness of a specialized education has the further effect of dispersing research energies, which in turn weakens any concentration on large historical schemes that cut across national lines. In the 1970s and 1980s, numerous American historians either lost interest in national history or became sharply critical of it. Their flight from nationalism, however, has not yet led to an alternative paradigm for interpreting large-scale changes and continuities. Although some brave spirits are undertaking a macrohistory of relations between cultures and between continents, world historians touch down only occasionally and lightly in the territory commanded by historians of the United States. The latter rarely take notice, for so many of them have turned inward, as Michael McGerr recently remarked, to microhistories that "measure experience on a small, intimate scale" of "private spaces, personal lives."[2]

The problem of connecting subnational particulars with supranational patterns has therefore become a major issue—perhaps *the* major issue—in formulating research strategies. The grand theories that once linked local history with universal history have faded. To bridge the huge discontinuities of scale between these levels, we must resort to less ambitious devices. One promising strategy points toward more rather than less attention to the mediating structure of nations. I want to suggest that the goal of transcending national history compels us paradoxically to revitalize it.

To grasp the scope of the problem, consider two contrasting ways in which modern historical studies involve nations. To choose a nation deliberately as the subject or protagonist of a history is to render it as actor, or at least as an active presence, in a story that includes other participants (individuals, groups, and institutions) within the nation and without. No single theater of action necessarily constricts the story. It may transport the historian to distant scenes, where external players and conditions impinge on a nation's destiny.

For many influential historians of the United States today, the nation has a different presence, passive and usually unexamined. In this second mode, the nation is simply a convenient arena within which some spectacle that interests the historian is easily observed. Here, too, the nation delimits attention, but now as a setting, not as a consciously chosen subject. Although the phenomenon under scrutiny may be visible in other national arenas, the historian ignores them. He or she is not interested in national questions or comparisons. For the most part, the current scholarship that forms the "field" of American history belongs to this second category: it is not about the United States but merely about what happens in the United States. The deliberate study of national behavior, institutions, and identity is relatively neglected in the United States at present. As subject or actor, the nation makes few forays into the arena of human behavior in which it used to play a starring role. The arena is still littered with inert memorials to the nation, but other actors have grabbed the spotlight.

From the middle of the nineteenth century until the 1960s, the nation was the grand subject of American history. The leading historians of the United States either devoted themselves to explaining the nation's distinctiveness, as a polity and a people, or took it for granted. The reality and importance of that distinctiveness were never in question. Quarreling over the causes of the country's uniqueness, historians divided into rival schools; but the clash of opposing interpretations veiled an underlying consensus on the inspiriting truth of American exceptionalism. The nation was both the preeminent subject of American history and very largely the arena in which it was observed.

Fortunately, not everyone was interested in American history. Some of the best historians the United States produced from the 1840s onward consciously turned away from the parochialism of their national history. Owing partly to the special influence of the Enlightenment on American thought and partly to the recoil of urban elites from the crass provincialism of a frontier society, conservative historians after the mid-nineteenth century identified themselves increasingly with a transatlantic world rather than with any single national origin. It is perhaps not surprising that the famous seminar in history that Herbert Baxter Adams directed at the Johns Hopkins University spent the better part of a month in 1889 developing a collective definition of "civilization."[3]

Accordingly, nineteenth-century Americans such as William H. Prescott, Henry C. Lea, Charles Homer Haskins, and Alfred T. Mahan produced major works on medieval Europe and on the growth and conflict of European empires overseas. They created a tradition of cosmopolitan scholarship, which outgrew the insularity of English historiography, although it drew on common Anglo-American values.[4] In the twentieth

century this transatlantic perspective has gradually lost its originally conservative, Anglophile bias and even its Eurocentric focus. Now reaching
outward to all parts of the globe, it remains to the present an impressive
feature of the American historical profession. Traveling in Europe, American scholars often notice that the schools they are visiting assign a considerably smaller proportion of academic positions to the history of other parts
of the world than do their own universities at home.[5]

In spite of the challenge that this impressive body of transnational
scholarship might seem to pose to writers of American history, at least until
recently it has not greatly affected them. One reason is simply the specialization I have already touched upon. Early in the twentieth century,
an informal segregation divided the tenders of the national garden from
all who labor in other vineyards. "They make their choice early," said
J. Franklin Jameson in the 1920s, "and for the rest of their lives the student
of European history knows very little of American history, the student of
American history very, very little of European." In the same vein, Jameson
wrote in 1924: "Most American history men suffer greatly from not having as their background a sufficient knowledge of European history and
its methods."[6]

An equally important reason why the transatlantic perspective made a
place for itself without altering the core of American history is that a
common theory of progress underlay both. Until fairly recent times, American and European history could be sequentially reconciled. American
students of European history generally chose periods and problems they
could interpret as earlier episodes in the history of liberty, which eventually
came to flower in the American republic. Thus, during the formative decades of the historical profession, internationally minded scholars linked
the British colonies in America closely to the antecedent history of England
and Europe. Wilsonian internationalism was in good measure a product of
that Anglo-American sense of cultural continuity, in which guiding values
broadened as they descended from remote, ancestral beginnings. After
1919, however, even that evolutionary connection receded into a dim background. With certain notable exceptions, American history from World
War I to the 1960s was a national story enclosed in a national arena.

Why did the encapsulation of American history within a national framework last so long? The question is unavoidable, for the effects of this
perduring separateness still weigh heavily on American historiography.
Fundamentally, historians treated the United States as unique and separate
from the rest of the world because a virtually unchallengeable national

myth identified it as a country created by removal from the corruptions and confinement of Europe. Exodus, celebrated initially by New England Puritans as the path to salvation, was secularized in the eighteenth century as the formative act of a virtuous people. Americans understood their revolution, not as the overthrow of an old, oppressive order, but as an escape from it and as the creation of a new order beyond the reach of the old. The Revolution was the birth of a people "conceived in liberty" but still confronting an evil world. The American, in J. Hector St. John Crèvecoeur's words, became "a new man, who acts upon new principles; he must therefore entertain new ideas, and form new opinions." Here "every thing has tended to regenerate" the downtrodden outcasts of Europe.[7] Conveying the same message, the official seal that the U.S. Congress adopted in 1782 depicted the nation as an unfinished pyramid, divinely blessed and emblazoned with a Vergilian motto, "Novus Ordo Seclorum"—a new order of the ages. The design still appears on the back of the American dollar bill, and the adjective "new" still reverberates in American speech as a redemptive promise.

In the nineteenth century, the myth of American newness diffused through daily life, spreading along with exceptional material abundance and exceptionally egalitarian social relations. The sense of separation from an Old World was perhaps especially underscored by an extraordinary level of geographical mobility. Everyone moved, or so it seemed. Conservative intellectuals such as Rufus Choate sometimes despaired over "our national humor . . . to be and do just what we please, go where we please, stay as long as we please and no longer; [holding] the State itself . . . to be no more than an encampment of tents on the great prairie, pitched at sun-down and struck to the sharp crack of the rifle next morning."[8] Accordingly the pioneer—the person who leaves home to claim a wilderness—became the archetypal American, just as the immigrant was perceived as the American-to-be, properly and inevitably; and beyond both of them loomed the self-made individual, the American who had fully achieved a new and larger identity. It is suggestive that the prototype of the self-made man, Benjamin Franklin, emigrated from his New England home at an early age to make his way in the distant city of Philadelphia; that the first known use of the designation "self-made men" came from a spokesman for the early American West, Henry Clay, who was championing "the American system" as a bulwark against aristocracy and foreign influence; and that the classic assessments of the United States by Europeans repeatedly stressed the migratory restlessness of the American people.[9]

From this cluster of attitudes and habits flowed a national vision so pervasive and compelling that even the most internationally minded historians absorbed it. Henry Adams's great nine-volume *History of the United States During the Administrations of Jefferson and Madison* (1889–1891) rested not only on research in the archives of Washington, London, Paris, and Madrid but also on Adams's lifelong familiarity with European history and culture. His *History of the United States,* largely concerned with foreign relations, was essentially a narrative of statecraft, yet the American leaders whose maneuvers Adams dissected minutely counted for little in the outcome of his story. Rather, Adams explained the rise of the new nation through a vivid contrast between America's "natural" development and the "artificial," class-ridden society of Europe. It was the energies of an uncowed people that redeemed their leaders' blunders and placed the United States on the path to greatness. Listen to the echoes of Crèvecoeur in Adams's invocation of "this new man": "Stripped for the hardest work, every muscle firm and elastic, every ounce of brain ready for use, and not a trace of superfluous flesh on his nervous and supple body, the American stood in the world a new order of man. . . . Compared with this lithe young figure Europe was actually in decrepitude."[10]

Henry Adams wrote as an independent gentleman. One might suppose that the professional historians who came after him would be more cautious about reifying a national type. And so they were—at least in picturing the physical attributes of a figure so aggressively masculine. Nevertheless, professional historians during the first half of the twentieth century featured frontiersmen and self-made men (though they often called the latter "robber barons") and continued to celebrate innovation, mobility, and the endogenous growth of a society shaped by its own institutions and ideals. The distinctiveness of the nation went unquestioned.

The strongest, most explicit version of the American-centeredness of American history was expounded by Frederick Jackson Turner and elaborated by countless disciples. Turner swept aside the significance that more conservative historians attached to the transatlantic "seeds" of American democracy. What really made the nation unique, according to Turner, was the natural environment in which it was formed. The most American part of the country was therefore the West. The frontier provided "the crucible" in which immigrants became Americans, and Americans self-made men.[11] The major alternative to Turner's vision of American history came from Charles A. Beard, a prodigiously productive scholar whose influence ultimately surpassed Turner's. Without denying the contribution of the frontier to American democracy, Beard stressed a broader clash of rival economic interests. Conflicts between shifting coalitions of property holders, he argued, had leveled "artifical" class privileges and undammed the democratizing power of science and technology.

On the surface Beard's history was far more sensitive than Turner's to a wider world. Beard had studied abroad, had written his first book on the Industrial Revolution in England, and remained in many ways a citizen of the world through most of his life. Widely read in German philosophy and social theory, he was fond of quoting the dictum *Weltgeschichte ist Weltgericht*. Recalling the excitement of Sunday visits at the Beard's home, Alfred A. Knopf remembered that the "talk would be about everything. . . . He had always been reading some German book, or some obscure somebody or other."[12] *The Rise of American Civilization*, Charles and Mary Beard's master work, pointed repeatedly to analogies with the social struggles of antiquity and the Middle Ages. Nevertheless, at the bedrock of their history was an unshakable belief in the uniqueness of *American* civilization. From all of his international engagements, Beard returned to his homeland with a renewed sense that here was the sanctuary of human progress—the last, best hope of universal history.[13]

Throughout the writings of the so-called Progressive historians, led by Turner and Beard, the distinctive character of the nation was presupposed rather than argued. Typically midwesterners, the Progressive scholars started from an inherited culture, absorbed in their early years in the heartland, and simply asked how it was changing or had changed. They could not address critically what they took for granted. I believe that was why Turner's thesis concerning the significance of the frontier did not lead him or others into an internationally comparative research program. Instead, he shifted from studying the frontier as a national experience to examining the shifting balance between major sections. By concentrating on internal conflicts, Progressive historians avoided everything that was problematical about national differences.

Additionally, the Progressives' preoccupation with internal conflict diverted them from any serious inquiry into the connective tissue that held the country together. While conservative scholars studied the slow evolution of central institutions, Progressives turned attention to the variety of groups contending for power. Ridiculing abstractions, they celebrated the American people, not by defining an all-embracing national character, but by describing the ceaselessly interactive movement of particular types: farmers, laborers, business leaders, women, inventors, immigrants, and so on. Although the Beards constructed their *Rise of American Civilization* on a conflict-driven, dialectical framework that was entirely different from the framework Henry Adams employed, the two works conveyed the same impression of a mysterious, never-resting energy, propelling the American people onward into the future.

In the 1940s and 1950s, under the weight of a broadly conservative shift of opinions, the progressive synthesis of American history broke down. Its critics assailed the progressive stress on dramatic antitheses and convulsive social change. Returning from World War II, a new generation of historians—many of them the children of immigrants—had seen the United States from the outside. It seemed to them, for better or worse, a stronghold of stability in a revolutionary world.

Accordingly, postwar historians called for recognition of the continuities in American history and belittled the magnitude of the many crises, upheavals, and "watersheds" that Progressive historians had reveled in. The commonalities that earlier scholars had taken for granted, notably a high level of mobility and the pervasiveness of capitalism, became foci of historical inquiry. So did rigidities, such as racism, that earlier scholars had passed over lightly.[14] Instead of presupposing an American national character, the so-called consensus historians puzzled over its paradoxes and contradictions. Instead of scoffing at unreal abstractions, they took national myths seriously as a force in history. By contrasting the United States with other countries, especially with a generalized image of Europe, they made the old myth of American newness explicit and adopted it as an analytical principle. The most influential of these revisionist works, Louis Hartz's *The Liberal Tradition in America,* opened with a dramatic declaration: "The analysis which this book contains is based on what might be called the storybook truth about American history: that America was settled by men who fled from the feudal and clerical oppressions of the Old World."[15]

Thus a new program of research and interpretation reconstituted the uniqueness of American history just when one might have expected the separation of American from world history finally to dissolve. Under the new program, the need to demonstrate how and why the United States differed from the rest of the world awakened a long-dormant interest in comparative, cross-cultural studies. This in turn opened exciting perspectives on topics as various as slavery, reform, social mobility, American fiction, and political theory.[16] American history suddenly gained an exhilarating international breadth, to which British and other foreign scholars now made contributions of the first order of importance.[17]

Yet the substance of this research largely reinforced the nationalism that its method seemed to challenge. On the whole, consensus historians looked only for the differences between the United States and other countries. Ideologically, their writings often had a conservative coloration. America was indeed—so it seemed—a very special place.

The consensus paradigm never became firmly rooted in the American historical profession. After a brilliant beginning, the internationally comparative scholarship that the new paradigm inspired failed to flourish, although isolated achievements continued to impress.[18] By the end of the 1960s, the study of national character and the respect for national myths was collapsing, not only in history but also in the other social sciences. The principal writers of consensus history were falling silent, or changing their points of view, or ceasing to make expansive claims. Louis Hartz left his professorship at Harvard University and abandoned the academic profession. An intellectual revolution, the kind of upheaval that postwar historians had tried to disprove, overturned their work.

Although the sources of the revolution are not easy to disentangle, two stand out. One was a profound revulsion, initially against the state, for the inhumanities it perpetrated or protected at home and overseas. The resulting alienation spread. Restless students and young intellectuals turned against all large, impersonal structures of authority, bringing scorn for the groups that maintain such structures and disbelief in their principles. Dominant nationalities, ruling elites, national states, and entrenched legal, economic, and educational systems turned vile. Creeds and universalistic ideals were ideological entrapments. Instead of investigating the foundations of liberty and justice, historians became more interested in demonstrating the inescapability of domination.[19]

Ironically, the other highly visible source of a new historiography that recoiled from distant and ruling powers was in European academic centers. Scholars in France and England, bent on recovering a premodern world that we had lost, found ways to reconstruct painstakingly the customs, mentalities, and choices of ordinary people in local communities long ago. What the French exuberantly called *l'histoire totale* opened windows into the private lives of hitherto neglected and often underprivileged groups with whom young scholars could feel a personal bond. By bringing to light the buried experience of vulnerable people of every description, the new paradigm of the 1970s and 1980s celebrated the authenticity of small or submerged communities rather than the uniqueness of any great community. And by orienting early American history toward premodern Europe, this intensely fragmented paradigm disconnected the colonial era from narratives of American uniqueness or identity.[20] The nation as actor became hard to find, except as a villain in other people's stories.

In the most influential historical scholarship, therefore, the myth of America, land of promise, either faded from sight or lived on as a target for critics. The downfall of belief in a unique American destiny did not happen all at once, nor is the demise complete. In hindsight we can follow an accumulation of doubts—beginning in the late nineteenth century—that the United States could ever possess some categorical exemption from the burdens and limits of history in other lands. A weaker form of the argument for American uniqueness persisted for several decades among many of those who clung to a vision of progress. For them history had given this nation the possibility of leading in the struggle of humanity for a better world.[21] As doubts about that prospect accumulated, consensus history provided a new foundation for exceptionalism by substituting continuity for progress.

Throughout the educated, professional classes, however, a sense partly of the destructiveness and partly of the declining power of the American national state spread during the seventies and eighties, along with the loss of belief in the reality of an overall American identity.[22] Laurence Veysey averred in 1979 that social historians now perceived the inhabitants of any nation-state not as a people but as a complicated mosaic, in which each element "must therefore have an utterly separate history. And there is little incentive to try to piece these histories together into a whole," Veysey continued, "because the parts are seen as the realities, the whole as an artificial construction sustained by politicians and financiers."[23]

Veysey's characterization of an American people (and presumably also the state) as artificial may suggest one reason why historians since the 1960s have made little headway in interpreting either a national community or the power of the national state. The ingrained contrast we have noted, in the American historiographical tradition, between what is "natural" (the indigenous society) and what is "artificial" (a remote European world) seems to persist in transmuted form. The national or spatial distinction between our own authenticity and those unnatural others who are far away has, in the scholarship of the 1970s and 1980s, turned into a hierarchical distinction between those who wield power from on high and those who suffer under it. Subordinate elements, wherever located, are the real. Dominant elements are contrivers; lofty principles, their contrivances. The onslaught on a traditional perspective perpetuates its categories.

Have we somehow entangled ourselves once more in an age-old American antipathy to power at a distance? Perhaps so; but contemporary culture now gives this ancient prejudice a voguish confirmation. Postmodern philosophies and critical theories imported from Europe lend a cachet of intellectual authority to our ingrained distrust of those who control the national state. Celebrating diversity and deconstruction, the insistent pluralism of our post-Marxist era rejects any claim to centeredness in the forms of experience. In short, postmodernism calls for destabilizing and decentering an integrated national history.[24]

"Why," a colleague asked me when I delivered an earlier version of this essay, "why must everything have a center?" I replied that everything doesn't, but large societies need one or more centers in order to hold together. Centers are too important to ignore, especially in complex systems such as nations—and academic professions.

Also, I might have added, identifying centers helps us to locate the margins of a culture, provided that we resist the facile assumption (carried over from Marxist colonial studies) that centers are by definition oppressive and peripheries necessarily exploited. A topological model tracing lateral ties between center and margins can go far toward rescuing us from the simplicities of a hierarchical model of domination and subordination.[25] Relations of sympathy, obligation, and social connectedness, extending across space as well as time, are just as essential to a nation as they are to an ethnic group. It would be helpful if these psychic bonds could be understood as simultaneously patriotic and ethnocentric: an inescapably supportive *and* exclusionary foundation of all large-scale collective identities that rest on a presumption of common origins.[26]

As yet, however, most American historians seem more or less content with the familiar pluralist paradigm. The recording of hitherto silent people in small communities or circumscribed settings has been the leitmotif of American social, cultural, and even political history during the last two decades. The nation, while seldom appearing as an actor, remains a vast arena in which a thousand voices are chanting their separate histories. Many subspecialties flourish—notably women's history, immigration history, African-American history, Native American history, and working-class history. But they function largely within the American arena and (except for early American history) make contact only intermittently with similar projects in other countries.

Logically, we might anticipate that the reaction against American exceptionalism would lead to strong transnational inquiries along comparative lines. If the United States is not significantly different from other countries, or different only as a variant within a larger system, shouldn't its relation to that system be spelled out? And wasn't Marxism ready at hand for the task? In the 1960s, virtually for the first time, a powerful strain of Marxist theory entered American historical writing. A major beneficiary of the failure of consensus, Marxism was particularly well suited to subsuming national experiences within a larger dialectic of historical change.[27]

Yet localism has prevailed here too, and the principal Marxist ventures in a comparative direction have left surprisingly little imprint on historians of the United States. Beginning in the 1960s, Eugene Genovese offered an original interpretation of the social structure of the Old South, designed to explain the American Civil War as a class struggle. Although focused on slavery, Genovese's work in its widest dimensions has looked toward a comparative history of ruling classes. To this, little attention has been paid. Instead, he is best known for an empathic, noncomparative book (*Roll, Jordan, Roll*) describing sympathetically the domestic and religious life of the slaves.[28]

The Marxist project that enlisted many young historians of the United States was not Genovese's but the intensive examination of working-class communities. Although this "new" labor history developed in the 1960s through contacts with English Marxism, it has now receded almost entirely into the American arena. The Marxist tradition lives on, either by turning inward and settling down in its own enclave of labor history, where a few traditional questions can be pursued without intrusion from outside, or by enlivening modern American cultural studies with the critical and conceptual fertility of a Jackson Lears. At neither level—one close to home, the other soaring far and wide—does explicitly comparative analysis play a continuing role.[29]

Although the comparative challenge to the separateness of American history is gradually winning converts, it lacks momentum. It has none of the things that made Marxism attractive in the 1970s: a clear theoretical direction, a strong political message, a visible institutional presence, and an effective network of scholarly communication. Since significant historical statements are at least implicitly comparative, the project of making crucial hypotheses more explicitly so meets little resistance among scholars. By the same token, what beckons to us everywhere belongs nowhere in particular. Since any historical journal will gladly print a well-crafted comparative article, the limited output of such work is highly scattered, and its diversity defeats an ongoing discussion of problems and models.[30] Comparative studies seem to flourish only when alternative interpretations clash. Until the subject matter that is being compared—in this case national history—becomes salient and passionately contested, the method is unlikely to be vigorously and cumulatively employed.

Some American historians, however, feel liberated by the fragmentation of their field. To the appeals for synthesis that have arisen in recent years, these happy individualists respond that synthesis is a weak ideal and integration not to be desired in historical scholarship. All calls for synthesis, Allan Megill warns, are attempts to impose one's own interpretation on others.[31] Such warnings quicken the pervasive distrust of domination that I have already remarked on.

On the other hand, a turn toward reintegration *is* under way. In general, two paths toward a wider historiography are opening up. One path seeks to follow the structures and movements that reach across political boundaries. I have in mind such institutions as religion, the family, and technology, as well as ecological systems and trading relations. Since these patterns typically extend beyond any single country, their study can and should lead historians outside the national arena. The second path returns to national history. In this direction historians are reinventing the nation and reconstituting the narrative of its development. I want to suggest that the two paths are interdependent. Neither a transnational nor a national history can properly flourish without the balance-weight of the other.

In a recent issue of the *American Historical Review,* Ian Tyrrell argued for the first of my two paths, and there is little I can add to his vigorous advocacy. It is regrettable, in my opinion, that he dwells on the failings of comparative history, instead of seeing national comparisons as one of the means of crossing national boundaries. Here, and in his hostility to any claims that the United States has been different from other countries, Tyrrell pits transnational history against national history instead of recognizing their complementarity.[32]

In our present historiographical situation, the special service of transnational history is to offer a means for building on the wealth of recent research in social and cultural history. A national-political framework can never hope to contain many of the new meanings and relations the past is disclosing.[33] Most notoriously, national history cannot treat women fully enough to do justice to *their* history, no matter how refined and extended the historian's notion of power becomes.[34] For any field of history in which national boundaries artificially cramp and distort a causal sequence or a cultural configuration, an alternative route toward a broadening level of interpretation is obvious. Instead of overburdening national history by loading it with social and cultural matters it cannot effectively contain, historians who seek a larger view of their field of study can move out of the national arena. As David J. Russo has pointed out, many of the nonpolitical aspects of life (demography, religion, technology, philosophy, communications) do not fit within political boundaries. "They have configurations and geographic territories of their own" and need to be understood historically in transnational contexts.[35]

Today historians who are pursuing thematic interests beyond the confines of any single national arena often have no special desire to compare nations. Their primary object may be to attain a wider human perspective, unclouded by nationalism and ethnocentrism. Philip Curtin, for example, has deliberately eschewed national comparisons, designing all of his books of the past two decades as studies of movement and encounter across continents or large economic regions.[36] This supranational social history can provide constructive vistas for the overspecialized microhistorians who came of age in the 1970s and 1980s. To an impressive degree, it is already doing so.[37]

The second path I have in mind—specifically, the reconstruction of a genuinely national history, a history of the connections through which state and society have defined one another and dealt with change—will also entail some venturing beyond the American arena. A need to rethink the vehicles of tradition and the agencies of authority in a chaotic world is upon us. The tenacity of nationalism and the widely different forms it takes in this country and in others—its capacity, on the one hand, to sustain a democratic partnership and, on the other hand, to plunge societies into endless ruin—will have to be understood comparatively before a new American history fully unfolds.

Accordingly, some historians are again asking the big questions that intrigued an earlier generation in the 1940s and 1950s. How were nations made? What have they achieved? Wherein have they failed?[38] Obviously a simple claim for incommensurable uniqueness will not help to locate the United States in the world of nations. We need responsible judgments of similarities and connections as well as differences, and we need a recognition of the societal forces, ranging across wider arenas, that delimit a nation's freedom of action more severely than its people may realize. To grasp the nation as subject must often pull historians beyond the national arena.

Modestly formulated and often skeptically expressed, a new, comparison-oriented literature on the changing contours of an American identity is emerging. To a considerable extent, initiatives are coming from scholars based in other countries, other disciplines, other fields of history.

Such is the case, for example, with the most grandly ambitious work to date, Liah Greenfeld's *Nationalism: Five Roads to Modernity,* a comparative study of the origins of English, French, Russian, German, and American national consciousness.[39]

There is also much to do within the American arena, where internal relations can count for more than international comparisons. Here the great challenge is to rebuild a structure for American history by revising or replacing the themes that have fallen apart in the past generation. For several years scholars have debated ways and means of formulating a synthesis more inclusive and coherent than textbooks currently offer. Their success has been limited, I sugggest, because they have tried to create a national framework without a national focus.

Some have designed a pluralistic synthesis based on the conflictual interplay between groups in American society or, in Robert Wiebe's version, on the spaces that separate those groups. The object is to bring out the many ways, both subtle and overt, in which power is exercised outside the political system as well as within it. Incorporating microstudies of social groups and situations is enriching political history greatly, and in the hands of Eric Foner and Wiebe this approach has yielded an unusually broad-gauged narrative. The best results to date span a period during which the nation moves, ambiguously rather than triumphantly, a certain distance toward its present condition.[40]

Valuable though such efforts are, they have the earmarks of an unstable compromise, as can be seen from Thomas Bender's theoretical attempt to reconcile "wholes" and "parts" in American history. Bender wants to show how a contest of diverse group cultures has shaped and reshaped a decision-making arena, which he calls "the public culture."[41] Although subtle and capacious, this formulation cannot satisfy the many social historians who refuse to grant such primacy either to public life or to any single center of history. It also disappoints those who insist, as I do, that at the center of American society there is not just an arena but a magnet. Bender's proposal fails to convey either the strengths and weaknesses of a national community or the inner life of less inclusive communities.

The inability of a multicultural project such as Bender's to illuminate the making and unmaking of a center suggests that a compelling synthesis of American history will have to deal with centers as well as margins and peripheries. From our present perspective, the most persistent and characteristic dialectic in American history is between centers and peripheries, or—to shift to a metaphor of process—between consolidation and differentiation. Centripetal force contends with centrifugal freedom. The prevailing pluralist paradigm allows no space for consolidation except as repression. It does not prompt us to ask whether some kinds of consolidation can engender diversity and whether some kinds of diversity can mask consolidation. How shall we ever grasp the great amorphous form of America without emphasizing the unceasing yet ever-changing tensions between its centers and its centrifugal energies?[42]

An important feature of American institutions is the distinctness of three centers or centralizing systems: the state, the economy, and the culture. A restructured history could clarify the separateness of the three systems, along with their conflicts and their phases of convergence. My own interest is most particularly in the third. It is in the sphere of culture that the dominant pluralist paradigm makes the lineaments of a people so hard to see.

To regain a national focus on a culture that is permeated by the energies of differentiation would seem to call for some readjustments in research priorities. Here are a few:

1. A recognition of assimilation as a legitimate, sometimes desirable, and often inescapable pathway in a heterogeneous but nonetheless cohesive culture. Our current language of "diversity" implies a stability and a permanence of social boundaries that neither the differentiating nor the integrative forces in American culture will sustain. Our current scholarship virtually ignores the remaking and blending of group identities throughout American history.[43]

2. Investigation of "Americanness" as a powerful though elusive level of national awareness. Research to date on the history of American nationalism has advanced on fairly explicit levels of myth, symbol, and ideology.[44] Below these conscious expressions of loyalty to and pride in a nation, however, there lie largely "unarticulated feeling[s] of belonging, of being at home," that inhere in mundane rituals and routines, in manners and in memories.[45] Whether historians can track, in diaries, journals, and travel literature, the emergence and persistence of such sentiments remains to be seen.

3. A return to broad-gauged regional studies. Questions about cultural contrasts between the major regions of the United States lost interest when the study of national character was jettisoned. The region as a mere arena remained, and historians have fruitfully examined many

subgroupings within it and powerful external forces that invaded it. As a distinctive presence within a larger national story, however, the credibility of the region suffered along with that of the nation.[46] If national propensities come alive again, regional peculiarities will enrich and complicate them.

4. An appreciation of social classes as national segments. In recent years the role of class in American history has to a large extent been subsumed within the study of ethnicity and gender. Enfolded within these specialized studies, class has been perceived less as an identity worthy in its own right than as a reinforcement of ethnic, racial, and sexual exploitation. Yet classes, like regions, are primarily constituent segments of *American* society. In the course of time, they became rivals for national honor with their own distinctive inflections of a national culture. A national focus can enable historians to see class relations and differences as a national configuration.[47]

To describe, as I have tried to do, the form of a future American history with only a slight anticipation of its content may seem an idle exercise. It is intended, however, not as a substantive blueprint but as a design for education—a design in which fragmentation is reduced because rival objectives are understood to complement one another. The design encourages young historians who are finding their way about in the arena of American history to choose, and to begin to work toward, a long-term goal: to either make national experience and identity one's subject or prepare to follow another subject beyond national lines, toward whatever periphery may help to define its center. To be sure, the two paths are interdependent; shifting from one to the other in the early years of a career should not be difficult. Both require some measure of comparative judgment and knowledge, but neither demands exhaustingly disjunctive research. What this choice of paths probably does require is more careful selection of graduate fields than many students now make.

At the same time there is a substantive point within this dual design. While doing fuller justice to what is transnational, it also seeks to end the quarrel of American historians with national myths and national character. The unquestioning rejection of American myths in recent scholarship perpetuates their intellectual tyranny. To put some weight at the center, the history of an American nation has to take account, in some relative way, of the beliefs of its people and the strength of its culture.

Notes

CHAPTER 1. *Hanging Together: Divergent Unities in American History*

1. John Higham with Leonard Krieger and Felix Gilbert, *History* (Englewood Cliffs, N.J., 1965), 221–26. For a more general post mortem see Thomas L. Hartshorne, *The Distorted Image: Changing Conceptions of the American Character Since Turner* (Cleveland, Ohio, 1968).

2. Michael Kammen, *People of Paradox: An Inquiry Concerning the Origins of American Civilization* (New York, 1972).

3. Michael H. Frisch, *Town into City: Springfield, Massachusetts, and the Meaning of Community, 1840–1880* (Cambridge, Mass., 1972); Michael Zuckerman, *Peaceable Kingdoms: New England Towns in the Eighteenth Century* (New York, 1970), 257; Sam Bass Warner, Jr., *The Urban Wilderness: A History of the American City* (New York, 1972), 3. See also Darrett B. Rutman, *Winthrop's Boston: Portrait of a Puritan Town 1630–1649* (Chapel Hill, N.C., 1965); Richard L. Bushman, *From Puritan to Yankee: Character and the Social Order in Connecticut, 1690–1765* (Cambridge, Mass., 1967); Kenneth Lockridge, *A New England Town, the First Hundred Years: Dedham, Massachusetts, 1636–1736* (New York, 1970). The vicissitudes of other collectivities are treated in Richard Sennett, *Families Against the City: Middle Class Homes of Industrial Chicago, 1872–1890* (Cambridge, Mass., 1970); Wilson Carey McWilliams, *The Idea of Fraternity in America* (Berkeley, Calif., 1973); Laurence Veysey, *The Communal Experience: Anarchist and Mystical Counter-Cultures in America* (New York, 1973); R. Jackson Wilson, *In Quest of Community: Social Philosophy in the United States, 1860–1920* (New York, 1968).

4. Most impressively, Anthony F. C. Wallace, *The Death and Rebirth of the Seneca* (New York, 1969). But see also Herbert G. Gutman, "Work, Culture, and Society in Industrializing America, 1815–1919," *American Historical Review*, 78 (June 1973), 531–88.

5. Clifford Geertz, "The Integrative Revolution: Primordial Sentiments and Civil Politics in the New States," in Clifford Geertz, ed., *Old Societies and New States: The Quest for Modernity in Asia and Africa* (New York, 1963), 105–57; Joshua A. Fishman and others, *Language Loyalty in the United States: The Maintenance and Per-*

petuation of Non-English Mother Tongues by American Ethnic and Religious Groups (The Hague, 1966).

6. Hazel W. Hertzberg, *The Search for an American Indian Identity: Modern Pan-Indian Movements* (Syracuse, N.Y., 1971).

7. Gunther Barth, *Bitter Strength: A History of the Chinese in the United States, 1850–1870* (Cambridge, Mass., 1964), 77–101; Theodore C. Blegen, *Norwegian Migration to America: The American Transition* (2 vols., Northfield, Minn., 1931–40), II, 582–84; Arthur A. Goren, *New York Jews and the Quest for Community: The Kehillah Experiment, 1908–1922* (New York, 1970), 20–21; Robert E. Park and Herbert A. Miller, *Old World Traits Transplanted* (New York, 1921), 145–51.

8. Harold Wentworth, *American Dialect Dictionary* (New York, 1944), 341; *Oxford English Dictionary* (13 vols., Oxford, 1933), V, 710.

9. C. Vann Woodward, *The Burden of Southern History* (New York, 1961), 23–24. The quotation is from Eudora Welty. See also David M. Potter, "The Enigma of the South," *Yale Review,* 51 (Autumn 1961), 150–51.

10. *The Annals of America* (18 vols., Chicago, 1968), IX, 146. See also William R. Taylor, *Cavalier and Yankee: The Old South and the American National Character* (New York, 1961).

11. See Clifford Geertz, "Ideology as a Cultural System," in David E. Apter, ed., *Ideology and Discontent* (New York, 1964), 47–76; and Willard A. Mullins, "On the Concept of Ideology in Political Science," *American Political Science Review,* 66 (June 1972), 498–510. I have resisted the special constructions the term has been given by Marxists and their successors, as in Ben Halpern, "'Myth' and 'Ideology' in Modern Usage," *History and Theory,* 1 (no. 2, 1961), 129–49, and by conservatives, as in Edward Shils, *The Intellectuals and the Powers and Other Essays* (Chicago, 1972), 23–41; but I have tried to avoid the sweep and elevation that ideology loses in the strictly functionalist definition employed in Talcott Parsons, *The Social System* (New York, 1951), 331–32, 348–58.

12. Michael Walzer, *The Revolution of the Saints: A Study in the Origins of Radical Politics* (Cambridge, Mass., 1965).

13. Sumner Chilton Powell, *Puritan Village: The Formation of a New England Town* (Middletown, Conn., 1963).

14. Timothy H. Breen and Stephen Foster, "The Puritans' Greatest Achievement: A Study of Social Cohesion in Seventeenth-Century Massachusetts," *Journal of American History,* 60 (June 1973), 5–22. See also Stephen Foster, *Their Solitary Way: The Puritan Social Ethic in the First Century of Settlement in New England* (New Haven, 1971).

15. Jack P. Greene, "Search for Identity: An Interpretation of the Meaning of Selected Patterns of Social Response in Eighteenth-Century America," *Journal of Social History,* 3 (Spring 1970), 189–220.

16. Bushman, *From Puritan to Yankee,* 183–95; Alan Heimert, *Religion and the American Mind from the Great Awakening to the Revolution* (Cambridge, Mass., 1966), 95–158.

17. Howard Miller, *The Revolutionary College: American Presbyterian Higher Education, 1707–1837* (New York, 1976); Sidney E. Mead, *The Lively Experiment: The Shaping of Christianity in America* (New York, 1963).

18. Ruth Miller Elson, *Guardians of Tradition: American Schoolbooks of the Nineteenth Century* (Lincoln, Neb., 1964), 46–55, 58; *McGuffey's Fifth Eclectic Reader*

(New York, 1962, reprint of 1879 edition), 296–97. See also Philip Schaff, *America: A Sketch of Its Political, Social, and Religious Character*, ed. Perry Miller (Cambridge, Mass., 1961), 72–95.

19. James Fulton Maclear, " 'The True American Union' of Church and State: The Reconstruction of the Theocratic Tradition," *Church History*, 28 (March 1959), 41–62; Lois W. Banner, "Religious Benevolence as Social Control: A Critique of an Interpretation," *Journal of American History*, 60 (June 1973), 35–41.

20. George Bancroft, *A History of the United States, from the Discovery of the American Continent* (10 vols., Boston, 1834–1874).

21. [Edward Johnson], *Johnson's Wonder-Working Providence, 1628–1651*, ed. J. Franklin Jameson (New York, 1910), 25. The importance and scope of the millennial idea are brought to the fore in Ernest Lee Tuveson, *Redeemer Nation: The Idea of America's Millennial Role* (Chicago, 1968); David D. Hall, "Understanding the Puritans," in Herbert J. Bass, ed., *The State of American History* (Chicago, 1970), 336–41; and Sacvan Bercovitch, "Typology in Puritan New England: The Williams-Cotton Controversy Reassessed," *American Quarterly*, 19 (Summer 1957), 179–91.

22. Heimert, *Religion and the American Mind*, 59, 94–96.

23. The most thoughtful effort to date to define an "American ideology" is Yehoshua Arieli, *Individualism and Nationalism in American Ideology* (Cambridge, Mass., 1964), but it needs to be corrected in the light of recent scholarship on republicanism, notably Gordon S. Wood, *The Creation of the American Republic, 1776–1787* (Chapel Hill, N.C., 1969); and Gerald Stourzh, *Alexander Hamilton and the Idea of Republican Government* (Stanford, Calif., 1970). I have also profited from: J. G. A. Pocock, "Virtue and Commerce in the Eighteenth Century," *Journal of Interdisciplinary History*, 3 (Summer 1972), 119–34; Edmund S. Morgan, "The Puritan Ethic and the American Revolution," *William and Mary Quarterly*, 24 (January 1967), 3–43; Perry Miller, *Nature's Nation* (Cambridge, Mass., 1967), 90–120; Max Savelle, "Nationalism and Other Loyalties in the American Revolution," *American Historical Review*, 67 (July 1962), 901–23; Eric Foner, *Free Soil, Free Labor, Free Men: The Ideology of the Republican Party Before the Civil War* (New York, 1970). Another formulation, different from mine, is presented in H. Mark Roelofs, "The Adequacy of America's Dominant Liberal Ideology," *Bucknell Review*, 18 (Fall 1970), 3–15.

24. Gaillard Hunt, *The History of the Seal of the United States* (Washington, D.C., 1909).

25. Jacob Cooke, ed., *The Federalist* (Middletown, Conn., 1961), 351–52.

26. On this point Ralph Barton Perry's classic treatise, *Puritanism and Democracy* (New York, 1944), is still worth reading.

27. John R. Howe, Jr., "Republican Thought and the Political Violence of the 1790's," *American Quarterly*, 19 (Summer 1967), 147–65; Richard Buel, Jr., *Securing the Revolution: Ideology in American Politics, 1789–1815* (Ithaca, N.Y., 1972).

28. Henry Steele Commager, ed., *America in Perspective: The United States Through Foreign Eyes* (New York, 1947), 112–13. See also Nils William Olsson, ed., *A Pioneer in Northwest America, 1841–1858: The Memoirs of Gustaf Unionius* (Minneapolis, 1950), 48; Timothy Flint, *Recollections of the Last Ten Years, Passed in Occasional Residences and Journeyings in the Valley of the Mississippi, from Pittsburgh and the Missouri to the Gulf of Mexico, and from Florida to the Spanish Frontier; in a Series of Letters to the Rev. James Flint, of Salem, Mass.* (Boston, 1826), 204–6. There is very likely a connection, not yet understood, between the rootlessness that Alexander

Mackay described and the predominance of intensely felt landscapes in American painting in this period. For an indication of the scope of the problem see Barbara Novak, "American Landscape: The Nationalist Garden and the Holy Book," *Art in America*, 60 (January, 1972), 46–57.

29. Michel Chevalier, *Society, Manners and Politics in the United States: Being a Series of Letters on North America* (Ithaca, N.Y., 1961), 306–10; [James Dawson Burn], *Three Years Among the Working-Classes in the United States During the War* (London, 1865), 116–17.

30. Paul C. Nagel, *One Nation Indivisible: The Union in American Thought, 1776–1861* (New York, 1964), 13–144.

31. Laurence Veysey, ed., *The Perfectionists: Radical Social Thought in the North, 1815–1860* (New York, 1973). But perfectionism was not confined to radicals, as can be seen in Timothy L. Smith, *Revivalism and Social Reform in Mid-Nineteenth-Century America* (New York, 1965), 103–34. For a discussion of interconnections between the religious and political crusades of this period—between evangelical Protestantism and nationalist expansionism—see Chapter 9 below.

32. Robert A. Nisbet, *The Social Bond: An Introduction to the Study of Society* (New York, 1970), 244–49; and Nisbet, "The Impact of Technology on Ethical Decision-Making," in Jack D. Douglas, ed., *The Technological Threat* (Englewood Cliffs, N.J., 1971), 39–54. See also Daniel Bell, "Technology, Nature and Society: The Vicissitudes of Three World Views and the Confusion of Realms," *American Scholar*, 42 (Summer 1973), 385–404; and Bell, *The Coming of Post-Industrial Society: A Venture in Social Forecasting* (New York, 1973).

33. Harold C. Syrett, ed., *The Papers of Alexander Hamilton* (17 vols., New York, 1961–), X, 256. On the further development and display of this aptitude in the nineteenth century, see Marvin Fisher, *Workshops in the Wilderness: The European Response to American Industrialization, 1830–1860* (New York, 1967), 46–75; and the illuminating documents in Carroll W. Pursell, Jr., ed., *Readings in Technology and American Life* (New York, 1969).

34. This distinction has been obscured by the tendency of many American intellectuals in recent decades to make technology, industrialism, urbanization, and materialism virtual equivalents of one another. Leo Marx's sensitive and evocative book *The Machine in the Garden: Technology and the Pastoral Ideal in America* (New York, 1964) contributed to the blurring of historical perspective by treating the machine in a highly metaphoric context, embracing a contrast between city and country and ultimately between head and heart. On that level of generality it becomes difficult to discriminate the intellectuals who were deeply concerned about technological power from those who were not. See Theodore R. Marmor, "Anti-Industrialism and the Old South: The Agrarian Perspective of John C. Calhoun," *Comparative Studies in Society and History*, 9 (July 1967), 377–406.

35. Nathan Rosenberg, *Technology and American Economic Growth* (New York, 1972), 25–36, 44–50, lists many other factors that contributed to the rapid rate of technological change in the United States in the nineteenth century. Some of Rosenberg's factors—a "utilitarian bent in American society," the "absence of inhibiting institutions," and a high level of education—may be regarded as consequences of the dominant ideologies.

36. Charles Sanford, *The Quest for Paradise: Europe and the American Moral*

Imagination (Urbana, Ill., 1961), 157–73; Perry Miller, *The Life of the Mind in America from the Revolution to the Civil War* (New York, 1965), 275–313; Hugo A. Meier, "Technology and Democracy, 1800–1860," *Mississippi Valley Historical Review,* 43 (March 1957), 618–40. Of special interest is Timothy Walker's reply to Thomas Carlyle, "Defense of Mechanical Philosophy," reprinted in Pursell, ed., *Readings in Technology in American Life,* 67–77.

37. Alfred D. Chandler, Jr., "The Coming of Big Business," in C. Vann Woodward, ed., *The Comparative Approach to American History* (New York, 1968), 223–25; Michael B. Katz, *Class, Bureaucracy, and Schools: The Illusion of Educational Change in America* (New York, 1971), 56–104; David Tyack, "Bureaucracy and the Common School: The Example of Portland, Oregon, 1851–1913," *American Quarterly* 19 (Fall 1967), 475–98; Roger Lane, *Policing the City: Boston, 1822–1885* (Cambridge, Mass., 1967), 95–105; Raymond H. Merritt, *Engineering in American Society, 1850–1875* (Lexington, Ky., 1969); Daniel H. Calhoun, *Professional Lives in America: Structure and Aspiration, 1750–1850* (Cambridge, Mass., 1965), 56–58, 186–97. For a detailed, illuminating study of one of the midcentury pioneers in technical integration—the first American to focus intensively on what he called in 1854 "the science of management"—see Alfred D. Chandler, Jr., *Henry Varnum Poor: Business Editor, Analyst, and Reformer* (Cambridge, Mass., 1956).

38. The decline in the rate of growth of patent office business in the twentieth century, as shown in the table, is discussed in Alfred B. Stafford, "Is the Rate of Invention Declining?" *American Journal of Sociology,* 57 (May 1952), 539–45.

39. Robert L. Carneiro, "Structure, Function, and Equilibrium in the Evolutionism of Herbert Spencer," *Journal of Anthropological Research,* 29 (Summer 1973), 77–95; Henry C. Carey, *Principles of Social Science* (3 vols., New York, 1858–60); Arnold W. Green, *Henry C. Carey, Nineteenth Century Sociologist* (Philadelphia, 1951), 55, 79–80. Herbert Spencer was a civil engineer before he became a social philosopher, and his philosophy can be understood as an application to nature of the principles of organization he learned in managing a railroad.

40. Katz, *Class, Bureaucracy, and Schools;* Robert L. Church, "Introduction," in Paul Buck, ed., *Social Sciences at Harvard, 1860–1920: From Inculcation to the Open Mind* (Cambridge, Mass., 1965), 1–17. The best compilation of Spencer's educational writings is in Andreas M. Kazamias, ed., *Herbert Spencer on Education* (New York, 1966).

41. James Willard Hurst, *Law and the Conditions of Freedom in the Nineteenth-Century United States* (Madison, Wis., 1967), 73–74; Daniel J. Boorstin, *The Americans: The Democratic Experience* (New York, 1973), 165–213.

42. David C. Huntington, *Art and the Excited Spirit: America in the Romantic Period* (Ann Arbor, Mich., 1972), 23–26.

43. Richard de Charms and Gerald H. Moeller, "Values Expressed in American Children's Readers: 1800–1950," *Journal of Abnormal and Social Psychology,* 54 (February 1962), 136–42. My understanding of the themes in popular fiction rests on an unpublished analysis by Raymond Detter of the thirty best-selling novels by American authors published between 1841 and 1874, as listed in Frank Luther Mott, *Golden Multitudes: The Story of Best Sellers in the United States* (New York, 1947), 306–10.

44. Richard Weiss, *The American Myth of Success: From Horatio Alger to Norman Vincent Peale* (New York, 1969), 11–14. For an early example, reprinted in 1970 with a

valuable introduction by Annette K. Baxter, see "Business Habits: Qualifications Essential to Success," in *The Universal Self-Instructor and Manual of General Reference* (New York, 1883), 484–86.

45. Some parts of this transition are noticed in John Tomsich, *A Genteel Endeavor: American Culture and Politics in the Gilded Age* (Stanford, Calif., 1971), 88; Frederic Cople Jaher, *Doubters and Dissenters: Cataclysmic Thought in America, 1885–1918* (New York, 1964); Richard L. Rapson, *Britons View America: Travel Commentary, 1860–1935* (Seattle, 1971), 174–77.

46. Samuel Haber, *Efficiency and Uplift: Scientific Management in the Progressive Era 1890–1920* (Chicago, 1964); Samuel P. Hays, *Conservation and the Gospel of Efficiency: The Progressive Conservation Movement, 1890–1920* (Cambridge, Mass., 1959); Joel H. Spring, *Education and the Rise of the Corporate State* (Boston, 1972); Jerry Israel, ed., *Building the Organizational Society: Essays on Associational Activities in Modern America* (New York, 1972). I am particularly indebted to the key book in this mode, Robert H. Wiebe, *The Search for Order: 1877–1920* (New York, 1967). I have differed from Robert Wiebe not only in trying to rescue the large kernel of truth in the older interpretation of progressivism but also in adopting a longer time perspective. Wiebe's concentration on dramatic change in a single decade at the turn of the century overlooks the gradual development of a technical order during the preceding fifty years. There was no "revolution in identity," no "Revolution in Values," no "intellectual revolution," and perhaps no "revolution that fundamentally altered the structure of politics and government early in the twentieth century." Wiebe, *Search for Order,* 113, 133, 145, 181. A longer perspective also permits a fuller appreciation of the ideological factor in America's "search for order." Wiebe argues that before the bureaucratic "revolution" America lacked cohesion; it was "a society without a core." Ibid., 12. This judgment depends on the presupposition that national integration is to be found only in and through a complex organizational structure. Having defined integration as bureaucratic, Wiebe naturally finds none prior to the appearance of his bureaucrats. I suspect his book might have been less subject to these criticisms if it had not been confined to a fixed, limited span of time by the requirements of a multi-authored series—another bureaucratic phenomenon!

47. For arguments that the ideological revival was Protestant as well as nationalist and that the two were closely connected, see Robert T. Handy, *A Christian America: Protestant Hopes and Historical Realities* (New York, 1971), 128, 139; Winthrop S. Hudson, *American Protestantism* (Chicago, 1961), 124–27; Jean B. Quandt, "Religion and Social Thought: The Secularization of Post-Millennialism," *American Quarterly,* 25 (October 1973), 390–409.

48. R. Laurence Moore, *European Socialists and the American Promised Land* (New York, 1970), 195–200.

49. For an excellent synthesis, see Otis L. Graham, Jr., *The Great Campaigns: Reform and War in America, 1900–1928* (Englewood Cliffs, N.J., 1971). On the role of science and technology, see Sidney Kaplan, "Social Engineers as Saviours: Effects of World War I on Some American Liberals," *Journal of the History of Ideas,* 17 (June 1956), 347–69; Ronald C. Tobey, *The American Ideology of National Science, 1919–1930* (Pittsburgh, 1971); Jean B. Quandt, *From the Small Town to the Great Community: The Social Thought of Progressive Intellectuals* (New Brunswick, N.J., 1970).

50. Jacques Ellul, *The Technological Society* (New York, 1964), 263–89. See also

H. H. Gerth and C. Wright Mills, eds., *From Max Weber: Essays in Sociology* (New York, 1958), 196–244.

51. Henry Adams, *The Education of Henry Adams: An Autobiography* (Boston, 1918), was the top nonfiction best-seller in 1919. See Alice Payne Hackett, *Seventy Years of Best Sellers, 1895–1965* (New York, 1967), 119.

52. John Dos Passos, *Three Soldiers* (New York, 1921); Elmer Rice, *The Adding Machine* (Garden City, N.Y., 1923); Aldous Huxley, *Brave New World* (London, 1932); and Huxley, "The Outlook for American Culture: Some Reflections in a Machine Age," *Harper's Monthly Magazine,* 155 (August 1927), 265–72. Some indications of the breadth of this concern in the 1920s are in Edward J. O'Brien, *The Dance of the Machines: The American Short Story and the Industrial Age* (New York, 1929); John M. Clark, "The Empire of Machines," *Yale Review,* 12 (October 1922), 132–43; "The Great Theme," *Saturday Review of Literature,* 2 (May 8, 1926), 765; Gilbert Seldes, "The Machine Wreckers," *Saturday Evening Post,* 200 (July 23, 1927), 27, 149–53. The most searing, as well as the first, of these attacks on the technical order came from Randolph Bourne, "Twilight of Idols," *Untimely Papers* (New York, 1919), 114–39.

53. Edward A. Purcell, Jr., *The Crisis of Democratic Theory: Scientific Naturalism and the Problem of Value* (Lexington, Ky., 1973), 25–29, 103–4; John Chynoweth Burnham, "The New Psychology: From Narcissism to Social Control," in John Braeman, Robert H. Bremner, and David Brody, eds., *Change and Continuity in Twentieth-Century America: The 1920s* (Columbus, Ohio, 1968), 351–98.

54. Lawrence K. Frank, "An Institutional Analysis of the Law," *Columbia Law Review,* 24 (May 1924), 495. See also *Recent Social Trends in the United States: Report of the President's Research Committee on Social Trends* (2 vols., New York, 1933), I, 393–96.

55. Purcell, *Crisis of Democratic Theory,* 135–231; Richard H. Pells, *Radical Visions and American Dreams: Culture and Social Thought in the Depression Years* (New York, 1973); Warren Susman, "The Thirties," in Stanley Cohen and Lorman Ratner, eds., *The Development of an American Culture* (Englewood Cliffs, N.J., 1970), 179–218.

56. Daniel Bell, *The End of Ideology: On the Exhaustion of Political Ideas in the Fifties* (Glencoe, Ill., 1960); Robert E. Lane, "The Decline of Politics and Ideology in a Knowledgeable Society," *American Sociological Review,* 31 (October 1966), 649–62.

CHAPTER 2. *America in Person: The Evolution of National Symbols*

1. Lawrence J. Friedman, *Inventors of the Promised Land* (New York, 1975), p. 302; Laurence Veysey, "The 'New' Social History in the Context of American Historical Writing," *Reviews in American History,* 7 (1979), p. 5.

2. Hans Kohn, *The Idea of Nationalism: A Study of Its Origins and Backgrounds* (New York, 1944).

3. John Murrin, "A Roof Without Walls: The Dilemma of American National Identity," in *Beyond Confederation: Origins of the Constitution and American National Identity,* ed. Richard Beeman et al. (Chapel Hill, N.C., 1987), pp. 333–48.

4. The scant references to the United States as a nation usually designated what the country was hopefully becoming, rather than what it was, as in George Washington's statement "We are a young Nation, and have a character to establish." Paul C. Nagel, *One Nation Indivisible: The Union in American Thought, 1776–1861* (New York, 1964),

p. 170. On republics, see Pauline Maier, "It Was Never the Same After Them," *New York Times Book Review,* March 1, 1992, p. 33.

5. The following discussion of the categories of place and principle is based on the fuller exposition and documentation in my extensively illustrated article "Indian Princess and Roman Goddess: The First Female Symbols of America," *Proceedings of the American Antiquarian Society,* 100, part 1 (1990), pp. 45-79.

6. Hugh Honour, *The European Vision of America* (Cleveland, Ohio, 1975), pp. 112-120; and Honour, *The New Golden Land: European Images of America from the Discoveries to the Present Time* (New York, 1975), pp. 84-89, 109-17.

7. David Beers Quinn, "New Geographical Horizons: Literature," in *First Images of America: The Impact of the New World on the Old,* ed. Fredi Chiapelli (Berkeley, Calif., 1976), vol. 2, pp. 642-51; Seymour I. Schwartz and Ralph E. Ehrenberg, *The Mapping of America* (New York, 1980).

8. The standard work by M. Dorothy George, *English Political Caricature to 1792: A Study of Opinion and Propaganda* (Oxford, 1959) can now be supplemented by the seven volumes of a splendid new series, *The English Satirical Print, 1600-1832,* ed. Michael Duffy (Cambridge, England, 1986).

9. Joan D. Dolmetsch, *Rebellion and Reconciliation: Satirical Prints on the Revolution at Williamsburg* (Williamsburg, Va., 1976), pp. 7-9, 42-43, 74-75. See also Donald H. Creswell, *The American Revolution in Drawings and Prints: A Checklist of 1765-1790 Graphics in the Library of Congress* (Washington, D.C., 1975).

10. Rayna Green, "The Pocahontas Perplex: The Image of Indian Women in American Culture," *Massachusetts Review,* 16 (1975), pp. 698-714; Jay B. Hubbell, "The Smith-Pocahontas Story in Literature," *Virginia Magazine of History and Biography,* 65 (1957), pp. 275-300.

11. Dolmetsch, *Rebellion and Reconciliation,* pp. 18-19, 45-46, 52-53. See also Creswell, *American Revolution,* no. 688; and Frank H. Sommer III, "Thomas Hollis and the Arts of Dissent," in *Prints in and of America to 1850* (Winterthur, Del., 1970), pp. 111-59.

12. Walt W. Ristow, *A la Carte: Selected Papers on Maps and Atlases* (Washington, D.C., 1972), p. 107.

13. Ted Schwarz, *A History of United States Coinage* (San Diego, 1980), pp. 63-73; Q. David Bowers, *The History of United States Coinage as Illustrated by the Garrett Collection* (Los Angeles, 1979), pp. 181-83.

14. Robert C. Smith, *"Liberty Displaying the Arts and Sciences:* A Philadelphia Allegory," *Winterthur Portfolio,* 2 (1965), pp. 84-102. For a wide-ranging treatment of liberty as idea and icon in American history see Michael Kammen, *Spheres of Liberty: Changing Perceptions of Liberty in American Culture* (Madison, Wis., 1986).

15. On the long-lasting popular vogue of this image see Elinor Lander Horwitz, *The Bird, the Banner, and Uncle Sam: Images of America in Folk and Popular Art* (Philadelphia, 1976), pp. 78-83.

16. Albert Bigelow Paine, *Th. Nast, His Period and His Pictures* (New York, 1904), p. 205.

17. Martha Banta, *Imaging American Women: Idea and Ideals in Cultural History* (New York, 1987), p. 411.

18. Cf. *Boston Magazine,* April 1784, frontispiece; and Henry Webber's statuette *Britannia Triumphant* (Josiah Wedgwood and Sons, ca. 1798-1802), in the New Or-

leans Museum of Art. Except for the head of Washington, the American etching was pirated from a French work by Montesquieu in 1772. Wendy C. Wick, *George Washington, an American Icon: The Eighteenth-Century Graphic Portraits* (Washington, D.C., 1982), pp. 16–18, 93.

19. Ibid., pp. 8–9, 79.

20. Barry Schwartz, *George Washington: The Making of an American Symbol* (New York, 1987), pp. 23, 41–42, 74–79.

21. Ibid., fig. 28; Patricia A. Anderson, *Promoted to Glory: The Apotheosis of George Washington* (Northampton, Mass., 1980), pp. 54–57.

22. Charles Lanman, quoted in William H. Gerdts and Mark Thistlethwaite, *Grand Illusions: History Painting in America* (Fort Worth, Tex., 1988), p. 87. On Washington's fixity of purpose see also Dixon Wecter, *The Hero in America: A Chronicle of Hero-Worship* (New York, 1941), pp. 103–4, 139–40.

23. Schwartz, *Washington*, p. 81. See also pp. 79, 85.

24. Friedman, *Inventors* (New York, 1975), pp. 60–78; Ruth Miller Elson, *Guardians of Tradition: American Schoolbooks of the Nineteenth Century* (Lincoln, Nebr., 1964), pp. 194–203; Nagel, *One Nation*, pp. 225–30; George Bancroft, *History of the United States of America*, ed. Russell Nye (Chicago, 1969), p. 174. See also *A Great and Good Man: George Washington in the Eyes of His Contemporaries*, ed. John P. Kaminski and Jill Adair McCaughan (Madison, Wis., 1989).

25. The Library of Congress Prints and Photographs Division has collected a large number of these (Lot 4407), printed between 1812 and 1889. Cf. Wick, *Washington*, pp. 99–101.

26. On diminishing fervor in the Washington cult and the glorification of the Founding Fathers around the middle of the nineteenth century, see Wilbur Zelinsky, *Nation into State: The Shifting Symbolic Foundations of American Nationalism* (Chapel Hill, N.C., 1988), pp. 34–36; and Zelinsky, "Nationalism in the American Place-Name Cover," *Names*, 31 (1983), pp. 6–7.

27. Albert Matthews, "Uncle Sam," *Proceedings of the American Antiquarian Society*, new series, 19 (April 1908), pp. 21–65. According to Matthews's still definitive research, this "cant name for our government" (*Troy Post*, September 7, 1813) became widespread in upstate New York that year as a result of the intrusion of U.S. wagons and troops into districts that were largely opposed to the War of 1812. The legend associating Uncle Sam with Samuel Wilson, a Troy meatpacker, first appeared in print in 1842; but when the latter died in 1854, none of the printed obituaries referred to Uncle Sam. Thus the legend may be understood as part of the long struggle to endow a governmental symbol with some tangible personal identity.

28. *Andrew Resolute, Uncle Sam's Faithful Teamster, Taking the Produce of the Farms to Another Storehouse* (1834) and *Old Jack, the Famous New Orleans Mouser, Clearing Uncle Sam's Barn of Bank and Clay Rats* (1832), American Political Prints, Z62-4831 and Z62-55185, Prints and Photographs Division, Library of Congress. See also [D. C. Johnston,] *Confab Between John Bull and Brother Jonathan* (1836), American Political Cartoons, C748, American Antiquarian Society.

29. George, *English Political Caricature*, pp. 177, 187–88; M. Dorothy George, *English Political Caricature, 1793–1832: A Study of Opinion and Propaganda* (Oxford, 1959); Jeannine Surel, "La première image de John Bull, bourgeois radical, Anglais loyaliste (1779–1815)," *Le Mouvement Social*, no. 106 (1979), pp. 65–84.

30. Michael Kammen, *A Season of Youth: The American Revolution and the Historical Imagination* (New York, 1978), pp. 17–19; Nagel, *One Nation*, pp. 170–73.

31. William Murrell, *A History of American Graphic Humor* (New York, 1933), vol. 1, pp. 136–37. See also Richard M. Dorson, "The Yankee on the Stage—a Folk Hero of American Drama," *New England Quarterly*, 13 (1940), pp. 467–93; and Dorson, *American Folklore and the Historian* (Chicago, 1971), pp. 100–107.

32. [Seba Smith,] *The Life and Writings of Major Jack Downing* (Boston, 1834); Francis Hodge, *Yankee Theatre: The Image of America on the Stage, 1825–1850* (Austin, Tex., 1964), pp. 96, 143–49, 170, 180. See also Henry Ladd Smith, "The Two Major Downings: Rivalry in Political Satire," *Journalism Quarterly*, 41 (Winter 1964), pp. 74–78, 127.

33. Albert Matthews, "Brother Jonathan," *Publications of the Colonial Society of Massachusetts*, 7 (1901), pp. 94–125; and "Brother Jonathan Once More," ibid., 37 (1935), pp. 374–86. A clear indication that Jonathan was recognizable in England before 1776 as a nickname for a New Englander or an American colonial is in *The American Moose-Deer, or Away to the River Ohio* [1754–55?], in English Political Cartoons, American Antquarian Society. See also Hodge, *Yankee Theatre*, pp. 45–54.

34. This process can be followed most closely in the monthly humor magazine *Yankee Notions*, which was published in New York from 1852 to 1875; but see also Cecil D. Eby, "Yankee Humor," in *The Comic Imagination in American Literature*, ed. Louis D. Rubin, Jr. (New Brunswick, N.J., 1973), pp. 77–84.

35. *The "Uncle Sam" Range Manufactured by Abendroth. Bros. New York* [1876], Negative File Catalog, no. 56261, Print Room, New-York Historical Society.

36. *Uncle Sam's Troublesome Bedfellows, Wasp*, February 8, 1879, in Henry E. Huntington Library; Homer C. Davenport, *Cartoons* (New York, 1898); Frederick Burr Opper, *A Fourth of July Soliloquy* (1903), in Thomas Craven, ed., *Cartoon Cavalcade* (New York, 1943), p. 48; *Cartoons of the War of 1898 with Spain from Leading Foreign and American Papers* (Chicago, 1898).

37. The fullest collection of political cartoons from American newspapers during World War I is in the G. W. Rehse Collection, Prints and Photographs Division, Library of Congress.

38. This was the most powerful of the numerous war posters that featured the Statue of Liberty. Anne Cannon Palumbo and Ann Uhry Abrams, "Proliferation of the Image," in *Liberty: The French-American Statue in Art and History*, ed. Pierre Provoyeur and June Hargrove (New York, 1986), pp. 230–64; George M. Dembo, "The Statue of Liberty in Posters: Creation of an American Icon," *P.S.: The Quarterly Journal of the Poster Society* (Winter 1985–86), pp. 18–21.

39. In contrast to this interpretation, Zelinsky stresses the permanence of monuments and associates the Statue of Liberty with a hardening of state worship and a loss of the national idealism of the early republic. *Nation into State*, pp. 23–27, 160, 219.

40. *The Great Gatsby*, in *The Portable F. Scott Fitzgerald*, ed. Dorothy Parker (New York, 1945), p. 167. The first U.S. postage stamp displaying the Statue of Liberty, issued in 1922, showed it solidly localized in New York Harbor. See Fig. 22.

41. John Higham, *Send These to Me: Immigrants in Urban America* (rev. ed., Baltimore, Md., 1984), pp. 71–80.

42. Compare Alton Ketchum, *Uncle Sam: The Man and the Legend* (New York, 1959), pp. 133–34, with Margaret Sherwood, "Uncle Sam," *Atlantic Monthly*, 121 (1918), pp. 330–33.

43. These changes may be traced in the annual volumes *Best Editorial Cartoons of the Year*, ed. Charles Brooks (Gretna, La., 1974–99).

44. Lorenz, Cover Drawing, *New Yorker*, 64 (July 4, 1988).

45. Toles, "Another Hostage Situation," *Boston Globe*, August 28, 1990; Flannery, "'Sometimes, for No Reason, I Suddenly Burst into Tears,'" *Baltimore Sun*, July 29, 1975; Andy Warhol, *Myths: Uncle Sam*, screenprint (1981).

CHAPTER 3. *Rediscovering the Pragmatic American*

1. Alexis de Tocqueville, *Democracy in America*, 2 vols. (New York, 1945), 2: 37.

2. *Pragmatism and American Culture*, ed. Gail Kennedy (Boston, 1950); *Benjamin Franklin and the American Character*, ed. Charles L. Sanford (Boston, 1955).

3. Henry F. May, "The Other American Tradition," in his *Ideas, Faiths and Feelings: Essays on American Intellectual and Religious History, 1952–1982* (New York, 1983), 52–64.

4. Compare Daniel J. Boorstin's *The Americans: The Colonial Experience* (New York, 1958) and his *The Americans: The National Experience* (New York, 1965) with his *The Americans: The Democratic Experience* (New York, 1973).

5. David Hollinger, "The Problem of Pragmatism in American History," *Journal of American History* 67 (June 1980): 91. For a thoughtful update on the literature of philosophical pragmatism, see James T. Kloppenberg, "Pragmatism: An Old Name for Some New Ways of Thinking," ibid., 83 (June 1996): 100–138.

6. J. G. A. Pocock, "Virtue and Commerce in the Eighteenth Century," *Journal of Interdisciplinary History* 3 (Summer 1972): 134.

7. Van Wyck Brooks, *America's Coming-of-Age* (1915), reprinted in *Van Wyck Brooks: The Early Years*, ed. Claire Sprague (New York, 1968), 83–84.

8. Lewis Mumford, *The Golden Day* (New York, 1926); Richard Hofstadter, *Anti-Intellectualism in American Life* (New York, 1963), 236. Entitled "The Practical Culture," this whole section of Hofstadter's book is probably the most trenchant of the hostile critiques of the American pragmatic temper.

9. Richard H. Thornton, *An American Glossary*, 3 vols. (New York, 1962), 2: 685–86; Mitford M. Mathews, ed., *A Dictionary of Americanisms on Historical Principles* (Chicago, 1956), 1278; Henry David Thoreau, "Life Without Principle," in *The American Transcendentalists: Their Prose and Poetry*, ed. Perry Miller (Baltimore, Md., 1981), 328; H. L. Mencken, *A New Dictionary of Quotations* (New York, 1942), 939.

10. John Swinton, "Caught Between Two Poles," *New York Times*, 25 July 1984.

11. James Bryce, "The American Character in the 1880s," in *The Character of Americans: A Book of Readings*, ed. Michael McGiffert (Homewood, Ill., 1964), 72. See also an expanded edition published in 1970.

12. Ibid., 186; Boorstin, *The Americans: The National Experience*, 3–48.

13. A briefer version of this quotation appears in Sally Foreman Griffith, *Home Town News: William Allen White and the Emporia Gazette* (New York, 1989), 67.

14. Nathan Reingold, "American Indifference to Basic Research: A Reappraisal," in *Nineteenth-Century American Science: A Reappraisal*, ed. George H. Daniels (Evanston, Ill., 1972), 38–62.

15. Stanley Hoffmann, *Gulliver's Troubles, or The Setting of American Foreign Policy* (New York, 1968), 144–49. Bourne's epochal assault on pragmatism in foreign policy appeared in the *Seven Arts* in October 1917 and is reprinted in Randolph

Bourne, *War and the Intellectuals,* ed. Carl Resek (New York, 1964), 53–64. See also John G. Stoessinger, *Crusaders and Pragmatists: Movers of Modern American Foreign Policy* (New York, 1979).

16. George Santayana, *Character and Opinion in the United States* (Garden City, N.Y., 1956), 108; Henry Adams, *History of the United States of America During the First Administration of Thomas Jefferson,* 2 vols. (New York, 1889), 1: 172.

17. See Chapter 1.

18. Sheldon Hackney, "The American Identity," *Public Historian* 19 (Spring 1997): 13–22, offers an exceptionally sophisticated summary of the many "fault lines" in American culture that can be seen in what Americans say about their national identity. He includes, but mentions only in passing, the contradiction between Americans' view of themselves as "practical and self-reliant" and their hospitality "to more utopian experiments in communal living than any other nation on earth."

19. Annie Kriegel, "Consistent Misapprehension: European Views of America and Their Logic," *Daedalus* (Fall 1972): 89.

20. *The Gallup International Public Opinion Polls: Great Britain, 1937–1975,* 2 vols. (New York, 1976), 2: 957, 1275–76; "What the World Thinks of America," *Newsweek,* 11 July 1983, p. 50.

CHAPTER 4. *Specialization in a Democracy*

1. Sally Gregory Kohlstedt, *The Formation of the American Scientific Community: The American Association for the Advancement of Science, 1848–1860* (Urbana, Ill.: University of Illinois Press, 1976); Robert A. McCaughey, "The Transformation of American Academic Life: Harvard University, 1821–1892," *Perspectives in American History* 7 (1974): 246–74.

2. See the illuminating discussion of these issues in Laurence Veysey's essay "The Plural Organized Worlds of the Humanities," in *The Organization of Knowledge in Modern America, 1860–1920,* ed. Alexandra Oleson and John Voss (Baltimore, Md.: Johns Hopkins University Press, 1979), pp. 51–106; and in Nathan Reingold's valuable corrective to the canonical distinction between professional and amateur, "Definitions and Speculations: The Professionalization of Science in America in the Nineteenth Century," in *The Pursuit of Knowledge in the Early American Republic,* ed. Alexandra Oleson and Sanborn C. Brown (Baltimore, Md.: Johns Hopkins University Press, 1976).

3. George H. Daniels, *American Science in the Age of Jackson* (New York: Columbia University Press, 1968), pp. 27–38; Howard S. Miller, "Science and Private Agencies," in *Science and Society in the United States,* ed. David D. Van Tassel and Michael G. Hall (Homewood, Ill.: Dorsey Press, 1966), p. 198. The advance of specialization in the first half of the century is ably treated in Stanley M. Guralnick, *Science and the Ante-Bellum American College,* Memoirs of the American Philosophical Society, vol. 109 (Philadelphia: American Philosophical Society, 1975).

4. Gulian C. Verplanck, "The Advantages and Dangers of the American Scholar," in *American Philosophic Addresses, 1700–1900,* ed. Joseph L. Blau (New York: Columbia University Press, 1946), p. 125. See also Merle Curti, *American Paradox: The Conflict of Thought and Action* (New Brunswick, N.J.: Rutgers University Press, 1956), pp. 40–56; James McLachlan, "The *Choice of Hercules:* American Student Societies in the Early Nineteenth Century," in *The University in Society,* 2 vols., ed. Lawrence Stone (Princeton, N.J.: Princeton University Press, 1974), 2: 468, 485; Samuel Haber,

"The Professions and Higher Education in America: A Historical View," in *Higher Education and the Labor Market*, ed. Margaret S. Gordon (New York: McGraw-Hill, 1974), pp. 246–52.

5. Emerson's address, "The American Scholar," is reprinted in Blau, ed., *American Philosophic Addresses*, pp. 153–70.

6. Quoted in Kohlstedt, *Formation of the American Scientific Community*, p. 134. See also Alexis de Tocqueville, *Democracy in America*, 2 vols., ed. Phillips Bradley (New York: Alfred A. Knopf, 1945), 2: 3–5.

7. Hugh Hawkins, *Between Harvard and America: The Educational Leadership of Charles W. Eliot* (New York: Oxford University Press, 1972), p. 288; George Rosen, "Changing Attitudes of the Medical Profession to Specialization," *Bulletin of the History of Medicine* 12 (July 1942): 343–54.

8. Quoted in William G. Rothstein, *American Physicians in the Nineteenth Century: From Sects to Science* (Baltimore: Johns Hopkins University Press, 1972), p. 211. For typical complaints about the cost of specialized education, see Clifford S. Griffin, *The University of Kansas: A History* (Lawrence, Kans.: Regents Press, 1974), especially pp. 118–19.

9. Charles E. Rosenberg, "Martin Arrowsmith: The Scientist as Hero," *American Quarterly* 15 (Fall 1963): 447–58.

10. J. G. A. Pocock, *The Machiavellian Moment: Florentine Political Thought and the Atlantic Republican Tradition* (Princeton, N.J.: Princeton University Press, 1975), pp. 498–503.

11. Adam Ferguson, *An Essay on the History of Civil Society*, 8th ed. (Philadelphia: A. Finley, 1819), p. 330.

12. Adam Smith, *An Inquiry into the Nature and Causes of the Wealth of Nations* (New York: Modern Library, 1937), pp. 10, 734–35.

13. Auguste Comte, *Cours de philosophie positive*, 2d ed., 6 vols. (Paris: Bachelier, Imprimeur-Libraire, 1864), 1: 26–29, 6: 384–89. See also Paul Robert, *Dictionnaire alphabétique et analogique de la langue française*, 6 vols. (Paris: Societé du nouveau Littré, 1964), 6: 523.

14. *Collected Works of John Stuart Mill*, 13 vols. (Toronto: University of Toronto Press, 1969), vol. 10: *Auguste Comte and Positivism*, pp. 312, 314; "Wordsworth and Professor Huxley on the Narrowness of Specialists," *Spectator* 58 (5 December 1885): 1611–12. See also *Oxford English Dictionary*, s.v. "speciality," "specialization."

15. Laurence R. Veysey, *The Emergence of the American University* (Chicago: University of Chicago Press, 1965), pp. 161, 200. See also Hawkins, *Between Harvard and America*, pp. 69–70, 272–77.

16. W. T. Harris, "The Use of Higher Education," *Educational Review* 16 (September 1898): 153–54, 161.

17. Elizabeth Donnan and Leo F. Stock, eds., *An Historian's World: Selections from the Correspondence of John Franklin Jameson*, Memoirs of the American Philosophical Society, vol. 42 (Philadelphia: American Philosophical Society, 1956), p. 22. See also S. W. Williston, "Specialization in Education," *Science*, n.s., 18 (31 July 1903): 129–38; W. A. Kellerman, "The Specialist," *Science* 19 (18 March 1892): 161–63; Henry Calderwood, "Risks and Responsibilities of Specialism," *Presbyterian Review* 6 (1885): 91–100; Henry J. Philpott, "Social Sustenance," *Popular Science Monthly* 31 (1887): 612–25.

18. Herbert Spencer, *Essays on Education and Kindred Subjects* (London: Every-

man's Library, J. M. Dent, n.d.), pp. 163–75; Spencer, *The Study of Sociology* (Ann Arbor: University of Michigan Press, 1961), pp. 301–6.

19. John Dewey, *The Early Works, 1882–1898,* 3 vols. (Carbondale: Southern Illinois University Press, 1969), vol. 3: *Early Essays and Outlines of a Critical Theory of Ethics,* pp. 319–20; Dewey, *Experience and Nature* (Chicago: Open Court, 1925), pp. 205, 409–10. A helpful chapter, "John Dewey and the Unity of Knowledge," with an emphasis somewhat different from mine, is in Jean B. Quandt, *From the Small Town to the Great Community: The Social Thought of Progressive Intellectuals* (New Brunswick, N.J.: Rutgers University Press, 1970), pp. 102–25.

20. The case is reexamined and qualified in I. Bernard Cohen, "Science and the Growth of the American Republic," *Review of Politics* 38 (July 1976): 370–84. For a thorough, convincing critique, see Nathan Reingold, "American Indifference to Basic Research: A Reappraisal," in *Nineteenth Century American Science: A Reappraisal,* ed. George H. Daniels (Evanston, Ill.: Northwestern University Press, 1972), pp. 38–62.

21. Robert M. MacIver, "Sociology," in *A Quarter Century of Learning, 1904– 1929,* Lectures delivered at Columbia University at the 175th Anniversary (New York: Columbia University Press, 1931), pp. 70–71. See also David A. Hollinger, *Morris R. Cohen and the Scientific Ideal* (Cambridge: MIT Press, 1975), pp. 147–48.

22. I have profited especially from Thomas Bender, "Science and the Culture of American Communities: The Nineteenth Century," *History of Education Quarterly* 16 (Spring 1976): 70–71; but see also Daniel Howe, *The Unitarian Conscience: Harvard Moral Philosophy, 1805–1861* (Cambridge: Harvard University Press, 1970), pp. 30– 38, and Daniels's chapter, 'The Reign of Bacon in America," in his *American Science,* pp. 63–85.

23. For an early assault on popular empiricism, and an appeal for "a minute sub-division in the pursuit of science" to overcome the evils of "charlatanism," see Alexander Dallas Bache's presidential address, *Proceedings of the American Association for the Advancement of Science,* August 1851, pp. xliii–liii. Subsequent complaints are quoted in Cohen, "Science," pp. 379–82.

24. Quoted in Charles Rosenberg's illuminating article "Science and Social Values in Nineteenth-Century America: A Case Study in the Growth of Scientific Institutions," in *Science and Values,* ed. Arnold Thackray and Everett Mendelsohn (Atlantic Highlands, N.J.: Humanities Press, 1974), p. 25.

25. A. Hunter Dupree, "The National Academy of Sciences and the American Definition of Science," in Oleson and Voss, eds., *Organization of Knowledge,* pp. 342– 63. See also Daniel J. Kevles, "On the Flaws of American Physics," in Daniels, ed., *Nineteenth-Century American Science,* pp. 148–51.

26. Veysey, "Plural Organized Worlds"; Rothstein, *American Physicians,* pp. 214– 15.

27. J. F. Jameson to Edward C. Armstrong, 21 July 1926, "A.C.L.S. Correspondence," American Historical Association Archives, Division of Manuscripts, Library of Congress, Washington, D.C.

28. James E. Russell, *German Higher Schools: The History, Organization and Methods of Secondary Education in Germany* (New York: Longman's Green, 1916), p. 358. See also Friedrich Paulsen, *The German Universities and University Study,* trans. Frank Thilly and William W. Elwang (New York: Charles Scribner's Sons, 1906), pp. 334–35, 408–28; Matthew Arnold, *Higher Schools and Universities* (London: Macmillan, 1882), pp. 145–50.

29. Fritz Ringer describes this spirit in his essay "The German Academic Community," in Oleson and Voss, eds., *Organization of Knowledge*, pp. 409–29.

30. Francesco Cordasco, *The Shaping of American Graduate Education: Daniel Coit Gilman and the Protean Ph.D.* (Totawa, N.J.: Rowman and Littlefield, 1973), pp. 85–88.

31. Walton C. John, *Graduate Studies in Universities and Colleges in the United States,* U.S. Department of Education, Bulletin no. 20 (Washington, D.C.: U.S. Government Printing Office, 1934), pp. 46–52.

32. James, quoted in Sol Cohen, ed., *Education in the United States: A Documentary History,* 5 vols. (New York: Random House, 1974), 5: 2755.

33. A few exceptions lingered. See John, *Graduate Study,* pp. 24–31, 201–2; Stephen H. Spurr, *Academic Degree Structures: Innovative Approaches* (New York: McGraw-Hill, 1970), pp. 16–17, 148–49; Walter Crosby Eells, *Degrees in Higher Education* (Washington, D.C.: Center for Applied Research in Education, 1963), pp. 6–7.

34. Richard J. Storr, *The Beginning of the Future: A Historical Approach to Graduate Education in the Arts and Sciences* (New York: McGraw-Hill, 1973), p. 48.

35. Joseph Ben-David, "The Universities and the Growth of Science in Germany and the United States," *Minerva* 7 (Autumn–Winter 1968–69): 1–35. See also Terry Nichols Clark, *Prophets and Patrons: The French University and the Emergence of the Social Sciences* (Cambridge: Harvard University Press, 1973), pp. 84–89.

36. Veysey, *Emergence*, pp. 304, 320–22. The resurgence of liberal culture in the early twentieth century, under the leadership of two strong university presidents (Woodrow Wilson and A. Lawrence Lowell), may perhaps be understood as a reaction against the increasing autonomy and parochialism of the departments.

37. Delaye Gager, *French Comment on American Education* (New York: AMS Press, 1925), pp. 2–3.

38. John Cole, "Storehouses and Workshops: American Libraries and the Uses of Knowledge," in Oleson and Voss, eds., *Organization of Knowledge*, pp. 364–85.

39. Raymond B. Fosdick, *The Story of the Rockefeller Foundation* (New York: Harper, 1952), pp. 15, 27–29; Nathan Reingold, "National Science Policy," in Oleson and Voss, eds., *Organization of Knowledge*, pp. 313–41.

40. F. Emerson Andrews, "Growth and Present Status of American Foundations," *Proceedings of the American Philosophical Society* 105 (1961): 158. See also Commission on Foundations and Private Philanthropy, *Foundations: Private Giving and Public Policy* (Chicago: University of Chicago Press, 1970), pp. 39–41.

41. In addition to Cole, "Storehouses and Workshops," see Arthur E. Bestor, "The Transformation of American Scholarship, 1875–1917," *Library Quarterly* 23 (July 1953): 175–77.

42. Roger W. Cooley, *Brief Making and the Use of Law Books*, 2 vols., 4th ed. (St. Paul, Minn.: West, 1924), 1: 67–68. See also Frederick C. Hicks, *Materials and Methods of Legal Research* (Rochester, N.Y.: Lawyers' Cooperative, 1923), pp. 250, 271.

43. I am indebted to an unpublished paper by Saul Benison on the Army Medical Corps, presented at the 1976 Newagen Conference sponsored by the American Academy of Arts and Sciences.

44. *The National Cyclopaedia of American Biography*, Current Series, vol. E, p. 361. See also John Lawler, *The H. W. Wilson Company: Half a Century of Bibliographic Publishing* (Minneapolis: University of Minnesota Press, 1950).

45. J. McKeen Cattell, ed., *American Men of Science: A Biographical Directory*

(New York: Science Press, 1906), p. v. See also Dorothy Ross's biography of Cattell in *Dictionary of American Biography,* Supplement Three, s.v. "Cattell, James McKeen."

46. Stephen Sargent Visher, "J. McKeen Cattell and American Science," *School and Society* 13 (December 1947): 450–52.

47. In another essay I have shown how the distinctive features of the American university press may be understood in the same terms. See "University Presses and Academic Specialization," *Scholarly Publishing* 10 (October 1978): 36–44.

CHAPTER 5. *Integrating America: The Problem of Assimilation at the Turn of the Century*

1. Gerald Mullin, *Flight and Rebellion: Slave Resistance in Eighteenth-Century Virginia* (New York, 1972), pp. 34–82; Ira Berlin, "Time, Space, and the Evolution of Afro-American Society on British Mainland North America," *American Historical Review* 85 (February 1980): 66–77.

2. Lawrence W. Levine, *Black Culture and Black Consciousness: Afro-American Folk Thought from Slavery to Freedom* (New York, 1977), pp. 4–30.

3. Jonathan D. Sarna, "From Immigrants to Ethnics: Toward a New Theory of 'Ethnicization,'" *Ethnicity* 5 (1978): 370–78.

4. Victor Greene, *For God and Country: The Rise of Polish and Lithuanian Ethnic Consciousness in America* (Madison, Wis., 1975), pp. 3–10.

5. Harry L. Golden, *Jewish Roots in the Carolinas: A Pattern of American Philo-Semitism* (Greensboro, N.C., 1955), pp. 25–27; Ray Stannard Baker, *Following the Colour Line: American Negro Citizenship in the Progressive Era* (New York, 1908), pp. 162–73; Carter G. Woodson, ed., *The Mind of the Negro as Reflected in Letters Written During the Crisis, 1800–1860* (New York, 1969), p. 273.

6. James Fenimore Cooper, *Notions of the Americans,* 2 vols. (New York, 1828), 1: 87, 305–6.

7. John Higham, *Strangers in the Land: Patterns of American Nativism, 1860–1925* (New Brunswick, N.J., 1955), p. 86.

8. Moses Rischin, ed., *Immigration and the American Tradition* (Indianapolis, Ind., 1976), p. 26.

9. Philip Rahv, ed., *Discovery of Europe: The Story of American Experience in the Old World* (Boston, 1947), pp. 137–38.

10. Holmes quoted in Merle Curti, *The Growth of American Thought,* 3d ed. (New York, 1964), p. 225; Bancroft quoted in Daniel J. Boorstin, *The Americans: The National Experience* (New York, 1965), p. 371.

11. Theodore Tilton, *The Negro: A Speech at Cooper Institute* (New York, 1863), reprinted in *The Burden of Race: A Documentary History of Negro-White Relations in America,* ed. Gilbert Osofsky (New York, 1967), pp. 102–3.

12. Francis P. Prucha, ed., *Documents of United States Indian Policy* (Lincoln, Nebr., 1975), p. 138.

13. Morton Cronin, "Currier and Ives: A Content Analysis," *American Quarterly* 4 (Winter 1952): 329–30; Edward A. Freeman, *Some Impressions of the United States* (New York, 1883), p. 150; Theodore Roosevelt to Henry Fairfield Osborn, 21 December 1908, in *Letters of Theodore Roosevelt,* ed. Elting Morison et al., (Cambridge, Mass., 1951–54), 6: 1434.

14. *Harper's Weekly*, 24 October 1874, p. 880; Moses Coit Tyler, *A History of American Literature*, 2 vols. (New York, 1878), 1: 10.

15. Heinz Kloss, "German-American Language Maintenance Efforts," in *Language Loyalty in the United States*, ed. Joshua Fishman et al. (The Hague, 1966), pp. 232–36. See also Selwyn Troen, *The Public and the Schools: Shaping the St. Louis System, 1838–1920* (Columbia, Mo., 1975), pp. 55–78.

16. James M. McPherson, *The Abolitionist Legacy: From Reconstruction to the NAACP* (Princeton, N.J., 1976); Gunther Barth, *Bitter Strength: A History of the Chinese in the United States, 1850–1870* (Cambridge, Mass., 1964), pp. 157–73.

17. Iris Podea, "Quebec to 'Little Canada': The Coming of the French Canadians to New England in the Nineteenth Century," *New England Quarterly* 23 (1950): 370–72; Massachusetts Bureau of Statistics of Labor, *Twelfth Annual Report, 1881*, pp. 469–70.

18. Robert Kelley, *The Cultural Pattern in American Politics: The First Century* (New York, 1979), pp. 31–80.

19. United States, Bureau of the Census, *Historical Statistics of the United States, Colonial Times to 1970* (Washington, D.C., 1976), pp. 428, 1103.

20. Robert H. Wiebe, *The Search for Order, 1877–1920* (New York, 1967), p. 12.

21. Quoted in Stanley M. Elkins, *Slavery: A Problem in American Institutional and Intellectual Life* (Chicago, 1959), p. 143. I am indebted to Elkins's discussion here of American institutions.

22. James's view was anticipated by Hegel, who observed that a true state appears "only after a distinction of classes has arisen, when wealth and poverty become extreme." In the absence of such pressure the state as a fundamental mode of expressing human solidarity has not developed. America remains an aggregation of individuals, whose government is "merely something external for the protection of property." Shlomo Avineri, *Hegel's Theory of the Modern State* (Cambridge, Mass., 1972), pp. 135, 236–37.

23. Daniel J. Boorstin, *The Americans: The National Experience* (New York, 1965), pp. 373–75. On the lack of a capital see James Bryce, *The American Commonwealth*, 2 vols. (London, 1891), 2: 660–66.

24. John Higham, "Hanging Together" (see Chapter 1).

25. *Our Old Home: A Series of English Sketches* (*The Centenary Edition of the Works of Nathaniel Hawthorne*, 1970), 5: 325. Henry James, Sr., grasped the same difference, without Hawthorne's ambivalence, in *The Social Significance of Our Institutions* (Boston, 1861), p. 28.

26. Compare the American situation with the relation between core and periphery in other countries, as described in Michael Hechter, *Internal Colonialism: The Celtic Fringe in British National Development, 1536–1966* (Berkeley, Calif., 1975), pp. 4–27.

27. Brinley Thomas, *Migration and Economic Growth: A Study of Great Britain and the Atlantic Economy*, rev. ed. (Cambridge, Mass., 1973), pp. 130–33.

28. Olivier Zunz, "Detroit en 1880: Espace et ségrégation," *Annales E.S.C.*, no. 1 (January–February 1977): 125–29; Kathleen Conzen, *Immigrant Milwaukee, 1836–1860: Accommodation and Community in a Frontier City* (Cambridge, Mass., 1976), pp. 126–53. See also Rowland Berthoff, "The Social Order of the Anthracite Region, 1825–1902," *Pennsylvania Magazine of History and Biography* 89 (July 1965): 266–70.

29. *The National Era*, 15 September 1853, p. 146; Thomas Wentworth Higginson,

"Americanism in Literature," in *Oxford Book of American Essays*, ed. Brander Matthews (New York, 1914), p. 218; and Gilbert Osofsky, "Wendell Phillips and the Quest for a New American National Identity," *Canadian Review of Studies in Nationalism* 1 (1973): 15–46.

30. James H. Kettner, *The Development of American Citizenship, 1608–1870* (Chapel Hill, N.C., 1978). See also James M. Banner's comments on this fine study in *Reviews in American History* 8 (1980): 23–24; and Arthur Mann's summary of continuing uncertainties in *The One and the Many: Reflections on the American Identity* (Chicago, 1979), pp. 88–93. On further contradictions in American culture see Michael G. Kammen, *People of Paradox: An Inquiry Concerning the Origins of American Civilization* (New York, 1972).

31. Henry James, *The American* (Boston, 1877), pp. 6–8. See James W. Tuttleton, *The Novel of Manners in America* (New York, 1974), pp. 14–27, 58–85.

32. The practical tendencies in the Enlightenment are discussed, from different points of view, in Peter Gay, *The Enlightenment: An Interpretation*, vol. 2: *The Science of Freedom* (New York, 1969): and Henry F. May, *The Enlightenment in America* (New York, 1976).

33. Quoted in Ronald A. Bosco, "Lectures at the Pillory: The Early American Execution Sermon," *American Quarterly* 30 (Summer 1978): 156. More broadly see Philip Greven, *The Protestant Temperament: Patterns of Child-Rearing, Religious Experience, and the Self in Early America* (New York, 1977), pp. 141–48; and Mary Douglas, *Purity and Danger: An Analysis of Concepts of Pollution and Taboo* (New York, 1966), pp. 53–54. There are some stimulating comments on the theme of contamination in Christopher Lasch, *The World of Nations: Reflections on American History, Politics, and Culture* (New York, 1973), pp. 13–15.

34. Sacvan Bercovitch, *The American Jeremiad* (Madison, Wis., 1978).

35. James Hastings, ed., *Encyclopedia of Religion and Ethics*, 13 vols. (New York, 1908–29), 10: 455, 515–16. See also David J. Pivar, *Purity Crusade: Sexual Morality and Social Control, 1868–1900* (Westport, Conn., 1973).

36. For an interesting discussion of this disjunction see Edward Morse Shepard, "Dishonor in American Public Life," in *Representative Phi Beta Kappa Orations*, ed. Clark S. Northup (New York, 1927), 2: 216–17.

37. David Grimsted, *Melodrama Unveiled: American Theatre and Culture, 1800–1850* (Chicago, 1968), pp. 204–48.

38. John Higham, *Send These to Me: Jews and Other Immigrants in Urban America* (New York, 1975), pp. 175–77, 184–86.

39. Thomas L. Haskell, *The Emergence of Professional Social Science: The American Social Science Association and the Nineteenth-Century Crisis of Authority* (Urbana, Ill., 1977), pp. 14–17, 27–47. I am also indebted to Robert H. Wiebe, *The Segmented Society: An Historical Preface to the Meaning of America* (New York, 1975).

40. Although writing with other questions in mind, Paul Boyer gives some of the evidence in *Urban Masses and Moral Order in America, 1820–1920* (Cambridge, Mass., 1978), pp. 252–63.

41. Lewis Mumford, *The Brown Decades: A Study of the Arts in America, 1865–1895* (New York, 1931).

42. David T. Day, "Light: The Civilizer," *American Magazine*, April 1906, pp. 658–64; Frederick S. Lamb, "Civic Treatment of Color," *Municipal Affairs* 2 (March 1898): 114–19; Edward S. Martin, "Manhattan Lights," *Harper's Monthly Magazine*, Febru-

ary 1907, pp. 359–67; Edward Bok, *The Americanization of Edward Bok* (New York, 1922), pp. 238–45, 251–53.

43. My own book, *Strangers in the Land,* in this respect has much in common with C. Vann Woodward, *Origins of the New South, 1877–1913* (Baton Rouge, La., 1951).

44. Woodward, *Origins,* pp. 326–27, reports that the primary reason given at the time for Negro disfranchisement was repugnance for corrupt elections. On crime and immorality see George M. Fredrickson, *The Black Image in the White Mind: The Debate on Afro-American Character and Destiny, 1817–1914* (New York, 1971), pp. 258–82. On blacks as a source of pollution see also *Literary Digest,* 22 September 1917, p. 34.

45. "The Psychology of the Race Question," *Independent,* 13 August 1903, pp. 1939–40; John Corrigan, "The Prohibition Wave in the South," *American Monthly Review of Reviews,* September 1907, pp. 328–34; John T. Graves, "The Fight Against Alcohol," *Cosmopolitan Magazine,* June 1908, pp. 88–89; P. H. Whaley, "Some Aspects of Prohibition in the South," *Collier's Weekly,* 31 May 1913, p. 32.

46. David A. Hollinger, "Ethnic Diversity, Cosmopolitanism, and the Emergence of the American Liberal Intelligentsia," *American Quarterly* 27 (1975): 133–51.

47. Richard Hofstadter, *The Age of Reform: From Bryan to F.D.R.* (New York, 1955), pp. 196–200.

CHAPTER 6. *Immigration and American Mythology*

1. Oscar Handlin, *The Uprooted: The Epic Story of the Great Migrations That Made the American People* (Boston: Little, Brown, 1951), p. 3; Alasdair MacIntyre, "The American Idea," in *America and Ireland, 1776–1976,* ed. David Noel Doyle (Westport, Conn.: Greenwood Press, 1980), p. 68.

2. Perry Miller, *The New England Mind: The Seventeenth Century* (Cambridge: Harvard University Press, 1939), pp. 463–91. John Randolph, *Considerations on the State of Virginia,* quoted in Max Savelle, "Nationalism and Other Loyalties in the American Revolution," *American Historical Review* 67 (July 1962), p. 912; James Otis, *Rights of the British Colonies,* quoted in Alden Vaughan, "From White Man to Redskin: Changing Anglo-American Perceptions of the American Indian," *American Historical Review* 87 (1982), p. 936.

3. Arthur Mann, *The One and the Many: Reflections on the American Identity* (Chicago: University of Chicago Press, 1979), p. 47.

4. J. Hector St. John Crèvecoeur, in *Immigration and the American Tradition,* ed. Moses Rischin (Indianapolis: Bobbs-Merrill, 1976), pp. 25–26.

5. *A Short Account of the Troubles and Dangers our Fore-fathers met with to obtain this Land . . . recommended to be preserved in the House of every true Friend to the Rights and Priviledges of America* (Danvers, Mass., n.d.), in William L. Clements Library, University of Michigan.

6. A revealing exception was Louisiana, where the French usage of "creole" has persisted as a means of affirming the social preeminence of *l'ancienne population* over the Anglo-Americans who poured in after annexation to the United States in 1803. Virginia Dominguez, "Social Classification in Creole Louisiana," *American Ethnologist* 4 (1977), pp. 589–602.

7. Francis Hodge, *Yankee Theatre: The Image of America on Stage, 1825–1850*

(Austin: University of Texas, 1964), is the fullest account but needs to be qualified, as in Richard Dorson, "The Question of Folklore in a New Nation," in his *American Folklore and the Historian* (Chicago: University of Chicago Press, 1971), pp. 94–107, and by the contemporary testimony in Theodore C. Blegen, ed., *Land of Their Choice* (Minneapolis: University of Minnesota Press, 1955), pp. 314–15.

8. Lester H. Cohen, *The Revolutionary Histories: Contemporary Narratives of the American Revolution* (Ithaca, N.Y.: Cornell University Press, 1980). While distinguishing between myth and ideology, I want to suggest that the difference is often one of degree and that each can contain elements of the other. See Ben Halpern, "Myth and Ideology in Modern Usage," *History and Theory* 1 (1961), pp. 129–49.

9. Michael Kammen, *A Season of Youth: The American Revolution and the Historical Imagination* (New York: Knopf, 1978), 15–26. See also J. Meredith Neil, *Toward a National Taste: America's Quest for Aesthetic Independence* (Honolulu: University Press of Hawaii, 1975).

10. Russel Ward, *The Australian Legend,* 3d ed. (Melbourne: Oxford University Press, 1978), pp. 284–309.

11. Owen Wister, *The Virginian: A Horseman of the Plains* (New York: Macmillan, 1902).

12. Henry Nash Smith, *Virgin Land: The American West as Symbol and Myth* (Cambridge: Harvard University Press, 1950), should be supplemented by Rush Welter, *The Mind of America, 1820–1860* (New York: Vintage Books, 1975), pp. 298–328.

13. Walt Whitman, *Representative Selections,* ed. Floyd Stovall (New York: American Book, 1939 [1865]), pp. 204–5.

14. Paul Nagel, *American Historical Review* 87 (October 1982), p. 1149 (book review).

15. See Chapter 9 below.

16. Werner Sollors, *Beyond Ethnicity: Consent and Descent in American Culture* (New York: Oxford University Press, 1986), pp. 66–101. For nineteenth-century comments on immigrant assimilation see Henry T. Tuckerman, *America and Her Commentators* (New York: C. Scribner, 1864), pp. 438–41; Oscar Handlin, ed., *This Was America* (Cambridge: Harvard University Press, 1949); Olga Peters Hasty and Susanne Fusso, eds., *America Through Russian Eyes, 1874–1926* (New Haven: Yale University Press, 1988), pp. 21–22.

17. Clyde A. Milner II, ed., *Major Problems in the History of the American West* (Lexington, Mass.: D. C. Heath, 1989), p. 13. Other important studies from Wisconsin were John R. Commons, *Races and Immigrants in America* (New York: Macmillan, 1907); and Selig Perlman, *A Theory of the Labor Movement* (1928; repr. Philadelphia: Porcupine Press, 1979).

18. Marcus Lee Hansen, *The Atlantic Migration, 1607–1860: A History of the Continuing Settlement of the United States* (Cambridge: Harvard University Press, 1940); Hansen, *The Immigrant in American History* (Cambridge: Harvard University Press, 1940); Theodore C. Blegen, *Norwegian Migration to America* (2 vols., Northfield, Minn.: Norwegian-American Historical Association, 1931–40); George M. Stephenson, *The Religious Aspects of Swedish Immigration: A Study of Immigrant Churches* (Minneapolis: University of Minnesota Press, 1932); Arthur M. Schlesinger, *New Viewpoints in American History* (New York: Macmillan, 1922), pp. 1–22.

19. For Turner's more orthodox followers the spirit of the frontier has persisted in

science, technology, and the American determination to make a better future; but concrete scholarship on the American West has concentrated increasingly on a region that is burdened and bounded rather than open and free. See Donald Worster, "New West, True West," in Milner, *Major Problems,* pp. 21–34.

20. John Higham, *Send These to Me: Immigrants in Urban America,* rev. ed. (Baltimore, Md.: Johns Hopkins University Press, 1984), pp. 5–15.

21. Stanley Lieberson, "Unhyphenated Whites in the United States," *Ethnic and Racial Studies* 8 (1985), pp. 159–80. To estimate the immigrant sector of American society, studies of the origins of the entire population are less helpful than the former practice of counting both first- and second-generation immigrants. Unfortunately, the U.S. Census gave up that tabulation after 1970. It should resume.

22. James P. Allen, "Changes in the American Propensity to Migrate," *Annals of the Association of American Geographers* 67 (1977), pp. 577–87; *New York Times,* December 12, 1994, p. 1.

23. Franz Schurmann, "The Country Is Becoming a Nation of Nomads," *Baltimore Sun,* August 3, 1986.

24. *Harvard Encyclopedia of American Ethnic Groups,* ed. Stephan Thernstrom (Cambridge: Harvard University Press, Belknap Press, 1980), Appendix 2, pp. 1047–49.

25. *Chicago Times,* January 7, 1874, in Chicago Foreign Language Press Survey, Reel 13, I C (Immigration History Research Center, University of Minnesota).

CHAPTER 7. *Pluralistic Integration as an American Model*

1. Leonard J. Fein, "The Limits of Liberalism," *Saturday Review,* 53 (June 20, 1970), 83–85, 95–96; Wilson Carey McWilliams, *The Idea of Fraternity in America* (Berkeley, Calif., 1973).

2. Michael Novak, *The Rise of the Unmeltable Ethnics: Politics and Culture in the Seventies* (New York, 1972).

3. Mary Antin, *The Promised Land* (Boston, 1912), xi, xiv.

4. Henry S. Lucas, *Netherlanders in America* (Ann Arbor, Mich., 1955); Arthur Mann, "The City as a Melting Pot," in *Lectures 1971–1972: History and the Role of the City in American Life* (Indiana Historical Society, Indianapolis, 1972), 18–19.

5. William Faulkner, *The Faulkner Reader* (New York, 1954), 143–44.

6. Harold Cruse, *The Crisis of the Negro Intellectual* (New York, 1967), 317, 394; Vine Deloria, *We Talk, You Listen: New Tribes, New Turf* (New York, 1970).

7. See Gilbert Osofsky's fine essay "Wendell Phillips and the Quest for a New American National Identity," *Canadian Review of Studies in Nationalism,* 1 (1973), 14–46.

8. Philip Gleason, *Speaking of Diversity: Language and Ethnicity in Twentieth-Century America* (Baltimore, Md., 1992), 3–31.

9. Israel Zangwill, *The Melting Pot* (New York, 1909), 37–38.

10. Ibid., 157, 196.

11. John Collier, *From Every Zenith* (Denver, Colo., 1963), 203.

12. Stokely Carmichael and Charles V. Hamilton, *Black Power: The Politics of Liberation in America* (New York, 1967), 44, 51.

13. Robert E. Park, *Race and Culture* (Glencoe, Ill., 1950).

14. See John Higham, *Send These to Me: Immigrants in Urban America*, rev. ed. (Baltimore, Md., 1984), 222–25.

15. Philippe Ariès, *Centuries of Childhood: A Social History of Family Life* (New York, 1962), 415. See also Margaret Hodgen, *Early Anthropology in the Sixteenth and Seventeenth Centuries* (Philadelphia, 1964).

16. Albert A. Sicroff, *Les controverses des statuts de "pureté de sang" en Espagne du XVe au XVIIe siècle* (Paris, 1960); Thomas F. Gossett, *Race: The History of an Idea in America* (Dallas, 1963), 3–53.

17. Ariès, *Centuries of Childhood*, 314. See also S. L. Bethell, *The Cultural Revolution of the Seventeenth Century* (London, 1951).

18. Robert Jay Lifton, *History and Human Survival* (New York, 1970), 311–31.

19. Robert Venturi, *Complexity and Contradiction in Architecture* (New York, 1966), 22–23.

20. For various indications of the growth of cultural differentiation see the report on religious trends in the *New York Times*, January 7, 1973, p. 55; "The Arts in America," *Newsweek*, 82 (December 24, 1973), 40; Richard Maisel, "The Decline of Mass Media," *Public Opinion Quarterly*, 37 (1973), 159–70.

21. Robert Kelley, *The Cultural Pattern in American Politics: The First Century* (New York, 1979).

22. The scope of this transition is most fully developed in Lawrence H. Fuchs, *The American Kaleidoscope: Race, Ethnicity, and the Civic Culture* (Hanover, N.H., 1990).

23. Christopher Jencks, *Rethinking Social Policy: Race, Poverty, and the Underclass* (Cambridge, Mass., 1992); Hugh Davis Graham, "Race, Language, and Social Policy: Comparing the Black and Hispanic Experience in the U.S.," *Population and Environment*, 12 (Fall 1990), 43–58.

24. Michael Kinsley, "Quota Bill?" *New Republic*, 204 (April 15, 1991), 4.

25. Heather MacDonald, "The Diversity Industry," *New Republic*, 209 (July 5, 1993), 22–25.

26. Peter H. Schuck, "The Great Immigration Debate," *American Prospect* (Fall 1990), 100–118. See also David E. Simcox, ed., *U.S. Immigration in the 1980s: Reappraisals and Reform* (Boulder, Colo., 1988).

27. Alejandro Portes and Rubén G. Rumbaut, *Immigrant America: A Portrait*, 2d ed. (Berkeley, Calif., 1996), 249–51; "Crowding Out Hope," *San Diego Union-Tribune*, August 22, 1999. For qualifications see Joel Perlmann and Roger Waldinger, "Immigrants, Past and Present: A Reconsideration," in *The Handbook of International Migration: The American Experience*, ed. Charles Hirschman et al. (New York, 1999), 233–34.

28. William H. Frey and Kao-Lee Liaw, "The Impact of Recent Immigration on Population Redistribution Within the United States," in *The Immigration Debate: Studies of Economic, Demographic and Fiscal Effects of Immigration* (Washington, D.C., 1998), 388–448; *Immigration and Opportunity: Race, Ethnicity and Employment in the United States*, ed. Frank D. Bean and Stephanie Bell-Rose (New York, 1999); James G. Gimpel, *Separate Destinations: Migration, Immigration, and the Politics of Places* (Ann Arbor, Mich., 1999); Jonathan Tilove, "The New Map of American Politics," *American Prospect* (May–June 1999), 34–42.

29. *The Economic Status of Americans of Southern and Eastern European Ancestry* (U.S. Commission on Civil Rights, Clearinghouse Publication 89, October 1986); W. Lloyd Warner, *Big Business Leaders in America* (New York, 1955), 190–93; "New

Names in the Board Room," *New York Times,* October 31, 1971; "Diversity on Boards Increases," ibid., June 13, 1999.

30. "Another Latin Boom, but Different," *New York Times,* June 27, 1999. On baseball see "Celebration in a Melting Pot," ibid., October 30, 1999.

31. Ronald H. Bayor, *Neighbors in Conflict: The Irish, Germans, Jews, and Italians of New York City, 1929-1941* (Baltimore, 1978); Melvin G. Holli, "*E Pluribus Unum:* The Assimilation Paradigm Revisited," *Siirtolaisuus—Migration,* 26 (February 1999), 5. On Serbo-Croatian relations see also *Baltimore Sun,* January 17, 1985; *New York Times,* December 17, 1991, and September 18, 1992.

32. *New York Times,* January 4, 21, 1993; March 26, 1996; January 12, 1999.

33. Joshua A. Fishman, *Language Loyalty in the United States: The Maintenance and Perpetuation of Non-English Mother Tongues by American Ethnic and Religious Groups* (New York, 1966); Portes and Rumbaut, *Immigrant America,* 207–25; Werner Sollors, ed., *Multilingual America: Transnationalism, Ethnicity, and the Languages of American Literature* (New York, 1998).

34. Gary B. Nash, "The Hidden History of Mestizo America," *Journal of American History,* 82 (December 1995), 941–62.

35. Chaim I. Waxman, *America's Jews in Transition* (Philadelphia, 1983), 25–26. Specifically, records are available for 699 marriages of Jews during this period, 201 with a non-Jewish spouse.

36. Richard Jules Oestreicher, *Solidarity and Fragmentation: Working People and Class Consciousness in Detroit, 1875–1900* (Urbana, Ill., 1986), 39. See also, on an earlier period, Aaron Spencer Fogleman, *Hopeful Journeys: German Immigration, Settlement, and Political Culture in Colonial America, 1717–1775* (Philadelphia, 1996), 80–83.

37. Reynolds Farley, "Racial Issues: Recent Trends in Residential Patterns and Intermarriage," in *Diversity and Its Discontents: Cultural Conflict and Common Ground in Contemporary American Society,* ed. Neil J. Smelser and Jeffrey C. Alexander (Princeton, N.J., 1999), pp. 108–9.

38. National Jewish Population Study, *Intermarriage: Facts for Planning* (New York: Council of Jewish Federations and Welfare Funds, n.d.), 1–10; Bruno Bettelheim, "Survival of the Jews," *New Republic,* 157 (July 1, 1967), 28–30; "Poll Shows Jews Both Assimilate and Keep Tradition," *New York Times,* June 7, 1991.

39. Stanley Lieberson, "Unhyphenated Whites in the United States," *Ethnic and Racial Studies,* 8 (January 1985), 161–80; Mary C. Waters, *Ethnic Options: Choosing Identities in America* (Berkeley, Calif., 1990).

40. Farley, "Racial Issues," 108–28; "Blending Races Making True Melting Pot," *USA Today,* September 7, 1999. See also David E. López, "Social and Linguistic Aspects of Assimilation Today," in *Handbook of International Migration,* 218–22, 266–67.

41. For an ingenious attempt to measure the racism that is masked by conservatism see Paul M. Sniderman and Thomas Piazza, *The Scar of Race* (Cambridge, Mass., 1993). For weariness and anger see Ellis Cose at Balch Round Table, Balch Institute for Ethnic Studies, Philadelphia, May 10, 1994; and *Baltimore Sun,* January 21, 1995.

42. "Years on Integration Road: New Views of an Old Goal," *New York Times,* April 10, 1994; George Fredrickson, "Far from the Promised Land," *New York Review of Books,* April 18, 1996, pp. 16–20.

43. Peter Skerry, *Mexican Americans: The Ambivalent Minority* (New York, 1993), 16–17, 300–302, 383; Linda Chavez, "Just Say Latino," *New Republic,* 208 (March 22,

1993), 19; Jack Miles, "Blacks vs. Browns," *Atlantic Monthly,* 270 (October 1992), 41–45; *New York Times,* June 20, 1993.

44. Portes and Rumbaut, *Immigrant America,* 68–75.

45. John Higham, "Introduction," in *Civil Rights and Social Wrongs: Black-White Relations Since World War II,* ed. John Higham (University Park, Pa., 1997), 13–18.

46. Gleason, *Speaking of Diversity,* 142.

47. This kind of leadership was prominent in the civil rights movement. Its importance in the formation of European immigrant communities is analyzed in Victor R. Greene, *American Immigrant Leaders, 1800–1910: Marginality and Identity* (Baltimore, Md., 1987).

48. Roger Sanjek, *The Future of Us All: Race and Neighborhood Politics in New York City* (Ithaca, N.Y., 1998), 393.

CHAPTER 8. *Three Postwar Reconstructions*

1. C. Vann Woodward, "From the First Reconstruction to the Second," *Harper's Magazine* 230 (April 1965): 127–33.

2. Ibid., 133; Eric Foner, "Slavery, the Civil War, and Reconstruction," in *The New American History,* ed. Foner (Philadelphia: Temple University Press, 1990), 83–89. The phrase comes from the title of Claude G. Bowers's influential book *The Tragic Era: The Revolution After Lincoln* (Cambridge, Mass.: Houghton Mifflin Co., 1929).

3. Gordon Wood, *The Creation of the American Republic, 1776–1787* (Chapel Hill: University of North Carolina Press, 1969), 91–124; Ernest Lee Tuveson, *Redeemer Nation: The Idea of America's Millennial Role* (Chicago: University of Chicago Press, 1968); Ruth H. Bloch, "Religion, Literary Sentimentalism, and Popular Revolutionary Ideology," in *Religion in a Revolutionary Age,* ed. Ronald Hoffman and Peter J. Albert (Charlottesville: University Press of Virginia, 1994), 308–30.

4. David Brion Davis, "American Slavery and the American Revolution," in *Slavery and Freedom in the Age of the American Revolution,* ed. Ira Berlin and Ronald Hoffman (Charlottesville: University Press of Virginia, 1983), 276–77.

5. David Brion Davis, *The Problem of Slavery in Western Culture* (Ithaca, N.Y.: Cornell University Press, 1966), 306–32; and Davis, *The Problem of Slavery in the Age of Revolution, 1770–1823* (Ithaca, N.Y.: Cornell University Press, 1975), 213–54.

6. Gary Gerstle, "The Working Class Goes to War," in *The War in American Culture: Society and Consciousness During World War II,* ed. Lewis A. Erenberg and Susan E. Hirsch (Chicago: University of Chicago Press, 1996), 105–27; and, in the same volume, Alan Brinkley, "World War II and American Liberalism," 313–30. See also Gerstle's "The Protean Character of American Liberalism," *American Historical Review* 99 (October 1994): 1043–74.

7. David M. Kennedy, *Over Here: The First World War and American Society* (New York: Oxford University Press, 1980), 245–50. For useful suggestions on the prewar milieu, see Joel Williamson, *The Crucible of Race: Black-White Relations in the American South Since Emancipation* (New York: Oxford University Press, 1984); and Kenneth L. Kusmer, "Toward a Comparative History of Racism and Xenophobia in the United States and Europe, 1870–1933," in Hermann Wellenreuther and Elisabeth Glaser, eds., *Bridging the Atlantic: Europe and the United States in Modern Times* (Cambridge University Press, 2001).

8. Willie Lee Rose, *Slavery and Freedom* (New York: Oxford University Press, 1982), 3–17; Ira Berlin, *Slaves Without Masters: The Free Negro in the Antebellum South* (New York: Random House, 1974), 20–50; Duncan J. MacLeod, *Slavery, Race, and the American Revolution* (New York: Cambridge University Press, 1974). See also Leonard P. Curry, *The Free Black in Urban America, 1800–1850* (Chicago: University of Chicago Press, 1981), 174–215.

9. James H. Moorhead, *American Apocalypse: Yankee Protestants and the Civil War, 1860–1869* (New Haven: Yale University Press, 1978); Edmund Wilson, *Patriotic Gore: Studies in the Literature of the American Civil War* (New York: Oxford University Press, 1962), 91–98.

10. Eric Foner, *Reconstruction: America's Unfinished Revolution, 1863–1877* (New York: Harper and Row, 1988), xxiv–28.

11. Ibid., 255–79, 446–59; Larry Kincaid, "Two Steps Forward, One Step Backward," in *The Great Fear: Race in the Mind of America,* ed. Gary Nash and Richard Weiss (New York: Holt, Rinehart and Winston, 1970). See also William Gillette, *Retreat from Reconstruction, 1869–1879* (Baton Rouge: Louisiana State University Press, 1979), ix–55.

12. Winthrop D. Jordan, *White over Black: American Attitudes Toward the Negro, 1550–1812* (Chapel Hill: University of North Carolina Press, 1968), 342–426; Berlin, *Slaves Without Masters,* 79–107.

13. Foner, *Reconstruction,* 281–88, 320–21, 449, 484–510.

14. Gary B. Nash, *Forging Freedom: The Formation of Philadelphia's Black Community, 1720–1840* (Cambridge: Harvard University Press, 1988), 172–83, 212–79; Stuart Bruchey, *Enterprise: The Dynamic Economy of a Free People* (Cambridge: Harvard University Press, 1990), 144–47, 161.

15. Robert Kelley, *The Cultural Pattern in American Politics: The First Century* (New York: Alfred A. Knopf, 1979), 228–55; Foner, *Reconstruction,* 523–27. On contemporary views of depressions, see Edward C. Kirkland, *Industry Comes of Age: Business, Labor, and Public Policy, 1860–1897* (Chicago: Quadrangle Books, 1967), 7.

16. *Southern Black Leaders of the Reconstruction Era,* ed. Howard N. Rabinowitz (Urbana: University of Illinois Press, 1982); Eric Foner, "The Tocsin of Freedom": The *Black Leadership of Radical Reconstruction* (pamphlet, Gettysburg College, Pa., 1992).

17. John Higham, "Introduction," in *Civil Rights and Social Wrongs: Black-White Relations Since World War II,* ed. John Higham (University Park: Pennsylvania State University Press, 1997), 3–18.

18. Stanley Crouch, "Race Is Over," *New York Times Magazine,* September 29, 1996, 170–71. In a more scholarly vein, see Gary B. Nash's important essay "The Hidden History of Mestizo America," *Journal of American History* 82 (December 1995): 941–62.

19. Tom Wicker, *Tragic Failure: Racial Integration in America* (New York: William Morrow and Co., 1996).

20. Robert Wiebe, *Self-Rule: A Cultural History of American Democracy* (Chicago: University of Chicago Press, 1995), 103, 126–30; Bruchey, *Enterprise,* 279; Foner, *Reconstruction,* 587–97, 612; Robert L. Woodson, "The End of Racism?" *New York Times,* September 23, 1995.

21. Tom Engelhardt, *The End of Victory Culture: Cold War America and the Disillusionment of a Generation* (New York: Basic Books, 1995). On the persistence of

the "American Dream" among lower-class blacks, see Jennifer L. Hochschild, *Facing Up to the American Dream: Race, Class, and the Soul of the Nation* (Princeton, N.J.: Princeton University Press, 1995).

CHAPTER 9. *From Boundlessness to Consolidation: The Transformation of American Culture, 1848–1860*

1. William W. Williams, *History of Ashtabula County, Ohio* (Philadelphia, 1878), 108–10. See also *Dictionary of American Biography* (20 vols., New York, 1937), XVII, 457; M. L. Dougherty, "History of Teaching Handwriting in America," *Elementary School Journal* 18 (1917), 280–86.

2. Henry Nash Smith, *Virgin Land: The American West as Symbol and Myth* (Cambridge, Mass., 1950), 85–112.

3. Perry Miller, *Nature's Nation* (Cambridge, Mass., 1967), 254–62. On Church as the culmination and conclusion of American romantic art, see David Carew Huntington, *Art and the Excited Spirit: America in the Romantic Period* (Ann Arbor, Mich., 1972).

4. "The Physical Training of Students," *Biblical Repertory and Princeton Review* 33 (April 1861), 183–214, is a review of *Education: Intellectual, Moral and Physical* (New York, 1861), in which Spencer reprinted four essays first published in British quarterlies during the 1850s.

5. Donald Fleming's "Social Darwinism," in *Paths of American Thought*, ed. Arthur M. Schlesinger, Jr., and Morton White (Boston, 1963), 123–46, surveys the influence of Spencer in the United States through the 1880s and the strong reaction against him thereafter.

6. Richard Hofstadter makes this point forcefully in *Social Darwinism in American Thought* (rev. ed., New York, 1959).

7. Daniel Boorstin, *The Americans: The National Experience* (New York, 1965), 219–324; Stanley Elkins, *Slavery: A Problem in American Institutional and Intellectual Life* (Chicago, 1959), 27–80; David Donald, "Toward a Reconsideration of Abolitionists," in his *Lincoln Reconsidered: Essays on the Civil War Era* (New York, 1956), 19–36.

8. "The Present Age," in *The Works of William E. Channing* (6 vols., Boston, 1848), VI, 150–54. For a more plebeian and bellicose statement of similar sentiments see George Miller, "The Present Age," *Western Literary Messenger* 9 (August 14, 1847), 25–26.

9. *The Complete Poetry and Prose of Walt Whitman* (2 vols., New York, 1948), I, 159.

10. Stow Persons, *American Minds: A History of Ideas* (Huntington, N.Y., 1975), 120–37.

11. Arthur O. Lovejoy, *The Great Chain of Being: A Study of the History of an Idea* (Baltimore, Md., 1936); E. M. W. Tillyard, *The Elizabethan World Picture* (New York, 1944); Alexandre Koyré, *From the Closed World to the Infinite Universe* (Baltimore, Md., 1957).

12. John G. Cawelti, *Apostles of the Self-Made Man* (Chicago, 1965).

13. C. Vann Woodward's "The Age of Reinterpretation," *American Historical Review* 66 (1960), 1–9, is expanded in Woodward, *The Future of the Past* (New York: Oxford, 1989), 75–118, to include a helpful criticism from W. Stull Holt.

14. Arthur O. Lovejoy, "The Meaning of Romanticism for the Historian of Ideas," *Journal of the History of Ideas* 2 (1941), 237–78.

15. I have lost the source of this quotation, but Jean V. Matthews presents an almost identical statement by Rufus Choate in *Rufus Choate: The Law and Civic Virtue* (Philadelphia, 1980), 87.

16. In a book that never received the recognition it deserved, Rowland Berthoff presents as a social breakdown what I am describing as an unbounded outreach. His vivid synthesis, *An Unsettled People: Social Order and Disorder in American History* (New York, 1971), 125–376, was first sketched out in Berthoff, "The American Social Order: A Conservative Hypothesis," *American Historical Review* 65 (1960), 495–514.

17. David Grimsted, *Melodrama Unveiled: American Theater and Culture, 1800–1850* (Chicago, 1968).

18. "American Hyperbole," *Harper's Weekly* 1 (April 11, 1857), 226; "Humor," in *Literary History of the United States*, ed. Robert E. Spiller et al., (3 vols., New York, 1948), II, 728–41.

19. *Inaugural Addresses of the Presidents of the United States from George Washington, 1789, to Lyndon Baines Johnson, 1965* (Washington, D.C., 1965), 105.

20. When this essay was written, the Whig party was only beginning to be studied intensively. It has now received its due from Daniel Walker Howe, *The Political Culture of the American Whigs* (Chicago, 1979).

21. Frank Thistlethwaite, *The Anglo-American Connection in the Early Nineteenth Century* (Philadelphia, 1959), 90–91.

22. William R. Taylor, *Cavalier and Yankee: The Old South and American National Character* (New York, 1961), 96–141; review of Fred Folio, *Lucy Boston: Women's Rights and Spiritualism*, in *Criterion* 1 (November 17, 1855), 38; "The Veto," *The New World* 4 (May 21, 1842), 327–28.

23. George Fredrickson, *The Inner Civil War: Northern Intellectuals and the Crisis of the Union* (New York, 1965; rev. ed., Urbana, Ill., 1993).

24. Both of the great national newspapers in New York City, almost always at loggerheads, reacted ecstatically in the first weeks. "Who shall longer hope to stay the swelling tide of Revolution?" the *New York Weekly Tribune* asked rhetorically (March 25, 1848). "A wonderful revolution," the *New York Weekly Herald* exclaimed (April 1, 1848). Scoffing at the Wall Street business press for depicting the new French republic as sliding toward socialism, the *Herald* replied that the "civilized world" is simply following in the footsteps of the United States. The Chicago *Gem of the Prairie* confessed "an ungovernable sympathy" and "uncontrollable solicitude" (March 25, 1848). See also the *Western Literary Messenger*'s reports of civic exuberance in Buffalo (March 25–April 8, 1848).

25. *Washington Union*, quoted in *New York Weekly Herald*, February 26, 1848. R. W. B. Lewis's masterful tracing of dialogic complication in literary images of youthful innocence reaches its climax in the 1850s. His writers may therefore be understood as interacting *within* the shift in public mood that is described here. Lewis, *The American Adam: Innocence, Tragedy and Tradition in the Nineteenth Century* (Chicago, 1955).

26. *Niles National Register* 74 (July 26, 1848), 64; *Literary World* 5 (July 2, 1849), 53.

27. *Western Literary Messenger* 10 (July 8, 1848), 363; *Harper's Weekly* 1 (April 4, 1857), 424–26; Thomas C. Grattan, *Civilized America* (2 vols., London, 1859), II, 469.

28. Charles B. Hosmer, Jr., *Presence of the Past: A History of the Preservation Movement in the United States Before Williamsburg* (New York, 1965), 33–59.

29. *Southern Literary Messenger,* quoted in Merle Curti, *Probing Our Past* (New York, 1955), 199.

30. Van Wyck Brooks, *The Times of Melville and Whitman* (New York, 1947), 211–12.

31. Putnam's letter to editor, *New York Evening Post,* July 1851, reprinted in *George Palmer Putnam: A Memoir* (New York, 1912), 207–8.

32. Perry Miller, *The Raven and the Whale: The War of Words and Wits in the Era of Poe and Melville* (New York, 1956), 189–258, 316; John Stafford, *The Literary Criticism of "Young America": A Study in the Relationship of Politics and Literature, 1837–1850* (Berkeley, Calif., 1952).

33. Merle E. Curti, *The American Peace Crusade, 1815–1860* (Durham, N.C., 1929); Norman Ware, *The Industrial Worker, 1840–1860* (Boston, 1924). On prisons, asylums, and mental illness, David J. Rothman's *The Discovery of the Asylum: Social Order and Disorder in the New Republic* (Boston, 1971), supersedes my sources; on Fourierism, see Carl J. Guarneri, *The Utopian Alternative: Fourierism in Nineteenth-Century America* (Ithaca, N.Y., 1991).

34. "Physical Training of Students," 189–90.

35. Norman H. Clark, *Deliver Us from Evil: An Interpretation of American Prohibition* (New York, 1976), 35–48, takes the place of earlier general accounts, but see also Frank L. Byrne, *Prophet of Prohibition: Neal Dow and His Crusade* (Madison, Wis., 1961).

36. *North American Review* 64 (1847) 406–7; "Literary Notices," *Knickerbocker Magazine* 35 (1850), 255, 259; Warren G. Jenkins, "Lowell's Criteria of Political Values," *New England Quarterly* 7 (1934), 115–41; Lewis, *American Adam,* 189–91.

37. The youngest of the causes emergent in the ethos of boundlessness, born at the Seneca Falls convention in 1848, is unhappily overlooked in my text, though very relevant to my story. That fledgling women's rights movement survived the widespread collapse of reform in the 1850s. It did so, I believe, not only because of its founders' tenacity but also because it was closely allied with and sustained by the radical, abolitionist wing of antislavery. A different women's project, dedicated to "moral purity" (i.e., exposing prostitution), dissolved in the late 1840s. It had no larger movement to give it leverage. Sara M. Evans, *Born for Liberty: A History of Women in America* (New York, 1989), 101–4; Bertha-Monica Stearns, "Reform Periodicals and Female Reformers, 1830–1860," *American Historical Review* 37 (1932), 681–84.

38. Fredrickson, *Inner Civil War;* Alfred D. Chandler, Jr., *Henry Varnum Poor: Business Editor, Analyst, and Reformer* (Cambridge, Mass., 1956).

39. Arthur C. Cole, *The Irrepressible Conflict, 1850–1865,* vol. 7 of *A History of American Life* (New York, 1934), 157; Stanley K. Schultz, *The Culture Factory: Boston Public Schools, 1789–1860* (New York, 1973), 132–33, 150–53. See also Richard H. Shryock, "The Origins and Significance of the Public Health Movement in the United States," *Annals of Medical History* 1 (1929), 645–65.

40. Frank Dekker Watson, *The Charity Organization Movement in the United States* (New York, 1922), 79–91.

41. Arthur Meier Schlesinger, *Learning How To Behave: A Historical Study of American Etiquette Books* (New York, 1947), is now largely superseded by John F.

Kasson, *Rudeness and Civility: Manners in Nineteenth-Century Urban America* (New York, 1999).

42. David Van Tassel and Michael G. Hall, eds., *Science and Society in the United States* (Homewood, Ill., 1966), 209.

CHAPTER 11. *The Reorientation of American Culture in the 1890s*

1. Henry Steele Commager, *The American Mind: An Interpretation of American Thought and Character Since the 1880s* (New Haven, 1950), ch. 2.

2. Marcus Cunliffe, "American Watersheds," *American Quarterly,* 13 (Winter 1961), 480–94.

3. Gerhard Masur, *Prophets of Yesterday: Studies in European Culture, 1890–1914* (New York, 1961); H. Stuart Hughes, *Consciousness and Society: The Reorientation of European Social Thought, 1890–1930* (New York, 1958); Morse Peckham, *Beyond the Tragic Vision: The Quest for Identity in the Nineteenth Century* (New York, 1962); Roger Shattuck, *The Banquet Years: The Arts in France, 1885–1918* (Garden City, N.Y., 1961); Carl E. Schorske, "Politics and the Psyche in *fin de siècle* Vienna: Schnitzler and Hofmannsthal," *American Historical Review,* 66 (July 1961), 930–46; and Eugen Weber, "The Secret World of Jean Barois: Notes on the Portrait of an Age," in *The Origins of Modern Consciousness,* ed. John Weiss (Detroit, 1965), 79–109.

4. Philippe Ariès, *Centuries of Childhood: A Social History of Family Life* (New York, 1965), 29–30; Ernest Earnest, *Academic Procession: An Informal History of the American College, 1636 to 1953* (Indianapolis, 1953), 204–36.

5. Robert H. Boyle, *Sport—Mirror of American Life* (Boston, 1963), 241–71.

6. Allan Houston Macdonald, *Richard Hovey, Man and Craftsman* (Durham, N.C., 1957), 128–29.

7. Frederick Rudolph, *The American College and University: A History* (New York, 1962), 373–93; Earnest, *Academic Procession,* 220–29; Foster Rhea Dulles, *America Learns to Play* (Gloucester, Mass., 1959), 264; John Allen Krout, *Annals of American Sport* (New Haven, 1929), 225.

8. Theodore Roosevelt, *The Strenuous Life: Essays and Addresses* (New York, 1900), 8, 20–21.

9. *The Selected Writings of John Jay Chapman,* ed. Jacques Barzun (New York, 1957), 248–50; Henry James, *The Ambassadors* (New York, 1930), 149. On James's significance in this respect, see Philip Rahv, *Image and Idea: Twenty Essays on Literary Themes* (Norfolk, Conn., 1957), 7–25.

10. *A Dictionary of Americanisms on Historical Principles,* ed. Mitford M. Mathews (Chicago, 1951). On "stuffed shirt" see also Thomas Beer, *Hanna, Crane, and the Mauve Decade* (New York, 1941), 97.

11. "Recording Time of Employees," *Scientific American,* 69 (Aug. 12, 1893), 101.

12. Frank Luther Mott, *A History of American Magazines, 1885–1905* (Cambridge, Mass., 1957), 369–70, 377–78; Frederick W. Cozens and Florence S. Stumpf, *Sports in American Life* (Chicago, 1953), 155; Harold Seymour, *Baseball: The Early Years* (New York, 1960), 345–58.

13. Dulles, *America Learns to Play,* 226–27; Krout, *Annals,* 227–31.

14. Mott, *American Magazines,* 316–17; Robert Lewis Taylor, "Physical Culture," *New Yorker,* 26 (Oct. 21, 1950), 47–50.

15. Roderick Nash, *Wilderness and the American Mind* (New Haven, 1967), 108–60; Lawrence A. Cremin, *The Transformation of the School: Progressivism in American Education, 1876–1957* (New York, 1961), 77; Margaret H. Underwood, *Bibliography of North American Minor Natural History Serials in the University of Michigan Libraries* (Ann Arbor, Mich., 1954). For general background see Hans Huth, *Nature and the American: Three Centuries of Changing Attitudes* (Berkeley, Calif., 1957), which reminds us that urban interest in the out-of-doors grew steadily during the preceding decades, although it increased most sharply after 1890.

16. Francis W. Halsey, "The Rise of the Nature Writers," *Review of Reviews,* 26 (November 1902), 567–71.

17. *Birds,* 2 (December 1897), back cover; *Bird Lore,* 1 (1899), 28.

18. James D. Hart, *The Popular Book: A History of America's Literary Taste* (New York, 1950), 214–15; Grant C. Knight, *The Critical Period in American Literature* (Chapel Hill, N.C., 1951), 121.

19. Macdonald, *Hovey,* 141–50.

20. David Ewen, *Panorama of American Popular Music* (Englewood Cliffs, N.J., 1957), 100–105, 142; *One Hundred Years of Music in America,* ed. Paul Henry Lang (New York, 1961), 143–47; Gilbert Chase, *America's Music from the Pilgrims to the Present* (New York, 1955), 433–45. See also the detailed account by Rudi Blesh and Harriet Janis, *They All Played Ragtime: The True Story of an American Music* (New York, 1959).

21. Bernarr Macfadden, *The Power and Beauty of Superb Womanhood* (New York, 1901), 23; William Dean Howells, *Suburban Sketches* (Boston, 1872), 96; James Fullarton Muirhead, *The Land of Contrasts* (London, 1898), 127.

22. Quoted from *Munsey's Magazine,* 1896, in Mott, *American Magazines,* 370–71.

23. Eleanor Flexner, *Century of Struggle: The Woman's Rights Movement in the United States* (Cambridge, Mass., 1959), 222–25.

24. James C. Malin, *Confounded Rot About Napoleon: Reflections upon Science and Technology, Nationalism, World Depression of the Eighteen-Nineties, and Afterwards* (Lawrence, Kans., 1961), 90, 185–97.

25. Cozens and Stumpf, *Sports,* 112–14. On cheerleaders see Muirhead, *Land of Contrasts,* 114; on jingoism, Richard Hofstadter, "Manifest Destiny and the Philippines," in *America in Crisis,* ed. Daniel Aaron (New York, 1952), 173–200.

26. Isaac Goldberg, *Tin Pin Alley* (New York, 1930), 166; Krout, *Annals,* 227; Theodore Roosevelt, "Value of an Athletic Training," *Harper's Weekly,* 37 (Dec. 23, 1893), 1236.

27. Halsey, "Rise of the Nature Writers," 571; Masur, *Prophets of Yesterday,* 356–59. The appeal of Haggard and Kipling in America is indicated in Hart, *Popular Book,* 309–10.

28. Frances Elizabeth McFall [Sarah Grand, pseud.], *The Heavenly Twins* (New York, 1893), 193; Frank Luther Mott, *Golden Multitudes: The Story of Best Sellers in the United States* (New York, 1947), 181–82. For a comparative study of the "New Morality" in England and in America see William L. O'Neill, *Divorce in the Progressive Era* (New Haven, 1967), 142–55.

29. Muirhead, *Land of Contrasts,* 106 ff.; *Sports and Athletics in 1908* (London, 1908), 13.

30. Paul de Rousiers, *American Life* (Paris, 1892), 324–33; Nat Fleischer, *The Heavyweight Championship* (New York, 1949), xiii.

31. Holbrook Jackson, *The Eighteen Nineties* (Harmondsworth, England, 1939), 28.

32. Harry Thurston Peck, "Migration of Popular Songs," *Bookman*, 2 (September 1895), 101; Chase, *America's Music*, 438.

33. Benedetto Croce, *History of Europe in the Nineteenth Century* (New York, 1933), 343. Croce gives a caustic appraisal of the new activism, which he views as a "perversion of the love of liberty" and holds responsible for the failure to avert a world war in 1914.

34. Duffield Osborne, "A Defense of Pugilism," *North American Review*, 146 (April 1888), 435; D. A. Sargent et al., *Athletic Sports* (New York, 1897), 4.

35. Walter LaFeber, *The New Empire: An Interpretation of American Expansion, 1860–1898* (Ithaca, N.Y., 1963), 63–101; Aileen S. Kraditor, *The Ideas of the Woman Suffrage Movement, 1890–1920* (New York, 1965), 97–101. There is an excellent discussion of this primitivistic theme in some of the leading novelists in Larzer Ziff, *The American 1890s: Life and Times of a Lost Generation* (New York, 1966), 173–228, 250–66.

36. Gertrude Atherton, "Why Is American Literature Bourgeois?" *North American Review*, 178 (May 1904), 778, emphasis added.

37. Boyle, *Sport*, 6–19; Dulles, *America Learns to Play*, 171; "Boxing," *Appleton's Annual Cyclopaedia, 1888*, 98–99; Duncan Edwards, "Life at the Athletic Clubs," *Scribner's Magazine*, 18 (July 1895), 4–23.

38. Lang, *One Hundred Years*, 147; Blesh and Janis, *They All Played Ragtime*, 152–53; James Weldon Johnson, *Black Manhattan* (New York, 1930), 105.

39. Richard Hofstadter, *The Paranoid Style in American Politics and Other Essays* (New York, 1967), 145–87; John P. Mallan, "The Warrior Critique of the Business Civilization," *American Quarterly*, 8 (Fall 1956), 218–30; Frederick Merk, *Manifest Destiny and Mission in American History: A Reinterpretation* (New York, 1963), 143–53.

40. Robert H. Wiebe, *The Search for Order, 1877–1920* (New York, 1967).

41. Maurice F. Brown, "Santayana's American Roots," *New England Quarterly*, 33 (June 1960), 147–63; Eric McKitrick, "Edgar Saltus of the Obsolete," *American Quarterly*, 3 (Spring 1951), 22–35; Max I. Baym, *The French Education of Henry Adams* (New York, 1951), 67.

42. Harold Frederic, *The Damnation of Theron Ware* (New York, 1896), 484.

43. Roger B. Salomon, *Twain and the Image of History* (New Haven, 1961), 199.

44. William Graham Sumner, *Social Darwinism: Selected Essays*, ed. Stow Persons (New York, 1963), 179–80; Rollo Ogden, *Life and Letters of Edwin Lawrence Godkin*, 2 vols. (New York, 1907), II, 186–87, 199, 202.

45. Brooks Adams, *The Law of Civilization and Decay* (New York, 1895); Henry Adams, *The Degradation of the Democratic Dogma* (New York, 1920).

46. Woodrow Wilson, *Congressional Government* (Boston, 1885), 5; Barrett Wendell, *A Literary History of America* (New York, 1900), 518.

47. Richard Burton, "Degenerates and Geniuses," *Critic*, 25 (Aug. 11, 1894), 85–86. For a general review of this intensely animated discussion see Milton Painter Foster, "The Reception of Max Nordau's *Degeneration* in England and America," University Microfilms, no. 1807 (Ann Arbor, Mich., 1954).

48. Quoted in George Mowry, *The Era of Theodore Roosevelt, 1900–1912* (New York, 1958), 88. See also Donald Pizer, "Romantic Individualism in Garland, Norris and Crane," *American Quarterly,* 10 (Winter 1958), 463–75; and Kenneth S. Lynn, *The Dream of Success: A Study of the Modern American Imagination* (Boston, 1955).

49. Van Wyck Brooks, *The Confident Years, 1885–1915* (New York, 1952), 218.

50. Arthur Beringause, *Brooks Adams, a Biography* (New York, 1955), 167–71, 186.

51. William E. Leuchtenburg, "Progressivism and Imperialism: The Progressive Movement and American Foreign Policy, 1898–1916," *Mississippi Valley Historical Review,* 39 (December, 1952), 483–504; John Higham, *Strangers in the Land: Patterns of American Nativism 1860–1925* (New Brunswick, N.J., 1955), 106–18, 144–45.

52. My indebtedness in the following pages to Morton G. White's *Social Thought in America: The Revolt Against Formalism* (New York, 1949) and to Henry F. May's *The End of American Innocence: The First Years of Our Own Time, 1912–1917* (New York, 1959) should be readily apparent, although they deal with other people and with a later period. I think the 1890s were more critically important than either book suggests.

53. On Turner's intellectual development see Fulmer Mood, "The Development of Turner as a Historial Thinker," Colonial Society of Massachusetts *Transactions,* 34 (1939), 283–352; and Lee Benson, *Turner and Beard: American Historical Writing Reconsidered* (Glencoe, Ill., 1960), 21–34.

54. Ralph Barton Perry, *The Thought and Character of William James,* 2 vols. (Boston, 1935), II, 251, 312.

55. "The Reminiscences of Guy Stanton Ford" (Oral History Research Office, Columbia University, 1956), 77–85; Ray Allen Billington, "Why Some Historians Rarely Write History: A Case Study of Frederick Jackson Turner," *Mississippi Valley Historical Review,* 50 (June 1963), 3–27.

56. Frank Lloyd Wright, *An Autobiography* (New York, 1943). On Wright's development and qualities as an architect I am especially indebted to Vincent Scully, Jr., *Frank Lloyd Wright* (New York, 1960).

57. Perry, *James,* II, 700.

58. See especially Frederick Jackson Turner, *Rise of the New West, 1819–1829* (New York, 1906).

59. Edward Bok, *The Americanization of Edward Bok* (New York, 1922), 238–45, 251–58.

60. Wright, *Autobiography,* 71. Cf. James's remark: "Your last two letters have breathed a . . . *Lebenslust,* which . . . nothing but mother earth can give." Perry, *James,* I, 414.

61. Quoted in Scully, *Wright,* 18; Frederick Jackson Turner, *The Frontier in American History* (New York, 1920).

62. William James, *The Will to Believe* (New York, 1931), 39–62; and James, *The Varieties of Religious Experience* (New York, n.d.). These books were first published in 1896 and 1902, respectively.

63. "Whitman and the Influence of Space on American Literature," Newberry Library *Bulletin,* 5 (December, 1961), 299–314.

64. James, *Varieties,* 84. In print, Turner quoted Whitman only once; he turned more readily to Kipling. *Frontier,* 262, 270, 336.

65. John Burroughs, *Whitman: A Study* (New York, 1896), 223. See also Burroughs's own response to Whitman (p. 103): "He kindles in me the delight I have in

space, freedom, power." On Whitman's reputation in the 1890s see Charles B. Willard, *Whitman's American Fame* (Providence, R.I., 1950), 28–29, 216.

66. Perry, *James,* II, 258; Wright, *Autobiography,* 126–28.

67. In addition to the sources cited in note 3 above, see Arthur Symons, *The Symbolist Movement in Literature* (London, 1899). I think it is pertinent that this kind of book about dramatic new trends in contemporary American culture was not written until the second decade of the twentieth century.

68. Hamilton Wright Mabie, *Essays on Nature and Culture* (New York, 1896), 231–32, 235–36, 241.

CHAPTER 12. *The Long Road to the New Deal*

1. E.g., Daniel T. Rodgers, *Atlantic Crossings: Social Politics in a Progressive Age* (Cambridge, Mass., 1998). See also Chapter 10.

2. Lizabeth Cohen, *Making a New Deal: Industrial Workers in Chicago, 1919–1939* (New York, 1990).

3. Gordon Donaldson, "Scots," in *Harvard Encyclopedia of American Ethnic Groups,* ed. Stephan Thernstrom (Cambridge, 1980), pp. 912–13. Since these figures very likely underrepresent unskilled rural labor, the variety of skilled trades may be more telling than the percentages.

4. Dale Light, "The Reformation of Philadelphia Catholicism," *Pennsylvania Magazine of History and Biography* 112 (July 1988), pp. 375–405, and Light, "The Role of Irish-American Organizations in Assimilation and Community Formation," in *The Irish in America: Emigration, Assimilation and Impact,* ed. P. J. Drudy, Irish Studies 4 (Cambridge, Eng., 1985), pp. 113–41, amplify aspects of an important argument summarized in Light's "Irish-American Organizations in Philadelphia," *American Catholic Studies Newsletter* 15 (Spring 1988), pp. 12–16.

5. Frederick Hale, ed., *Danes in North America* (Seattle, 1984), pp. 106, 116; H. Arnold Barton, ed., *Letters from the Promised Land: Swedes in America, 1840–1914* (Minneapolis, 1975), p. 247; Theodore C. Blegen, ed., *Land of Their Choice: The Immigrants Write Home* (St. Paul, Minn., 1955), pp. 86, 199, 203, 433–34.

6. Sean Wilentz, *Chants Democratic: New York City and the Rise of the American Working Class, 1788–1850* (New York, 1984), pp. 220–23, 250–51, 364–86; Steven J. Ross, *Workers on the Edge: Work, Leisure and Politics in Industrializing Cincinnati, 1788–1890* (New York, 1985), pp. 142–57, 172–91; Susan E. Hirsch, *Roots of the American Working Class: The Industrialization of Crafts in Newark, 1800–1860* (Philadelphia, 1978); Amy Bridges, "Becoming American: The Working Classes in the United States Before the Civil War," in *Working-Class Formation: Nineteenth-Century Patterns in Western Europe and the United States,* ed. Ira Katznelson and Aristide R. Zolberg (Princeton, N.J., 1986), pp. 171–89.

7. Michael F. Holt, *The Political Crisis of the 1850s* (New York, 1978), pp. 184–99, 242–56; Tyler Anbinder, *Nativism and Slavery: The Northern Know Nothings and the Politics of the 1850s* (New York, 1992); William Dusinberre, *Civil War Issues in Philadelphia, 1856–1865* (Philadelphia, 1965).

8. James W. Sanders, *The Education of an Urban Minority: Catholics in Chicago, 1833–1965* (New York, 1977); Iver Bernstein, *The New York Draft Riots: Their Significance for American Society and Politics in the Age of the Civil War* (New York, 1990).

9. Jay Dolan, *The Immigrant Church: New York's Irish and German Catholics,*

1815–1865 (Baltimore, Md., 1975); Eric L. Hirsch, *Urban Revolt: Ethnic Politics in the Nineteenth-Century Chicago Labor Movement* (Berkeley, Calif., 1990); Kathleen Neils Conzen, *Immigrant Milwaukee, 1836–1860: Accommodation and Community in a Frontier City* (Cambridge, Mass., 1976), pp. 208–24; Kathryn Kish Sklar, *Florence Kelley and the Nation's Work* (New Haven, 1995), pp. 124–29.

10. James Livingston, "The Social Analysis of Economic History and Theory: Conjectures on Late Nineteenth-Century American Development," *American Historical Review* 92 (February 1987), p. 83.

11. William Dean Howells, *A Traveler from Altruria* (New York, 1908), pp. 44–45. Explicit class awareness, centered especially in the middle class, pervaded the short stories in the *Saturday Evening Post*, e.g., Emery Pottle, "The Weekend: A Story for Those Who Earn and Spend a Modest Competence," July 30, 1904, pp. 6–9. See also Reed Ueda, *Avenues to Adulthood: The Origins of the High School and Social Mobility in an American Suburb* (New York, 1987); and the classic study by Robert S. and Helen M. Lynd, *Middletown: A Study in Contemporary American Culture* (New York, 1929).

12. P. K. Edwards, *Strikes in the United States, 1881–1974* (New York, 1981), pp. 15–16. See also David Montgomery, "The 'New Unionism' and the Transformation of Workers' Consciousness in America, 1909–1922," *Journal of Social History* 7 (Summer 1974), pp. 509–29.

13. Peter Roberts, *The Anthracite Coal Industry* (New York, 1901), p. 172. See also Paul Krause, "Labor Republicanism and 'Za Chlebom': Anglo-American and Slavic Solidarity in Homestead," and James R. Barrett, "Unity and Fragmentation: Class, Race, and Ethnicity on Chicago's South Side, 1900–1922," in *"Struggle a Hard Battle": Essays on Working-Class Immigrants*, ed. Dirk Hoerder (DeKalb, Ill., 1986), pp. 143–69, 229–53; Victor R. Greene, *The Slavic Community on Strike: Immigrant Labor in Pennsylvania Anthracite* (Notre Dame, Ind., 1968).

14. Robert A. Slayton, *Back of the Yards: The Making of a Local Democracy* (Chicago, 1986), pp. 110–48; John J. Bukowczyk, "The Transformation of Working-Class Ethnicity: Corporate Control, Americanization, and the Polish Immigrant Middle Class in Bayonne, New Jersey, 1915–1925," *Labor History* 25 (Winter 1984), pp. 61–65, 70–71.

15. The eastern European Jews did find an entrenched middle class waiting for them in America; but so different was it from themselves in religion and culture, as well as class, that the newcomers would not submit to its guidance or control. Howard M. Sachar, *A History of the Jews in America* (New York, 1992), pp. 128–39, 150–214; Irving Howe, *World of Our Fathers* (New York, 1976), pp. 135, 229–35, 360–71.

16. *Statistical Abstract of the United States*, 1925, p. 31.

17. Bukowczyk, "Transformation of Working-Class Ethnicity," pp. 58–59; Ewa Morawska, *For Bread with Butter: The Life-Worlds of East Central Europeans in Johnstown, Pennsylvania, 1890–1940* (New York, 1985), pp. 224–43; Josef Barton, "Eastern and Southern Europeans," in *Ethnic Leadership in America*, ed. John Higham (Baltimore, Md., 1978), pp. 159–68. The multiethnic and interracial company towns of West Virginia offer an extreme example of the working-class solidarity that could develop in the absence of a countervailing ethnic middle class. See David Corbin, *Life, Work, and Rebellion in the Coal Fields: The Southern West Virginia Mines, 1880–1922* (Urbana, Ill., 1981).

A further inducement to solidarity in both the workplace and the neighborhood surely stemmed from the ascriptive cultures of eastern Europe, in which individual achievement was less valued than communal goals. Gwendolyn Mink, *Old Labor and New Immigrants in American Political Development* (Ithaca, N.Y., 1986), p. 29.

18. Joseph P. O'Grady, ed., *The Immigrants' Influence on Wilson's Peace Policies* (Lexington, Ky., 1967); Robert E. Park, *The Immigrant Press and Its Control* (New York, 1922), pp. 309–12; M. M. Stolarik, "The Role of American Slovaks in the Creation of Czecho-Slovakia, 1914–1918," *Slovak Studies* 8 (1968), pp. 7–82.

19. Melvin I. Urofsky, *American Zionism from Herzl to Holocaust* (Garden City, N.Y., 1975), pp. 117–245; Naomi W. Cohen, *American Jews and the Zionist Idea* (New York, 1975), pp. 3–24.

20. Circular [1918], reproduced in *The Marcus Garvey and Universal Negro Improvement Association Papers*, ed. Robert A. Hill (Berkeley, Calif., 1983), vol. 1, p. 315. See also Judith Stein, *The World of Marcus Garvey* (Baton Rouge, 1986).

21. At its height Garvey's movement enrolled a million members in the United States and perhaps as many more in other countries. Its only rival as a protest organization, the National Association for the Advancement of Colored People, reached a peak of ninety-one thousand members around the same time. Emory J. Tolbert, *The UNIA and Black Los Angeles: Ideology and Community in the American Garvey Movement* (Los Angeles, 1980), p. 3.

22. Victor R. Greene, "Slavic American Nationalism, 1870–1918," in *American Contributions to the Seventh International Congress of Slavists*, ed. Anna Cienciala (The Hague, 1973), vol. 3, pp. 197–215.

23. Ewa Krystyna Hauser, "Ethnicity and Class in a Polish American Community" (Ph.D. diss., Johns Hopkins University, 1981), pp. 165–68.

24. American Scenic and Historic Preservation Society, *Twenty-fourth Annual Report*, 1919, pp. 125–29; George Creel, *How We Advertised America* (New York, 1920). There is a particularly vivid record of ecstatic mobilization in the Czech-American daily, *Denni Hlasatel*, 1917–18, in Chicago Foreign Language Press Survey, Reel 2, I G (Immigration History Research Center, University of Minnesota).

25. Alexander M. Bing, *War-Time Strikes and Their Adjustment* (New York, 1921), pp. 236–240; Leo Wolman, *The Growth of American Trade Unions, 1880–1923* (New York, 1924), pp. 34–37.

26. David Montgomery, *The Fall of the House of Labor: The Workplace, the State, and American Labor Activism, 1865–1925* (Cambridge, Eng., 1987), pp. 384–85; Paul H. Douglas, "The Socialist Vote in the Municipal Elections of 1917," *National Municipal Review* 7 (March 1918), pp. 131–39; James Weinstein, *The Decline of Socialism in America, 1912–1925* (New York, 1969), pp. 145–62. On trade unions as a powerfully Americanizing agency during this period, linking "Kaiserism" in Europe with corporate Kaiserism in the United States, see James R. Barrett, "Americanization from the Bottom Up: Immigration and the Remaking of the Working Class in the United States, 1880–1930," *Journal of American History* 79 (December 1992), pp. 996–1020.

27. Nancy Gentile Ford, "'Mindful of the Traditions of His Race': Dual Identity and Foreign-Born Soldiers in the First World War American Army," *Journal of American Ethnic History* 16 (1997), pp. 35–57. John Radzilowski finds in his reading of Polish-American newspapers during World War I a "continuous fusion of American and homeland symbols." H-ETHNIC@H-NET.MSU.EDU (September 5, 1999).

28. David Saposs, "The Mind of Immigrant Communities," in *Public Opinion and*

the Steel Strike, ed. Interchurch World Movement (New York, 1921), pp. 228–41; David Brody, "Labor," in *Harvard Encyclopedia of American Ethnic Groups*, ed. Stephan Thernstrom (Cambridge: Harvard University Press, 1980), p. 615.

29. Irving Bernstein, *The Lean Years: A History of the American Worker, 1920–1933* (Boston, 1960), pp. 83–143, 334–57; *Historical Statistics of the United States, Colonial Times to 1970* (Washington, D.C., 1976), pp. 178–79.

30. Cohen, *American Jews*, pp. 25–32; Higham, *Strangers*, p. 311.

31. John W. Allswang, *A House for All Peoples: Ethnic Politics in Chicago, 1890–1936* (Lexington, Ky., 1971), pp. 117–18; William Preston, Jr., *Aliens and Dissenters: Federal Suppression of Radicals, 1903–1933* (Cambridge, Mass., 1963).

32. Louis Adamic, "Thirty Million New Americans," *Harper's* 169 (November 1934), pp. 684–94.

33. Adamic's impressions on this point were very widely shared, as Richard Weiss points out in "Ethnicity and Reform: Minorities and the Ambience of the Depression Years," *Journal of American History* 66 (December 1979), pp. 583–84.

34. Kristi Andersen, *The Creation of a Democratic Majority, 1928–1936* (Chicago, 1979), pp. 30–38, 105–14; John H. Shover, "The Emergence of a Two-Party System in Republican Philadelphia, 1924–1936," *Journal of American History* 60 (March 1974), pp. 996–98; Edward H. Litchfield, *Voting Behavior in a Metropolitan Area*, Michigan Governmental Studies no. 7 (Ann Arbor, Mich., 1941), pp. 38, 41.

35. On the role of the second generation in a revitalized labor movement see Peter Friedlander, *The Emergence of a UAW Local, 1936–1939: A Study in Class and Culture* (Pittsburgh, 1975); and Thomas Göbel, "Becoming American: Ethnic Workers and the Rise of the CIO," *Labor History* 29 (Spring 1988), pp. 173–98.

36. Gary Gerstle, *Working-Class Americanism: The Politics of Labor in a Textile City, 1914–1960* (New York, 1989). On the Statue of Liberty see Higham, *Send These to Me*, pp. 71–80. On "democracy" in American usage note its centrality in major college textbooks such as Ralph H. Gabriel's *The Course of American Democratic Thought* (New York, 1940) and Robin M. Williams, Jr.'s *American Society: A Sociological Interpretation* (New York, 1951), and note also the extraordinary vogue that a new edition of Alexis de Tocqueville's *Democracy in America* (2 vols., New York, 1945) awakened.

37. John A. Garraty, "Radicalism in the Great Depression," in *Essays on Radicalism in Contemporary America*, ed. L. H. Blair (Austin, Tex., 1972), pp. 102–14; John A. Garraty, *Unemployment in History: Economic Thought and Public Policy* (New York, 1978), pp. 177–87.

38. Francis G. Castles, *The Social Democratic Image of Society: A Study of the Achievements and Origins of Scandinavian Social Democracy in Comparative Perspective* (London, 1978). Cf. L. C. Seaman, *Post-Victorian Britain, 1902–1951* (London, 1966), pp. 232–37, and J. R. Robertson, "1930–39," in *A New History of Australia*, ed. F. W. Crowley (Melbourne, 1974), pp. 421 ff. On the conservative influence of postwar Australian immigration see Ronald Taft, "The Myth and Migrants," in *Australian Civilization: A Symposium*, ed. Peter Coleman (Melbourne, 1962), pp. 191–206.

39. Julian Jackson, *The Popular Front in France: Defending Democracy, 1934–1938* (Cambridge, Eng., 1988), pp. 17, 46, 85–112; Eugen Weber, *The Hollow Years: France in the 1930s* (New York, 1994), pp. 42–49, 114–65.

40. Garraty, "Radicalism," pp. 113–14; Jackson, *Popular Front*, p. 286; James Joll,

"The Making of the Popular Front," in *The Decline of the Third Republic*, ed. Joll (New York, 1959), pp. 36–66.

41. Thomas J. Archdeacon, *Becoming American: An Ethnic History* (New York, 1983), pp. 113–15.

42. Mark Falcoff and Ronald H. Dolkart, eds., *Prologue to Perón: Argentina in Depression and War, 1930–1943* (Berkeley, Calif., 1975). See also Carl Solberg, *Immigration and Nationalism: Argentina and Chile, 1890–1914* (Austin, Tex., 1970); and James R. Scobie, *Argentina: A City and a Nation* (New York, 1971).

43. Walter Nugent, *Crossings: The Great Transatlantic Migrations, 1870–1914* (Bloomington, Ind., 1992), pp. 138–40; M. Mark Stolarik, *Slovaks in Canada and the United States, 1870–1990: Similarities and Differences*, Occasional Papers no. 1 (Ottawa, 1992), p. 6.

44. Nicholas DeMaria Harney, *Eh, Paesan! Being Italian in Toronto* (Toronto, 1998), pp. 14–22. On Toronto's population mix see Robert A. Murdie, *Factorial Ecology of Metropolitan Toronto, 1951–61* (Chicago, 1969), pp. 56–57; John Porter, *The Vertical Mosaic: An Analysis of Social Class and Power in Canada* (Toronto, 1965), pp. 77–80. We have no exactly comparable data, but it is suggestive that native whites of native white parentage made up no more than half of the population in any of the ten largest American cities in 1920. Niles Carpenter, *Immigrants and Their Children, 1920*, U.S. Bureau of the Census, Census Monographs, vol. 7 (Washington, D.C., 1927), p. 24.

45. Irving Abella, *Nationalism, Communism, and Canadian Labour* (Toronto, 1973), pp. 29–77.

46. Robert R. Alford, *Party and Society: The Anglo-American Democracies* (Chicago, 1963), pp. 250–86, 354; Donald Creighton, *Canada's First Century, 1867–1967* (New York, 1967), pp. 173–260.

47. Gad Horowitz, *Canadian Labour in Politics* (Toronto, 1968), pp. 24, 43–44.

48. Kenneth D. McRae, "The Structure of Canadian History," in *The Founding of New Societies*, ed. Louis Hartz (New York, 1964), pp. 246–47.

CHAPTER 13. *Multiculturalism and Universalism: A History and Critique*

An earlier version of the present paper was delivered in Berlin at the annual meetings of the German Association for American Studies in June 1992. For helpful comments and criticism, I am indebted, first, to fellow participants in the Berlin meetings—especially Berndt Ostendorf and Willi Paul Adams, together with Werner Sollors, Henry Louis Gates, Jr., and H.-J. Puhle—and, second, to a close reading of the present version by Robert Kelley and David Hollinger.

1. John Higham, "From Process to Structure: Formulations of American Immigration History," in *American Immigrants and Their Generations: Studies and Commentaries on the Hansen Thesis After Fifty Years*, ed. Peter Kivisto and Dag Blanck (Urbana, Ill., 1990), 18–41.

2. Gunnar Myrdal, *An American Dilemma: The Negro Problem and Modern Democracy* (New York, 1944), 8–27. See also Walter A. Jackson, *Gunnar Myrdal and America's Conscience: Social Engineering and Racial Liberalism, 1938–1987* (Chapel Hill, N.C., 1990).

3. Dorothy Ross, *The Origins of American Social Science* (Cambridge, Mass., 1991).

4. Quoted in Robert W. Tucker and David C. Hendrickson, *Empire of Liberty: The Statecraft of Thomas Jefferson* (New York, 1990), 83.

5. Rogers M. Smith, "The 'American Creed' and American Identity: The Limits of Liberal Citizenship in the United States," *Western Political Quarterly* 41 (June 1988): 225–51.

6. James Fenimore Cooper, *Notions of the Americans*, 2 vols. (Philadelphia, 1828), 1: 239; Henry James, *The Social Significance of Our Institutions* (Boston, 1861), 28.

7. Gordon S. Wood, *The Radicalism of the American Revolution* (New York, 1992), 222–23. See also Chapter 2.

8. I share much common ground with David A. Hollinger; see his important article "Postethnic America," *Contention* 2 (Fall 1992): 79–96. His definitions of universalism and cosmopolitanism, however, seem too restrictive and too precisely differentiated to designate, as I wish to do, substantial bodies of social thought. I have not, for example, run into any universalists "for whom the [human] species as a whole can be community enough" (84), except possibly Henry David Thoreau.

9. Thomas Paine, "Common Sense" (1776), in *American Issues*, ed. Willard Thorp, Merle Curti, and Carlos Baker (Philadelphia, 1955), 1: 83–84; *Speeches, Correspondence, and Political Papers of Carl Schurz*, ed. Frederic Bancroft (New York, 1913), 1: 48–59, 71–72; Richard Conant Harper, *The Course of the Melting Pot Idea to 1910* (New York, 1980), 118–23, 132–48, 176–86. See also Kathleen Neils Conzen, "German-Americans and the Invention of Ethnicity," in *America and the Germans: An Assessment of a Three-Hundred-Year History*, ed. Frank Trommler and Joseph McVeigh (Philadelphia, 1985), 1: 131–47; Kathleen Neils Conzen et al., "The Invention of Ethnicity: A Perspective from the U.S.A.," *Journal of American Ethnic History* 12 (Fall 1992): 3–41.

10. Wendell Phillips, "Idols" (1859), in *Speeches, Lectures, and Letters* (Boston, 1900), 1: 243. See also "The United States of the United Races," *National Era* 7 (Sept. 15, 1853): 146; John Todd, "The Future of the Pacific Slope and the Chinese Question," *Home Missionary* 42 (March 1970): 253–59; David Herbert Donald, *Charles Sumner and the Rights of Man* (New York, 1970), 422; Waldo E. Martin, Jr., *The Mind of Frederick Douglass* (Chapel Hill, N.C., 1984), 197–224; Charles Shanabruch, *Chicago's Catholics: The Evolution of an American Identity* (Notre Dame, Ind., 1981), 76.

11. See David A. Gerber's account of an increasing ethnicization of native-born Americans in *The Making of an American Pluralism: Buffalo, New York, 1825–60* (Urbana, Ill., 1989), 96–109.

12. David A. Hollinger, "Ethnic Diversity, Cosmopolitanism, and the Emergence of the American Liberal Intelligentsia," in *In the American Province: Studies in the History and Historiography of Ideas* (Bloomington, Ind., 1985), 56–73; Ross, *Origins*, 143–71, 195–216, 303–19; James T. Kloppenberg, *Uncertain Victory: Social Democracy and Progressivism in European and American Thought, 1870–1920* (New York, 1986). The accompanying expansion of women's rights and women's issues must not be forgotten. I am concentrating, however, on relations between class and ethnicity because those seem to me to have produced the problematic structure of multiculturalism, within which academic feminism has located itself.

13. Jack M. Bloom, *Class, Race, and the Civil Rights Movement* (Bloomington, Ind., 1987), 204–13.

14. Murray Kempton, "Brother, Can You Spare a Dime?" *New York Review of Books,* 23 Apr. 1992, p. 55.

15. Ira Katznelson, "Was the Great Society a Lost Opportunity?" in *The Rise and Fall of the New Deal Order,* ed. Steve Fraser and Gary Gerstle (Princeton, N.J., 1989), 185–211.

16. Nathan Glazer cites both usages in a perceptive article, "The Problem of Ethnic Studies" (1977), reprinted in his *Ethnic Dilemmas, 1964–1982* (Cambridge, Mass., 1983), 107. The principal handbook for teachers was James A. Banks, *Multi-ethnic Education: Theory and Practice* (Boston, 1981), and he retained that title in a second edition in 1988. The new works that Banks edited in the late 1980s, however, were *Multicultural Education in Western Societies* (New York, 1986) and *Multicultural Education: Issues and Perspectives* (Boston, 1989).

17. The recent Banks-edited text for teachers devotes a chapter to social class but treats it only as an obstacle to multiculturalism, not as a subject for classroom discussion. See Banks, *Multicultural Education: Issues and Perspectives,* 67–86.

18. Paul Lauter, *Canons and Contexts* (New York, 1991), ix.

19. James A. Miller, "American Studies at Trinity College," *American Studies Association Newsletter* 14 (December 1991): 7. See also Jane De Hart, "Report on the Program for the 1988 Convention," *American Studies Association Newsletter* 12 (March 1989): 1, which raises but then allays concerns about "this celebration of multicultural diversity." For a semiofficial account of "the speed with which we have discovered diversity of race, class, gender, and ethnicity," see Linda Kerber, "Diversity and the Transformation of American Studies," *American Quarterly* 41 (September 1989): 415–31.

20. Stuart M. Blumin, *The Emergence of the Middle Class: Social Experience in the American City, 1760–1900* (Cambridge, Mass., 1989); Olivier Zunz, *Making America Corporate, 1870–1920* (Chicago, 1990); Michael Denning, *Mechanic Accents: Dime Novels and Working-Class Culture in America* (New York, 1987).

21. "Democratic Platform Shows Shift in Party's Roots," *New York Times,* 14 July 1992.

22. David Brion Davis, "The American Dilemma," *New York Review of Books,* 16 July 1992, pp. 13–17.

23. Jonathan Okamura, "Situational Ethnicity," *Ethnic and Racial Studies* 4 (October, 1981): 452–65; William L. Yancey et al., "Emergent Ethnicity: A Review and Reformulation," *American Sociological Review* 41 (June 1976): 391–403.

24. Compare Stow Persons's *Ethnic Studies at Chicago, 1905–45* (Urbana, Ill., 1987) with R. Fred Wacker's more sympathetic assessment in *Ethnicity, Pluralism, and Race: Race Relations Theory in America Before Myrdal* (Westport, Conn., 1983).

25. Randolph Bourne, "Trans-National America," in *The Radical Will: Selected Writings,* ed. Olaf Hansen (New York, 1977), 248–64. The assimilationist position is best represented in Robert E. Park, *Race and Culture,* vol. 1: *The Collected Papers of Robert E. Park,* ed. Everett C. Hughes et al. (Glencoe, Ill., 1950). See in general John Higham, "Ethnic Pluralism in Modern American Thought," in *Send These to Me: Immigrants in Urban America,* rev. ed. (Baltimore, Md., 1984), 198–232; Philip Gleason, "American Identity and Americanization," in *Harvard Encyclopedia of American Ethnic Groups,* ed. Stephan Thernstrom (Cambridge, Mass., 1980), 31–58; and especially Philip Gleason, *Speaking of Diversity: Language and Ethnicity in Twentieth-Century America* (Baltimore, Md., 1992).

26. Hollinger's *In the American Province*, 56–65, contrasts Bourne's "cosmopolitanism" with the "cultural pluralism" of his immediate precursor, Horace Kallen. In my terms both were pluralists. To the key question, "Where are authentic cultures located?" both men gave in effect the same fateful answer: "Only in minorities." Bourne's minorities included a "young intelligentsia," with whom he identified himself. But the masses of Americans who had lost their Old World ties were only "half-breeds . . . without a spiritual country, cultural outlaws, without taste, without standards but those of the mob. . . . They become the flotsam and jetsam of American life, the downward undertow of our civilization . . . which we see in our slovenly towns, our vapid moving pictures, our popular novels, and in the vacuous faces of the crowds on the city street." Bourne, *Radical Will*, 254–55.

27. See, for example, J. Christopher Eisele, "John Dewey and the Immigrants," *Journal of Education Quarterly* 15 (Spring 1975): 67–85.

28. Diane Ravitch, "Multiculturalism: E Pluribus Plures," *American Scholar* 59 (Summer 1990): 337–54; Molefi Kente Asante, "Multiculturalism: An Exchange," *American Scholar* (Spring 1991): 271; Robert Fullinwider, "Multicultural Education," *University of Maryland Institute for Philosophy and Public Policy* (Winter 1991): 12–14. See also Banks's manual for teachers, *Multiethnic Education: Theory and Practice*, 2d ed. (Boston, 1988), 115–25.

29. Horace M. Kallen, *Cultural Pluralism and the American Idea: An Essay in Social Philosophy* (Philadelphia, 1956). See also John Higham, "The Redefinition of America in the Twentieth Century," in *German and American Nationalism: A Comparative Perspective*, ed. Hartmut Lehmann and Hermann Wellenreuther (Oxford, Eng., 1999), 301–25.

30. James B. Gilbert, "Popular Culture," *American Quarterly* 35 (Spring–Summer, 1983): 141–54. See also the polling data in Louis Harris, *The Anguish of Change* (New York, 1973).

31. Mary Ann Glendon, *Rights Talk: The Impoverishment of Political Discourse* (New York, 1991); Jeffrey C. Goldfarb, *The Cynical Society: The Culture of Politics and the Politics of Culture in American Life* (Chicago, 1991).

32. Compare two columns by Chuck Stone in the *Detroit Free Press:* the first a militant appeal, "Black Nationhood Antidote to Gangs," 25 Sept. 1972; the second a complacent and apolitical article, "Black Crime Syndicates Grow Across Nation," 21 June 1973.

33. Paul Ruffins, "Interracial Coalitions," *Atlantic Monthly* 265 (June 1990): 28–34. See also *New York Times*, 2 Dec. 1991, on intermarriage, and 24 July 1992, on the black-white income gap; Lawrence H. Fuchs, *The American Kaleidoscope: Race, Ethnicity, and the Civic Culture* (Hanover, N.H., 1990), 190–205, 425–30, 482–84; Reynolds Farley, "Trends in Racial Inequalities: Have the Gains of the 1960s Disappeared in the 1970s?" *American Sociological Review* 40 (April 1977): 189–208; Charlotte Steeh and Howard Schuman, "Young White Adults: Did Racial Attitudes Change in the 1980s?" *American Journal of Sociology* 98 (September 1992): 340–67.

34. Alan Peshkin, *The Color of Strangers, the Color of Friends: The Play of Ethnicity in School and Community* (Chicago, 1991). On other well-integrated school districts, in places where low-income minorities have not been highly ghettoized and public schools link city and suburb, see David Rusk, "America's Urban Apartheid," *New York Times*, 21 May 1992. More generally, on convergence between blacks and whites, see Bob Blauner, *Black Lives, White Lives: Three Decades of Race Relations in America*

(Berkeley, Calif., 1989), 163–71, 332; Andrew Hacker, "The Myths of Racial Division," *New Republic* 206 (23 Mar. 1992): 21–25; and the powerful, broadly based argument of Fuchs's *American Kaleidoscope*.

35. *New York Times*, 8 Jan. 1992.

36. *New York Times*, 2 Jan. 1987, 16 Mar. 1987, 29 Mar. 1987. In New York City the first of the dramatically inflamed confrontations over crime occurred in December 1986, when a pack of white youths in Howard Beach chased three black men, one of whom was killed by a passing car. In May of that year, a more deliberately murderous assault by whites had taken place in Coney Island without receiving any special notice. The Howard Beach incident, however, released a paroxysm of televised rage. Jim Sleeper, *The Closest of Strangers: Liberalism and the Politics of Race in New York* (New York, 1990), 138–40, 183–88; *New York Times*, 20 Dec. 1992.

37. Jon Wiener, *Professors, Politics and Pop* (London, 1991), 136–51; *New York Times*, 3 Oct. 1990, 18 May 1991. On 23 Dec. 1986 the *Times* published a perceptive editorial linking, but not explaining, the resurgence of racism on campuses and on city streets.

38. *New York Times*, 28 Oct. 1991: Dinesh D'Souza, *Illiberal Education: The Politics of Race and Sex on Campus* (New York, 1991), 59–93.

39. *New York Times*, 22 June 1991; Ravitch, "Multiculturalism," 339; and Ravitch, "A Culture in Common," *Educational Leadership* (December 1991–January 1992): 8–11; Robert K. Landers, "Conflict over Multicultural Education," *Editorial Research Reports* (Congressional Quarterly, 1990): 681–95. See also Robert J. Cottroll, "America the Multicultural," *American Educator* (Winter 1990): 18–21, 38.

40. David A. Kirp, "Textbooks and Tribalism in California," *Public Interest* 104 (Summer 1991): 20–36; *Washington Times*, 13 Nov. 1990; Abdul R. JanMohamed and David Lloyd, eds., *The Nature and Context of Minority Discourse* (New York, 1990), 8; Molefi Kente Asante, "Afrocentric Curriculum," *Educational Leadership* (December 1991–January 1992): 28–31.

41. Catharine Stimpson, "Presidential Address, 1990: On Differences," *PMLA* 106 (May 1991): 404.

42. I discuss this central issue more fully in Chapter 7.

43. For a related point, stressing the needs of black educators, see Nathan Glazer, "In Defense of Multiculturalism," *New Republic* 205 (2 Sept. 1991): 18–22.

44. Frances Fitzgerald, *America Revised: History Schoolbooks in the Twentieth Century* (Boston, 1979), 80–105; Eva Moskowitz, "Lessons in Achievement in American History High School Textbooks of the 1950s and 1970s," *Pennsylvania Magazine of History and Biography* 112 (April 1988): 268–69.

45. Elliott Robert Barkan, "Strategies for Multicultural Teaching: The Quest for Social Justness and a Multicentric Perspective," in *Changing College Classrooms: The Challenge of Educating Students for the Twenty-first Century*, ed. Diane F. Halpern (San Francisco, 1994). This racial dualism may be partly understandable as an expression of a Hispanic tendency in the American West to label all whites as Anglos, but it does suppress a vital span of the nation's diversity.

46. Personal communication.

47. Andrew Delbanco, *The Puritan Ordeal* (Cambridge, Mass., 1989). On subgroups see David Hackett Fischer, *Albion's Seed: Four British Folkways in America* (New York, 1989).

48. Leonard J. Moore, *Citizen Klansmen: The Ku Klux Klan in Indiana, 1921–1928*

(Chapel Hill, N.C., 1991); Stuart C. McConnell, *Glorious Contentment: The Grand Army of the Republic, 1865–1900* (Chapel Hill, N.C., 1992).

49. Kenneth Lauren Burns, *The Civil War,* PBS Home Video (Beverly Hills, Calif., 1990). The series incorporates a dignified black perspective, but leaves it quite muted. What viewers overwhelmingly experience is the death of white men.

50. Kirp, "Textbooks and Tribalism," 33–35, and Robert Fullinwider, "Multicultural Education," *University of Chicago Legal Forum* (1991): 88–91, review several sociological studies that failed to find any relation between low self-esteem among black youth and "any problematic behavior," such as teen pregnancy or drug use.

51. Sandra Stotsky, "Multicultural Education in the Brookline Public Schools: The Deconstruction of an Academic Curriculum," *Network News and Views* (June 1991), in *Multicultural Education: A Compilation of the Literature,* ed. Ruth McGrath (Office of Multicultural Education, Pittsburgh Public Schools, 1992).

52. *American Studies Association Newsletter* 15 (February 1992): 1–8. Election results were reported in the *American Studies Association Newsletter* (May 1992): 1.

53. David Hollinger has brought to my attention a partial exception: Iris Marion Young, *Justice and the Politics of Difference* (Princeton, N.J., 1990), an argument for strengthening divergence institutionally, which captures the spirit of multiculturalism without ever invoking the name.

54. Kwame Anthony Appiah, *In My Father's House: Africa in the Philosophy of Culture* (New York, 1992), 176–77.

CHAPTER 14. *The Future of American History*

1. "Reconstructing Nations and States," special issue, *Daedalus,* 122 (Summer 1993); Crawford Young, "The Dialectics of Cultural Pluralism: Concept and Reality," in *The Rising Tide of Cultural Pluralism: The Nation-State at Bay?,* ed. Crawford Young (Madison, Wis., 1993), 3–35.

2. Michael McGerr, "The Price of the 'New Transnational History,'" *American Historical Review,* 96 (October 1991), 1065.

3. Marvin E. Gettleman, ed., *The Johns Hopkins University Seminary in History and Politics: The Records of an Educational Institution. 1877–1912* (4 vols., New York, 1987), III, 634–38, 645–53.

4. William H. Prescott, *History of the Conquest of Mexico* (3 vols., New York, 1843); Henry C. Lea, *History of the Inquisition of the Middle Ages* (3 vols., New York, 1888); Charles Homer Haskins, *Norman Institutions* (Cambridge, Mass., 1918); Haskins, *Studies in the History of Medieval Science* (Cambridge, Mass., 1924); Alfred T. Mahan, *The Influence of Sea Power upon History, 1660–1783* (Boston, 1890). See also John Higham, Leonard Krieger, and Felix Gilbert, *History* (Englewood Cliffs, N.J., 1965), 39–51, 263–87; and Edward Sculley Bradley, *Henry Charles Lea: A Biography* (Philadelphia, 1931). The breadth of this transatlantic perspective is seen in Charles McLean Andrews, "Some Recent Aspects of Institutional Study," *Yale Review,* 1 (February 1893), 381–410.

5. Ian Tyrrell, "A View from the Periphery," *OAH Newsletter* (August 1991), 7.

6. J. Franklin Jameson, quoted in Jean Jules Jusserand et al., *The Writing of History* (New York, 1926), 131; John Franklin Jameson to Hiram Bingham, Jan. 11, 1924, in *An Historian's World: Selections from the Correspondence of John Franklin Jameson,* ed. Elizabeth Donnan and Leo F. Stock (Philadelphia, 1956), 296. See also

Raymond Grew, "The Comparative Weakness of American History," *Journal of Interdisciplinary History*, 16 (Summer 1986), 87–101; and John Higham, "Paleface and Redskin in American Historiography: A Comment," ibid., 111–16.

7. J. Hector St. John Crèvecoeur, *Letters from an American Farmer* (1782), in *Immigration and the American Tradition*, ed. Moses Rischin (Indianapolis, 1976), 24–26. See also Andrew Delbanco, "The Puritan Errand Re-Viewed," *Journal of American Studies*, 18 (1984), 343–60.

8. Rufus Choate quoted in John P. Diggins, *The Lost Soul of American Politics: Virtue, Self-Interest, and the Foundations of Liberalism* (New York, 1984), 177. See also James P. Allen, "Changes in the American Propensity to Migrate," *Annals of the Association of American Geographers*, 67 (December 1977), 577–87.

9. John G. Cawelti, *Apostles of the Self-Made Man: Changing Concepts of Success in America* (Chicago, 1965), 9–21, 40–47. For Henry Clay's remarks, see *Register of Debates in Congress*, 22 Cong., 1 sess., Feb. 2, 1832, pp. 263–77. Alexis de Tocqueville, *Democracy in America* (1835, 1840; 2 vols., New York, 1945), II, 144–45; Alexander Mackay, *The Western World* (1849), in *America in Perspective: The United States Through Foreign Eyes*, ed. Henry Steele Commager (New York, 1947), 111–13; Thomas Colley Grattan, *Civilized America* (2 vols., London, 1859), II, 99.

10. Henry Adams quoted in what remains the finest study of this remarkable work: William H. Jordy, *Henry Adams: Scientific Historian* (New Haven, 1952), 82–83.

11. Frederick Jackson Turner, *The Frontier in American History* (New York, 1920). See also Ray Allen Billington, *America's Frontier Heritage* (New York, 1966); and John Higham, *Writing American History: Essays on Modern Scholarship* (Bloomington, Ind., 1970), 118–29.

12. Ellen Nore, *Charles A. Beard: An Intellectual Biography* (Carbondale, Ill., 1983), 113, also 106–11, 129, 269; "Reminiscences of Alfred A. Knopf," p. 151, Oral History Collection (Oral History Research Office, Butler Library, Columbia University, New York).

13. Charles A. Beard and Mary R. Beard, *The Rise of American Civilization* (2 vols., New York, 1927), II, 747, 797–800. See also Charles A. Beard, "The Idea of Progress," in *A Century of Progress*, ed. Beard (New York, 1932), 3–19; and Nore, *Beard*, 111. On Mary R. Beard's coauthorship of a number of the later books the couple produced, see Nancy F. Cott, ed., *A Woman Making History: Mary Ritter Beard Through Her Letters* (New Haven, 1991).

14. It was, in fact, a "consensus" historian, Oscar Handlin, who (together with his wife) raised the first probing questions concerning the genesis of race prejudice on the North American mainland: Oscar Handlin and Mary Handlin, "Origins of the Southern Labor System," *William and Mary Quarterly*, 7 (April 1950), 199–222. More generally, see Higham, Krieger and Gilbert, *History*, 212–32.

15. Louis Hartz, *The Liberal Tradition in America: An Interpretation of American Political Thought Since the Revolution* (New York, 1955), 3. On the exploration of myth, see especially R. W. B. Lewis, *The American Adam: Innocence, Tragedy, and Tradition in the Nineteenth Century* (Chicago, 1955); and the writings of Henry Nash Smith, John William Ward, and Leo Marx.

16. Stanley M. Elkins, *Slavery: A Problem in American Institutional and Intellectual Life* (Chicago, 1959); Frank Thistlethwaite, *The Anglo-American Connection in the Early Nineteenth Century* (Philadelphia, 1959); Seymour Martin Lipset and Reinhard Bendix, *Social Mobility in Industrial Society* (Berkeley, Calif., 1959); Lionel Trilling,

The Liberal Imagination: Essays on Literature and Society (New York, 1950); Daniel J. Boorstin, *The Genius of American Politics* (Chicago, 1953). See also C. Vann Woodward, ed., *The Comparative Approach to American History* (New York, 1968).

17. Brinley Thomas, *Migration and Economic Growth: A Study of Great Britain and the Atlantic Economy* (Cambridge, Eng., 1954); Marcus Cunliffe, *Soldiers and Civilians: The Martial Spirit in America, 1775–1865* (Boston, 1968); Yehoshua Arieli, *Individualism and Nationalism in American Ideology* (Cambridge, Mass., 1966); Gerald Stourzh, *Alexander Hamilton and the Idea of Republican Government* (Stanford, Calif., 1970).

18. George M. Fredrickson, *White Supremacy: A Comparative Study in American and South African History* (New York, 1981); Peter Kolchin, *Unfree Labor: American Slavery and Russian Serfdom* (Cambridge, Mass., 1987). For contrasting assessments of accomplishments in the 1970s, see Peter Kolchin, "Comparing American History," *Reviews in American History,* 10 (December 1982), 64–81; and George M. Fredrickson, "Comparative History," in *The Past Before Us: Contemporary Historical Writing in the United States,* ed. Michael Kammen (Ithaca, N.Y., 1980), 457–73. Ten years later the continuing record looked disappointing to a younger scholar: Alan L. Karras, "Of Human Bondage: Creating an Atlantic History of Slavery," *Journal of Inderdisciplinary History,* 22 (Autumn 1991), 285–93.

19. John Patrick Diggins, "Language and History," *Reviews in American History,* 17 (March 1989), 8–9.

20. Joyce Appleby, "A Different Kind of Independence: The Postwar Restructuring of the Historical Study of Early America," *William and Mary Quarterly,* 50 (April 1993), 245–67. See also John Higham, *History: Professional Scholarship in America* (Baltimore, Md., 1989), 235–64; Fred Matthews, "'Hobbesian Populism': Interpretive Paradigms and Moral Vision in American Historiography," *Journal of American History,* 72 (June 1985), 92–115; and David A. Gerber, "Local and Community History: Some Cautionary Remarks on an Idea Whose Time Has Returned," *History Teacher,* 13 (November 1979), 7–30.

21. On the genesis of this revised exceptionalism, see Dorothy Ross, *The Origins of American Social Science* (Cambridge, Eng., 1991), 150–57.

22. On recent perceptions of a broad and fundamental decline of the United States, see, for example, Theodore Caplow, "Is America Declining?," *Social Change Report* (Ball State University), 2 (July 1988), 1; Alan Brinkley, "The New World in the Evening," *Times Literary Supplement* (London), Sept. 23–29, 1988, pp. 1046, 1050; James Fallows, "Wake Up, America!" *New York Review of Books,* Mar. 1, 1990, pp. 14–19; and Paul Kennedy, "Fin-de-Siècle America," ibid., June 28, 1990, pp. 31–40. On the academic onslaught on lofty American ideals, see Frederick Crews, "Whose American Renaissance?" ibid., Oct. 27, 1988, pp. 68–81. These gloomy announcements provoked remarkably little alarm. Gallup polls taken at the same time showed a relatively high level of satisfaction with "the way things are going in the U.S." *New York Times,* Dec. 25, 1988, p. 18.

23. Laurence Veysey, "The 'New' Social History in the Context of American Historical Writing," *Reviews in American History,* 7 (March 1979), 5. Disparaging the state as artificial or irrelevant seems hard to reconcile with a perception of pervasive domination from above, but some current scholarship, following Michel Foucault, treats power as so subtly ubiquitous that no single institution, even the state, stands out as a specific locus.

24. Frank Ankersmit, "Historiography and Postmodernism," *History and Theory,* 28 (no. 1, 1989), 137–53.

25. John Higham, "Finding Centers Among the Margins," *American Literary History,* 3 (Winter 1991), 745–46. The classic analysis, in the Marxist tradition, of geopolitical relations between a dominating "core" and dominated peripheral regions is Immanuel Wallerstein, *The Modern World-System: Capitalist Agriculture and the Origins of the European World-Economy in the Sixteenth Century* (New York, 1974).

26. In my terminology nationalism includes patriotism but is more complex and various in its configurations. Within a specific territory, nations claim sovereignty (or at least cultural autonomy), in the pursuit and exercise of which they employ coercive force and elaborate one or more ideologies advertising the nation's scope, structure, and goals. By avoiding the conventional view of patriotism and ethnicity as good and nationalism as evil, one can recognize that all three are flammable, but none will burn the house down unless fanned that way.

27. Jonathan M. Wiener, "Radical Historians and the Crisis in American History, 1959–1980," *Journal of American History,* 76 (September 1989), 399–434; John Higham, "Changing Paradigms: The Collapse of Consensus History," ibid., 460–66. See also Ian Tyrrell, *The Absent Marx: Class Analysis and Liberal History in Twentieth-Century America* (Westport, Conn., 1986).

28. Compare Eugene D. Genovese, *Roll, Jordan, Roll: The World the Slaves Made* (New York, 1974), with Genovese, *The Political Economy of Slavery: Studies in the Economy and Society of the Slave South* (New York, 1965); Genovese, *The World the Slaveholders Made: Two Essays in Interpretation* (New York, 1969); Elizabeth Fox-Genovese and Eugene D. Genovese, *Fruits of Merchant Capital: Slavery and Bourgeois Property in the Rise and Expansion of Capitalism* (New York, 1983); and Eugene D. Genovese, *The Slaveholders' Dilemma: Freedom and Progress in Southern Conservative Thought, 1820–1860* (Columbia, S.C., 1992).

29. A similar tendency for the American radical history of the late 1960s to become narrowly focused on the United States alone was noticed years ago in Hans Rudolf Guggisberg, *Alte und neue Welt in historischer Perspektive* (Bern, 1973), 136–50. For a perceptive assessment of the present state of the field and a hopeful anticipation of a "yet 'newer' labor history," see Jonathan Prude, "Directions in Labor History," *American Quarterly,* 42 (March 1990), 136–44. For a creative reformulation and application of Marxist theory to modern American culture, see T. J. Jackson Lears, *Fables of Abundance: A Cultural History of Advertising in America* (New York, 1994).

30. The two journals in the United States that make an effort in that direction, both outgrowths of the Annales school, are so eclectic that comparative perspectives are secondary to their embrace of *l'histoire totale: Comparative Studies in Society and History* (1958–) and *Journal of Interdisciplinary History* (1969–).

31. Allan Megill, "Fragmentation and the Future of Historiography," *American Historical Review,* 96 (June 1991), 693–98.

32. Ian Tyrrell, "American Exceptionalism in an Age of International History," *American Historical Review,* 9 (October 1991), 1031–55. For a bibliographically indispensable riposte, see Michael Kammen, "The Problem of American Exceptionalism: A Reconsideration," *American Quarterly,* 45 (March 1993), 1–43.

33. These criticisms were widely aired at the 1989 meetings of the Organization of American Historians.

34. At the same time, comparative studies of women's influence in different coun-

tries are adding significantly to an understanding of American national history. Donald Meyer, *Sex and Power: The Rise of Women in America, Russia, Sweden, and Italy* (Middletown, Conn., 1987); Seth Koven and Sonya Michel, eds., *Mothers of a New World: Maternalist Politics and the Origins of Welfare States* (New York, 1993).

35. David J. Russo, "The Case Against 'American' History," unpublished paper, 1990.

36. Philip D. Curtin, *Cross-Cultural Trade in World History* (Cambridge, Eng., 1984); Curtin, *Death by Migration: Europe's Encounter with the Tropical World in the Nineteenth Century* (Cambridge, Eng., 1989); Curtin, *The Rise and Fall of the Plantation Complex: Essays in Atlantic History* (Cambridge, Eng., 1990). A ringing summons in this direction is a presidential address to the American Historical Association: Bernard Bailyn, "The Challenge of Modern Historiography," *American Historical Review*, 87 (February 1982), 1–24.

37. See, for example, Alfred W. Crosby, *Ecological Imperialism: The Biological Expansion of Europe, 900–1900* (New York, 1986); Alfred D. Chandler, Jr., *Scale and Scope: The Dynamics of Industrial Capitalism* (Cambridge, Mass., 1990); Virginia Yans-McLaughlin, ed., *Immigration Reconsidered: History, Sociology, and Politics* (New York, 1990); Walter Nugent, *Crossings: The Great Transatlantic Migrations, 1870–1914* (Bloomington, Ind., 1992); John Bodnar, *The Transplanted: A History of Immigrants in Urban America* (Bloomington,Ind., 1985); Albert S. Lindemann, *The Jew Accused: Three Anti-Semitic Affairs (Dreyfus, Beilis, Frank), 1894–1915* (Cambridge, Eng., 1991); Jon Butler, *Awash in a Sea of Faith: Christianizing the American People* (Cambridge, Mass., 1990); W. R. Ward, *The Protestant Evangelical Awakening* (Cambridge, Eng., 1992); Thomas P. Hughes, *Networks of Power: Electrification in Western Society, 1880–1930* (Baltimore, Md., 1983); Thomas P. Hughes, *American Genesis: A Century of Invention and Technological Enthusiasm, 1870–1970* (New York, 1989); Rebecca J. Scott, "Exploring the Meaning of Freedom: Postemancipation Societies in Comparative Perspective," *Hispanic American Historical Review*, 68 (August 1988), 407–28; and Peter Coclanis, "Distant Thunder: The Creation of a World Market in Rice and the Transformations It Wrought," *American Historical Review*, 98 (October, 1993), 1050–78.

38. On the widest scale the problem of nationalism was reopened by three authors, none of whom dealt seriously with the United States: Ernest Gellner, *Nations and Nationalism* (Ithaca, N.Y., 1983); Benedict Anderson, *Imagined Communities: Reflections on the Origin and Spread of Nationalism* (London, 1983); and Anthony D. Smith, *The Ethnic Origins of Nations* (Oxford, 1986). Anderson has now added two new chapters to a revised edition of *Imagined Communities* (1991).

39. Liah Greenfeld, *Nationalism: Five Roads to Modernity* (Cambridge, Mass., 1992). See also Rupert Wilkinson, *American Tough: The Tough-Guy Tradition and American Character* (Westport, Conn., 1984); Rupert Wilkinson, *The Pursuit of American Character* (New York, 1988); Wilbur Zelinsky, *Nation into State: The Shifting Symbolic Foundations of American Nationalism* (Chapel Hill, N.C., 1988); Byron E. Shafer, ed., *Is America Different? A New Look at American Exceptionalism* (Oxford, 1991); J. C. D. Clark, *The Language of Liberty, 1660–1832: Political Discourse and Social Dynamics in the Anglo-American World* (Cambridge, Eng., 1993); and Catherine Collomp, "Unions, Civics, and National Identity: Organized Labor's Reaction to Immigration, 1881–1897," *Labor History*, 29 (Fall 1988), 450–74. For contributions by U.S. historians, see John M. Murrin, "A Roof Without Walls: The Dilemma of American

National Identity," in *Beyond Confederation: Origins of the Constitution and American National Identity,* ed. Richard Beeman, Stephen Botein, and Edward C. Carter II (Chapel Hill, N.C., 1987), 333–48, and other essays in the same volume; Michael Kammen, *Mystic Chords of Memory: The Transformation of Tradition in American Culture* (New York, 1991); Kammen, "Problem of American Exceptionalism"; John Bodnar, *Remaking America: Public Memory, Commemoration, and Patriotism in the Twentieth Century* (Princeton, N.J., 1992); Chapters 2 and 6 in this book.

40. Eric Foner, *Reconstruction: America's Unfinished Revolution, 1863–1877* (New York, 1988); Robert H. Wiebe, *The Opening of American Society: From the Adoption of the Constitution to the Eve of Disunion* (New York, 1984).

41. Thomas Bender, "Wholes and Parts: The Need for Synthesis in American History," *Journal of American History,* 73 (June 1986), 120–36. See also the ensuing symposium, "A Round Table: Synthesis in American History," ibid., 74 (June 1987), 107–30.

42. This formulation arises from reflections summarized originally in *From Boundlessness to Consolidation: The Transformation of American Culture, 1848–1860* (Chapter 9 in this book), and now reinforced by a report on a planning conference on May 28–29, 1993, for the series A History of the Book in America: Carl Kaestle and Janice Radway, *The Book: Newsletter of the Program in the History of the Book in American Culture* (nos. 29–30, March–July 1993), 4. For a thoughtful exposition of centrifugal forces, see R. Laurence Moore, *Religious Outsiders and the Making of Americans* (New York, 1986).

43. Andrew Hacker, "'Diversity' and Its Dangers," *New York Review of Books,* Oct. 7, 1993, pp. 21–25.

44. In addition to the titles in note 39, see Gordon S. Wood, *The Creation of the American Republic, 1776–1787* (Chapel Hill, N.C., 1969); Ruth Bloch, *Visionary Republic: Millennial Themes in American Thought, 1756–1800* (Cambridge, Eng., 1985); Edward Millican, *One United People: The Federalist Papers and the National Idea* (Lexington, Ky., 1990); and Fred Somkin, *Unquiet Eagle: Memory and Desire in the Idea of American Freedom, 1815–1860* (Ithaca, N.Y., 1967).

45. Katherine Verdery, "Whither 'Nation' and 'Nationalism'?" *Daedalus,* 122 (Summer 1993), 41.

46. How the absence of a national context impoverished and distorted a major corpus of regionally specific scholarship during the 1970s and 1980s is brilliantly illuminated in James L. Huston, "The Experiential Basis of the Northern Antislavery Impulse," *Journal of Southern History,* 56 (November 1990), 609–40. "In current studies of abolitionism," Huston demonstrates, "one never encounters a slave at all." The national context in which antebellum northerners had experienced slavery was no longer meaningful to scholars intent on a microscopic view of one small group within its own social setting.

47. For an outstanding model, see Melvin L. Kohn and Carmi Schooler, *Work and Personality: An Inquiry into the Impact of Social Stratification* (Norwood, N.J., 1983).

Index

Aaron, Daniel, 166
abolition. *See* antislavery movement
academies, national, 75–76
activism, 172; as form of accommodation, 184–85; manifestations of, 177–83; as response to pessimism, 189–90
Adamic, Louis, 211
Adams, Brooks, 187, 188, 189–90
Adams, Henry, 20, 63, 148, 187, 189, 240, 246, 248
Adams, Herbert Baxter, 243
Adams, John, 159
Adams, John Quincy, 159
Addams, Jane, 225
affirmative action, 134
African Americans, 86, 87, 92, 98–99; and American universalism, 226; and educational reform, 226–27; and other ethnic groups, 130–32; political strength of, 231–32; voting rights for, 140, 231; during World War I, 138, 207. *See also* antislavery movement; Black Power; race relations; racism; slaves
Akin, James, 42
Allen, James Lane, 179
Amendments. *See* Fourteenth Amendment; Thirteenth Amendment
America: British views of, 25, 28–29; as immigrant society, 100; national character of, 56; personifications of, 22, 25, 28–39, 41–55; regional differences within, 96–97, 256–57

American Association for the Advancement of Science, 67
American Creed, 110, 136, 144, 145, 222
American culture, 2, 3–5; ideological unity, 7–14, 15, 18–21; primordial unity, 5–7, 21; purity in, 84, 95–96, 98–99; technical unity, 14–21
American Digest: Century Edition, 80–81
American Federation of Labor, 204
American history: comparative studies, 252–53; intellectual revolution in, 249–54; Marxist approaches to, 252; multicultural approaches to, 255; scholarly approaches to, 243–57
American Idea, 231
American ideals, 11–14, 93–94, 143; and scientific-technical methods, 19–20
American identity, 90–91, 104–6
American Medical Association, 69, 165
American Men of Science: A Biographical Directory, 81–82
American Revolution, impact of, on race relations, 134, 136
American Society for Civil Engineers, 165
American Studies Association, 220, 227, 237
Anderson, Benedict, 22
Antin, Mary, 113, 114
antislavery movement, 136–37, 139, 141, 142, 161, 162–63
architecture, 122. *See also* Wright, Frank Lloyd
Argentina, immigration to, 214–15

Ariès, Philippe, 121
Art Nouveau, 174
Ashmore, Harry, 110
Asian Americans, 131
assembly line, 70
assimilation, 85–89, 127–28, 130, 224–25, 256; through education, 88–89; of Indians, 88; and the individual, 113; as path to equality, 229–30; versus pluralism, 110, 112–19, 122–23
Association of American Universities, 77
athletics. *See* sports
Attucks, Crispus, 129
Australia, as immigrant society, 100, 101–2, 103–5, 106

bald eagle, 35
Bancroft, George, 10, 88
Barnum, P. T., 155
Bartoldi, Frédéric Auguste, 48
Barton, Josef, 84
baseball, 184
Beard, Charles, 240, 246–48
Beard, Mary, 247–48
Bederman, Gail, 84
Beecher, Henry Ward, 162
Bellamy, Edward, 166, 167–68, 169, 170, 171
Bellew, Frank H. T., 43, 44
Bender, Thomas, 66, 255
bicycling, 178
Bierce, Ambrose, 187
Bilingual Education Act, 128
bilingualism, 128–29
Billings, John Shaw, 81
birds, 179
Black Codes, 140
Black Power, 118–19, 230
Blum, Léon, 213–14
Bodnar, John, 22
Bok, Edward, 192
Book Review Digest, 81
Boorstin, Daniel, 2, 3, 58, 61, 152
Boston Tea Party, 29
Boundlessness, Age of, 154–57, 163
Bourne, Randolph, 62, 99, 230; as elitist, 300n26
boxing, 181, 182, 184
Britannia, 28–29, 31
Brooks, Van Wyck, 60, 62, 189
Brother Jonathan, 44
Brown Decades, 98

Bryce, James, 61
Bryce, Lord, 75
bureaucracy, 14, 18; in Progressive era, 266n46
Burns, Ken, 235–36
Burroughs, John, 193

California, multicultural curriculum in, 233
Calvinism, 153
Camp, Walter, 176
camp meetings, 13
Canada: immigration to, 214–16; labor movement in, 215–16
capital punishment, 161
card catalogs, 80
Carey, Henry C., 16, 164
Carmichael, Stokely, 118
Carnegie Foundation for the Advancement of Teaching, 79
cartoons, 35, 36. *See also* Nast, Thomas
Cattell, James McKeen, 81–82
Chambers, C. E., 52
Chandler, Alfred, 2
Channing, William Ellery, 152–53
Chapman, John Jay, 176–77
charitable trusts, 79
Chinese in American West, 128
Choate, Rufus, 245
Christianity, 9, 154. *See also* Protestant ideology; Puritanism
Church, Frederick, 150
citizenship, 93–94
civil rights, 125–26, 128, 140, 145
civil rights movement, 137–38, 144
Civil War, 14, 158; black migration during, 136
class: in America versus Europe, 202; as focus of scholarly study, 257; universalist view of, 223
class consciousness: and ethnic identity, 198, 201–6, 208–9; and the labor movement, 204–6; and multiculturalism, 221–22
Clay, E. W., 42
Clay, Henry, 245
Cleveland, Grover, 47
Clinton, Bill, 125
coal industry, 204
Cohen, Lizabeth, 198, 200
Cole, John, 79
Collier, John, 117–18
Collomp, Catherine, 198
colonies. *See* English colonies

Columbia. *See* Liberty

Commager, Henry Steele, 173

community: conceptions of, 2, 3–5, 230; integration and pluralism in, 112

Comte, Auguste, 70–71

Congress of Industrial Organizations, 212

Congress of Physicians and Surgeons, 75

Conkin, Paul K., 66

Connor, Ralph, 179

consensus and community, 3–4

consensus historians, 248–49

conservatism, 157, 162–63

consolidation, 165, 255–56

Constitution, U.S., 124

Continental Congress, 11

Conzen, Kathleen, 100

Cooper, James Fenimore, 223

Cooperative Commonwealth Federation, 216

Corbett, "Gentleman Jim," 178

Crane, Stephen, 188, 189

Crèvecoeur, J. Hector St. Jean de, 87, 102–3, 245

Croats in Midwest, 128

Crunden, Robert, 84

Cruse, Harold, 115

Cudahy Bros. Packers, 46

cultural history, 172, 174–75

Cunliffe, Marcus, 173

Curtin, Philip, 254

Cutter, Charles A., 80

Dana, Charles A., 162

Dartmouth College, 175–76

Darwin, Charles, 150, 187

Darwinism, 188

Darwinism, Social. *See* Spencer, Herbert

Davis, David Brion, 228

Debs, Eugene, 19, 166

Debussy, Claude, 182

decentralization, 8, 89–92

Deloria, Vine, 115

democracy and ethnic diversity, 119–20, 200

Democratic Party, 142. *See also* Jacksonian Democrats

Depression, impact of, on ethnic minorities, 212–14

determinism, 187–88

Dewey, John, 56, 72–73, 190, 196, 225

Dewey, Melvil, 80

Dewey decimal system, 80

diversity: and technological uniformity, 119–

20; and unity, 110, 111–12, 124–33. *See also* assimilation; multiculturalism

Dix, Dorothy, 161

doctoral degree, 69, 76–78

Donald, David, 152

Dos Passos, John, 20

Douglas, Ann, 84

Douglass, Frederick, 140

Downing, Jack, 42–43

Dreiser, Theodore, 189

Du Bois, W. E. B., 225

Dupree, A. Hunter, 75

Dutch Americans, 114

Duyckinck, Evert, 160

Duyckinck, George, 160

Dwight, Louis, 161

eagle, bald, 35

Early, Gerald, 220

economic reform, 167–71

education, multiculturalism in, 227–29, 234–39

education, higher. *See* universities

education, public, 88–89

educational reform, 226–27

Edwin, David, 38

Elkins, Stanley, 152

Ellison, Ralph, 21

Ellul, Jacques, 2

Emancipation Proclamation, 140

Emerson, Ralph Waldo, 69, 162

encyclopedias, 80

English colonies, 90

English-Only movement, 128

equality: demands for, 221–22; pursuit of, 225–26

Erenberg, Lewis A., 172

ethnic boundaries, 112, 113–14, 120–22, 123, 132

ethnic groups, 84–89, 91–92, 96–97, 107–9; during the Depression, 212–14; rivalries among, 128; social recognition of, 127–28; solidarity of, 114, 119, 294–95n17. *See also* African Americans; assimilation; German Americans; immigrants; Indians; Irish Americans; *and other groups by name*

ethnic identity, 7, 24, 86–87; Americanization of, 210–11; and class consciousness, 198, 201–6; as a social force, 236–37

ethnicization, 5–7, 86, 91–92

ethnic nuclei, 120, 123

ethnic relations, 85–86, 130–33. *See also* race relations

ethnic studies programs, 235, 238

etiquette books, 165

Europe, 174; history, 243–44

evangelical Christianity, 154

evolutionism, 119

exceptionalism, American, xiv, 56, 166, 172, 222, 251–52

exclusive possession, myth of, 103

expansionism, 155–56, 160. *See also* Boundlessness, Age of

experimentalism, 60, 62

Fabian socialism, 170

Faulkner, William, 114–15

feminism, roots of, 238

Ferguson, Adam, 70

Field, Eugene, 179

Fish, Stanley, 56

flag, American, 91

flag ceremonies, 181

Flagg, James Montgomery, 54

Fletcher, Robert, 81

Foner, Eric, 255

Ford, Henry, 20

foreign policy, 62

Forrest, Edwin, 155

foundations, private, 79

Fourteenth Amendment, 140

Fourth of July, 159

France, Popular Front in, 213

Franklin, Benjamin, 32, 60, 153, 245

Frederic, Harold, 187

Fredrickson, George, 148, 158

Free Soil Party, 137

French Canadians, 89

French Huguenots, 87

Freud, Sigmund, 195

Frisch, Michael H., 4

frontier, as American myth, 104–5

frontiersman, 104–5, 192

frontier thesis, 95, 106, 113, 191, 246–47

Garraty, John, 213–14

Garrison, William Lloyd, 143

Garvey, Marcus, 207

Geertz, Clifford, 2, 5

Genteel Tradition, 71

George, Henry, 148, 166, 167, 168, 169, 185–86

George III (king), 37

Gerber, Richard A., 166

German Americans, 87, 89, 109, 202, 203, 206, 208

Germania, 46, 47

Germany, 24; Ph.D. degree in, 76–77

Gibson, Charles Dana, 47, 50

Gilded Age, 172, 177

Gillam, Bernhard, 47

Glassberg, David, 22

Gleason, Philip, 132

globalization, 126, 144

Göbel, Thomas, 198

Godkin, E. L., 187

Graham, Sylvester, 161

Grand, Sarah, 182

Grant, Ulysses S., 141

Great Seal of the Republic, 11

Greeley, Horace, 162

Green, Thomas Hill, 185

Greene, Victor, 86

Greenfeld, Liah, 255

Griffith, Sally F., 66

Guarneri, Carl J., 2

Guinier, Lani, 125

Haggard, H. Rider, 181

Hall, G. Stanley, 175

Hamilton, Alexander, 14–15

Hamilton, Charles V., 118

Hamilton, Grant, 49

Handlin, Oscar, 100, 106

handwriting, 149–51

Hapgood, Hutchins, 99

Harris, William T., 71

Hartz, Louis, 3–4, 248, 249

Hasbrouck House, 159

Haskins, Charles Homer, 243

Hawaii, annexation of, 49

Hawthorne, Nathaniel, 91

health, gospel of, 178

Hearst, William Randolph, 181

Heimert, Alan, 11

Henry, Joseph, 67

Hindus in Chicago, 128

Hispanic Americans. *See* Latinos

histoire totale, l', 249

historic preservation movement, 159

historiography, 3–4; future of, 240, 241–57

history: progressive interpretation of, 119–20, 153; transnational approach to, 243–44. *See also* American history

Hoffmann, Stanley, 62

Hofstadter, Richard, 3–4, 60–61
Hollinger, David, 59, 100
Holmes, Oliver Wendell, Jr., 191
Holmes, Oliver Wendell, Sr., 88, 164
Hoover, Herbert, 20
Hovey, Richard, 175–76, 179–80
Howe, Julia Ward, 139, 184
Howells, William Dean, 180, 185–86, 204
humor, American, 155
Hutchins, Robert, 110
Hutchinson, Anne, 183
Huxley, Aldous, 20
Huxley, Thomas, 71

idealism, 60–61, 63–65. *See also* American ideals
ideological unity, 7–14, 15, 18–21
ideology: defined, 7–8; and ethnicity, 92; national, 11–14, 91; Protestant, 9–13
immigrants: assimilation of, 85–89, 107–8, 224–25; backlash against, 44; communal values of, 294–95*n*17; defined, 100, 107; eastern European, 199–217 passim, 294–95*n*17; origins of, 108–9; as political force, 216; and social change, 199–200, 201; and Statue of Liberty, 50–51, 52. *See also* ethnic groups
immigration: to Argentina, 214–15; to Canada, 214–16; controls for, 125–27; myths of, 101–2, 106; role of, in American history, 100, 101–9, 200–217
Immigration and Reform Law of *1965*, 126
imperialism, 18, 45–46, 190
Independence Day, 159
Independence Hall, 159
Index-Catalogue of the Surgeon General's Library, 81
Index-Medicus, 81
Indian Princess, 25, 28–30
Indians: attitudes toward, 88; rights of, 117–18. *See also* Indian Princess
individualism, 151, 164
industrialization, 15, 164, 201, 203
injustice, 167
integration, democracy of, 112–13. *See also* assimilation
intellectual history, 66, 67, 148. *See also* specialization; universities
intellectuals: and American universalism, 225–26; in the late nineteenth century, 185–90
interdependence, 97

intermarriage, 129, 231
International Index to Periodicals, 81
inventions, 16–17
Irish Americans, 44, 45, 109, 128, 202, 203, 205, 206
Irish Catholics, 87, 203
isolationism, 122
Italians, 207, 209

Jackson, Andrew, 39, 42
Jacksonian Democrats, 155–56
James, Henry, 90, 94, 177, 223
James, William, 56, 59, 69, 77, 190–96
Jameson, J. Franklin, 75–76, 244
Jefferson, Thomas, 139, 159, 222
Jeffersonian embargo, 142
Jennings, Samuel, 33
Jerusalem, 27
Jews, 87, 128, 202, 206; intermarriage of, 129–30; and Zionism, 206–7, 208, 210
Jim Crow laws, 140
jingoism, 180, 181, 184
John Bull, 41
Johns Hopkins University, 77
Johnson, Edward, 10
Johnson Reed Act of *1924*, 210
journalism, sensational, 181
Joyce, William L., 56

Kammen, Michael, 4, 22
King, Martin Luther, Jr., 144, 226
King, Rodney, 239
Kipling, Rudyard, 181
Kirby, Rollin, 50
Knickerbocker Magazine, 162
Knopf, Alfred A., 247
Know-Nothing movement, 96, 104
Kohn, Hans, 22, 23–24
Korean Association for American Studies, 56, 57
Kossuth, Louis, 158
Ku Klux Klan, 98
Kung Fu, 123

labor movement, 169–70, 208; and class consciousness, 204–6; political strength of, 211–12; and U.S. Steel strike, 210
laissez-faire individualism, 151, 164
Landi, Gaspare, 34
language, politics of, 128–29
Latinos, 127–28, 131
Lauter, Paul, 227

law reference books, 80–81
Lawson, Alan, 220
Lea, Henry C., 243
Lears, Jackson, 252
Leutze, Emanuel, 37, 39
Lewis, Robert, 100
Lewis, Sinclair, 70
liberal education, 71
Liberty (Columbia): as goddess, 31, 34;
    Statue of, 47–51, 52, 53, 212; as symbol of
    American republic, 31–35, 37, 40, 45, 46
libraries, 79
Library of Congress, 80
Lifton, Robert Jay, 122
Lincoln, Abraham, 140, 160, 163
Literary World, 160
literature, American, 160; fiction of the
    1890s, 179; naturalistic novel, 188, 189
Lloyd, Henry Demarest, 166, 167–68, 169–
    70, 171
localism, 5–6, 8, 89–90, 97, 252
London, Jack, 179, 189
Looking Backward (Bellamy), 169, 170
Lopez, Jennifer, 128
Louis Philippe, King, 158
Lowell, James Russell, 160, 162
Lowell, Josephine Shaw, 184

Mabie, Hamilton Wright, 196
Macfadden, Bernarr, 178, 180
MacIver, Robert, 73, 119, 120
Mackay, Alexander, 13
Madison, Dolley, 159
Madison, James, 12
Mahan, Alfred T., 243
Maine Law of 1851, 161–62
manifest destiny, 160
Mann, Arthur, 102, 114
manumission, 139, 141
Marx, Leo, 15
Marxist approaches to history, 251, 252
Masaryk, Thomas, 206
materialism, 60
Matthews, Albert, 269n27
May, Henry, 58, 59
McClay, Wilfred M., 148
McConnell, Stuart, 148
McGerr, Michael, 242
medical reference books, 80, 81
Megill Allan, 253
melting pot, as American image, 87, 106,
    113, 116–17

Melting Pot, The (Zangwill), 116–17
Melville, Herman, 87–88, 150, 162
Mencken, H. L., 61
Merriwell, Frank, 175
Mexicans in Southwest, 126
military values, 180–81
Mill, John Stuart, 71
millennialism, 10–11, 156
Mitchell, John, 28
modernism, 99
Montanus, Arnoldus, 26
moral teachings, 17–18
Muir, John, 179
multiculturalism, 134, 220; and class con-
    sciousness, 227–28; dilemmas underlying,
    234–39; in education, 227–29, 234–39;
    limitations of, 233–34
Mumford, Lewis, 21, 60, 98, 171
music, American, 179–80, 182
Muslim Americans, 128
mutual avoidance, 92, 126
Myrdal, Gunnar, 110, 113, 136, 222
myths, national, 100, 101–3, 104–7, 245,
    249, 250, 257

Nagel, Paul, 105
Napoleon, 181
Nast, Thomas, 35, 36, 43, 44, 45
National Association for the Advancement of
    Colored People, 99
national character, 56
nationalism: in America, 24–25, 54–55,
    224; as area of scholarly study, 254, 256;
    cultural, 24; defined, 305n26; among eth-
    nic groups, 207–9; and gender, 25, 35–37;
    jingoism, 180, 181, 184; liberal versus eth-
    nic, 24; in western versus eastern Europe,
    23–24. See also America: personifications
    of
Nationalism (collectivist program), 170, 171
national parks, 178
nation-state: challenges to, 241–42; as focus
    of American history, 243
Native Americans. See Indian Princess;
    Indians
nativism, 84, 98
nativist movement, 104
naturalistic determinism, 187–88
naturalistic novel, 188, 189
nature, attitudes toward, 149–51, 178–79,
    196
New Deal, 199–201

New Directions in American Intellectual History (Higham and Conkin), 66
New England towns: cohesiveness of, 4; ideological unity in, 8–9; public education in, 89; Puritanism in, 95
New Woman, 180, 182, 183
Niebuhr, Reinhold, 21
Nixon, Richard, 141
Nordau, Max, 188
Norris, Frank, 189
North American Review, 160, 162
Northwest Ordinance of 1787, 139
novel, naturalistic, 188, 189
Nugent, Walter, 100

Oleson, Alexandra, 68
Olmsted, Frederic Law, 164
Olympic Games, 182
Organization of Knowledge in Modern America, 1860–1920 (Oleson and Voss), 66, 68
Other Tradition, 58
Otis, Harrison Gray, 159
Otis, James, 102
Otto, Max, 56
outdoor movement, 178–80
Ownby, Ted, 134

Paderewski, Ignace, 206
Paine, Thomas, 224
Park, Robert E., 118–19, 120, 229–30
Parkman, Francis, 150
patriotism, 180–81, 305n26. *See also* myths, national
Peirce, Charles, 56, 190, 196
penmanship, 149–51
Pennell, Joseph, 49
periodization, 173–74
Perón, Juan, 215
Peshkin, Alan, 232
pessimist philosophies, 172, 186–90
Ph.D. *See* doctoral degree
Phillips, Wendell, 116, 224–25
Pierce, Franklin, 156
pioneers, 104–5, 245
place, sense of, 24, 25–29
Pledge of Allegiance, 181
pluralism, 99; cultural, 230, 234–39, 300n26; versus assimilation, 110, 112–19
pluralistic integration, 110, 111–33; and ethnicity, 209; and racism, 121–22
Pocahontas, 30, 129

Poles, 206, 207, 208, 209, 211
political conventions, 14
political parties, 124; and race relations, 142
Poor, Henry Varnum, 164
popular culture, 127–28, 179–80
Popular Front, 213
postage stamps, U.S., 53
postmodernism, 251
Potter, David, 3–4
Powell, Colin, 127
Powell, Sumner Chilton, 8
practicality. *See* pragmatism
pragmatism, 56, 190–91; and experimentalism, 60, 62; and idealism, 60–61, 63–65; as way of life, 57–65
Prescott, William H., 243
presidents as national symbols, 37–41
primordial unity, 5–7, 21
Princeton Review, 150–51
producerism, 170–71
professionalization, 67–68
professional societies, 165
professorships, 78. *See also* universities
progress, idea of, 136, 186–89, 233, 249
Progressive era, 18–19; bureaucracy in, 266n46
Progressivism, 2, 18–19, 84, 98, 99, 190, 199
Protean Man, 122–23
Protestant ideology, 9–13; and American nationalism, 11–12, 92–93, 95
provincialism, 99
public health, 164
Puritanism, 8–9, 93, 95, 111
purity, 84, 95–96, 98–99; and ethnic diversity, 116, 122
Putnam, Hilary, 56
Putnam's Monthly, 160

Quakers, as antislavery activists, 137

race relations, 118–19, 134, 226; after the American Revolution, 134, 136; college courses in, 229; progress in, 138–45, 231–32; and universities, 232–33; and World War I, 138; and World War II, 136, 137, 140
racism, 18, 84, 98–99, 118–19, 121–23, 130–31, 141–42
railroad strike of 1877, 168
Randolph, John, 102
Ravitch, Diane, 233
reason, 153

reconstruction: after the American Revolution, 136; defined, 136. *See also* race relations
Reconstruction (post–Civil War), 135, 143
reference books, 80–82
reference tools, 79–82
regional differences, 96–97, 256–57. *See also* frontier; New England towns; southerners
Reingold, Nathan, 62, 79
Renan, Ernest, 187
Republican Party, 163
research: American approach compared with German, 73; as function of universities, 78
Revere, Paul, 29
Revolutions of *1848*, 158–59, 287*n*24
Rice, Elmer, 20
Richardson, George, 27
riots, interracial, 128, 221
rituals, 13–14
Roberts, Peter, 204–5
Rockefeller, John D., 79
Rockefeller Foundation, 79
Rockefeller Institute for Medical Research, 79
Rodgers, Daniel, 2
Rogers, William Allen, 48
romanticism, 148
Roosevelt, Franklin D., 212
Roosevelt, Theodore, 176, 184, 191
Rorty, Richard, 56
Rossiter, Margaret, 75
Russo, David J., 254

Sack, Steve, 55
Saltus, Edgar, 187, 189
Sanjek, Roger, 132, 133
Santayana, George, 63, 187, 189
Savage, Edward, 34, 35
Schlesinger, Arthur M., 106, 172
science, 19, 62; specialization in, 74–75
Science, 165
Scots, 201–2
secularization, 16–17, 185
self-made man, 153, 245
Serbs in Midwest, 128
Seton, Ernest Thompson, 179
Sherman, Roger, 24
Sklar, Kathryn Kish, 240
slaves, 102, 129; emancipation of, 139–40. *See also* antislavery movement

Slavs, 207
Smith, Adam, 70
Smith, Alfred E., 211
Smith, Henry Nash, 150
Smith, John, 30
Smithsonian Institution, 67
socialism, 18–19, 170, 171
Socialist party, 166
social protest, 169–70
social reform, 156–57. *See also* economic reform
Society for the Promotion of Agricultural Science, 75
"Song of the Open Road" (Whitman), 153
Sousa, John Philip, 181, 182
southerners, 6–7
specialization: American attitudes toward, 66, 68–82; in historical studies, 242, 244, 251; institutions evolving from, 82
Spencer, Herbert, 16, 72–73, 148, 150–52, 153, 165, 187, 188, 265*n*39
Spencer, Platt Rogers, 149–50, 151
sports: American enthusiasm for, 183–84; American superiority in, 182; at universities and colleges, 175, 176, 177
Standard Oil, 168
state, incompleteness of the American, 90–91
stereotypes, 65, 202, 232
Stimpson, Catharine R., 233
Stowe, Harriet Beecher, 162
Sullivan, John L., 178
Sullivan, Louis, 191
Sumner, William Graham, 187, 189
symbols, American, 13–14, 224, 245. *See also* America: personifications of

tall tales, 155
Tammany Tiger, 35, 36
Tarbell, Ida, 181
Taylor, William R., 157
technical unity, 14–21, 56; and despiritualization, 17–18
technology, attitudes toward, 152, 154
temperance, 161–62
Thirteenth Amendment, 140
Thistlethwaite, Frank, 156
Thomas, John L, 166, 167, 170–71
Thoreau, Henry David, 61, 150
Tocqueville, Alexis de, 57–58, 152
Trollope, Anthony, 105
Truman, Harry, 144

Turner, Frederick Jackson, 95, 106, 113, 191–93, 194, 240, 246–47
Twain, Mark, 187, 189
Tyrell, Ian, 253

Uncle Sam, 36, 41–43, 45, 46, 47, 48, 52–55; origin of, 269n27
unions. *See* labor movement
United States Catalog, 81
United States Steel Company, strike against, 210
unity: and diversity, 110, 111–12, 124–33; ideological, 7–14, 15, 18–21; primordial, 5–7, 21; technical, 14–21, 56
universalism, American, 84, 220, 222–25, 229–31
universities: American versus European, 66; and academic degrees, 76–78; departmental structure of, 78; and liberal education, 71; minority students at, 232–33; research function of, 78; specialization in, 68–69; sports at, 175, 176, 177; and youth culture, 175
urbanization, 164–65
utopians, 166

van Meur, Jacob, 26
Veblen, Thorstein, 225
Vecoli, Rudolph, 110
Venturi, Robert, 122
Verplanck, Gulian C., 69, 74
Veysey, Laurence, 23, 68, 75, 250
Victorian culture, 149–50
Virgil, 11
Voltaire, 122
Voss, John, 68

Wallis, John, 32
Ward, Artemus, 160

Ward, Lester F., 185
Ward, Russel, 104
Warner, Sam Bass, Jr., 4
Warner, W. Lloyd, 127
Washington, George, 24, 32, 35–39, 104
Washington Monument, 91, 159
Wealth of Nations, The (Adam Smith), 70
Webster, Daniel, 157
welfare state, 199, 201
Whig Party, 156
White, William Allen, 62, 64
Whitman, Walt, 105, 152–53, 162, 193–94
Whittier, John Greenleaf, 162
Wiebe, Robert, 2, 90, 145, 148, 255, 266n46
Wilde, Oscar, 187
Wilder, Thornton, 6
Williams, Robin, 61
Wilson, Halsey William, 81
Wilson, Samuel, 269n27
Wilson, Woodrow, 47, 58, 188
Wister, Owen, 179
women: in historiography, 253; rights of, 288n37. *See also* feminism, roots of; New Woman
Woodward, C. Vann, 6, 100, 135
World War I and race relations, 138, 207
World War II and race relations, 136, 137, 140
Wright, Frank Lloyd, 171, 191, 192, 194, 195
Wuthnow, Robert, 2

Yankee, 104
Young Americans, 158–59, 160

Zangwill, Israel, 116–17
Zionism, 206–7, 210
Zuckerman, Michael, 4
Zunz, Olivier, 110